CLEVELAND'S SPORTS FACILITIES

CLEVELAND'S SPORTS FACILITIES

A 35 Year History

KEN SILLIMAN

THE PAPER HOUSE
PUBLISHING

CONTENTS

PREFACE

For a thousand years, every city in the western world poured all of their wealth, natural resources, artistic vision, civic pride, and faith in God into building cathedral churches.

Now they build football stadiums....

The cathedrals of old engaged in centuries-long games of one-upmanship: they constantly grew bigger, better and more beautiful. NFL stadiums are no different. Cowboys Stadium is currently the biggest and best, but the next one is always on the horizon.[1]

This comparison led off a 2012 entry in the sports blog Bleacher Report. Does it work for you? Or, at a time when pro athletes are injecting *politics* into sports—are they standing or kneeling for the national anthem?—does a *religious* analogy strike you as "piling on?"

We shouldn't be too quick to dismiss the cathedral/stadium parallels. In addition to their similar roles as community and cultural icons, both churches and stadia historically have drawn upon financing from common citizens for their construction costs: medieval churches via citizen payments to the Roman Catholic Church, and sports stadia via taxes on property, sales, alcohol, tobacco, hotels and motels, and rental cars.

Yet the similarities end when considering longevity. Medieval churches have lasted 700 years and longer and many—Seville Cathedral in Spain, Florence Cathedral in Italy, York Minster in England, and Canterbury Cathedral in England—were constructed over periods of a century or more. Contrast Atlanta in 2017, where a downtown baseball park and a downtown football stadium were replaced prior to their respective 25-year anniversaries.

Local politicians cringe when they face requests for public financing of professional sports facilities, as they know they will face conflicts on many fronts, including:

- Sports culture versus arts culture (recalling clashing high school cliques);
- Class warfare (common citizens versus billionaire team owners);
- Downtown development versus neighborhood development; and
- Historic preservation versus new construction.

The story told in these pages begins in 1988 when I joined the Cleveland Law Department, determined to play a role in my hometown city's turnaround. At that time, Mayor George V. Voinovich and Council President George Forbes had forged a productive collaboration. Yet Cleveland was then confronting its most significant sports facilities decisions since its voters approved a bond issue for Cleveland Municipal Stadium on November 6, 1928. That lakefront stadium, constructed at a $3 million cost, was upon its July 2, 1931, public opening date the largest stadium in the world to feature individual seats rather than bleacher-type seating.[2]

But in 1988 (over half a century later)—and after years of deferred maintenance on the Stadium—Cleveland's elected officials knew that it was past time to take action to retain the Stadium's sports team tenants (baseball's Indians and football's Browns). This book tells the story of over thirty years of decisions regarding Cleveland's sports facilities.

Depending on your point of view, I was either fortunate enough—or philistine enough—to play a role in sports facility decisions for all three of Cleveland's major pro sports franchises. My childhood loyalties certainly motivated me to seek out these opportunities. As one of three sports-addicted brothers growing up in several of the city's western suburbs, I was a hard-core Browns and Indians fan when I began college at Case Western Reserve University in September of 1970.

The first Browns home game I attended as a college student was the historic inaugural Monday Night football game against the Super Bowl champion New York Jets. In my four years of college, I attended every single Browns home game. Despite the pressure of studying for finals every April and May, I attended more Indians ballgames than was good for my academic health.

And, as a timely bonus, the National Basketball Association welcomed the Cleveland Cavaliers as an expansion franchise: the team played its first game on October 14, 1970. I quickly learned the schedule of the Euclid Avenue #6 bus route that delivered me to innumerable Cavaliers games.

But when my dad first delivered me to my dormitory room in September 1970, I made the mistake of bragging that my dorm window commanded a superb view of the Browns full-time practice field located across the street. That ill-advised boast came back to haunt me at Christmas vacation when I toted back to my family a woeful 2.3 first semester grade point average: my dad hadn't forgotten about that view out my window.

Having confessed my sports-fan upbringing, my team loyalties were nevertheless tempered by a strong populist strain I had acquired during my time at Case Western Reserve. My undergraduate major was Urban & Environmental Studies, and several of my professors shaped my goal as a future public servant "to increase choices for those who have the fewest choices in life." The competing motives in my own upbringing have certainly played out in the local government decisions described in the pages of this book.

My Book's Target Audiences

A core policy question—the extent to which, if at all, local governments should fund professional sports facilities—has split Northeast Ohio citizens and even led to referenda. Local sports fans who care about urban policy and politics are one audience that will want to know the particulars of how Cleveland and Cuyahoga County answered this question.

But my "case studies," if you will, are relevant to a broader national audience that will develop as state and local public investments in individual facilities approach and exceed one billion dollars. That said, this book makes no attempt to add to the considerable "economic impact of sports facilities" literature that has surfaced over the last three decades. Authors[3] including Baade, Coates and Humphries, Noll and Zimbalist, Quirk and Fort, Rosentraub, and many others have pursued this topic in depth, and I do not pretend to match their rigorous academic treatments.

Rather, my national target audience is the legion of government careerists, in office now or studying to become so, who will find that sports facility negotiations can consume much of the oxygen in a room. My experiences will be relevant not only to those doing the negotiating, but also to those officials tangentially impacted by the outcomes. A billion dollars invested in a sports facility is a billion dollars that could otherwise be spent on education, housing, or urban infrastructure.

20th Century Harvard philosopher George Santayana famously observed that "Those who cannot remember the past are condemned to repeat it." Our Cleveland outcomes, good and bad, _do_ translate to other cities. My book is a ground-level, in-the-trenches account of how sports teams go about getting what they want from the public sector. As such, it is akin to several case studies of sports facility negotiations in particular cities.[4] But it's told from an "inside City Hall perspective" that is only shared with Pittsburgh's study[5]; and it tracks at least _eight distinct negotiations with three separate sports teams and one sports league (the National FootbaL League in 1996)_ occurring over 30 years of time.

To derive the most benefit from those eight sessions, view each as its own laboratory testing the public's negotiating outcome. Some initial definitions are needed:

... a Least Acceptable Result (L.A.R.)... is the point at which you would be better off walking away and forgetting the deal rather than accept less.[6]

... your Maximum Supportable Position... (M.S.P.) is the point furthest in the direction of meeting all your goals that (you) can justify in some way, shape or form[7]

The reader can then judge each outcome under a two-step test:

How real was the team's stated or unstated threat of franchise relocation? That answer will greatly impact step two:

Your ultimate success in any negotiation... can be measured by how well you can move your opponent toward your Maximum Supportable Position and reach a settlement at or near his Least Acceptable Result.[8]

Sports Facility Community Impacts

The national competition for professional sports franchises is but one battlefront of a broader economic development "arms race" in which local business incentives offered to owners of private enterprises constitute the "armaments." A city that underestimates its competition is at risk of losing its sports franchise to a faster growing city that lavishes superior incentives on the franchise's owner. In a 2004 study on the effect of development incentives, Alan Peters and Peter Fisher found:

The most fundamental problem is that many public officials appear to believe that they can influence the course of their state or local economies through incentives and subsidies to a degree far beyond anything supported by even the most optimistic evidence. We need to begin by lowering their expectations about their ability to micromanage economic growth and making the case for a more sensible view of the role of government—providing the foundations for growth through sound fiscal practices, quality public infrastructure, and good education systems —and then letting the economy take care of itself.

Against that general background, there is still a role for specific programs aimed at improving worker employability and mobility (both occupational and geographic) and for community development efforts. But continuing on the path of traditional incentive-based economic development policy will simply produce an unending merry-go-round of tax cuts and subsidies whose net effect is to starve government of the resources it needs to finance the services it should be providing and to make the state and local tax system ever more regressive.[9]

Although economic questions predominate in sports facility debates, several other factors are usually present. One is the use of sports facility investments to drive district redevelopment, and this approach is discussed in Chapters 10 and 11.

You will read about a 2004 study published in the Journal of the American Planning Association that compared Baltimore and Cleveland outcomes in achieving these goals.

Second, there is an argument that sports facilities can enhance a city's image. In their efforts to retain or attract businesses, residents, or tourists, Cleveland officials often cite the presence of three professional sports facilities within easy walking distance of the downtown core. Intuitively, the sports facilities' presence matters to downtown employers and employees. And if the teams are performing well and winning playoff games, so much the better: consider the city's free national publicity in the form of Goodyear blimp shots, scenic images displaying the city's attractions, and exciting crowd shots.

Though there's little stateside research on sports facilities and city image, a 2001 United Kingdom research paper has tackled this topic.[10] The 2001 study examined the efforts of UK cities with declining manufacturing bases—Birmingham, Manchester, and Sheffield—to upgrade their images via sports initiatives. The author validated this strategy, though that conclusion centered more on "the potential of sports reimaging, rather than any objective assessment of a strategy's success."[11]

Third, there is the "opportunity cost" of making a sports facility investment.

Consider the following quote from a book entitled FIELD OF SCHEMES from stadium-financing critics Joanna Cagan and Neil deMause:

> Like other sports fans of long standing, we had worried over the yearly ritual of watching our teams declare their intentions to move to another city unless bribed with a new stadium or a new lease. As journalists concerned with urban issues, we wondered about the wisdom of city governments spending millions of dollars on these stadiums at a time when public housing, libraries, and schools were being dismantled at an unprecedented pace.[12]

Most of us would agree that—given a choice between padding sports owners' wallets and funding public housing, libraries, and schools—we would opt for the latter choice. But the question is rarely that simple. More often, the franchise-granting professional sports leagues will condition the retention of a team in a particular city upon that city's willingness to provide some minimal level of public incentives. In weighing the level of incentive needed to retain or attract a sports franchise, local officials will want to know what's been done in comparable cities.

Fortunately, there are at least three superb resources for information on sports facility deals in American cities. One is the work product of FIELD OF SCHEMES co-author Neil deMause: his "Field of Schemes" blog averages 20+ stories a month on latest trends in public financing of sports facilities. The second source is the National Sports Law Institute of Marquette University Law School, which publishes lease summaries for professional baseball, basketball and football franchises.

The third source is a 2013 book published by University of Michigan Professor Judith Grant Long entitled PUBLIC/PRIVATE PARTNERSHIPS FOR MAJOR LEAGUE SPORTS FACILITIES. As Professor Long explained in her Preface:

> My primary aim is to inform the ongoing national and local debates over public investments in sports facilities, and by extension, to contribute to the discourse surrounding public spending on sports and tourism infrastructure as a priority in contemporary urban agendas. My central questions are concerned with the nature and interpretation of public/private partnerships—who pays, how much, and why—as revealed in over 100 recent deals struck to build new major league ballparks, stadiums, and arenas, in over 50 host cities located throughout the US and Canada.[13]

As you read about my personal and unvarnished sports facility experiences in the pages of this book, you will naturally reach your own conclusions on whether the various investments were worthwhile. For those of you who are willing to lose a sports franchise, you will rightly disapprove of some of the decisions. For others, who believe it's important to retain the franchises, you may agree with the decisions and want to know how Cleveland bargained in comparison to comparable cities.

CHAPTER ONE

CLEVELAND'S UNIQUE POLITICAL ENVIRONMENT

For any company seeking public subsidies from the City of Cleveland, the upper management team is wise to acquire an understanding of the City's political idiosyncrasies. And that applies double for sports franchise applicants. Cleveland's politics are unique in a number of ways, including the features listed below.

One Party System

The 21st century has yet to witness the election of a Republican member to Cleveland's 17-member City Council. George V. Voinovich (1980-1989) was the most recent Republican mayor. Thus, the agreements and disagreements amongst City Council members cannot be explained by partisan differences. Every Monday at noon, the entirely Democrat Council members attend a party caucus that covers legislative topics of current interest.

Though not defined by party lines, political divergences do occur. In Cleveland, the Council members break into several camps defined by the extent to which the members agree or disagree with major policy pursuits of the current mayor's administration. Further, those members who often oppose administration policies can be clustered into two subgroups:

- Outspoken critics (via floor speeches and media quotes) who, notwithstanding their public stances, still engage the mayor and his or her administration behind the scenes to advance projects and initiatives of interest in their wards; and
- "Brick throwers" who rarely pursue behind the scenes discussions for improvements in their wards (apparently out of the belief that such discussions might leave them "beholden" and might diminish their status as critics of the administration).

Urban Populism

Cleveland is unique amongst Midwestern cities in the extent to which a strong urban populism informs its major political debates. This phenomenon dates back over a century to the mayoral terms of Mayor Tom L. Johnson in the early 1900's. In the introduction to his book "My Story," Mayor Johnson said:

> The greatest movement in the world to-day may be characterized as the struggle of the people against Privilege.

On the one side the People—slow to wake up, slow to recognize their own interests, slow to recognize their power, slow to invoke it. On the other, Privilege—always awake and quick to act, owning many of the newspapers, controlling the election and appointment of judges, dictating to city councils, influencing legislatures and writing our national laws.[1]

In relaying an account of how overzealous Cuyahoga County tax officials allegedly drove industrialist John D. Rockefeller out of town (taking his millions of charitable bequests to New York rather than Cleveland), Cleveland Magazine writer Michael D. Roberts cited Cleveland politicians' "populist character focused on the status quo, never heading warnings or embracing benefactors."[2]

In a 1995 article recapping his tenure as Cleveland City Planning Director in the 1960's and 1970's, Norman Krumholz spoke of his realization that in a city of limited resources, we must promote more choices for those Cleveland residents who had few, if any, choices.[3] He then cited how he and his planning staff members had practiced what they preached by tackling downtown commercial development, public transit, and lakefront development.

Then came Cleveland Mayor Dennis Kucinich for a brief (1977-1979) tenure:

> Kucinich attracted attention by doing the unexpected, poking his finger into the belly and face of corporate Cleveland over important decisions. He had successfully thwarted the sale of Muny Light (Cleveland's municipally-owned electric company) and actively continued an antitrust suit in federal court against (private electric company) CEI, claiming damages of a third of a billion dollars. He fought public subsidies for an iron-ore dock, dearly desired by Republic Steel. Business interests found themselves

frustrated at every turn by Kucinich, who proudly proclaimed a "new urban Populism."[4]

Finally, there was the writer of the preceding passage—journalist Roldo Bartimole—whose publications decrying public subsidies to sports team owners and sports facilities comprised a major battle-front in his lifetime war against corporate welfare.

Bartimole began as a conventional journalist and worked for Cleveland's Plain Dealer and the Cleveland office of the Wall Street Journal. But the day after Martin Luther King's assassination in April, 1968, he resigned the latter position. Inspired by Michael Harrington's book, *The Other America: Poverty in the United States*, he commenced publication of a biweekly newsletter entitled Point of View that jabbed corporate Cleveland until 2000. In a 30th anniversary edition of that publication in 1998, he explained his role in public discourse:

> Not from any special ability but because the news media refuse to examine power and particularly avoid the power wielded by corporate interests and the many institutions such as Cleveland Tomorrow formed to do their bidding. The conventional news media refuse to confront honestly the nature of how and who makes community decisions. Refuse to ask the most important questions about who pays and who benefits from decisions made by edict of the few. The reasons for media indifference are simple: because they are a part of the establishment and because they depend upon the elite and their institutions for their revenue.[5]

Bartimole has also appeared in other alternative press publications such as *The Free Times* and *Cleveland Scene*. He still contributes to

Thomas Mulready's online Cool Cleveland. Ralph Nader's website League of Fans had this to say about Point of View in 2005:

> While the waves of myopia, indentured status, titillation and trivia continue to advance on the media, the maverick newsletter by Cleveland's Roldo Bartimole gives some of us in Washington a respite.
>
> His (biweekly) Point of View (POV) punctures the balloons of the city's political surrender to corporate fat cats who shake down the Mayor and City Council for huge tax escapes shaping their Stadiums, Arenas, galleries and other baubles built on the backs of tenants, homeowners and small business.

Whenever Bartimole highlighted a particular topic headed toward City Council action, the legislative sponsor could expect to see that "point of view" echoed by several reviewing Council members (the specific number depending on the magnitude of the issue). During my 1990-1995 tenure as Chief Assistant Director of Law for Development, I encouraged the attorneys in my section to read all of Bartimole's articles.

As Bartimole evolved to a senior statesman over the last decade, Cleveland Scene Senior Writer Sam Allard has emerged as a logical successor. Bearing strong journalist credentials, Allard is a graduate of the Medill School of Journalism at Northwestern University and the NEOMFA at Cleveland State. Prior to joining Scene, he was encamped in Sarajevo, Bosnia, on an investigative reporting fellowship with the Organized Crime and Corruption Reporting Project. Although Allard is apt to cover any local political issue, he addresses corporate welfare to sports franchises in a manner that must make Bartimole very proud.

Downtown Versus the Neighborhoods

Though it is a byproduct of urban populism, the theme of "downtown versus the neighborhoods" deserves its own mention. The political argument that a proposed downtown project is occurring at the expense of the City's neighborhoods has been a reliable tool for City Council members who seek to either derail a proposal or hold it hostage. Apart from its use during debates on particular projects, this proposition has been regularly adopted every four years by virtually every candidate or candidates running in opposition to the sitting mayor.

Catering to Suburbanites

If you appear before a Cleveland City Council committee hearing seeking any kind of public support for a professional sports facility, it won't be long before you are accused of "catering to suburbanites." Inevitably, one or more Council members will lament that "my constituents in my ward can't afford to attend events in the facility." And, as a result, "most of the attendees are coming from the suburbs and we can't afford to be subsidizing their playground."

Community Benefits and Affirmative Action

It is not unusual for community benefits/affirmative action questions and speeches to consume half or more of the total City Council review time for a particular project. Developers and sports teams appearing before Council can be shockingly unsophisticated on this point, failing to prepare for— and fumbling their answers to —predictable Council cross examinations on their company's equitable practices.

Naively, corporate presenters often assume that they can sidestep hard community benefits/affirmative action inquiries by promoting their charitable giving histories or their economic impact studies. But the long City Council Finance Committee table is haunted by the ghosts of past CEO's and CFO's who were eviscerated after entering with such assumptions.

In some cities, nonprofit groups or neighborhood organizations negotiate community benefits from sponsors of major projects on a case-by-case basis. But in Cleveland, most desired community benefits are spelled out in advance via detailed codified ordinances. The major examples include:

- Best efforts in contracting for minority business enterprises ("MBE's), female business enterprises (FBE's), and small business enterprises ("SBE's);
- Percentages requirements for hiring Cleveland/low-income residents;
- Workforce development requirements;
- Bidding incentives for local procurement; and
- Living wage requirements.

Sponsors of large projects (particularly those located downtown) should view these codified ordinances as a floor—and not a ceiling— for their obligations. Their chances of City Council passage can be enhanced via additional offered benefits such as stated percentages of permanent jobs for City residents, job training offers, and grants or loans to community groups.

Affirmative action in company hiring practices is equally important. Here, the usual corporate misstep is to assume that an African-American face in the presenting team can mask years of "affirmative inaction." City Council members sometimes obtain photos of the company's leadership team and board of directors in advance of the Council hearing. If that profile is nearly or entirely "White Male," the company's presenter will have a lot to answer for at the Committee table.

"Voodoo Economics"

When preparing for Cleveland City Council members' responses to economic testimony, the best advice I ever got came from Mayor Frank Jackson: "Remember," he said. "What's the truth got to do with it?" Over the years I learned to handle economic testimony by hitting it quickly and moving on, not letting the deal's common-sense appeal get buried by a debate over numbers. Two examples help make the point.

First, as noted above, major development project presenters often include an economic impact study that quantifies direct and indirect project benefits. Some dissenting Council members will entice you down the rabbit hole of an endless numbers debate which detracts from your core message; others will feign naivete re the study's methodology—broadly dismissing it as "voodoo economics"—and proceed directly to a conclusion that "this won't benefit my constituents" (alleging that it only serves downtown residents and suburbanites).

Second, suppose you are testifying in support of a deal where most of the proposed City payments or receipts do not occur upfront;

rather, they are spread out over a period of 10-20 years or longer. Deals that involve payments or receipts of money over long periods of time require an understanding of "the time value of money." Simply stated, a dollar paid or received five years from today is not worth as much as a dollar paid or received today, since the dollar paid or received today can be invested and accumulate interest over the next five years.

Anyone who is paying off a home mortgage understands this concept. Nevertheless, in Cleveland politics, it's not unusual for a council member who opposes your project to pretend ignorance. To exaggerate the amount the City is paying, he or she will simply add up all the future payments and harangue you over the gross amount, making no allowance for the time value of money. That's because the larger number better serves his or her purpose of making the deal look worse to the general public.

Certainly, every city has its own political rituals. West coast cities are extremely hard sells on sports subsidies. By contrast, the City of Indianapolis—which has successfully staked its downtown vitality on both amateur and professional sports (witness the city's capture of the entire 2021 NCAA Basketball Tournament)—is usually receptive to any project that further enhances the local sports environment.

Cleveland lies somewhere in between, but the political quirks described above will always drive the discussion at the City Council Finance table.

CHAPTER TWO

CLEVELAND'S SPORTS FACILITY SETTING IN 1988

Cleveland had three major professional sports franchises in 1988. The Cleveland Browns and Cleveland Indians played in Cleveland Municipal Stadium on the downtown lakefront, and the Cleveland Cavaliers played in the semi-rural Richfield Coliseum.

The Browns were thriving, in the midst of playing in three conference championship games in a four-year period. So were the young and improving Cavaliers, on the verge of challenging Michael Jordan's Chicago Bulls for Eastern Conference dominance over the next five years. The Indians remained a disappointment, failing to deliver on promise shown during a standout 1986 season.

Cleveland Municipal Stadium 1931-1988

Designed to seat 78,189 for baseball and 83,000 for football—giving it the largest individual seating capacity of any outdoor arena in the world-- Cleveland Municipal Stadium opened in 1931 at a $3 million construction cost. It was truly innovative in its conception: at a time when nearly all ballparks were privately financed by team owners, Cleveland voters approved $2.5 million of city bonds to fund the Stadium. Stadium historian James Toman explained their rationale:

> Baseball, however, was not to be the main thrust of a civic campaign designed to sell the project to the voters. A citizens committee was formed, chaired by long-time civic and business leader Charles A. Otis. Otis's blue-ribbon committee consisted of forty-seven of the city's foremost educational, business, political, and religious leaders (including Floyd Rowe). The committee detailed some sixty possible uses for a city-owned stadium, including pageants, dramatic offerings, musical entertainments, civic gatherings, business expositions, in addition to a variety of athletic events. In athletics alone, the committee foresaw the stadium being used for: boxing, wrestling, gymnastics, track and field events, skating, hockey, tennis, soccer, and even cricket, in addition to the standard favorites of baseball and football. The sponsors also envisioned the facility used for all levels of sporting events, from the pros, to college games, and even for high school contests.[1]

Over time, Cleveland Municipal Stadium hosted virtually all of these events. So did its west-coast counterpart, Los Angeles' Memorial Coliseum. These two facilities were forty years ahead of their time, previewing the late 1960s and early 1970s popularity of city-financed multi-use stadiums in Cincinnati, Pittsburgh, Philadelphia, Washington, D.C., and Atlanta. The Cleveland and Los Angeles citizenries got their money's worth from their investments in multi-purpose stadia.

Notable Stadium events with respective attendances included a World Heavyweight Championship boxing match between Max Schmeling and Young Stribling in 1931 (37,000); the 7th National Eucharistic Congress of 1935 (125,000); a Notre Dame/Navy 1947 college football game (84,090); the Indians drawing 72,434 fans to a 1948 night game (featuring the first start of Satchell Paige) and 86,288 fans to Game 5 of the 1948 World Series; the Browns winning NFL Championship games against the Rams in 1950 (29,751), the Lions in 1954 (43,827) and the Colts in 1964 (79,544); the Beatles performing in 1966 (24,000); the first-ever Monday Night Football game in 1970 (85,703); Frank Robinson hitting a home run in 1975 on opening day in his debut as the Major League's first African-American manager (56,000+); hosting the "World Series of Rock" from 1974-1980, including Pink Floyd in 1977 (83,199) and the Rolling Stones in 1978 (82,238); hosting the Billy Graham Crusade in 1994 (230,000); and hosting the Concert for the Rock and Roll Hall of Fame in 1995 (65,000+).

But, as historian James A. Toman observed:

> Even a new facility is not without its share of problems. And as a facility ages, the challenges which it faces increase. Regular mainte-nance and extraordinary repairs, of course, must be undertaken. But changes in the needs of the tenants, in the expectations of the patrons, and in the surrounding area all bring pressure on a facility to stay "up to date." Over the years, Cleveland Stadium has faced many challenges and witnessed many changes.[2]

Ideally, the rents paid by the sports teams and the revenues from other concession agreements would have been sufficient to allow the City to pay the annual bond debt service *and* contribute annual amounts toward capital improvements. But, after leasing the

Stadium for the 1932 and 1933 seasons, the Indians became disenchanted with the venue's suitability for baseball. The meager Depression-era attendance totals didn't square with the Stadium's 78,000 capacity, and die-hard fans preferred the intimacy of the smaller League Park facility still owned by the club at East 66th and Lexington.

Consequently, from 1934-1946, the Indians played most of their weekday games at League Park and used the Stadium only on weekends, night games, and for special games promising large crowds.

This unexpected development laid waste to the City's original financial projections:

> Only once in its history did the Stadium operate completely in the black. That was 1948.... The reality of this kind of financial situation meant that changes to the Stadium and its surroundings would generally have to depend on resources other than the facility's owner.[3]

Though their initial Stadium financial model had been undermined, City officials still found money for some Stadium investments. The below table lists Stadium improvements from 1932-1972, focusing on city expenditures but including—when discernable—some team funded improvements.[4]

YEAR	IMPROVEMENTS	COST IN $
1936	Construct Donald Gray Gardens north of Stadium	Unknown
1939	Replace 250 field lights	55,000
1944	Paint brickwork, replace concrete, roof/sheet metal, painting, pipe rail & wire rods, enamel repair, box seats repair, install electrical standby, plumbing and electrical repairs	200,000
1945	Increase field lights to 716 lamps	89,288
1947	Rest room improvements	5,319
1948	Increase field lights to 796 lamps	25,000
1949	Construct new pedestrian bridge replacing Great Lakes Exposition's "Bridge of the Presidents" that connected Mall C to the lakefront	134,719
1949	Parking lot fence	1,084
1949-50	Painting and repairs, new box office at Gate A, increase field lights to 1,318 lamps ($77,000), two baseball scoreboards	350,000
1953	Renovate original scoreboard Add clock and football timer Rehabilitate bleacher wall	122,000 35,000 6,893
1954	Paint all structural steel Repair expansion joints, concrete ceilings, bleachers	118,378 133,970
1958	Carpeting Pedestrian bridge repairs	40,260 8,311
1960	Install football press box	81,779
1961	Reconstruct/rehab roof, flashing, expansion joints	61,152
1962	Install Chief Wahoo sign at Gate D	Unknown
1965	Install new baseball press box Install public address systems Renovate/rehab rest rooms	200,000 62,690 65,000
1966-69	New office addition to Towers A and B, open Stadium Club, clean all bricks, install 1,000 field boxes, install two new escalators, replace 920 field lights with halite lights	3,375,000
TOTAL IMPROVEMENTS 1932-1972		5,170,852

In late 1973, the City of Cleveland executed a 25-year lease with Cleveland Browns owner Art Modell's Cleveland Stadium Corporation under which the latter entity took over operation and maintenance of the Stadium and subleased to the Cleveland Indians. The lease required the lessee to complete $10 million of capital improvements during the lease term.

Over time, Modell more than fulfilled the capital investment requirement. In fact, as of the November, 1995, date when he sought to breach the lease and relocate the Browns to Baltimore, Modell had invested over *$18 million* in Stadium capital improvements. The specific investments actually made by Cleveland Stadium Corporation over the lease term—the cost of which were almost entirely financed by borrowings at interest rates ranging from 6.2% to 19.9%--are listed in the following table.

YEAR	CLEVELAND STADIUM CORPORATION IMPROVEMENT	COST IN $
1974	Construct 108 bi-level loges	1,500,000
1975	Install new playing field and drainage tiles	4,600,000
1976	Install additional drainage tiles	1,000,000
1977	Install new scoreboard	504,000
1978	Replace 11,000 wooden box seats with molded plastic seats	676,000
1979		200,000
1980		177,000
1981	Install additional drainage tiles	260,000
1982	Replace plumbing and wiring	1,700,000
1983	Improve concession stands	15,000
1984		212,000
1985		100,000
1986		380,000
1987		437,000
1988		225,000
1989	Install new scoreboard	5,352,000
1990	Renovate locker rooms	538,000
1991	Renovate rest rooms	290,000
1992		325,000
1993		390,000
TOTAL INVESTMENT 1974-1993		18,281,000

Note: Sources are MICHAEL POPLAR, FUMBLE, and a "Stadium Capital Improvements" table submitted by the Browns as part of their relocation application submitted to the National Football League in November, 1995.

Summarizing, the City of Cleveland did not have a strong record of maintaining its Stadium, particularly in the last decade (1964-1973) of the City's sole control of the facility when there was more need for repairs than in the early history of the facility. During Art Modell's 20+ years (1974-1995) of control pursuant to his Cleveland Stadium Corporation lease, he significantly upped the level of capital investment (but not by enough to offset years of the City's deferred maintenance). As will be seen in later chapters, the City learned its lesson from this experience and made capital repairs a major point of emphasis when planning its new sports facilities.

At the end of 1987, the Stadium—which seated 78,189 persons in 1931—had revised seating capacities of 74,483 for baseball and 80,098 for football. And in 1988, the City commissioned a financial review of the Stadium lease: Toman's summary of this milestone was:

> Time has also allowed observers to gain a better perspective on the merits of the city's lease of the Stadium to the Stadium Corporation. In 1980, Cleveland Mayor George Voinovich stated that, "If the city had held onto the Stadium, it probably would be closed today." In 1988 a comprehensive analysis of the lease was undertaken on behalf of the City of Cleveland by the accounting firm of Laventhol and Horwath. Laventhol and Horwath's report found that "Cleveland's financial return from Stadium operations is substantially higher than that of the average return of eight comparable cities." The study found that in 1986, stadiums in the other eight cities had suffered an average net loss of $3.7 million, while the City of Cleveland took in $647,815 from Stadium receipts.[5]

Basketball Arenas 1971-1988

The Cleveland Cavaliers joined the National Basketball Association in 1970 and commenced play in the Cleveland Arena located at 3717 Euclid Avenue. This historic but dated building seated 11,000 for basketball and 9,900 for hockey. Privately constructed in 1937 by Albert C. Sutphin at a cost of $1.5 million, the Arena became famous as the site of the world's first Rock & Roll concert—the Moondog Coronation Ball—in 1952.

Real estate operative Nick Mileti purchased the arena and its principal tenant—the Cleveland Barons hockey team—in 1968 and shortly thereafter acquired the rights to the Cavaliers NBA expansion franchise. But to Mileti, the Cleveland Arena was a short-term proposition: he envisioned a day when the metro areas of Cleveland and Akron would merge in the vicinity of semi-rural Richfield Township. It was there, at a farmland site located 10 miles north of downtown Akron and 18 miles south of downtown Cleveland, that Mileti targeted for the construction of a new arena.

But the Cavaliers played their first four seasons—1970-1974—at the old arena on Euclid Avenue. I began following the early woes of the Cavaliers in their inaugural season by taking the Euclid #6 bus from my Case Western Reserve University dormitory to the aging yet intimate Cleveland Arena. The new expansion team struggled mightily, with these years symbolized by a 1970 play in which Cavalier guard John Warren made a basket at opposing team Portland's basketball hoop.

Mileti's move to his new privately-financed $36 million Richfield Coliseum in the fall of 1974 attracted its share of critics, most of whom believed that the basketball team should remain within the City of Cleveland. A Cleveland Magazine writer observed that Mileti was unfazed:

> Mileti says the whole thing was very simple. The people were not downtown and would not come downtown and one had to realize that.[6]

And so:

> For 25 years, the hulking shape of the Richfield Coliseum hunkered incongruously above the cornfields of northeast Ohio, visible for

miles above the plunging ravines, hidden streams, and dense, leaf-carpeted forests of the Cuyahoga River Valley.[7]

For those who undertook the long wintry commutes—the final segment being a narrow, bending country road with scenery reminiscent of the *Polar Express* movie—and navigated their way into the huge rectangular parking lot, the game day experience inside the well-designed Coliseum usually made the "getting there" seem worthwhile. Players felt the same: Boston Celtic legend Larry Bird called Richfield his favorite arena.

CHAPTER THREE

THE GATEWAY SPORTS COMPLEX (ARENA, BALLPARK, AND COMMON AREAS)

When I started work in the Cleveland Law Department in January 1988, two of the City's sports franchises were thriving and the third was challenged yet showing signs of hope.

The Cleveland Browns were legitimate Super Bowl contenders led by youthful offensive stars—quarterback Bernie Kosar, running backs Earnest Byner and Kevin Mack, and receivers Webster Slaughter, Reggie Langhorne, and Brian Brennan—who were all approaching their prime years, and anchored by veteran tight end Ozzie Newsome. In 1988, they would record their second highest annual attendance total of 615,525 (averaging 77,000 attendees per regular season game).

The Cleveland Cavaliers, playing in the still-fresh 14-year-old Richfield Coliseum, would finish the 1988-1989 season with a then-franchise record 57 wins. Led by a trio of youthful NBA All-Stars—guard Mark Price, center Brad Daugherty and forward Larry Nance—they would duel Michael Jordan's emerging Chicago Bulls team in a back-and-forth playoff Game 5 at Richfield Coliseum that was only decided when Jordan sank a foul line jump shot just above Cavalier guard Craig Ehlo's outstretched hand (memorialized since in NBA history as "The Shot").

The regular season attendance total of 730,925 (an average of 17,827 attendees per game) was a franchise record. In a city historically defined by football prowess, the Cavaliers were carving out a niche.

However, baseball remained a challenge in Cleveland. Unlike football—where attendance would remain high despite periodic team losing spells—baseball attendance in Cleveland was a "What have you done lately?" proposition. When the front office produced an exciting pennant-contending team, the fans would turn out: the 1948 Indians team set attendance records that lasted for decades. But, unlike football, Cleveland fans would not show up to support a mediocre product. And, since 1959, the baseball product in Cleveland was less than mediocre.

As a result, as an Indians fan growing up in the 1950's and 1960's, I had to endure frequent threats of the team's departure: to Houston or Minneapolis-St. Paul in 1958, to Seattle or Atlanta in 1964, to Dallas in 1970, to New Orleans in 1971. When I began to learn to read baseball box scores, I checked not only the players' statistics but also the daily attendance numbers.

But, in 1988, there were no immediate threats of franchise relocation. Wealthy real estate entrepreneurs Richard and David Jacobs had purchased the team in 1986 and had hired respected baseball executive Hank Peters to oversee a long-term rebuild of the team and its player procurement process (i.e., "farm system"). The team would compile a 76-84 record in 1988 and attendance would reach 1,411,610 (an average of 17,427 per game, below league average yet the second highest Indians' total since 1959).

Nationally, though it was in the process of surrendering its top popularity ranking to pro football, baseball was rekindling its sentimental roots: two popular and critically acclaimed baseball-themed movies opened in this time period. John Sayles' Eight Men Out contrasted the superb regular season play of the 1919 Chicago White Sox team with the playoff scandal in which eight Sox players conspired with gamblers to throw the World Series. Sayles' film highlighted pitcher Ed Cicotte's family-driven choice to lose two games, third-basemen Buck Weaver's fine Series play (he was banned not because he took money but because he kept silent about those who did), owner Charles Comiskey's miserly treatment of his players, and the gamblers' icy cynicism in locking in the conspirators.

One year later, Phil Alden Robinson's Field of Dreams juxtaposed the same 1919 scandal with an Iowa cornfield to spin out what film critic Roger Ebert called a "religious picture, but the religion is baseball." Themes of fathers and sons, family physician practice, pivotal life choices, and 1960's idealism all combine to create what USA Today ranked as the #2 all-time sports movie (trailing only Hoosiers, released in 1986).

The Effort to Build a New Downtown Ballpark

Of Cleveland's three sports franchises, it was clear that the baseball team was in the most need of new accommodations. Within the past five years, several unrelated initiatives had been launched:

- In 1983, Republican Cuyahoga County Commissioner Vince Campanella—a potential challenger to Ohio Democrat Governor Richard Celeste—proposed a County property

23

tax increase to fund a $150 million multipurpose domed stadium to be located in downtown's Central Market area. Though he convinced fellow County Commissioners Tim Hagan and Virgil Brown to place the issue on the May 1983 primary ballot, he quickly encountered Governor Celeste's strong opposition and saw his issue lose by a 2-1 margin. Adding insult to injury, that fall his Democrat Commissioner opponent Mary Boyle bounced him from office by reminding County voters of his ill-fated property tax proposal;

- In 1985, architect Robert Corna proposed a six-sided "Hexatron" stadium. This proposal never made it to the voters: Mayor Voinovich nixed it in the spring of 1985. However, the Hexatron did attract the interest of Ohio State Representative Jeff Jacobs—son of Dick Jacobs—who proposed an alcohol and cigarette "sin tax" as the funding source. More would be heard from this sin tax proposal.
- Also, in 1985, Cleveland business leaders coalesced to form the Greater Cleveland Domed Stadium Corporation, a nonprofit entity that—presumably due to the high profile of its corporate founders—quickly procured over $20 million of bank loans and began assembling property in the Central Market area to comprise a future site for a multipurpose domed stadium. Reflecting the civic composition of the new nonprofit, its operations were managed by Dennis Lafferty, VP of the Greater Cleveland Growth Association.

Meanwhile, per historian Jack Torry's book detailing the Indians' business history, Mayor Voinovich was conducting his own quiet inquiry into the future of the Cleveland Indians:

The Indians were beginning to worry George Voinovich.... (he) held long talks with Baseball Commissioner Bowie Kuhn and American League President Bobby Brown. The rest of the American League owners, they told Voinovich, had lost their patience with Cleveland. They were fed up with playing before crowds of 5,000 in old Cleveland Stadium, losing money every time they came to town.... With its vast size, Cleveland Stadium offered no incentive for anyone to buy a season ticket. People in downtown Cleveland on a July evening knew perfectly well they could walk down to the stadium and find a seat... He once hosted a cocktail party for some of the baseball owners during a Browns playoff game. Instead of talking football, the owners nagged Voinovich "When are you going to do something? We're getting a little tired of this.[1]

By the beginning of 1989, with the knowledge that over 80% of the land was assembled, most community leaders had settled on a site several blocks south of Public Square (then known as the "Central Market site" but to be renamed "Gateway" a year later) as the location for Cleveland's new sports facility. Less certain was exactly what would be built there.

Clearing the air on a number of topics in a February 1989 Plain Dealer interview, Browns owner Art Modell delivered a prophetic statement of his (and the community's) facility needs:

The only facility that we will be interested in talking about at the Central Market will be a TWIN (emphasis added) facility... a smaller facility for baseball and a larger one for football. We have a dual purpose now. Why should we move? I am happy with the Browns' occupancy of the stadium. Obviously, Dick Jacobs (Indians' co-owner) is not. And I am saying that the city and county direct their efforts toward accommodating his needs for a smaller baseball-only grass facility. If the developers cannot do a twin complex, then they should concentrate on baseball, and maybe an arena...Should the community end up building a baseball-only stadium for the Indians, I expect the city fathers and powers that be to give Cleveland Stadium Corp. some help to keep this place going absent a baseball tenant.[2]

This placed Modell in the same frame of mind as Dick Jacobs:

The Indians, meanwhile, were growing cool to playing under a dome.... (Soon after Jacobs bought the Indians) it quickly became apparent to Lafferty that Jacobs was more interested in an open-air baseball-only park. Without a firm commitment from the Indians, the domed corporation's work could not proceed. Finally, on November 2, 1987, Dick Jacobs made public what Lafferty had suspected: The Indians would move to the Central Market but only in a small, intimate ballpark. Real grass. No dome.[3]

In quieter, "under the radar" fashion, Jacobs and his baseball executive were investing in the team's farm system in a manner not seen in Cleveland since the ballclub's last heyday in the mid 1950's. At that time the Indians' player procurement methods were the envy of baseball. Their rich farm system yielded plenty of players from traditional sources, among them pitchers Herb Score and Jim Perry and outfielders Roger Maris and Rocky Colavito. But where they really outpaced their American League rivals was in the procurement of players from nontraditional groups; African-Americans (Satchel Paige, Larry Doby, Al Smith, Luke Easter, Jim "Mudcat" Grant), and Hispanics (Minnie Minoso, Mike Garcia, Bobby Avila).

But except for a brief period in the early 1960's (when the farm system delivered pitchers Sam McDowell, Tommy John and Luis Tiant, outfielder Tommy Agee, and third baseman Max Alvis), for thirty years the Indians had watched their competitors snap up the best prospects.

After persuading Jacobs to invest big dollars in the farm system, Peters was starting to change that dynamic. In the annual draft, the Indians added outfielder Albert Belle (1987), pitcher Charles Nagy (1988), third baseman Jim Thome and outfielder Brian Giles (1989), and outfielder Manny Ramirez and pitcher Chad Ogea (1991). Peters also tested the fans' patience by trading major league stars for future prospects: outfielder Joe Carter for catcher Sandy Alomar, second baseman Carlos Baerga, and outfielder Chris James in 1989, and catcher Ed Taubensee for outfielder Kenny Lofton in 1991.

In their book looking back on this period, writer Terry Pluto and broadcaster Tom Hamilton concluded:

> "The best decision that Dick Jacobs made after buying the Indians was to bring in Hank Peters as team president," said (Indians' broadcaster) Tom Hamilton. "Hank has never received the credit that he is due. It's Hank Peters who made the Joe Carter trade, bringing in Sandy Alomar and Carlos Baerga. It's Hank who hired John Hart and Danny O'Dowd. It's Hank who had the vision of how to build up the farm system, and he knew how to do it because he was (general manager) in Baltimore when the Orioles had a great farm system. It was Hank who took all the shots from the media when the Indians were slowly building the teams that would be so good in the 1990s. The fact that Dick Jacobs knew enough to hire Hank Peters was the first sign that Dick Jacobs was a very smart man when it came to owning a baseball team."[4]

By the spring of 1989, the community seemed to be answering two of the three questions concerning the Indians' facility: *what to build* (an open-air baseball-only stadium) and *where to build it* (Central Market). The third question—how to finance it—had yet to be answered.

It was then that Governor Dick Celeste asked his former cabinet member and 20-year colleague and friend, lawyer Tom Chema (they had first met at the 1968 Democratic National Convention), to "go to the public-sector players in town and try and develop a consensus behind putting public money in the pot."[5] Easier said than done, particularly in an election year where Cleveland mayoral candidates included County Commissioner Tim Hagan, Cleveland City Council President George Forbes, and Ohio State Senator Michael R. White. Chema bided his time and awaited the outcome of the election.

Browns owner Art Modell grew concerned when he learned of an option to design the new 44,000 seat stadium to allow for another 28,000 seats for football. Acting on a February, 1989, invitation from Mayor Voinovich to develop his own proposal, Modell called an August 16, 1989, press conference at second base of the Stadium field. There he and his architect, Ron Labinsky of HOK, unveiled a 5-foot model of an $80 million modernization of Cleveland Municipal Stadium into a roofless, column-less facility with retractable seating (allowing for 72,000 for football and 52,000 for baseball), and double the number of restrooms.

Though Mayor Voinovich delivered a supportive quote, neither he nor his upper staff members attended the press conference, leaving Modell—who showed off his model like a cat delivering a fresh-caught mouse to the feet of its owner—more than a little bit peeved. As noted in a book by Modell's VP/Treasurer Mike Poplar:

While the conference was well-attended, conspicuous by their absence were Mayor George Voinovich and his aide Ed Richard. In the years to come, Modell often referred to the snub he received by City Hall that day.[6]

Within five days of the Modell press conference, Mayor Voinovich was calling for a "stadium summit" to discuss the two competing sports stadium proposals. Nevertheless, with the benefit of hindsight, Mayor Voinovich's absence at the Modell event was a mistake. Modell was a public relations professional prior to his purchase of the Browns, and he was always extraordinarily sensitive to media and public opinion.

Earlier that year he had asked for the Cleveland City Council session where he informed the Council that he would construct a new scoreboard with his funds without benefit of a lease extension. Shortly thereafter, Mayor Voinovich asked Modell to determine whether the Stadium could be refurbished as an alternative to a costly new stadium. Obviously proud of his work product, he was clearly miffed at City Hall's "no show" and never forgot the snub.

Adding A New Downtown Arena to the Mix

Two days after the November election, Chema met with Mayor-elect White. It didn't take Chema long to realize he was dealing with a very unconventional politician.

White had grown up in the Glenville neighborhood on Cleveland's northeast side and attended The Ohio State University where he became the school's first African-American student body president.

From there he returned to Cleveland and commenced his political career as a Cleveland City Councilman, acquiring a reputation as both a quick study and an effective enforcer (his enemies would have said "hatchet man") for Council President George Forbes' agenda. Next came a stint as a State Senator, followed by his upset victory over George Forbes in the 1989 mayor's race.

But internally, White's political aspirations were atypical. Most politicians govern with one eye on their current constituency and one eye on the constituency they seek to serve in the future as they proceed up a career political ladder. By contrast, Mayor White had decided back as a teenager in Glenville that his sole political aspiration was to become Mayor of Cleveland: not for the title or the trappings of office, but *to serve*. Once in office, he would commit his limitless energies to advancing the choices for those Clevelanders who had the fewest choices in life.

He had definite ideas on how to improve the quality of life in Cleveland neighborhoods: if you invested in public safety enhancements, you could encourage more people to take a chance on staying in—or moving into—a Cleveland neighborhood; conversely, if you invest in new housing construction in that same neighborhood, you add new neighbors who will by their presence make the neighborhood safer. He was also preparing to take an extremely active role in the improvement of the city's public schools.

Though he admitted to Chema that he was not much of a sports fan, he displayed a competitive fire—a willingness to obliterate any obstacle standing in the way of the accomplishment of his goals— that any of Cleveland's pro athletes would be proud to own. Chema realized that the "trophy" of a new sports edifice would by itself prove insufficient to induce Mayor White to lead a campaign to the voters.

When Chema went on to ask what *would* be a sufficient incentive, Mayor White responded that there had to be real economic development that would benefit rank-and-file Clevelanders. Standing alone, a new 40,000-seat ballpark would fall short, since it would only replace jobs that already existed in downtown Cleveland. Indians' historian Torry set forth the solution:

> To Chema, the only possibility was to (add) a large indoor arena for basketball, ice hockey, and shows. Chema calculated that an indoor arena packed with nightly events would draw an additional 2.5 million people downtown every year. They would spend their money downtown for dinner, parking and tickets to the arena, and satisfy White's demand that the project provide a long-term boost to Cleveland.[7]

In short, Art Modell's prophesy of the best solution to Cleveland's sports facility dilemma was taking shape. But there were at least three problems: The Cavaliers were reasonably happy with their still fairly new Richfield Coliseum, Cleveland State University had just invested in a brand-new 11,000-seat arena less than a mile to the east, and a ballpark plus arena project was twice as complicated (and nearly twice as costly) as a ballpark-only project.

Confronted with these new challenges, Chema updated County Commissioner Tim Hagan, who was still smarting from his elimination from the mayoral race in the September, 1989 primary. Historian Torry observed:

> But in Cleveland politics, there are no permanent enemies, just temporary allies. A few days after the election, Hagan asked White about a new stadium. "If we're going to do this, you've got to be with us," Hagan told the mayor-elect. "You've got to be a co-chair

with me." White repeated what he already told Tom Chema: "I want to make sure we get the Cavaliers downtown as part of the deal."[8]

By December, 1989, Chema was on his third round of talks with Cleveland business and political leaders and was receiving consensus on a plan for an open-air ballpark and an indoor basketball arena, with funding derived half from public sources and half from private sources.[9] The private money would come from the team owners; directly via cash payments and indirectly via loge and club seat purchases.

The public money decision was more difficult. Some potential sources (property taxes and sales taxes) were quickly eliminated: the "ghost of Vince Campanella" and his failed domed stadium property tax levy still haunted northeast Ohio's political officials. The ideal tax would be one that could be avoided if the voters so chose and would be linked in some fashion to the actual users of the sports facilities.

At this point Chema and his confidents made one of the most important decisions in the long effort to fund new Cleveland sports facilities: they turned to Jeff Jacobs' 1985 proposal for a sin tax on alcohol and cigarettes. It fared better than other options in the early polling, and the title itself—*sin tax*—also helped. Its chief drawback, which critic Roldo Bartimole immediately publicized, was its regressive nature: it disproportionately taxed poor people.

The Gateway Campaign

In January, 1990, Chema took stock of his progress: he had achieved consensus that the community would construct a ballpark and arena at the Central Market site. But he still faced a dizzying array of issues: when to hold the sin tax election, who would manage the campaign, and how to reach basic agreements with the Indians and Cavaliers. He began by setting a deadline and working backwards. He knew that he had to sell the bonds for the project by the end of 1990 in order to take advantage of expiring federal tax incentives.

That deadline drove the decision to set the vote for the May primary. Though that early date set a staggering agenda for the next four months—Chema and the public officials would be negotiating the teams' letters of intent while simultaneously running the sin tax campaign—it did have the advantage of leaving the rest of the year available for negotiating the far more complicated team leases and bond closing documents. Moreover, the "quick strike" May voting date gave the opponents less time to mobilize an opposition.[10]

So Chema and the public officials began negotiating nonbinding letters of intent with the teams. On the other side of the negotiations were Dick Jacobs and Cavaliers general counsel Dick Watson. At first glance, the Cavaliers appeared to present the tougher hurdle. They had considerable leverage: they were doing just fine in Richfield, and they would only move to the Central Market site if their economics at the new site were equal to or better than their Richfield arrangements. And no one who had dealt with Dick Watson in the past could say he didn't take full advantage of every leverage point.

Superficially, the Jacobs negotiations looked easier: the Indians would be getting a brand-new state-of-the-art baseball facility and would pay less rent than they paid to Art Modell in Cleveland Municipal Stadium. Moreover, over the last five years Jacobs had sunk millions of dollars into nearby downtown investments: Society Tower (Cleveland's tallest building, since renamed Key Tower), the Galleria shopping mall, and a parking lot upon which Jacobs hoped to construct a new Ameritrust skyscraper. Did anyone think that Jacobs would walk away from ballpark negotiations when he had these adjacent major investments to consider?

But Dick Jacobs did not become Cleveland's strongest real estate investor without accumulating a few scalps along the way. As frequent Jacobs critic Roldo Bartimole put it:

> Dick Jacobs once said "I believe in the quantum theory of profits to the nth power." He lived by that motto.... (Then quoting Jacobs' response to a George Forbes request for a community contribution) "Bye, bye, Pasadena. No way. There's no deal. It's not in the deal. It's as simple as that. The figures are here for everyone to see...The patient is breathing heavily. Don't kill it."[11]

The letter of intent negotiations dragged...and dragged...and dragged. That made it difficult for campaign spokespeople to answer basic questions about the deal structure until the last days of the campaign. As Torry explained:

> Not until the spring of 1990 did the Indians and Cavaliers officially sign an agreement with Chema. The public would contribute half the estimated cost of $344 million for a 45,000-seat stadium and 20,000-seat arena. *Chema also insisted that the teams manage the facilities and that taxpayers not be handed an annual bill to cover operating*

deficits. The rest would be raised by the teams through the sale and rental of luxury loges and club seats in the two facilities. The Indians would provide $20 million at the very beginning and nearly $3 million annually for the capital costs of construction.[12] (Emphasis added)

As for the campaign itself, Chema and the public officials identified their endeavor as the "Gateway Project" and selected Jones Day attorney Oliver "Pudge" Henkel to manage the effort. Henkel's long list of accomplishments included managing Senator Gary Hart's longshot 1984 presidential campaign into near-contention.

Campaign ads embedding promises are always tricky. Viewing through the prism of the Great Depression of the 1930's, Democrats gleefully mocked the 1928 Republican campaign promise of "a chicken in every pot." Similarly, Gateway critics in 1990—and throughout the years since—have had a field day with the campaign's signature newspaper ad:

"Who wins with Issue 2?" blared a newspaper ad just days before the 1990 vote. "We All Do," answered the placard held by a multi-cultural rainbow of Cleveland schoolchildren. "Gateway will create a development that will generate $33.7 million in public revenues every year and provide: 28,000 good-paying jobs for the *jobless*; Neighborhood housing development for the *homeless*; $15 million a year for schools for our *children*; revenues for City and County clinics and hospitals for the sick; energy assistance for the *elderly*." The ad went on to promise what wouldn't be taken from taxpayers' wallets or given to team owners: "No property tax; no sales tax; no income tax; no tax abatement...Gateway: the next chapter in our future."[13]

Henkel and Chema then decided to ask Mayor White to highlight his support of the issue via television ads. The new mayor's decision on whether to accept such a high- profile role was not without risk; a failure at the polls could have slowed or stalled his momentum in developing programs to advance Cleveland neighborhoods and schools. A more cautious politician would have sought a background role in the campaign: "Wasn't this a county tax, after all? Shouldn't the County Commissioners be leading the charge? That way, if the thing craters, I don't end up taking the main hit just five months into my mayoral term."

Mayor White didn't see it that way; "half-stepping" was just not in his nature. His history was to run *to* fights, not *away* from them. He enthusiastically embraced his TV-spokesman role, freely spending the political capital he had built up with city and county residents during his energetic campaign for mayor.

The campaign's most contentious event occurred less than a week before the election when Major League Baseball Commissioner Fay Vincent came to town. Vincent had been in office less than a year, having been elevated from his Deputy Commissioner role upon Bart Giamatti's sudden death from a heart attack.

He was immediately challenged by the October 1989 earthquake during the San Francisco/Oakland World Series. After some tense sparring with San Francisco Mayor Al Agnos, the Series resumed ten days after the quake and a national poll found that 85% of the public approved of the way that Major League Baseball handled the situation.[14]

Shortly thereafter he angered many MLB owners by prematurely (at least in the dissenting owners' view) settling a March, 1990 owners' lockout of Spring Training. And storm clouds were already gathering ahead of a pending National League decision to add two teams via expansion. Owners disliked expansion because it diluted their product and, in the words of baseball historian John Helyar:

> ...removed some of the scarcity that undergirded the value of the franchises. When a city without a team—like St. Petersburg—made a play for another city's team—like the (Chicago) White Sox —it opened up delicious possibilities.[15]

In that White Sox example, the team's owners successfully parlayed their St. Petersburg relocation threat into a brand new Comiskey Park Stadium approved by a last-minute, June 30, 1988 vote of the Illinois legislature. St. Petersburg was still out there as a stalking horse, with its $100 million spec-built domed ballpark (later enhanced with $30 million interior improvements approved by the Florida legislature).

Thus, when Dick Jacobs invited Fay Vincent to attend City Council President Jay Westbrook's Finance Committee meeting on May 2, 1990—less than a week before the sin tax election date—the newly-minted Baseball Commissioner knew what to do. I was present at that Finance Committee meeting, and that session began my education on the roles that the major sports leagues play in local stadium building decisions.

The next day's Plain Dealer top-fold, front-page headline said it all: "Baseball Chief opposes city losing Indians, but says move is possible." The story quoted Vincent's warning:

> "Should the facility not be available in Cleveland, should the vote be a negative one, we may find ourselves confronting a subject that we want to avoid...." and added: Vincent indicated that the Indians met at least three of the four criteria for moving. He said the team has lost a substantial amount of money since owners Richard E.

and David Jacobs bought it, has had poor attendance, and plays in a stadium poorly regarded by other teams. Vincent added that defeat of Issue 2, the Gateway proposal, would be one indicator that the team had lost community support.[16]

Election day arrived on May 8, 1990. By late morning it was apparent there would be a very high turnout. It was less apparent whether the turnout was good or bad news. After the polls closed, early returns from the City wards showed the issue losing. But later results from the eastern suburbs turned the tide, and the final tally showed a narrow 51.7% approval outcome. Per Torry, Commissioner Hagan and Mayor White grabbed sunglasses and did a Blues Brothers celebratory routine.

But Tom Chema was not ready for sleep. He drove down to Dpoo's in the flats. Ahead of him was a year of tough negotiations with Dick Jacobs on a long-term lease, petty squabbles with the two teams over construction of Gateway, and a funding gap that had to be closed. But none of that mattered on this night. Tom Chema ordered a drink. It was fun, he thought, to win.[17]

Planning the Gateway Neighborhood

In 1991, the Gateway sponsors hired landscape architects Sasaki, Inc., to do a plan for the neighborhood surrounding the project. In doing so, they were anticipating a national shift in the principal justification for sports facility investments, as explained in a 2004 article in the Journal of the American Planning Association:

Many of these (economic impact) studies miss the mark in assessing the rationale for public investments in sports facilities. A major shift in the economic development rationale has occurred in the past decade. While previous decades saw stadium proponents emphasize the indirect economic benefits of a new facility, using terms such as *spinoff, multipliers*, and *job creation*, the current economic development rationale for almost all of these projects rest upon the idea of district redevelopment.[18]

By building new sports facilities in the heart of downtown, the public officials were hoping to add vitality and spur restoration and adaptive reuse of the adjacent older buildings. They were aware— from examples in Baltimore and other cities—that if left unchecked, parking lot operators would buy up the buildings within a half-mile radius, demolish them, and construct parking lots to serve the new sports facilities. They undertook at least six initiatives to ensure that this scenario would not play out in Cleveland.

First, as noted in the above-referenced Journal article, they made an early commitment to district planning:

> The intention to utilize the Gateway Complex as an urban redevelopment catalyst is detailed in both the Cleveland Civic Vision 2000 Downtown Plan (Cleveland City Planning Commission, 1988) and the Gateway Project Notebook (Sasaki Associates, Inc., 1991) ....Unlike Camden Yards (in Baltimore), the Gateway project emphasized not just visual connections with the city but physical connections to the surrounding district in the form of planned, funded, and constructed pedestrian pathways to other nearby activity centers.[19]

Second, they included two new parking garages, physically-connected to the sports facilities, in the Gateway project: the 2100-space East Garage, and the 1100-space North Garage. Third, knowing that the 3,200 new garage spaces would fall far short of the parking needs for the new sports facilities, they gambled that most downtown office workers would decide to leave their cars at their workplaces and walk the short distances to and from the sports facilities.

Fourth, they worked with Ron Tober, General Manager of the Greater Cleveland Regional Transit Authority, to cause construction of a $10 million underground tunnel connecting the ballpark and arena to the regional public transit hub located in Forest City's recently-opened 360,000 square-foot, $387 million mixed-use Tower City Center redevelopment project.

Fifth, to coordinate district projects, they formed a development corporation:

> The Historic Gateway Neighborhood (HGN) association (origi-
> nally the Gateway Economic Development Corporation) was
> created by combining local business groups to help oversee the
> project and push local redevelopment efforts.[20]

Sixth, acting on the advice of his Planning Director Hunter Morrison, Mayor White instructed his attorneys to draft a new "Public Land Protective District" ordinance. The ordinance created a district in an approximate-one-mile radius surrounding the new ballpark and arena: within this district you could not demolish older buildings without first documenting to the Cleveland City Planning Commission the "present and potential economic viability of the subject building or structure, given its physical condition and marketability." In this ordinance, passed by Cleveland City Council on June 19, 1995, lay the key to the preservation of—and future flourishing of—the East 4th Street entertainment district.

Constructing the Gateway Project

Gateway did not have the luxury of a lengthy construction timeline: if it did, it could have set its contracts with flexible completion dates, thereby encouraging more competitive, lower bids (based on bidders' knowing they would have a cushion against bad weather and other contingencies outside their control).

But Gateway did have the services of a national construction law expert: Cleveland-based ThompsonHine's Jeff Appelbaum. I had been watching Jeff in action as a construction attorney for nearly a decade, and he was simply the best in the field. He earned a B.A. degree with distinction from Cornell University in 1974, and a law degree, cum laude, from Cornell in 1977.

Since 1980, he had served the construction industry in the varying roles of trial and transactional attorney, project counsel, project management consultant, mediator and partnering facilitator. He represented public and private owners, design professionals, construction managers and contractors on important projects throughout the United States and Canada.

Though Gateway was one of his first major sports facility clients, over the succeeding two decades he would go on to serve as project counsel or owner's representative for 20 major league sports facilities and other projects throughout North America (including facilities for the Jacksonville Jaguars, San Francisco 49ers, Minnesota Twins, Orlando Magic, Pittsburgh Penguins, Miami Marlins, Kansas City Royals, St. Louis Cardinals, Minnesota Wild, Chicago Bears, Toledo Mud Hens, Pittsburgh Pirates, and Golden State Warriors).

Appelbaum and his ThompsonHine colleagues faced many challenges on the Gateway construction project,[21] but none was more daunting than the compressed construction timeline. Gateway's July 3, 1991, lease to the Cleveland Indians and its December 20, 1991, lease to the Cleveland Cavaliers each required completion of facilities by the teams' respective 1994 opening dates. This tight timeline not only led to higher bids; it also precluded Gateway from using a traditional design-bid-build construction approach. Instead, Gateway used a phased fast-track process.

The contractor selection process commenced in the summer of 1990 when Gateway issued Requests for Proposals ("RFP's") for the following services:

- A Program and Planning Consultant;
- A Stadium Architect;
- An Arena Architect;
- A Service Level Architect;
- A Parking Garage Architect; and
- A Cost and Constructability Consultant.

When awarded, the respective contracts departed from many of the standard terms embedded in the American Institute of Architects form agreements that were widely used on privately-funded construction projects. The Gateway agreements' phased fast-track approach allowed design and construction phases to overlap, placed heavy emphasis on joint development of facilitating programs through use of partnering techniques, minimized surprises by wrapping "reimbursables" and "additional services" into a lump-sum fee for services, and minimized litigation through use of an Alternative Dispute Resolution process.

In the fall of 1991, Gateway selected separate construction managers for the Stadium and Arena projects.

As a non-public entity (a status later confirmed in federal court litigation), Gateway was able to have its attorneys structure pre-hire multiple project labor agreements ("PLA's") with the construction trade unions. The PLA's prohibited work stoppages and assured access to quality tradespeople, and the Cleveland Building and Construction Trades Council was a key player in enabling this arrangement. Multiple PLA's were signed on November 26, 1991, and the individual unions later ratified them (as did the Gateway board in a February, 1992 meeting).

The Associated Builders and Contractors—an organization of non-union builders—was less enthusiastic about the PLA's, but that entity's request for an injunction in its March 30, 1992, lawsuit in U.S. District Court was denied in a May 12, 1992, decision issued by Judge Ann Aldrich (a decision later confirmed on appeal).

The Gateway board valued diversity and inclusion, and instructed its attorneys to draft provisions for participation by minority and female business enterprises, employment of minorities and women in construction and operation of the facilities, and monitoring of work by the Black Trades Council and Hard-Hatted Women. The attorneys also drafted strong provisions in the PLA's which—among other remedies— gave Gateway the opportunity to refer individuals to the trade unions.

Apart from defending Gateway in two lawsuits, Gateway's attorneys participated in numerous arbitrations, mediations, and negotiations in furtherance of the project and its aggressive timelines.

Other than our role in preparing the deed from the City to Gateway's predecessors in title, my colleagues in the Cleveland Law Department were minimally involved in the 1990-1991 negotiations which resulted in the major bond financings and the team leases.

Many of Cleveland's major law firms were involved in one way or another in these highly pressurized negotiations.

However, by 1992 the Gateway public costs were growing beyond the limits of the sin tax. Then-Finance Director Steve Strnisha conceived a way for the City to take on $37 million worth of the escalating costs. Strnisha and his successor Kathryn Hyer proposed to package the two new Gateway garages with the City's then-deteriorating 1,500-space underground garage serving City Hall—Willard Garage—into a three-garage, $73 million parking revenue bond issue. The bond proceeds would fund the new 2,100-space L-shaped Gateway East Garage, the new 1,100-space Gateway North Garage, and the renovation of Willard Garage.

Since the City administration would need authorizing legislation to take on ownership and operation of the $37 million worth of new garages at Gateway, Strnisha asked my Law Department colleagues and I to prepare the legislation. That became our entrance into the group of the City's top public financiers and attorneys who were crafting the slew of Gateway agreements.

Two attorneys in my section worked with me on the parking revenue bond issue: Assistant Director of Law Barbara Langhenry (who went on to become Law Director 20 years later) and Assistant Director of Law Debra Rosman (who would become the principle legal advisor to the Finance Department). Both were bright and hardworking Case Western Reserve University Law School graduates. Before we could focus on the specific parking revenue bond documents, we had to take some time to understand the flow of moneys as they channeled through the labyrinths of the previous Gateway deal structures.

A word of advice to in-house attorneys coming late to parties such as this: bury your egos, work harder than anyone else, and watch your backs.

In-house city attorneys throughout the nation quickly learn that their counterparts in the private firms (some consciously and others subconsciously) can treat them in a patronizing fashion. There's an unstated premise that the in-house attorneys are in their low-paying public-sector jobs because they just aren't as good as the attorneys in the big law firms.

Moreover, in our case, we were late entrants to an incredibly complex deal that had been negotiated throughout 1990 and 1991. The last thing the veterans of those delicate negotiations needed were last minute complications thrust upon them by the newly minted city attorneys.

Our experience on this project highlights a significant—and far too common—dynamic in big city mayor's offices. It begins when a mayor conceptualizes basic deal terms in discussions with a private sector actor. The mayor then usually assigns to his or her senior staff the responsibility of hammering out deal specifics that are sufficient to enable the city's law department to prepare authorizing legislation.

In an ideal policy world, the mayor's point person would call in a city lawyer and involve that lawyer in the process of assembling the deal. But the real world often diverges from this ideal. Sometimes the mayor's point person is so focused on the task at hand that he or she inadvertently fails to include the city's lawyers in on the ground floor of the negotiations (*even with* my law department background, I made this mistake more than once during my tenures in mayors' offices). Other times the mayor's point person will *intentionay* exclude the city lawyers, acting on a fear that the lawyers' naysaying might implode the deal before it even takes shape.

Under either scenario, the city lawyers may find themselves charged with enabling a deal that has fundamental legal flaws: flaws which, if they could have been explained to the mayor's point person before the deal was locked in place, might have led to a different deal outcome.

The dilemma facing both the deal-makers and the attorneys when these situations arise is that the mayor's office has already spent valuable capital on the existing deal terms: to backtrack at this late stage would cause the mayor to lose face with the other party and—if the deal has already gone public—with the media and general public as well.

There is a municipal practice lesson for city attorneys placed in these situations. To underscore your commitment to preserving your deal-making client's business reputation, begin by assuring that client that you *know* that bad faith deal revisions are a bad thing, and *then* present your advice to your client on how to *tweak* the deal (rather than blowing it up). I regard the 1974 made-for-TV movie *The Missiles of October* to be a superb negotiating primer. In the movie's depiction of the peaking of tensions during the Cuban missile crisis of 1962, there is a scene in which Soviet Premier Nikita Khrushchev lectures his Presidium:

> We must make it possible for Kennedy to negotiate...without *appearing* to negotiate. We must make it possible for him to compromise...without *appearing* to compromise.

I can offer no better advice to city attorneys forced to walk a tightrope between a legally flawed deal on one side, and a mayoral face-losing calamity on the other side.

Not surprisingly, our early sessions with the Gateway negotiators recalled a Thanksgiving dinner. The Gateway veterans were at the grown-ups table, and we were at the kids table (strictly confined to drafting authorizing legislation for the garage deal and being cautioned not to interrupt or complicate the sophisticated deal implementation actions occurring at the grown-ups table).

But the legislation we were drafting wasn't the simple "find a way to get the parking garages done and don't ask questions about the bigger deal" proposition desired by the Gateway veterans. Once we learned all the complicated money flows and pointed out some concerns to our City financial team clients, we were eventually invited to join the grown-ups table and effect some deal term revisions that better protected the City's interests.

Ultimately, when the dust had settled on the financial and legal documents, the final deal showed significant private participation that nevertheless fell well short of the "50% private, 50% public" format promoted during the Gateway project's early stages. A 1996 tabulation[22] compiled by Squire attorney Barbara Hawley (with assistance from Gateway staff) depicted sources and uses as follows:

ITEM	CONSTRUCTION COSTS ($)	CONSTRUCTION & OPERATING COSTS ($)	SOURCE
USES			
Stadium	180,100,000	180,100,000	
Arena	157,200,000	157,200,000	
Site	41,811,000	41,811,000	
Garages	37,000,000	37,000,000	
Land	21,102,000	21,102,000	
Property Taxes		1,800,000	
Operations		20,001,571	
New Stadium Corp. Debts		1,885,000	
Total Uses	437,213,000	460,899,571	
SOURCES			
Luxury Tax Bonds	86,014,607	86,014,607	Private
Stadium Revenue Bonds	26,740,000	26,740,000	Private
Cuyahoga County Bonds	114,300,000	114,300,000	Public
Prepaid Stadium Seating	20,000,000	20,000,000	Private
Luxury Tax Receipts	44,769,374	44,769,374	Public
Cleveland Development Partnership	28,115,000	28,115,000	Private
Arena Premium Seating Deposits	3,877,257	3,877,257	Private
State Capital Grant	25,000,000	25,000,000	Public
State Stadium Guarantee	12,000,000	12,000,000	Public
State Issue II Proceeds	2,319,585	2,319,585	Public
Interest Income	6,650,000	9,850,000	Private
Parking Revenue		1,170,945	Private
Foundations	1,750,000	1,750,000	Private
Team Contributions	9,295,000	9,295,000	Private
City Garages	37,000,000	37,000,000	Public
Total Sources	415,830,824	439,517,395	
DEFICIT	21,382,176	21,382,176	
Public Funding	235,388,960	252,819,586	
Private Funding	180,441, 854	186,697,809	
Total	415,830,824	439,517,395	
Public Funding Percentage	56.61	57.52	
Private Funding Percentage	43.39	42.48	

Several points from this table are worth noting. First, at that time the chart still showed a $21,382,176 deficit. As described later, the City and County and State were in the process of identifying funding for this gap. Second, an article by Jack DeVries contained in a program distributed on Opening Day, April 4, 1994, described one key private financing source:

One of the more interesting scenarios that played out was the sale of luxury suites and Club Seating before the ballpark was built. "We structured this project as a public-private partnership," (Gateway Executive Director Tom) Chema commented about the plans. "Our principal source of private sector revenue would come from the leasing of Suites and Club Seats. We thought we could convince large numbers of Cleveland corporations to pay the entire lease payment for these seats upfront—something which was never done before.... By pre-selling Suites and Club Seating, $20 million was raised for the construction fund. Jacobs and the Indians agreed to this unusual method of generating revenue, even making large financial concessions and future payments to ensure its success.... This revenue would result in a corporate investment of $71 million on the part of Dick Jacobs and the Indians, generated over the course of several years.[23]

Third, the chart shows a significantly higher private contribution for the ballpark than for the arena. This difference reflects the Cavaliers' strong negotiating position stemming from their ownership of the still relatively-new Richfield Coliseum (it was less than twenty years old at the time) with its acres of surrounding income-generating parking.

Opening Days: Ballpark and Arena

The first ballgame played at the new ballpark was on April 2, 1994: it was an exhibition game against the Pittsburgh Pirates played on a cool but clear day under bright blue skies. The first official game was two days later, with the Indians hosting the Seattle Mariners before another sellout crowd that included President Bill Clinton.

Mariners' pitcher Randy Johnson took a no-hitter into the eighth inning but the Indians rallied to win 4-3 in extra innings on Wayne Kirby's single to left field.

The team' s excellent recent draft record began to pay dividends in the 1994 season, as young players Manny Ramirez and Jim Thome joined the club and made strong contributions. By August, the Indians were fighting the Chicago White Sox for the division lead and were in position to claim a wild card spot in the playoffs that would never arrive: a baseball strike brought a premature end to the season. Nearly 2 million fans had attended games by the time of the August strike.

On the other side of Gateway Plaza, Gund Arena opened its 20,562 seats on October 17, 1994 to a Billy Joel concert. The Cavaliers played their first regular season game there several weeks later, losing to the Houston Rockets who were led by Hakeem Olajuwon's 21 points and 12 rebounds. The Cavaliers were led by point guard Terrell Brandon's 19 points and 7 assists.

The Construction Overruns Problem

But while the Cleveland sports fans were reveling in the brand-new facilities, there were some troubling signs coming from contractors who had worked at Gateway. Browns VP Mike Poplar began hearing concerns in December, 1994.

> ...contractors began to tell me about financial difficulties at Gateway Corp. Many of these contractors, who also performed work for us at the Stadium, were saying their Gateway invoices were not getting paid.

Some bills were about a year old, and vendors were coming to realize that the project had run out of money, although no one had yet come up with a complete and accurate accounting for the public. One rumor cited a $12 million shortfall, another had it as large as $20 million.[24]

When I was promoted to my position in Mayor White's office in early 1995, one of my new responsibilities was to be the City's Gateway board representative. Former Cleveland law director and practicing real estate attorney Craig Miller—one of my early mentors in the Cleveland Law Department—had recently been appointed Gateway Board Chair (succeeding former Nestle executive James Biggar). In an April 24, 1995 briefing for Mayor White and me, Miller told us that contractors were starting to file liens, the County was envisioning large dollars losses from its SAFE financial investments, and Doan Electric was going to sue Gateway (alleging fraud by prior board members). Mayor White asked Miller to talk to Cavaliers attorney Dick Watson to get their read on things (the County Commissioners had been expecting the Cavaliers to help out via a $9 million equity contribution).

Next came a May 19, 1995, Gateway board meeting. Miller began with a statement that we needed to come to some conclusions as to the real deficit number (in a previous board meeting he had mentioned $29 million). In reviewing records, he noted that, beginning in December 1993, cost reports were saying there were $15 million in Arena overruns; yet there was no reference to this in the Gateway minutes. He acknowledged that Gateway's board and staff had done a remarkable job getting the facilities built but reminded us that the board members have to answer to the public. He added that the teams are the only source of funds at this point: the public entities had been clear that they couldn't solve this. And, apart from the $29 million capital issue, there was a projected $800,000 1996 operating deficit.

The board met again five days later. Executive Director Chema started the meeting by explaining the primary cause of the 1996 operating deficit: it was the baseball strike, resulting in dramatically less Indians rent for the 1994 season. He then informed us that the Cavaliers had advanced Gateway $9 million. Miller then moved that we go into executive session to discuss specific contractors' claims, and the motion carried despite Bartimole's voiced objections.

In the executive session, Gateway's consulting construction attorney Appelbaum began the review by citing three issues: 1) a need to examine large change orders to determine whether their scope of work should have been covered under the original contracts; 2) whether there was "unjust enrichment" under the teams' leases; and 3) a need to ascertain whether the *amounts* of the change orders were excessive.

Appelbaum then addressed the specific Gateway construction claims. On the ballpark, the biggest claimant was structural steel contractor Kilroy at just under $5 million. Chema believed that $2.1 million of this claim was clearly owed but thought that Kilroy would settle its remaining $2 million-plus amount for $400,000. Appelbaum discussed the next biggest claimant—Higley—and told us that he had spent 22 days with them in alternative dispute resolution ("ADR"). Re designer HOK, —who had submitted a claim for $3 million extra in November, 1993, and who had been paid $750,000 of this amount by Gateway despite Appelbaum's objection—Appelbaum believed that HOK "was nervous" about its position and recommended that we authorize him to present a comprehensive claim against the design firm.

On the Arena claims, Appelbaum warned us that if we didn't pay the Arena contractors, we would be looking at a "huge delay claim:" $13 million in claims could become $25 million. Itemizing, he believed that Doan Electric had "the best claim on the whole Gateway project" while Automatic Sprinkler's $4 million claim was only worth $400,000.

We met again on May 31, 1995, and we again went into executive session to discuss claims. Miller advised us that he had just received the formal proposal from the Cavaliers and suggested that we now do some analysis of how we got from a $124 million Arena cost to a $152 million cost, and then determine what portion of the excess was Gateway's obligations. Chema reminded us that at the time of the lease signing, the underlying base of the deal to get the Cavaliers to come to Cleveland was that they'd get a building that was in every respect better than Richfield Coliseum. The public-sector decision makers were all on board and the 1990-1991 lease negotiations reflected that approach. That said, we did try to get the Cavaliers to agree on what "state of the art" meant.

County Administrator (and County board appointee) Tom Hayes suggested we take the position that, at $130 million, we gave them a "state of the art" facility and the rest of the cost is the Cavaliers' responsibility. Miller asked what would have happened if, as a practical matter, we had said "no" to the terrazzo floors. Appelbaum responded that a key provision in the ballpark lease was referral to federal mediation on cost excesses. The Cavaliers had been able to keep that mediation option out of their Arena documents.

Nevertheless, by the next Gateway board meeting—on June 7, 1995 —Chairman Miller was able to report that "in the past week there has been some success in resolving claims in Gateway's favor," and over the next several months the board and the public-sector players came together on a four-pronged solution to the problems. That summer the Indians placed six players on the American League All-Star team, and Miller and the public-sector players deployed an equivalent team of all-stars in attacking the $29 million Gateway overrun.

First, we needed to hold the line on the known $29 million. To that end, the Gateway board turned Applebaum loose on the pending claims. That authorization, and the standout construction attorney's prompt and aggressive actions in response, led to Miller's positive report to the board. Appelbaum brought a quick halt to the escalation of contractor claims and beat back HOK's claims for extras.

Second, there was the $9 million Cavaliers contribution, and for this issue a new player entered the arena: 59-year-old former City Council President Anthony Garofoli. Garofoli was a legendary figure in Cleveland politics. In his late teens he had moved from Pittsburgh to Cleveland to attend John Carroll University, and he obtained his law degree from Cleveland Marshall College of Law at Cleveland State University. He was elected to Cleveland City Council in 1965 and served as Council President until 1972. Since leaving City Council and commencing a private law practice, he had become one of Cleveland's "can-do" fix-it leaders on major civic issues. I had last seen him prowling the Council halls when Council President George Forbes brought him in to massage the Council on the 640-acre Chagrin Highlands office park legislation in 1989.

Garofoli had been hired several months ago by Mayor White to assist in putting together the Cleveland Browns deal, so he was available to help out on the Gateway issue. As was his practice, it didn't take long to see results: at an August 14, 1995 meeting with Mayor White, he reported that "the Cavaliers have agreed to spread out $25 million over a number of years. That commitment has a present value of $9 million. They have already advanced Gateway $9 million, and now they just won't ask to be paid back." The Cavaliers action left a balance of $21.5 million that required action.

Third, through hard work and shuttle diplomacy by County Administrator Hayes, the hard-pressed County Commissioners agreed to make an $11.5 million interest-free loan to Gateway. The loan would be repaid over a 10-year term via several parties' contributions:

- $300,000 per year from the City of Cleveland;
- $500,000 per year from the Convention and Visitors Bureau; and
- $400,000 per year from Gateway's capital funds.

Fourth, on the last $10 million envisioned to come from the State of Ohio, attorney/lobbyist Tim Cosgrove went to work. The original State ask had been the full $21.5 million, but State Budget Director Greg Browning shot that down after which the County took on the $11.5 million loan. A local bank loaned Gateway $10 million in expectation of reimbursement from a 1996 State capital grant. However, the State legislature instead provided Gateway a $10 million interest-free loan to be repaid over a 20-year term by both the County and the City of Cleveland equally from State Local Government monies.

By December 9, 1995, Bartimole's Point of View article, "Boyle, Hagan morally deficient again," was slamming two of the County Commissioners for their (admittedly successful) efforts to resolve the Gateway deficit; he characterized the Cavaliers contribution slightly differently, calling it a "loan" of $9 million in which the Cavaliers would forego repayment in exchange for a ten-year extension on their naming rights purchase that resulted in the name "Gund Arena."[25]

Looking back on the Gateway cost overrun problem with the benefit of over 20 years of hindsight, we can derive several lessons. But first, we need to recall Chema's points about the negotiating positions of the parties when the team leases were drafted: to get the Cavaliers to come to Cleveland, we needed to lease them a building that was in every respect better than Richfield Coliseum. Given that impediment, it was inevitable that the Cavaliers lease would end up more "team-friendly" than that of the Indians (who had less negotiating leverage). Those lease terms, in turn, led to a good percentage of the overruns: Bartimole estimated that $22 million of the overruns occurred at Gund Arena, with $5 million occurring at Jacobs Field.[26]

That said, the "state-of-the-art" clause in the Cavaliers lease should have been fleshed out via reference to a specific example such as the America West Arena in Phoenix (opened in 1992 at a construction cost of $90 million: it is now known as Talking Sticks Resort Arena).

Second, although the original Gateway board properly focused on meeting timelines and achieving quality work products, the board and staff could have—and should have—been more proactive in anticipating claims. If the board and staff had used Appelbaum more at the front end, he would have saved them a lot of money and prevented much of the bad will that arose when contractors found it necessary to file liens or sue in order to get paid.

Success in the 1990s

Nevertheless, Northeast Ohio residents were justly proud of their new entertainment and sports complex, and Pluto and Hamilton explained how those residents displayed their approval:

By opening day of 1994, the Tribe had sold 17,000 season tickets. Compare that to 3,330 in 1992, when the team had the $8 million payroll. The Indians had sold about 2 million tickets before the first pitch....

- In 1994, the average attendance for a Major League Baseball (MLB) game was 31,256 before the strike. The Indians averaged 39,121.
- In 1995, the MLB average dropped to 25,022. The Tribe was at 39,483.
- In 1996, the MLB average was 26,510. The Tribe was at 41,477.
- In 1997, the MLB average was 28,261. The Tribe was at 42, 034.[27]

Fittingly, the Indians' 1995 post-season had just as many thrills as the regular season: there was Tony Pena's 13th inning game-winning home run against the Boston Red Sox to start things off, and Kenny Lofton scored from second base on a wild pitch thrown by the Seattle Mariners' Randy Johnson in the eighth inning of Game 6 of the American League Championship Series, breaking open a tight contest in which 39-year-old Dennis Martinez pitched the playoff game of his life to outduel the Mariners' ace and send the Indians to the World Series.

And I was in my customary seat down the third base line on October 24 when Eddie Murray lined a single up the middle in the bottom of the eleventh inning to give the Indians a 7-6 win over the Atlanta Braves (their first Series win since 1948). It was probably my favorite live sporting event, but little did I know what was brewing with another team soon after this exhilarating Series win.

As a long-time Cleveland sports fan, one naturally acquires some abnormal superstitions and emotional baggage to cope with the teams' history of falling just short ever since the Browns' 1964 championship. In my case, I'd come to believe that there was a short supply of euphoria that had to be sparingly distributed amongst the city's three sports teams. Accordingly, when one team wins a big game, I'd expect one of the other teams to lose a game (evening out the limited supply of good sports karma). And if a Cleveland team not only wins but does so in unbelievably dramatic fashion such as the Indians did against the Braves that night, then a compensating calamity lay in store for another Cleveland team.

Thus, it was that less than three days later, after another dramatic 5-4 Indians' Series win featuring a Jim Thome missile launched to straight-away centerfield, a surrealistic scene played out in the early morning hours at Cleveland's lakefront. In the words of Baltimore Sun reporter Jon Morgan:

> As the tiny jet lifted off the runway Oct. 27 on its fateful mission, the passengers caught a view of Cleveland Municipal stadium in the pre-dawn light—a great hulking structure between glistening skyscrapers and inky black Lake Erie. Most of the city was still asleep, recovering from celebrations the previous night…. Little could Clevelanders know that a clandestine mission was then under way to steal their football team from them. On the private plane were four men who had spent much of their lives at Municipal Stadium and knew it better than the masons who had built it: Browns owner Art Modell; his son David; and two of his closest advisors, Jim Bailey and the jet's owner, Al Lerner.[28]

After the 1995 world Series, it was clear that the community had fully embraced their baseball team in a manner not seen since the late 1940's; it was only a matter of time until that embrace began turning profits for the owner. Though Jacobs lost money in his first seven years of ownership, revenues began flowing once the new ballpark opened: $6.7 million in 1995; $10.2 million in 1996, $22.6 million in 1997, and $13.6 million in 1998.[29]

The Importance of Player Drafting

Cleveland's status as a small or medium market team in all three sports leagues—baseball, basketball, and football—means *now*, and has *always meant*, that the quality of the teams' player procurement processes (primarily through the respective leagues' annual drafts) is/are critically important.

With rare exceptions (the Indians in the 1990's; the Cavaliers during LeBron James' return in 2014-2018), Cleveland does not operate as a major-market franchise and can rarely outbid its competitors for quality free agent players. Rather, Cleveland sports franchises must instead rely on the annual player drafts to replenish the players they lose as they reach their free-agent years. When you're playing by these rules, you can't afford to miss on your draft picks (*Browns from 1987-2017*), you can't blow operating budgets on expensive free agents (Browns in 1995), and you can't afford to package too many of your future stars in trades for established veteran players.

Somewhat understandably, as they were desperately trying to win a World Series before their late 1990s/early 2000s window closed, the Indians' front office violated the last of these principles after their near-miss at a World Series championship in 1997. In three trades the Indians gave up: Brian Giles (248 home runs over the next eleven years) for Ricardo Rincon in 1998; Sean Casey (batted .305

over the next eight years) for Dave Burba in 1998; and Richie Sexson (248 home runs after leaving the Indians) for Bob Wickman, Jason Bere, and Steve Woodward in 2000.[30]

These trades, coupled with a very poor drafting record from 2000-2007, signaled the end of the Indians' remarkable run in the 1990's and—with brief exceptions in 2005 and 2007—regaled the team to also-run status until Mark Shapiro began turning the ship around by promoting Brad Grant to scouting director in 2007 (and completed the turnaround by hiring Terry Francona as manager in 2012).

An article published on the eve of the Indians' June 2018 player draft contrasted the team's mediocre drafting record from 2000-2007 with Grant's strong drafting record in the decade from 2008-2017:

> ... since Brad Grant's promotion to scouting director in late 2007 the Indians drafting and player development has been revitalized....
>
> In the accounting, of 64 players from the (2000-2008) group, 45 represented busts, a 71 percent failure rate. This was actually very close to the overall rate of busts found by McKinney using Baseball America top 100 from 1990-2003 (69.2 percent). Likewise, the amount of successes for the Indians prior to 2008 (18/63, 28.5 percent) was very similar to McKinney (30.8%), and the amount of superior successes was also right on target (17.4 vs. 16.8 percent)
>
> .... the Grant years live up to their expectations. Only 14 of 32 players can be considered busts (43.7%) whereas 14 can be considered successes (43.7 percent), with 11 of the 14 successes already reaching the superior success level (34.4 percent). Against McKinney's findings, the Grant years come out far ahead of the averages.[31]

Turning to the NBA, we can compare five comparable Midwestern franchises—Chicago, Milwaukee, Cleveland, Indiana and Detroit—according to their performances in the NBA draft from 1995 (the first year after the opening of Gund Arena) through 2017. We will first count premium players (i.e., players who became either NBA All-Stars or All-NBA performers) and then count "solid" players (non- All-Stars who nevertheless made significant contributions).

The Chicago Bulls were the best performing Midwestern franchise in this 1995-2017 time period, with six premium selections (Elton Brand, Ron Artest, Lamarcus Aldridge, Joakim Noah, Derrick Rose, and Jimmy Butler) and five solid selections (Kirk Hinrich, Ben Gordon, Taj Gibson, Norris Cole, and Tony Snell).

The Cleveland Cavaliers were a close second, though they were significantly aided by their periodic *abysmal records that a owed them to claim the overaL number one draft slot four times.* They selected four premium players (LeBron James, Zydrunas Ilgauskas, Kyrie Irving and Andrew Wiggins) and six solid players (Derek Anderson, Brevin Knight, Andre Miller, Jamal Crawford, Tristan Thompson, and Dion Waiters).

Next best were the Milwaukee Bucks with four premium players (Stephon Marbury, Dirk Nowitski, Andrew Bogut, and Giannis Antetokounmpo) and four solid players (Danny Fortson, Gary Trent, James Posey, and Jabari Parker). Unfortunately for the Bucks, many of these players had their best years away from Milwaukee.

Then came the Indiana Pacers with three premium players (Danny Granger, Paul George and Kawhi Leonard) and five solid players (Travis Best, Erik Dampier, Austin Croshere, Miles Plumlee, and Myles Turner).

The Detroit Pistons trailed the pack, with two premium players (Theo Ratliff and Andre Drummond) and six solid players (Scot Pollard, Bonzi Wells, Tayshaun Prince, Rodney Stuckey, Greg Monroe, and Brandon Knight).

Assessing Gateway

Gateway was a bold project, as evidenced by the narrow voting margin for the countywide sin tax that ushered the project into existence in 1990. Its on-time opening in 1994 accomplished many goals: retention of baseball in Cleveland, return of the Cavaliers and other arena activities to downtown Cleveland, good design of the facilities and the connecting plaza, economic development of the Gateway neighborhood (most notably, East 4th Street), increase in tourism, and improvement of Cleveland's national image. These economic impacts are more fully described in Chapter 9.

But, apart from economic impacts, how did Gateway fare when measured by promises to citizens regarding its construction and its ongoing operations? Starting with construction, the main drawback was the construction overrun problem and the shadow it would cast on other proposed public projects in general, and on the Browns stadium project in particular (Art Modell's attorneys would cite the Gateway overruns as evidence why the community's planned renovation of Cleveland Municipal Stadium "wouldn't work").

Specifically, the sources and uses table shown earlier in this Chapter showed construction and operating costs of $440 million including a $21.5 million deficit and $20 million for (initial) "operations." As noted above, the deficit was closed via two public loans which have since been repaid: $11.5 million from Cuyahoga County and $10 million from the State of Ohio. The sources and uses table also showed a $9,295,000 "team contribution" which was probably the Cavaliers advance that was subsequently written off by the team via the efforts of Garofoli and others. Finally, the chart did not show the $10 million public cost of the RTA connecting tunnel between Tower City and Gateway. Consolidating, these updates yielded a revised project cost of $450 million of which the public funded 58% ($263 million) and the private sector funded 42% ($187 million).

Turning to ongoing operations, we have to revisit the pledges made in the Gateway campaign ad. Ironically, the promise that the White Administration took the most flak for in Gateway's early history—the 28,000 jobs—may have, over time, come closest to realization. That is due to the revitalization of the entire neighborhood as described in Chapter 13. Instead, the most vulnerable pledges turned out to be the ad's promise of "no tax abatements," the ad's promise of "$15 million annually for our school children," and the Administration's 1992 statements to Cleveland City Council that the Gateway Garages would likely pay for themselves.

Though the Gateway land was not abated, the ballpark and arena buildings were. The impact of those abatements was estimated as follows:

In Cleveland, for example, the value of property tax exemptions over 2008 and 2009 for the MLB Progressive Field was estimated at $3.8 million per year (based on an assessed value of approximately $69 million); and $3.8 million for the Quicken Loans Arena (based on assessed value of just over $50 million).[32]

Turning to the Gateway Garages, soon after their opening it became apparent that the large number of spaces reserved to the teams by their respective leases would undermine the predictions made to

Cleveland City Council that the Garages would "pay for them-selves." In practice, they ran an average annual deficit of several million dollars. As of December 31, 2019, City financial statements had this to say:

> In accordance with an agreement with Gateway Economic Devel-opment Corporation (Gateway), Gateway is required to reimburse the City for the excess of the debt service requirements of the Parking Facilities Refunding Revenue Bonds attributed to the two Gateway garages over the net revenues generated by the two Gateway garages.... In 2019, net revenues generated by the remaining Gateway garage were less than the debt service payments attributed to that garage by $896,000. Cumulative debt service payments funded by the City that are due from Gateway totaled $54,286,000 at December 31, 2019.[33]

And Gateway owed the County a comparable amount of money on account of County bond debt service payments.

Summarizing, could the Schools/City/County and other property tax beneficiaries have used another $8-10 million annually over the past thirty years? Certainly. And could the City and County have each used another several million dollars a year from Gateway on account of parking and bond payments? No doubt. And certainly, there are lessons to be learned in explaining financial risks to Cleveland City Council.

But I strongly believe that if all these financial factors _were_ known in advance, the community would have still moved forward on the Gateway adventure. There was really *that much* at stake.

CHAPTER FOUR

CLEVELAND BROWNS STADIUM (FOOTBALL)

Since their triumphant 1950 entry into the National Football League as an expansion team title winner (this followed four years of dominance in the All-American Football Conference), the Cleveland Browns have embedded themselves in Northeast Ohio's psyche and culture. Among their accomplishments:

- In their first 30 years in the NFL (1950-1979), they won four titles (1950, 1954, 1955, and 1964) and endured only four losing seasons;
- For each of the seasons from 1964-1973, they averaged over 70,000 attendance per game;
- The Browns Backers Worldwide is considered to be one of the largest organized fan clubs in all of professional sports;
- Founding coach Paul Brown and running back Jim Brown are many experts' choice as all-time best NFL coach and player;

- They are tied for seventh—joined by the Dallas Cowboys and Oakland Raiders—in the number of franchise Hall of Fame inductees;
- Despite consistent losing records since the franchise returned to Cleveland in 1999 (two winning seasons in a span of 18 years), in 2017 CBS Sports still ranked the fan base 14th among the NFL's 32 franchises.

When I joined the City of Cleveland Department of Law in January, 1988, the City had truly become "Brownstown." It had been less than a year since Denver Broncos quarterback John Elway had led his team on a fourth quarter drive to tie the Browns in a playoff game at Cleveland Municipal Stadium: The Broncos' ensuing overtime victory denied the Browns a trip to the Super Bowl.

Led by quarterback Bernie Kosar on offense, and by two cornerbacks (Hanford Dixon and Frank Minnifield) whose dog-barking motivational tool was embraced by hard core fans in the Stadium's east end zone who branded themselves as the "Dawg Pound," the Browns were embarking on a second consecutive playoff run that would again be vanquished by Elway and the Broncos in heartbreaking fashion.

In the spring of 1988, Law Director Marilyn Zack assigned me the task of drafting legislation to authorize a 10-year extension of Art Modell's lease of Cleveland Municipal Stadium. Having grown up in Cleveland suburbs in the 1950s and 1960s and become a lifetime fan of Cleveland sports teams, I had kept track from afar of the teams' dealings with the City. I knew that the City had leased the Stadium to Modell in 1973 for a 25-year term due to expire in 1998, and that Modell had subleased the Stadium to the Cleveland Indians baseball team. I also knew that the original lease terms required Modell to invest $10 million in Stadium capital improvements.

The origins of the 10-year lease extension proposal derived from a question Modell had asked his upper management staff in 1987: if his Cleveland Stadium Corporation invested in a new scoreboard—with the latest video replay technology—for the Stadium, could the cost of that investment be amortized from additional scoreboard advertising revenue derived over the 11 years remaining on the original lease term? His VP/Treasurer Michael Poplar answered "no," and—per Poplar's autobiographical book—that response led Modell to a proposal:

> ...Modell told us that he intended to present the scoreboard renovation as part of a $10 million capital improvement program which would include a $1 million locker room renovation...and public restroom expansion and renovation ($1.5 million), along with the $7.5 million scoreboard.[1]

As with the original $10 million investment, the City would get title to the new improvements at the expiration of the lease term. In return, the City would extend the lease term by 10 years—to 2008—if Cleveland City Council approved the authorizing legislation.

Journalist Bartimole quickly registered his objections. Convinced that the original 1973 lease was a sweetheart deal, he critiqued the 1988 proposal as more of a bad thing, reminding his readers that most of Modell's investment would go toward income-producing improvements (rather than rehabilitation that improves the City's property).[2]

While Modell and his management team were by this time accustomed to Bartimole's "point of view," they were far less forgiving when the *Plain Dealer* piled on via an editorial:

The Plain Dealer ran a lead editorial...entitled THE BROWNS'
DEFENSIVE LINE, challenging Modell's position on the lease
extension request and his tactics, referring to his original 25-year
lease in the editorial as a "sweetheart deal" and questioning his
right to recoup money from the eventual move of the Indians.[3]

Time passed: a year since the extension legislation was introduced.
Cleveland City Council hadn't even held a hearing on the proposal.
Poplar depicted Modell's mood:

Deep down inside, though, I could tell that Modell's mind was not
on the scoreboard. He knew something was terribly wrong.
Despite the fans' love affair with the team, the politicians seemed
to have an entirely different view of both the Browns and the
Stadium Corporation's efforts. We thought it strange. Any other
city would love to have a major sports tenant invest its own money
in a public sports complex, but Cleveland apparently wanted no
part of it. What had happened, we wondered? (Browns president)
Jim Bailey concluded that plans were being developed for the lakefront that would extend farther west of the Inner Harbor and
which did not include the Stadium on that land beyond 1998.[4]

Modell eventually lost his patience and requested an audience
before Cleveland City Council. In February, 1989, Bartimole had this
to say about Modell's appearance:

Modell—probably a little jealous of all the attention given to
(Cleveland Indians' owners) the Jacobses lately and not eager to
lose his sweet deal for the present stadium—went to city council
this week to cry a little more in public....(he stated) that he was
withdrawing his request because some people were saying nasty
things about him and his motives in wanting to stay at the old

stadium....(he) again said that his request was being "misunder-stood, distorted, and not put in a proper context by this body, by members of the business community, who are close, intimate colleagues of mine, I might add, who had their own private and personal agenda, and editorial comments." (Modell later promised) that the present stadium was solid for at least another 75 years.[5]

I was at that same City Council meeting. As a Browns fan I knew that Art Modell was on edge: two years ago in the Stadium, Denver quarterback John Elway had blocked the Browns' path to the Super Bowl in a game immortalized in NFL annals as "The Drive;" one year ago in Denver Elway had again ejected the Browns a win short of the Super Bowl in a 38-33 game ironically known as "The Fumble" (ironic because Earnest Byner's late-game fumble on what would have been a tying touchdown overshadowed Byner's superb efforts driving a comeback from a 21-3 deficit); and just two months ago the Browns had exited the playoffs via a frustrating 24-23 loss to the Houston Oilers.

I was not aware that Modell's upper management team had studied whether the scoreboard cost could be amortized by 1998 and concluded "no," I was not aware that the same management team had concluded that the North Coast Harbor expansion plans were a major obstacle to Modell's proposal, and I was not aware of Modell's personal financial situation.

But as I watched Modell withdraw his request for a 10-year lease extension (could the heartbreaking playoff losses have played a role?), I knew that the City was the beneficiary of a great deal: Modell was still going to pay the scoreboard, locker room and restroom costs, thereby increasing—from $10 million to $15 million —his investment in Stadium capital improvements. By appearing before City Council to confirm that he would spend an additional $5 million and get nothing in return, he was refuting both his media critics and a "corporate whispering campaign."

But one key thing the City did not get—and that Modell himself had proposed—was a 10-year lease extension which would have changed the lease end-date from 1998 to 2008. The significance of this lost opportunity was not appreciated in 1989 and would be lost in the shuffle of the events that later transpired in 1995.

Modell and the City would be back in negotiations before long: the 1998 Stadium lease expiration date was less than 10 years away, the Cleveland Indians' facility needs had to be addressed even sooner, and the Stadium was nearly 60 years old. It was clear to me then that—when we did resume negotiations—Modell and his management team would remember this concession they were now making.

Timeline From 1989 to 1993

In one sentence, Browns investor Al Lerner captured the essence of Modell's financial challenges as they developed over the years: "... Stadium Corp. did with borrowed money what others did with public money."[6] I would make a slight amendment: *Stadium Corp. did with borrowed money what others did with public money or owner investments.* Unlike many of his fellow NFL owners, Modell did not have profits from other businesses to invest in his football team.

In the Browns' decision-making in 1989-1993, many of the negative issues that developed during this time period are traceable directly or indirectly to Art Modell's gradual withdrawal from an active role in Cleveland Stadium Corp. management, and a similar withdrawal from an active role in Browns financial management.

In the 1970's and 1980's, Modell had practiced a very inclusive management style. VP/Treasurer Poplar has described daily lunch meetings at a round table at the Stadium Club restaurant. Modell made himself available to department heads to hear their updates and give appropriate directions. The department heads learned what was going on in the different departments, and "in those days Art liked to get opinions from as many people as he possibly could."[7] Coincidentally, these meetings were quite similar in style and approach to weekly Cabinet meetings I had experienced through the tenures of successive Cleveland mayors.

Modell's decision-making withdrawal began in 1989. That year, as the Browns upper management narrowed its candidates for a coach to succeed Marty Schottenheimer, Modell allowed his management team to make the ultimate selection of Bud Carson. Per Poplar's book:

> It must have been the accumulation of all the tribulations of the prior months that finally caught up with the normally indefatigable Art Modell. The disappointing end to the 1988 season, the firing of another head coach, and what he regarded as a slap in the face from the politicians and corporate elite left him too depleted to continue the selection process. What had always been Arthur B. Modell's most important decision, selecting his head coach, he left to others.[8]

By 1990, Browns' Executive VP/legal counsel Jim Bailey was assuming Stadium-related decision-making responsibilities that had previously been performed by Modell himself. This occurred on the development of the new training facility in Berea, Ohio (and the opening of the new facility in 1991 itself contributed to more segregated decision-making). In April, 1990, Modell endured his second quadruple bypass operation (the first operation occurred in 1983), and shortly thereafter he redesigned "his modus operandi so as not to talk to the different department heads individually as he had for the previous 30 years."[9]

Several years later, Bailey became the leader of a three-man management committee that included Modell's son David Modell and head coach Bill Belichick. Poplar's accounts of this committee (and similar examples of a more closed management approach) raised many concerns: "protection" of Art Modell from staff members with dissenting views, conflict avoidance ("don't tell Art, it'll just upset him"), exclusion of the most capable finance people from a seat at the table. Poplar concisely summarized his concerns in the following passage (emphasis added):

> *It has been my experience that strong, secure managers demand to hear about problems as soon as they crop up, so they can nip them in the bud. If, on the other hand, a leader does not solicit reports on impending problems from his top executives, then it is not surprising to find a myriad of problems lurking just below the surface. When these problems eventually break through, they are usually too overwhelming to correct.*[10]

As we now turn to the major events that occurred in the 1989-1993 timeframe, many of them can be connected back to this key observation.

The Browns' strong on-field performance in the late 1980's came to a screeching halt in the 1990's. In the years 1990-1995, the Browns recorded a disappointing 39-57 won-loss record. This declining performance was largely due to poor draft choices over time. The annual NFL draft is the League's main source of procuring players and is designed to achieve competitive balance amongst the 32 franchises. The order of selection in each of the draft's seven rounds is "worst-first" based on the teams' records in the preceding season. Success in the draft is the best strategy for success for NFL teams: a strong drafting record will minimize the need to pay large sums for free agent acquisitions and avoid speculative player trades.

With that background, consider the Browns' draft record in years 1987-1995: in those nine years they drafted 7 players who appeared in the NFL Pro Bowl and drafted no players who became NFL Hall of Fame inductees. By contrast, their chief rival—the Pittsburgh Steelers—over the same time period drafted *14 Pro Bowl players and two Hall of Fame inductees (Rod Woodson, Dermontti Dawson).*

The Browns' poor draft record during this period led Modell, still desperate for a Super Bowl appearance, to pursue costly—and largely unsuccessful—free agent signings in the mid-1990s. Poplar made the same points. First, going back to the Browns' 1970s drafts, he quoted Bill Levy, author of the book Sam, Sipe & Company, as concluding that the Browns had been "...poor judges of talent in both the draft and in trading. If they hope to remain in the National Football League's elite, they must do a better job."[11]

> But in the 80s that was not the way it played out. The Browns went on a trading binge, exchanging high draft picks for aging former All-Pro players Lyle Alzado and Joe Delamielleure.... The Browns then kept the phone lines open with Buffalo and dealt with the Bills in two more major trades...to acquire Tom Cousineau and Bernie Kosar. To acquire the aforementioned four starters, the Browns surrendered draft picks that should have yielded 10 very good players for years to come... One has to wonder how much these trades helped up the balance of power to propel the Bills to the Super Bowl during the 90s, while relegating the Browns to subpar years.[12]

The 1990s also marked a sea change in what until then had been Modell's generally positive media image. Though there was some degree of fan backlash to the team's 3-13 record in 1990 under the second, and last, year of Bud Carson's head coaching tenure, the real problems began with Modell's 1991 decision to hire coach Bill Belichick. If Cleveland fans then had had the benefit of seeing into Belichick's future as a sure Hall of Fame coach with six Super Bowl trophies, perhaps they would have been more patient with the young coach's approach.

As it was, they quickly soured on Belichick's "defense-first" conservative play-calling approach and his willingness to strip the team of most of the offensive stars who had developed strong fan followings during the team's late-1980s glory years. One by one the fan favorites were either traded or cut—Webster Slaughter, Reggie Langhorne, Brian Brennan—as Belichick sought to remake the team in the mold of the bigger, stronger NFC conference teams that had prevailed in the last seven Super Bowls.

After guiding the team to records of 6-10 in 1991 and 7-9 in 1992 and slipping after a fast early start in 1993, Belichick concluded that it was time for a major culture change. He benched quarterback Bernie Kosar in favor of recently acquired Vinnie Testaverde. Though Kosar's elbow and other injuries had clearly limited both his throwing and his mobility, the fans largely sided with Kosar's belief that he could still win games if only his coach would adopt more imaginative play calling.

The controversy came to a boiling point after a 29-14 home loss against, ironically, the Denver Broncos. That evening, Modell decided to release Kosar. In their Monday press conference, Modell and Belichick cited Kosar's "diminishing skills." The fan base and the local media erupted, and their bitterness continued years after the decision.

Viewed 20 years later, the Kosar release was probably Modell's second most costly public relations error. The 1995 move of the team ranks first, the Kosar press conference ranks second, and the 1962 dismissal of Hall of Fame coach Paul Brown ranks third (the latter event, though more impactful than the Kosar release, was moderated by the 1964 NFL title achieved two years later).

In terms of negative staying power with both the fan base and the media, the Kosar decision is comparable to the Indians' 1960 trade of outfielder Rocky Colavito. But Colavito was traded in the prime of his career, while Kosar, as even his strongest supporters would concede, was clearly approaching an injury-induced downslope. Why, then, did the backlash from the Kosar decision have such staying power? The answer lies not in the decision itself, but in how it was handled. As Modell himself later admitted, an owner as trained in public relations as he was should have realized that his caustic handling of the news was disastrous.

Kosar was not just a star quarterback who had led the Browns to five playoff appearances: he was also a local kid—from Boardman, Ohio just outside of Youngstown—who had manipulated the NFL draft process so he could come *to Cleveland* (at a time when the fan base was used to seeing star athletes manipulate themselves *away Lom Cleveland*).

He was a cultural icon the likes of which this city had not seen since Colavito nor would see again until the coming of LeBron James. Poplar's capsule summary nailed it:

> In retrospect, the event marked a major milestone in the erosion of respect by Cleveland fans for Art Modell. The style and manner in

which Kosar was dismissed were so distinctly "un-Modell-like" that it was evident that Belichick had gained tremendous influence over the owner. I believe that from this time on real Browns' fans finally quit on Art Modell, and finding themselves in a kind of sports vacuum, they turned to the newest darlings in town, the Indians.[13]

While the Kosar incident's damage to Modell's public image was self-induced, there was a parallel negative media theme for which Modell was blameless and the local media was blameworthy: that was the growing perception of Modell as a profiteer and an extortionist by reason of, respectively, his 1973 Stadium lease deal and his request for a renovated Cleveland Municipal Stadium.

In the Preface I discussed the importance of the question "Compared to What?" Bartimole's ongoing Stadium critiques rarely, if ever, dealt with this question. Rather, Bartimole assaulted public funding of sports team facilities on a philosophical basis: it was fundamentally wrong for any city to significantly subsidize a private sports facility—let Jacobs/Modell pay!

If you accept this notion philosophically—I do, and I suspect most citizens would concur—that doesn't mean you accept it practically in todays' political world in which the U.S. Congress has to date granted the respective sports leagues a relatively free hand in allocating, removing and relocating sports franchises. If you operate in that political environment, and if you regard the retention of existing sports franchises as a worthy goal, then you have to subordinate your philosophical desires to the practical political question of how your local sports facility deal compares to those in comparable cities.

I made earlier reference to a 1988 audit that concluded that Cleveland's stadium lease deal compared favorably to stadium deals in six other cities. The deal continued to improve through the 1990's:

- The Stadium lease was worth $3 million a year in cash benefits to the city, taking into account rent, real estate tax, annual maintenance, and annual principal and interest payments on capital improvements;
- Capital improvement investments grew to over $18 million, almost double the investment required by the 1973 lease;
- Cleveland Stadium Corp. aggressively promoted special events throughout the 1990's—Paul McCartney in 1990, Ohio State/Northwestern in 1991, Phil Collins/Genesis in 1992—and earned $900,000 in 1994 upon the Indians departure to Gateway, booking a major carnival, the Billy Graham Crusade, World Cup Soccer, Monster Truck Jam, Pink Floyd, the Eagles, and the Rolling Stones; and
- Modell was seeking a stadium *renovation* at a time when fellow owners were demanding *brand new stadiums*.

Yet throughout 1994 and 1995, the Plain Dealer added its voice to that of persistent critic Bartimole via its columnists (Joe Dirck, "One last chance for EXTORTion," May 7, 1995) and its editorial cartoonists ("Go Browns! But leave the Indians here.")

1994-1995: The Stadium Funding Negotiations

The beginning of 1994 was pivotal in the chain of events leading to Modell's decision to move the Browns to Baltimore. In April, 1994, the Indians would move into their new home at Gateway, triggering Modell's request for compensation for loss of his major tenant. And, given the Stadium lease's 1998 expiration date, it was time to do early planning on a Stadium construction project that needed to be complete by August, 1999, to insure s smooth transition for the Browns.

Poplar's book listed four causes for Modell's move:

- Things that Modell failed to do;
- The lack of political leadership;
- A hypercritical media environment; and
- Too many good intentions (e.g., Rock and Roll Hall of Fame and Museum, Great Lakes Science Center, the 1996 Bicentennial Celebration, and the Gateway Project).

I have a different view, or rather, a different emphasis among Poplar's points. The predominant cause of the move was the things that Modell or his advisors failed to do, and first and foremost amongst those things was the dismal record of drafting players and trading for players. Even a league-average performance level would have led to a better team in the 1990's and could have substantially reduced the Browns' debt level by avoiding the signing of costly free agents.

Secondarily, Modell's gradual shift to a less-inclusive management style led to exclusion of his best financial advisors from key decisions; this in turn led to the shock waves when Modell realized the extent of his debts in September 1995.

Poplar's last three factors played much lesser roles than he, Modell, or Modell's advisors on the Baltimore move (principally, Executive VP Jim Bailey and the Jones Day lawyers) would have us believe:

- While the political leaders did suffer from a major unexpected barrier—in the form of the County's October,

1994, SAFE financial crisis—within six months' time after that crisis all political players were back on track under Mayor White's strong leadership;

- While media outlets, including the Plain Dealer, were unjustly critical of Modell in 1994, by the spring of 1995 the media (Bartimole excepted) was largely supportive of the Stadium renovation project; and
- While it's true that Cleveland and Cuyahoga County had an extraordinary number of civic projects in the mid-1990's that tapped many of the potential stadium-funding sources available to other cities, Cleveland Finance Director Steve Strnisha and his successor Kathryn Hyer developed a list of less obvious funding sources that proved successful.

By 1994, Modell faced three revenue challenges—two new and one old—that made it difficult for him to service his by-then extraordinary debt levels. The new challenges were the loss of the Indians as a tenant (an annual revenue hit of over one million dollars) and declining loge sales (30 of the 102 loges went vacant, a revenue hit of over $1.5 million). The longstanding revenue challenge was the relatively small (compared to other NFL stadia) number of revenue-producing parking spaces.

ESTIMATED CLEVELAND BROWNS DEBT

YEAR	MAIN CAUSES OF NEW INDEBTEDNESS	SOURCE	TOTAL $ DEBT (MILLIONS)
1982	Unstated	Poplar, p. 39	2
1982	NFL Player Strike of 1982	Poplar, p. 88	6
1982	Purchase of Cleveland Stadium Corp.	Poplar, p. 39	12
1986	Ohio Supreme Court decision rescinds purchase of Cleveland Stadium Corp.	Poplar, p. 48	6
1986	Unstated	PD 1/7/96	11
1987	Unstated	PD 1/7/96	19
1988	Unstated	PD 1/7/96	21
1989	Unstated	PD 1/7/96	27
1994	$40 million signing bonuses in last three years ($23.6 million of that occurring in 1995)	PD 1/7/96; Poplar, p. 250	40
1995	Unstated	Poplar, p. 241	48
1995	Andre Rison $5 million signing bonus financed by Modell personally via Star Bank loan	Lerner, quoted at Poplar, p 300	60

ESTIMATED CLEVELAND STADIUM CORP. DEBT

YEAR	MAIN CAUSES OF NEW INDEBTEDNESS	SOURCE	TOTAL $ DEBT (MILLIONS)
1975	Construction of 108 loges	Poplar	5
1978	Acquire 200 acres in Strongsville from Modell; limited partnership in Stouffer Hotel	Poplar, p. 34	9
1978	New scoreboard	Poplar, p.25	10.6
1980	Stadium concession improvements	Poplar	12.6
1982	Sale of Cleveland Stadium Corp. to Cleveland Browns	Poplar, p. 39	6.6
1986	Ohio Supreme Court decision rescinds purchase of Cleveland Stadium Corp.	Poplar, p. 48	12.6
1986	Through corporate transactions, Modell effectively conveys 50% of his interest to Al Lerner; legal fees from past 4 years	Poplar, p. 52	15.6
1989	New scoreboard; freshen loges	Poplar, p. 139	20.6
1990	$10 million bank loan for Berea training facility; $25 million from prior bank loans	Browns NFL submission	35
1994	Pay down of debt from profits	PD 1/7/96	33.6
1995	Payoff $20 million Huntington Bank loan		13.6

Poplar contended that Modell did not comprehend the magnitude of the Browns' debt level until *September, 1995*.[14] If true, this fact underscores Poplar's critique of Modell's exclusion of financial staff from decision-making throughout the 1990s.

As the Gateway complex neared completion in 1994, City of Cleveland and Cleveland Browns representatives commenced negotiations on the Browns' stadium renovation proposal. As the Browns later summarized in a statement to the NFL:

In early 1994, representatives of Cleveland and the Browns began a series of protracted negotiations designed to address the issues of stadium renovation and the terms of a lease arrangement between Cleveland and the Browns. Extensive negotiations between Cleveland and the Browns continued on a regular basis for a period of nine months from January, 1994, through September, 1994. During these negotiations the Browns representatives repeatedly made it clear to Cleveland that unless the parties were able to agree upon an arrangement which provided for the renovation of Cleveland Stadium without monetary contribution from the Browns and provided the Browns with substantially increased revenues from Cleveland Stadium, the Browns would have no alternative but to relocate.[15]

But in October, 1994, news broke concerning a Cuyahoga County financial crisis. The County's investment in its Secure Assets Funding Earnings ("SAFE") turned into a $115 million loss. This cloud over the County's finances caused the City/Browns negotiators to temporarily hit a "pause" button.

Yet by December 9, 1994, Mayor White was meeting with area sports writers to warn that the Browns could leave town if Modell didn't get what he wanted.[16] One day later, the Plain Dealer quoted the Mayor stating that the Stadium issue was now a top priority. That month he appointed the "Cleveland Stadium Task Force" to make construction and financing recommendations, and by January, 1995, the Task Force was recommending Stadium renovation at a then undetermined cost.

Mayor White was reacting to at least two very real relocation threats—St. Louis and Baltimore—each of which was desperate to replace football teams that had departed in the previous decade. Both cities had tried, and failed, to land NFL expansion teams: they were thwarted when the League's owners opted instead to issue franchises to Charlotte and Jacksonville in late 1993.

St. Louis responded by building a new facility to spec: the $258 million public-funded Trans World Dome (later renamed the Edward Jones Dome) attached to and a part of the St. Louis convention center, with 113 luxury boxes and 6,500 club seats. By early 1995 St. Louis was negotiating with Los Angeles Rams football owner Georgia Frontiere. Professor and author Mark Rosentraub explained:

> To entice the Rams from Anaheim, the city and county of St. Louis offered the team a wonderful lease for the use of their new dome. The St. Louis Rams would receive 100 percent of all concession revenues, 75 percent of advertising income from the facility, and 90 percent in any year that more than $6 million in advertising income was earned. A local corporate group guaranteed that 85 percent of the luxury boxes and club seats would be sold for fifteen years and the Rams could keep all this income. Through the sale of seat options to prospective fans, the city and county of St. Louis also agreed to provide the funds to pay the team's indemnity to Anaheim, all moving expenses, and the costs associated with building a practice facility.[17]

Oh, and there was one more thing: the proposed lease contained a "state of the art" clause where the lessor promised to keep the stadium within the top 25% of all NFL facilities as measured in years 2005 and 2015. After some initial hesitation—that quickly dissipated following litigation threats from both the Rams and the Missouri Attorney General—the NFL owners approved the Rams' relocation to St. Louis by a 23-6-1 vote on April 12, 1995.

But Baltimore was still out there, having tried every way possible to lure a team for the past eight years. The Colts had left town in 1984, and the Maryland legislature had responded in two phases. First, in 1986, it established the Maryland Stadium Authority for the purpose of retaining the Baltimore Orioles baseball team and procuring a football team. Second, in 1987, it provided massive public funding for the Authority via redirection of $16 million a year from the state's lottery proceeds.

Armed with these powerful tools, Maryland Governor William Donald Schaefer and Maryland Stadium Authority Chairman Herb Belgrade set to work, subject to some agreed rules of engagement:

> The two had put together a three-part anti-raiding test that they applied before talking to a franchise. First, the team had to have made an irrevocable decision to move. Second, it must have communicated this decision to the authorities in its hometown. And third, the league had to be aware of the talks.[18]

They struck gold with the Baltimore Orioles and constructed Oriole Park at Camden Yards which, immediately after its 1992 opening, became the prototype for new ballparks. But after their exhaustive efforts to obtain an expansion football franchise were rebuffed by the NFL owners' choice of Charlotte and Jacksonville in late 1993, they had to pass the baton to their respective successors in early 1995: Maryland Governor Parris Glendening and Maryland Stadium Authority Chairman John Moag, Jr.

Desperate to claim a scalp by the end of the year, the two new players adopted very different rules of engagement:

> Moag told Glendening that NFL expansion wasn't likely to happen in the next year. If Baltimore was going to get a team, it would have

to steal one from another city. Neither Moag nor Glendening raised the ethics of NFL team raiding or the other gentleman's rules of engagement that Schaefer and Belgrad had espoused. This was not going to be an operation performed under the auspices of the U.S. Conference of Mayors.[19]

In February, 1995, I was promoted from the Law Department to Mayor White's office—succeeding Steve Strnisha as Executive Assistant for Development—and assumed a much more active role in Cleveland's Stadium discussions. Strnisha had just moved to Cleveland Tomorrow, a corporate civic group, and in that new role he continued his involvement with the Stadium issue.

Shortly before moving from the Law Department to the Mayor's Office, I had met and begun to work with Mayor White's outside counsel on the Stadium project, Squire Sanders Dempsey partner Fred Nance. Nance had a rare blend of legal skills: he was both an aggressive litigator and a tactful negotiator of sensitive business deals (where patience and the ability to thread a needle through competing interests were essential skills). He was an African-American in his mid-thirties with a shaved head and a strong physique that hadn't slipped since his high school days as a St. Ignatius football player.

In fact, back in November, 1970, Nance had played in Cleveland Municipal Stadium as a St. Ignatius offensive guard in the then-annual charity game held on the Saturday after Thanksgiving (Ignatius lost that game to Benedictine). While at Ignatius, he had watched the National Guard turn out to stem riots in Glenville and began thinking about a legal career to become an effective player in urban America. This motivation carried him to Harvard University for an undergraduate degree and the University of Michigan for a law degree. After joining Squire Sanders as a young attorney, he gained Mayor White's confidence by successfully representing him in a 1991 Grand Jury investigation of the Mayor's investments.

On February 15, 1995, I attended a Task Force meeting including Nance, Cleveland Tomorrow representatives Joe Roman and Strnisha, City Architect Ken Nobilio, and Law Department attorney Therese Sweeney Drake. Roman referenced a Task Force budget of $450,000 (the Browns contributed $125,000) and an estimated April 15, 1995, due date for a Turner Construction Company project cost estimate. Nance discussed the next challenge: identifying a funding source for the full design cost estimate of $6 million. Roman passed on some recent comments from Browns President Jim Bailey: that other NFL teams are paying less and less on their leases; and that August, 1999, may be a project completion deadline.

It was not unusual for the Cleveland Tomorrow organization to be involved in an important public-private endeavor such as the Cleveland Stadium project. Created in 1981 to improve the region's long-term economic health, it was a private civic entity made up of chief executive officers of the largest companies in the Cleveland-area. Its priorities included attracting and retaining businesses, encouraging innovation in industry, and revitalizing Cleveland neighborhoods.

When founding Executive Director Richard Shatten stepped down in 1993, Cleveland Tomorrow had already played a significant role in some catalytic development projects: the $400 million Gateway project, the nation's largest downtown movie theater renovation (four theaters in Playhouse Square), the $400 million Tower City project in Terminal Tower, the Rock and Roll Hall of Fame and Museum, and some major neighborhood housing projects. Cleveland Tomorrow was recognized by Harvard Business School as one of the most innovative and successful regional business organizations in the country.

Roman succeeded Shatten in 1993. A native Clevelander, he earned a bachelor's degree from the State University of New York and a master's degree in public administration from Harvard University. Prior to joining Cleveland Tomorrow, he had worked on Capitol Hill as both a congressional staff person and as a lobbyist for manufacturing trade associations, and in the City of Cleveland's Department of Economic Development. Having worked under Shatten during most of Cleveland Tomorrow's early accomplishments, he was well-prepared to continue the entity's progress throughout the 1990s.

I had known Roman since the late 1980s, and we shared the experience of having grown up in Greater Cleveland during the 1950s and 1960s with the same sports allegiances. In 1995 and beyond, he would become a major player in public-private negotiations involving all three of the city's major sports franchises (where, like me, his involvement would often land him in the crosshairs of journalist Bartimole). He would later go on to co-lead the March, 2004, merger of Cleveland Tomorrow, the Greater Cleveland Growth Association, and the Greater Cleveland Roundtable into a new entity known as the Greater Cleveland Partnership. He would also help to found regional economic development entities BioEnterprise, JumpStart, NorTech and the Cleveland Plus Marketing Alliance.

On February 16, 1995, in a meeting with City staff, Nance summarized next steps: Mayor White had decided that the City would build the project as a public improvement and that Nance, Silliman, and an undetermined business CEO will continue the lease negotiations with the Browns; the project timeline was set as design (June 1995-June 1996), bidding (June 1996-September 1996), and a January 1, 1996 construction start date.

By mid-April, 1995, our City team was meeting with designers HOK and Turner Construction Company to discuss the details of the construction process. By May, Turner had presented a $154 million project cost estimate, and we were beginning to look at site development and infrastructure costs that had not been included in Turner's estimate. On May 12, 1995, I met with City Council President Jay Westbrook and he advised me that we need to "lower the political temperature" on the Stadium project and that we need to "get this resolved where people start to see their own agendas addressed; just selling this on the merits won't be enough; I will tell you what those other agendas will be."

By now, the County Commissioners—still recovering from their October, 1994, SAFE financial crisis—were returning to the negotiating table. On May 12, 1995, -- the same day I met with Council President Westbrook—I met with County Commissioner Lee Weingart and he proposed, as an alternative to the City's proposed new 10% parking tax, a sales tax approach that would look less like a tax increase. Later that month, I met with County Commissioner Tim Hagan to receive his proposal that the Gateway sin tax be extended from its 2005 expiration date to a new date of 2025, with 80% of the extended tax being allocated to the Stadium renovation and 20% being allocated to a $30 million Gateway cost overrun.

Additionally, in a May 17, 1995, Stadium Task Force meeting, Mayor White characterized the State of Ohio's commitment to the Stadium renovation project via a 12-15% participation level as "fairly firm" (with "12" probably being the operative number). Later, when the far more aggressive state roles played by Maryland and Pennsylvania in stadium funding became more widely known, Poplar and others could afford to be critical of Ohio's role.

But Maryland only had one city in the state to worry about. Ohio Governor Voinovich knew that anything done for Cleveland would probably have to be replicated in Cincinnati and—given the extensive college athletic facility demands in the state—may even have to be replicated at the college level.

In that May Stadium Task Force meeting, Mayor White was in full throttle. By then, he had cemented his mayoral leadership style. On previous issues such as the Cleveland schools, new housing construction in City neighborhoods, and public safety in those neighborhoods, he had mobilized both City staff and outside business and civic leaders in all-out attacks on the obstacles in his way. It was now time for the Stadium issue, and his remarks in this meeting left no doubt:

> The loss of a professional sports team couldn't come at a worse time. The Stadium renovation is more important than any other current issue. I don't like a world that's set up that way, but I have to deal with reality.... I'm willing to take a fairly unpopular package to the public. The most we can do (now) is confirm our slice of the pie. Once we do our part, we'll spend the summer on the other pieces—the County and the State. This group must show consensus soon or we'll be looking at a moving van.[20]

He had recently met with Modell and Lerner, and he characterized the Browns' owner's present state of mind:

> He feels set upon by the media and is facing debt structure issues. At least two cities are barking at the door, one of which is offering $150 million as a start. He's weary, is feeling abandoned and betrayed, and can't wait much longer because the deals to be done

won't be there. And he needed to go to the bank to get Andre Rison's contract signed.[21]

The City's proposed funding package had evolved into a 10-15% parking tax, a 2% increase in the City's admissions tax (from 6 to 8%), and a 2% motor vehicle license tax. Re next steps, the Mayor focused on resolving the parking tax percentage with the parking lot operators and business leaders: he noted that at 15% the tax would draw "buzzards to the carcass," but that at 10% we're left with a hole.

We had a preview of their views. A week earlier, I met with former federal judge Alvin "Buddy" Krenzler who had become a bowtie-wearing millionaire real estate developer. He had expressed major concerns about the parking tax, warning that downtown parking was a "weak and fragile thing." He contrasted Pittsburgh's captive market (surrounded as it was by mountains which precluded suburban shopping malls) with Cleveland's more vulnerable downtown office and shopping market. When I asked him whether there was some percentage of parking tax that he (I didn't ask him to speak for his colleagues) *would support*, he responded: "If it's 5% and its part of a package, then I wouldn't recommend us fighting it."

Then, on May 17, 1995, Nance presided over a "cast of thousands" meeting with downtown parking lot operators and business leaders. He started by describing the funding components of the proposed $154 million project. He warned the group that competing cities Los Angeles and Baltimore would not remain silent for long, and the Browns needed an August, 1999, construction completion date. Turning to the parking tax component, he stated that we were not stuck on a 15% rate, but the group needed to recognize that any substantial reduction in rate would need to be made up from some other source.

Judge Krenzler responded that we're in competition with the suburbs, the financing should be broad-based (the parking tax is too narrow), and that a regional solution is preferable. He specifically mentioned a ¼% County sales tax (which the County Commissioners could pass without a public vote), with half the proceeds going to the Stadium and half going to resolve the County's SAFE financial crisis.

Parking operator John Coyne (whose company owned half the lots in downtown) described a free fall in parking rates since 1990 due to white collar layoffs, and cited Minneapolis' recent experience: the city cut a 22% office vacancy rate in half after making a decision to *subsidize* parking. Krenzler summarized that the group would vigorously oppose parking rate percentages of 15, 10, or 8.

On May 26, 1995, I met with Mayor White to summarize the various recommendations and prepare a legislative package for introduction in Cleveland City Council on June 5, 1995. The Mayor decided to reduce the parking tax rate to 10% (with a portion going to recreation programming for Cleveland schools), coupling it with the 2% admissions tax increase and the new 2% motor vehicle license tax. He reacted favorably to Commissioner Hagan's sin tax extension proposal. He planned weekend briefings with City Council members, to be later followed by "enlisting everyone we know" to assist in the lobbying.

A week later, Cleveland Tomorrow's Strnisha reported back to a group of us—Mayor White, Nance, and myself—on his assessment of City Council's stance on the legislation: most Council members would support an 8% parking tax, a 2% increase in the admission tax, a twenty-year extension of the sin tax with half of the tax proceeds applied to the Stadium debt, and no element to appease the schools. Nance reminded us that the Browns will look at the admissions tax as a contribution from them. He also said the Browns were looking for more dollars out of the lease. Mayor White responded that he needed the schools in the deal, and he would talk to Council President Westbrook.

At the beginning of June, Mayor White hired local attorney Anthony Garofoli to coordinate the negotiations with City Council. As with his work on the Gateway cost overrun issue described above, it didn't take Garofoli long to get rolling. The Mayor needed City Council's passage of the Stadium legislation by the end of June. By a June 12 executive staff meeting, Mayor White was telling us that "Garofoli is doing a very good job: there's a framework of a deal."

But Mayor White's pipeline from Modell had just closed. Angered by an incident when a reporter had badgered Browns quarterback Vinny Testaverde with a barrage of questions about the Stadium renovation plans, and intently focused on preparing his team toward a march to the Super Bowl, Modell fired off a June 5, 1995, letter to Mayor White, copied to the Plain Dealer, that decried the current media environment and imposed a moratorium—until the end of the football season—on the team's participation in further Stadium renovation discussions.

Undaunted, on June 21, the Mayor assembled a large group to assess our progress. Attendees included Garofoli, Nance, myself, Finance Director Hyer, Council leaders (Jay Westbrook, Jim Rokakis, and Roosevelt Coats), and Council's outside counsel Craig White. Garofoli kicked off the meeting by stating a legislative goal of raising $144 million toward the then $170 million project (with the private sector funding the $26 million balance). We were attempting to avoid a City guaranty of the debt, offering in its place a pledge of the City's entire 8% admissions tax.

From the proceeds of the new motor vehicle lessor tax and accumulated revenues from the parking tax (the Stadium bonds would not be issued until 1996), he envisioned an annual $2 million contribution toward the schools' recreational programming.

Mayor White identified a "$46 million funding gap" which he itemized as:

- $10 million private;
- $10 million from the Browns;
- $6 million from naming rights; and
- $20 million to deal with site issues outside the consultants' $154 million Stadium renovation estimate (these included lead abatement, utilities, and site improvements).

Westbrook seemed certain that Cleveland Tomorrow would be good for $10 million of this gap, and he speculated that city utilities could absorb much of the utilities cost. He then pledged to have Council meet sometime in the next week.

One day later, Mayor White gathered key players for a conference call with Governor Voinovich: the participants were Westbrook, County Administrator Tom Hayes, Cleveland Tomorrow President Roman, State Senator Stanley Aronoff and State Representative Patrick Sweeney via phone links, Growth Association President Carole Hoover, and me.

In his brilliant history of power and politics in the Kennedy and Johnson administrations—The Best and the Brightest—David Halberstam described one of the key inside players:

> For Robert Lovett understood power, where it resided, how to exercise it. He had exercised it all his life yet was curiously little

known to the general public. The anonymity was not entirely by chance, for he was the embodiment of the public servant-financier who is so secure in his job, the value of it, his right to do it, that he does not need to seek publicity, to see his face on the cover of a magazine, or on television, to feel reassured. Discretion is better, anonymity is safer, his peers know him, know his role, know that he can get things done.[22]

This passage nails Hoover's role in Cleveland's civic agenda in general, and in the Stadium negotiations in particular. She began her professional career as a 19-year-old ingenue on Dr. Martin Luther King's staff during a pivotal time when he was mobilizing against the Vietnam war. In Cleveland she joined the Greater Cleveland Growth Association in 1971 and in 1994 her elevation to President of that entity had made her the first African-American President of a major city chamber of commerce. But she was even more impressive as a behind-the-scenes player, including a key role in the Gateway project. Her involvement now in the Stadium issue signified its importance for the region.

Mayor White started the discussion with Governor Voinovich by referencing the City's pending 55% slice of the Stadium funding pie and identifying the key remaining slices: 15% from the State, the sin tax extension, $26 million from the private sector, and a yet-unidentified source for the $20 million site costs.

Senator Aronoff informed us of a vehicle for State legislation on sin tax extension authorization—a July 11/12 Jobs Bill—and advised that we needed strong support from our legislative delegation. Governor Voinovich recommended a revised pie chart showing a greater private role, and a smorgasbord approach to funding. He also suggested that "people closest to Art need to call."

The critical City Council meeting occurred on June 29,1995, via a "Committee of the Whole" meeting. Early in the meeting West-brook and his leadership team had to fight back a host of offered amendments: no municipal dollars for parking in and around the Stadium (defeated 14-6), competitive bidding for the lease (defeated 13-7), creating a maintenance fund when the taxes expire (defeated 11-9), striking the motor vehicle lessor tax (defeated 17-3), lease payments equal to no less than assessed value (defeated 17-3), repeal of taxes if outside funding pieces don't materialize (defeated 15-5), passage of an operating levy for the schools cancels out the school contributions (defeated 14-6).

Then, after agreeing on amendments to enhance minority and female business participation, the Council passed the legislation by a 14-6 vote.

Now Mayor White turned his full attention to the Ohio legislature. He led our team to a week's expedition to Columbus, and there we watched him parlay his prior experience as a State legislator into an around-the-clock lobbying effort. Enlisting support from aide Cheryl Davis and outside consultants Tim Cosgrove and Andy Juniewicz, he renewed acquaintances, hovered over committee meetings, and stalked legislators in the lobbies and corridors. Responding to his full-court press, the Ohio Legislature passed the sin tax extension authorization, giving the County Commissioners the discretion on whether to subject the decision to a public vote.

But at this very time—in July, 1995—when we were so intently focused on the Ohio legislature, John Moag was about to cash in on his exhaustive efforts in Maryland.

Moag (had) set in motion a plan that was the opposite of the city's expansion strategy. He focused primarily on NFL team owners and totally ignored Tagliabue and the league office. An owner in financial trouble, he reasoned, would have to consider the city's lucrative stadium offer.[23]

In the five months since he was appointed Chairman of the Maryland Stadium Authority in February, 1995, Moag had already discussed the Maryland incentive package with owners of the Cincinnati Bengals, Houston Oilers, Chicago Bears, Los Angeles Raiders, Tampa Bay Buccaneers, and Arizona Cardinals. For varying reasons none of these approaches had yet been successful. He had also reached out to the Browns—in the spring of 1995—only to be informed that team president Jim Bailey had checked with Modell who was "not interested."[24]

But Moag was relentless, and a July conversation with a local banker led to an indirect contact to Cleveland Stadium Corporation co-owner Al Lerner. Ethics aside, the negotiating strategy that Moag pursued with Lerner and the Browns over the course of the next two months was chock full of best practices worthy of a Harvard Business School case study. First, he capitalized on *scarcity*: whether true or not (and it probably wasn't), Moag led Lerner to believe that the Maryland incentive package would expire at the end of the year. Second, he injected *competition*: he made sure the Browns knew that the Cardinals and Buccaneers were still in the hunt (though this too was an exaggeration, since negotiations with these two owners had by then slowed to a standstill). Third, by shrouding the discussions in *secrecy*, he protected his dealings from the reach of the rabid Browns' fan base.

Moag was also lucky: he made his second contact with the Browns right about the time that the Browns owner was finally beginning to comprehend the full extent of his escalating debts. So, this second inquiry to the Browns developed traction, and Lerner invited Moag to meet in the former's private jet at BWI Airport on July 28.[25]

We were blissfully naïve as to these latest doings in Maryland. By August, 1995, parking tax opponents were mobilizing for a referendum, and pollster Bob Dykes offered to try to get a copy of the group's petition. Regarding a possible November sin tax vote by the public, he warned that "people will be reluctant to extend the sin tax without some word from Modell."

At an August 21 strategy meeting, State Representative Patrick Sweeney presented Mayor White with a House Resolution designating the Cleveland mayor as "Lobbyist of the Year." As the group discussed the question of whether the sin tax extension could survive a public vote, Dykes opined that the issue "was not completely dead in the water:" with a major effort and expenditure ($900,000), it could pass. I suggested that the Browns' on-field performance may become relevant, and Dykes agreed.

Over the next several weeks, in meetings with legislative consultants, Mayor White predicted—correctly, as it later turned out—that Commissioner Boyle would vote to submit the sin tax extension to the County's voters. So far, Mayor White's strategy was playing out. Negotiate the parking tax percentage. Check. Get City Council to pass legislation for the City's slice of the Stadium renovation pie. Check. Get the State legislature to authorize the County to extend the sin tax. Check. Get the County Commissioners to place the sin tax extension—now reduced to ten years as opposed to the previously proposed twenty years—on the November ballot. Check.

There were three major remaining challenges: run the campaign to pass the sin tax extension, close the last holes in the financing package, and negotiate the Stadium lease with Modell and his attorneys. On September 5, Commissioner Tim Hagan, Hoover, Roman, Garofoli, Nance, and I met to launch the campaign. Pollster Dykes summarized an early poll:

- 54% for the sin tax extension;
- 38% against the sin tax extension;
- 8% undecided.

Further data included: 83% agreed that the Stadium needed repairs and improvements; 32% were convinced that Modell wants to keep the Browns here (40% were unsure); senior citizens are the most opposed; and people generally think that Gateway benefits exceed costs. Dykes stressed the importance of reminding voters that this would not be a tax increase. The Mayor stated that Arnold Pinkney (a local political guru who had become nationally known for managing Jesse Jackson's presidential campaign) and jack-of-all-trades Dennis Roche would manage the campaign.

Ironically, unbeknownst to all of us, on that same September 5 date Modell had gathered his key advisors to assess his options. By the time the meeting concluded at 1 PM, Modell had made a decision that—in his mind and in those of his advisors—would render moot the outcome of the November sin tax extension vote.

The meeting[26] convened at 10 AM at the offices of the Jones Day law firm, and included Modell, his son David Modell, Jones Day managing partner Pat McCartin, Jim Bailey, media advisor David Hopcraft, and Lerner. Hopcraft summarized the media environment and—wrongly, as it later turned out—concluded that the sin tax extension would fail at the ballot. Lerner reported on the Baltimore stadium funding plan and its looming "deadline." Bailey recapped the team's dire financial situation but apparently failed—as later detailed by Poplar in his analysis[27]--to explain that one of the key Baltimore relocation incentives—a $75 million payment derived from expected permanent seat license sales—would be largely offset by Browns relocation expenses (including a $29 million NFL relocation fee and an immediate payoff of the debt on the Berea practice facility).

Moreover, though Modell had complained bitterly in the spring when Cleveland included an admissions tax increase (from 6% to 8%) in its Stadium funding plan, there is no record of whether the meeting participants discussed the higher Maryland-imposed 10% admission tax that would be assessed to Baltimore ticket purchasers. Nevertheless, by the end of the meeting, Modell concluded that he had no choice (but to accept the Baltimore offer), and Lerner concurred.

Ignorant of that momentous Jones Day meeting, on September 22, Nance, Roman, Hyer, and I met to review a financial source and uses table for our project. At that time, the numbers were:

SOURCES OF FUNDS	$ COST MILLIONS	USES OF FUNDS	$ COST MILLIONS
Local bond issue (including passage of a 10-year sin tax extension)	125	Hard construction	130
State of Ohio @15%	26	Contingency	13
City utilities	5	Architecture/engineering	10
GCRTA	5	Testing & inspections	1
Premium seating	14	Utilities	6
Naming rights		Lead abatement	8
Browns contribution		Site improve/project manager	4
		GCRTA rail stop	3
TOTAL	175	TOTAL	175

On September 23, in a meeting including LTV Steel CEO Dave Hoag, Roman, and me, Mayor White summarized a very grim recent Modell discussion: apart from the renovation, Modell also had a revenue issue (having lost $21 in the last two years); thus, in Modell's words, he needed: "...revenues comparable to those in the recent Charlotte and St. Louis stadium deals; there's a $50 million hole in the Stadium proposal, and you can't ask local businesses—who aren't even buying loges—to cover this gap; (my wife) Pat wanted to leave town (given the media environment) and I had to calm her down...I won't jeopardize your ballot issue."

The Mayor and Hoag asked Roman and I to draft a letter to Modell stating: our current deal status, the campaign status, and a gross articulation of the "holes" with our approach to filling them. After delivery of the letter, we would then seek a meeting with Modell.

This meeting, and a September 27 follow up meeting including Carole Hoover, was the origin of a new mini-task force focused on "closing the holes" in our deal—Modell had said $50 million, Mayor had said $46 million in the spring— by a November deadline (Hoover said that she'd heard that the next 60 days was a critical time period). The foot soldiers in this effort would be me, Finance Director Hyer, Roman, financial advisor Tim Offtermatt and Squires bond attorney Barbara Hawley.

Offtermatt took the two biggest pieces. First, he was able to add $15 million to our bond issue: he did this by adjusting for a drop in interest rates since the beginning of the year, and by adding a public guaranty to our bond issue (primarily in the form of a pledge of the City's entire 8% admission tax revenues) to reassure the bond market. These measures increased the bond proceeds to a new total of $140 million.

Second, he removed the $14 million Browns/private contribution to the construction project (Modell had strongly objected to this piece even though both the Cavaliers and Indians had contributed greater amounts at Gateway) and replaced it with a separate $14 million *payment to Modell* on account of the Browns' previous capital investments at Cleveland Municipal Stadium. This new $14 million would be funded via the first $4 million generated from our projected capital repair fund (more on this later), and a $10 million loan from

Cleveland Tomorrow and other private sources (which would eventually be repaid from our debt reserve).

Next, we knew that Governor Voinovich had pledged a 15% State contribution. Since our project had increased from $154 million in the spring to $175 million in the fall, we were able to increase the State amount from $23 million to $26 million.

We had already discussed with City Council a $6 million contribution from City utilities (the Division of Water and Cleveland Public Power), and we were in the early stages of discussions with the Greater Cleveland Regional Transit Authority on a $3 million contribution.

Finally, though it made no contribution to our $175 million Stadium construction budget, we structured a unique long-term capital repair budget to ensure the renovated Stadium would not suffer from the deferred maintenance history at our Stadium and those in many other cities.

> In Cleveland, $57.6 million will be set aside for the next twenty years for capital improvements in the 64-year-old Stadium. The money for the fund would come from excess tax revenues on parking and admissions not used to retire bonds. The capital improvement money figure assumes that the parking tax and admissions tax will increase 2.5 percent annually.[28]

On September 26, we met with Browns' minority owner Bob Gries and heard these observations and suggestions:

- Currently the Browns have perhaps the worst economic deal of the NFL's 32 franchises; to be competitive, the City needs to improve Modell's lease economics to place him 8th or 9th;

- At least eight other team owners (Seattle, Phoenix, Cincinnati, Houston, Tampa, Washington, Chicago, and New England) are looking for new stadiums.

In the midst of our "hole-closing" efforts, on October 5, 1995, Modell sent Mayor White a letter— copying Governor Voinovich, Dave Hoag, and Commissioner Tagliabue— to reinforce in writing the points he'd made to the Mayor in their last phone conversation. The key paragraph warned:

> Merely fixing up the stadium, or even building a new stadium as some have urged, will not solve the problem. Many of our NFL competitors receive as much as $18 million more than the Browns in annual revenues before the first ticket is sold. They use that money to sign players. Indeed the Browns have suffered a cash loss of more than $21 million since we first met on this subject.

Nevertheless, by mid-October, Mayor White was confident enough of our "hole-closing campaign" that he was able to write Modell to assure him that we had closed the gap with no required contribution from the Browns. He requested a meeting with Modell to elaborate, but the Browns owner declined (in three short weeks we would learn why).

Moreover, since June—acting on Nance's advice—the Mayor had been copying NFL Commissioner Paul Tagliabue on letters summarizing our deal status as each respective piece was laid in place. Now, fearing the worst, we began meeting with Nance and his litigation attorneys (Damon Mace, John Stipancic) to project lawsuits in the event that Modell did try to leave Cleveland. The legal theories included a State antitrust action, a claim based on NFL rules, and an eminent domain action.

This was the state of our Stadium efforts as of Friday noon, November 3, 1995, when Law Director Sharon Sobol Jordan and I were on the corner of St. Clair Avenue and East 9th Street. We were returning to City Hall after she had defended my deposition in a major lawsuit involving the Figgie Corporation's and the Richard E. Jacobs Group's respective roles in the City-owned 640-acre Chagrin Highlands real estate development in Cleveland's east side suburbs. Each of our pagers went off simultaneously (with a "00" code signifying we were being summoned by the Mayor). When we arrived at the Mayor's office 10 minutes later, he informed us that Modell was soon going to announce his relocation of the Browns to Baltimore.

I had known Sobol Jordan for five years and accumulated a lot of respect for her in that time. She earned a B.A. degree in public administration from Indiana University and a law degree from The Ohio State University. She joined the Cleveland Law Department as Chief Counsel in 1990, and in 1992—at age 32—she became one of the youngest directors of law in the City's history. She was energetic, smart, and attractive, and she was equally adept at litigation and negotiation. Her later career would include roles of Chief Operating Officer/general counsel and President/CEO of Centers for Families and Children during that entity's remarkable growth (2000-2015), Chief of Staff to County Executive Armond Budish (2015-2018), and CEO of the Unify Project (2018), and President and CEO of United Way of Greater Cleveland (2022).

Did the Politicians Drop the Ball?

In the days and weeks immediately following Modell's press conference, there were many who believed that it was the local politicians who dropped the ball and virtually pushed Modell out the door to Baltimore. The critiques were usually imprecise, but presumably "the politicians" refers to some combination of Mayor White, Cleveland City Council, the three Cuyahoga County Commissioners, and Governor Voinovich. A sampling of the responses:

Former NFL player and author Tim Green:

> It's all well and good for any of us (especially our slippery politicians) to stand back and cry foul at Modell's apostasy.... You are about to learn what happened in those back rooms of power over the years, the events that made Modell's move from Cleveland inevitable. For the first time, you will be privy to all the political shenanigans, false promises and shady deals you always suspected were occurring.[29]

John Helyar of the Wall Street Journal:

> In some ways, the furor at his pending exit reflects as badly on Cleveland as on Mr. Modell. It betrays a cynical bent in politicians, who failed to make a stadium deal with Mr. Modell when they could have and now make political hay by flailing him. It raises questions about priorities, in a city whose school system is under state receivership. It also suggests, for all its comeback-city swagger, the fragility of Cleveland's self-esteem.[30]

Art Modell:

> The reason I'm taking so much heat now is that every politician is
> covering his backside for failing to do anything at all...They took
> me for granted.[31]

Many others shared this view, so we knew we had some major
communications work to do. If the NFL owners and staff adopted
this version of history, the Browns would have a very strong chance
of establishing their eligibility to relocate under the League criteria.
And if the local and national media also accepted it, the City's
national image—which was in the midst of a revival over the last
several years—would surely suffer.

The person who would bear most of the responsibility for getting
this narrative right was an unlikely candidate. Throughout his 12-
year mayoral tenure, Mayor White never got enough credit for his
willingness to entrust major responsibilities to young, unproven City
staffers who made up for their lack of experience with relentless
energy, hard work, and raw intelligence. At this most critical time,
the Mayor's faith in his 25-year-old Press Secretary, tall and dark-
haired Nancy Lesic, would be tested on a national stage.

Armed with a B.A. from Cleveland State University and a short stint
at the Lake County News Herald, Nancy had been in her position of
Press Secretary for a little over a year when Modell held his Baltimore relocation press conference. Yet Mayor White entrusted her
with—and she confidently and capably assumed—our lead communications role in what was to become a four-month national
campaign to "Save Our Browns." After establishing a local media
base (she authored a fierce Op-Ed piece on the Plain Dealer editorial page under the title "The Art of Deception"), she quickly
became our point person for all the national media that was

descending upon Cleveland. The New York Times. The Wall Street Journal. The Washington Post. USA Today. The Baltimore Sun. Sports Illustrated. ESPN. NBC-TV.

The Save Our Browns National Campaign

In an interview with NBC-TV's Bob Costas that aired on "NFL on NBC" on December 17, 1995, Mayor White captured the essence of what would become a four-month national campaign to "Save Our Browns:"

> We have been wronged: The League knows it, the lawyers know it, Commissioner Tagliabue knows it, and America knows it. I think it is incumbent upon the Commissioner, the League, and Mr. Modell to make it right. We are very reasonable people, but this must be made right.

By the time of that interview, he was over a month into a fight that would evolve into a national campaign. He had started the ball rolling on Monday, November 6, 1995, with a lawsuit, borne out of hard work over the weekend by a team of lawyers led by Law Director Sobol Jordan, Chief Assistant Director of Law William Ondrey Gruber, and Squire attorneys Nance and George M. von Mehren. Baltimore Sun reporter Jon Morgan described what happened next.

> On 9:30 a.m. on the Monday of (Modell's) announcement, ...White launched a public relations jihad. The city filed a lawsuit in Cuya-hoga County Common Pleas Court alleging that the Browns were breaking their contract with Cleveland and that the City would

suffer irreparable harm as a result. Cleveland asked a judge to block the move.... Cleveland went from a frenzied, behind-the-scenes appeasement of Modell to an all-out war of vilification. All announcements of upcoming city events, which normally appeared on electronic signs at the airport, in downtown tourist kiosks, and at the convention center now carried two simple exhortations: "Stop Art" and "Save Our Browns!"[32]

The next day—Tuesday, November 7, 1995—was the County vote on the sin tax extension, and the Mayor urged County residents to make this a referendum on saving the Browns: the voters responded with a 72% "yes" vote (campaign manager Arnold Pinkney commented a day later that tracking polls had been predicting a 60-62% affirmative vote: thus, the extra 10% was a "stick it to Modell vote").[33]

Returning to the City's lawsuit, much credit was due to former Director of Law Dick Hollington and his staff: they had the foresight to insert a "specific performance" clause in Modell's 1973 lease requiring that the Browns play all home games during their lease term at Cleveland Municipal Stadium.

The City's request for a preliminary injunction, requiring Modell to honor the pledge to play home games in Cleveland, was heard by Common Pleas Judge Kenneth R. Callahan over three days (Tuesday, November 22 through Thursday, November, 24).

In addition to the City versus Modell angle, there was the spectacle of two of the city's biggest law firms—Squire Sanders Dempsey for the City versus Jones Day for Modell—battling each other in court (noted Jones Day litigator Robert C. Weber represented Modell in this and other move-related matters). A front-page Plain Dealer photo of a break in the proceedings showed a symbolically isolated

Art Modell in a witness chair on one side of the Judge's bench and a gaggle of attorneys—including Sobol Jordan—at the other end of the bench.

On Friday, November 24, 1995, Judge Callahan announced his decision granting the City's preliminary injunction, thereby ensuring that no permanent move could occur until the trial on the merits could resolve the question several months later. Maryland Governor Glendening's office took the news in stride:

> "The ruling was not unexpected," said Dianna Rosborough, a spokeswoman for Maryland Gov. Parris N. Glendening. "We are extremely confident that Mr. Modell will be free to move the team from Cleveland, so this doesn't affect our plans in Maryland. We have an extremely strong and binding contract."[34]

The next salvo from Mayor White was a letter-writing campaign:

> Mayor Michael R. White and Browns fans worldwide yesterday launched their own version of The Drive that might last until the Super Bowl. White, in an effort named "Save the Browns" is appealing to 120 Browns fan clubs with a combined membership of 46,000 to start a massive letter-writing campaign to keep the football team in Cleveland.... Browns Backers Central, the lead Browns Backers club, will spearhead the mail drive, said Bob Grace, chapter president.... (who) asked Browns fans yesterday to write, call or fax their protests to the NFL headquarters in New York and to the 30 team owners.[35]

Plain Dealer reporter Tony Grossi captured the NFL's perspective on all this in a November 26, 1995, article:

> Joe Browne, NFL vice president of communications...said the NFL
> office has felt the impact of negative reaction from Clevelanders
> and Browns fans across the country. He would not quantify the
> number of protests lodged with the NFL office. One report esti-
> mated the numbers to be 15,000 calls and 12,000 faxes.[36]

The Mayor's schedule took on a national perspective: to Baltimore
the day of Modell's press conference; to the NFL Owners' Meeting
in Houston the weekend after Modell's announcement, trips to NFL
headquarters in New York in November and December, leading a
caravan of Browns supporters traveling to Pittsburgh to attend a
Browns/Steelers Monday Night Football Game, testifying before
Congress in late November, hosting ten cities in a conference at the
Sheraton Cleveland on December 14-15, and addressing NFL
Owners' Stadium and Finance Committees on January 4, 1996.

Negotiating with the NFL: November 1995- April 1996

Though we had just filed a $300 million antitrust lawsuit against the
Browns, and had effectively shut down the NFL office's fax machine
and otherwise created headaches for League owners and staff via the
mobilized "Save the Browns" campaign, the NFL reached out to
provide some early guidance in our efforts to quell what was
becoming known as "franchise free agency." On November 29, 1995,
the NFL encouraged Pittsburgh Steelers owner Dan Rooney to
dispatch his staff member Mark Hart to Cleveland to advise us on
how the League and owners viewed our situation.

In a meeting with Squire Sanders attorneys Barbara Hawley and
Terry Clark, and me, Hart informed us that our Stadium renovation

proposal's lack of club seats was viewed as a weakness. He relayed the NFL staff's observation that we needed club seats in an amount "comparable to the local market" (and Jacobs Field had 2,058).

He then walked us through a side-by-side comparison of the Baltimore and Cleveland proposals, noting that Baltimore's would yield annual owner revenues of $22.9 million while ours would yield $16.2 million. He offered advice on how to improve both our financial and graphics presentations to the owners (apparently, Steelers owner Rooney had been impressed with neither). He concluded by agreeing with Clark that "we should prepare as though we were submitting an expansion application" and cautioned that "you don't have 8 'no' votes now."

The meeting with the Steelers' Hart was an early prelude to a six-month period of intense negotiations with the NFL staff. Within a week we would meet five leading NFL officials— Commissioner Paul Tagliabue, President Neil Austrian, Executive Vice President and Chief Operating Officer Roger Goodell, Senior Vice President, Business Affairs/legal counsel Frank Hawkins, and Vice President Joe Ellis—who had guided the League through a tumultuous period of relocation/labor relations/expansion in the past five years.

Tagliabue, then 55, had been Commissioner since August of 1989, having succeeded longstanding Commissioner Pete Rozelle who led the League through a twenty-year period of unprecedented growth. The 6'5" Tagliabue grew up in New Jersey and attended Georgetown University on a basketball scholarship. After graduating from New York University School of Law in 1965, he joined the Washington, D.C. law firm of Covington and Burlington in 1969 and had served the League as outside legal counsel until his appointment as NFL Commissioner. He entered that office committed to League expansion and had presided over the controversial 1993 selection process which admitted Charlotte and Jacksonville as the NFL's 29th and 30th franchises.

Austrian, also then 55, had received an MBA from Harvard Business School. He had been with the NFL since 1991 and as President he managed a wide range of NFL business interests including television contracts, branding, and expansion.

Goodell, then 36, grew up in Jamestown, New York. The son of United States Senator Charles Ellsworth Goodell of New York, he starred in football, basketball, and baseball in high school and was named athlete of the year. He graduated from Washington & Jefferson College with a degree in economics. He began as an NFL intern in 1982, joined the New York Jets as an intern in 1983, and returned to the NFL in 1984 where he had he had performed a variety of roles leading to his present executive role.

Hawkins was a Harvard Law School graduate and—like Commissioner Tagliabue—had practiced law at Covington & Burling. He joined the NFL in 1993 and was performing a wide range of contractual and negotiating roles.

Lastly, there was Joe Ellis, then 37, who had joined the NFL in 1990 after a stint with the Denver Broncos front office (after eight years with the NFL he would go on to return to the Broncos, rising in the ranks until he succeeded Pat Bowlen as President of the team in 2011). As the NFL's Vice President of Club Administration and Stadium Management, he would become our main contact for our stadium design and construction activities.

When Tagliabue took office in 1989, he inherited a 28-team League along with Rozelle's commitment to expansion, and there were a host of cities (many located in in high-growth Sunbelt regions) promising new territories and new TV markets: Charlotte, Raleigh-

Durham, Jacksonville, Memphis, Nashville, Sacramento, and Honolulu. But he had also inherited three team relocations—the Raiders from Oakland to Los Angeles in 1983, the Colts from Baltimore to Indianapolis in 1984 and the Cardinals from St. Louis to Phoenix in 1987—where the fans and political leaders of the abandoned cities were still agitating for teams.

All these cities—the eight emerging markets and the three abandoned markets—responded to the NFL's September 16, 1991, expression of interest concerning a proposed two-team expansion. Rozelle had previously suggested an informal goal of placing one team in a new market and one team in an abandoned market.[37] As the evaluations moved toward a 1994 two-team expansion, Raleigh-Durham, Nashville, Sacramento, Oakland and Honolulu either dropped out or were eliminated for failure to produce a potential team owner satisfying the NFL's vetting process.

By mid-1992, then, there were five cities competing for two franchises: Charlotte, Jacksonville, Memphis, St. Louis, and Baltimore. The new owners would each be required to pay a $140 million expansion fee. Per Morgan of the Baltimore Sun, Tagliabue was particularly enamored with the new markets:

> The fact was Tagliabue and his staff had internally developed a "Sun Belt strategy," their idea being to steer teams to fast-growing regions which could capture fans and dollars not otherwise committed to professional sports. The NFL Commissioner's buzzwords had become "hot markets" and virgin territory." ...Tagliabue...dismissed the "old city/new city" approach Rozelle had discussed, thus depriving Baltimore of credit for helping the NFL to get off the ground.[38]

Presented with this new approach from their staff in October, 1993, the NFL owners' joint finance and expansion committees voted 12-0 to award Charlotte a franchise. The next month— despite Baltimore's last-minute insertion of Modell's Cleveland Stadium Corp. Partner Al Lerner as an ownership candidate— the joint committees voted 10-2 to award the remaining franchise to Jacksonville (thus leaving an angry Baltimore contingent in their wake).

As Tagliabue and his staff proceeded through their expansion process, they developed several ancillary themes that would prove very significant in future NFL decision making: a quest for new football stadia and a fascination with a new stadium financing tool known as permanent seat licensing.

They were bristling over the NFL's inability to procure new stadiums in cities where Major League Baseball had scored beautiful new edifices. Cleveland was one example, but Seattle was a particular sore point. In September, 1995, that city's voters had turned down a ballot measure to fund a new ballpark to replace the Kingdome; however, after the team's exciting October playoff run which included an upset of the dreaded Yankees, the Washington State legislature stepped in and provided alternate funding for what would become the $517 million Safeco Field. But, in the NFL's view, the Seahawks football team had been left at the altar.

They were aware of cities' rationale for prioritizing baseball facilities —economic impacts of 81 home dates versus 10 home dates—but, though football had eclipsed baseball as the country's most popular sport in the 1970's and the NFL had the TV contracts to prove it, the NFL staffers intensely resented what they perceived as an inequity in local sports facility decision-making. The Cleveland debacle—and that's what it was to the NFL – had at least the potential saving grace of breaking the ice on the football stadium building dilemma.

The second ancillary theme—the new tool of personal seat licensing —grew out of Charlotte owner Jerry Richardson's financing plan for the new Charlotte football stadium. Working under the guidance of advisor Max Muhleman, Richardson sold seat licenses in his new stadium for prices ranging from $600 to $5,400, thereby raising $100 million towards the facility's $248 million construction cost. The NFL leaders viewed this new technique as a potential break-through in their quest to accelerate construction of new football stadiums.

The NFL staff and owners were particularly enamored of two models: Charlotte's stadium construction and St. Louis's lease. We would hear a lot about both in the coming weeks and months. And it was probably no coincidence that recently-admitted Carolina Panthers owner Jerry Richardson had already been installed by the owners as chairman of their newly-formed stadium committee.

The NFL leaders had been nearly as surprised as we were by Modell's preemptive move: franchise relocations in general—and ours in particular—were thorny problems. When Raiders Owner Al Davis sought to relocate his team from Oakland to Los Angeles in 1980, the NFL owners had voted 22-0 to block the move. Davis sued the League on antitrust and other claims, and a lengthy trial and appellate process ensued. When the dust settled, the courts had allowed the move— *and* tagged the NFL with a $34.65 million judg-ment in favor of Davis and a $14.58 million judgment in favor of the L.A. Coliseum. Per Baltimore Sun's Morgan:

> The decision was not a carte blanche inviting sports teams to move. But the stiff damage award took the fight out of the NFL.

Rozelle drew up some guidelines, tailored to the judge's directions, to govern team relocations. The new rules required a team to demonstrate a lack of governmental and fan support, as well as financial distress, before it could move. But the legality of these rules wouldn't be known until the NFL went to court to stop another club from moving. And there was little stomach to do that after the Raiders debacle.[39]

Commissioner Tagliabue explained the NFL's concerns regarding franchise relocation—and potential antitrust liability for the League—in a November 25, 1995, statement he presented to the Subcommittee on Antitrust, Business Rights and Competition of the Committee on the Judiciary of the United States Senate.

He cited six factors bearing upon "team location controversies:" 1) differences in size and attributes of the markets in which sports teams compete; 2) labor changes including player revenue sharing with owners and unrestricted free agency for veteran players; 3) a steady increase in the number of pro sports franchises; 4) a need to repair or replace numerous dual-purpose stadiums built in the 1960's; 5) stadium funding disparities; and 6) uncertainty about federal antitrust laws as they apply to the location and relocation of sports teams. Then, as to NFL approaches:.

In the past decade, the NFL's member clubs have modified and focused their revenue-sharing policies to support new stadium construction and renovation. By deciding to waive a portion of the game receipts that otherwise would be shared by visiting clubs, all League clubs effectively contribute to the payment of stadium construction (or related financing) costs. Through this mechanism, the League's member clubs have collectively supported the construction of new stadiums in a number of communities (e.g.,

Atlanta, Miami), The clubs are also collectively supporting the extensive renovation of existing stadiums in a number of communities, including Buffalo, New Orleans, and San Diego.[40]

Turning to the antitrust issue, he explained:

In this context, an internal decision of a professional sports league —whether it relates to funding stadium construction or determining where to locate its franchises—bears no resemblance whatsoever to a "contract, combination or conspiracy" among independent economic competitors that provides a coherent basis for applying the antitrust laws....[41]

Since the Raiders decision, federal courts, seeing the Raiders precedent, have failed to recognize (and potential litigants have elected to ignore) the economic reality of a sports league—that league members are co-producers of a joint product, and thus together constitute a single league enterprise in competition with other entertainment providers. Instead, courts and others have tended to raise form over substance, viewing each team franchise as an independent competitive entity that is portable and transient without regard to its commitments as a member of the league enterprise, the needs and the preferences of the league, or the interest of the league's fans.[42]

The legal decisions, he went on to explain, tied the League's hands and left it powerless to prevent the Raiders' move from Oakland to Los Angeles in 1983, the Colts' move from Baltimore to Indianapolis in 1984, and the Rams' move from Los Angeles to St. Louis in 1995.[43]

This was the setting when we traveled to New York on December 7, 1995, for our first negotiating session with the NFL in the League headquarters at 310 Park Avenue. Representing the NFL were Goodell, Hawkins, Ellis, VP Jay Morgan, CFO Tom Speck, and "financial wizard" Ken Saunders. Mayor White led our team of Nance, Hawley, myself, Finance Director Kathryn Hyer, Planning Director Hunter Morrison, and our premium seat advisor Hamp Howell.

The NFL staff members were extremely interested in how our renovated Stadium would fit in amongst the other North Coast Harbor attractions. We quickly learned that they envisioned Cleveland "breaking the ice" of getting new football stadia built nationwide, and if that did occur, they wanted our facility located in an attractive, bustling and scenic national setting. In short, we had to construct on the lakefront because that site had the most potential for making a national statement.

This was all the encouragement that Director Morrison needed, and for the next hour the NFL officials were putty in the hands of Cleveland's outstanding planning director. The Director described how the individual harbor attractions (Rock and Roll Hall of Fame and Museum, Great Lakes Science Center, Donald Gray Gardens, and Cleveland Municipal Stadium) were linked together via walkways, lakefront elements, and public transit infrastructure as called out in the harbor design standards prepared by the internationally-known Sasaki design team.

Nance summarized Osborn Engineering's Stadium renovation plans, after which Goodell suggested a comparison to Jacksonville's planned Gator Bowl upgrade (on the low end) and Charlotte's planned stadium (on the high end) and offered Joe Ellis's assistance in this analysis. He then asked: "When is the earliest we could see passage of legislation on the $26 million State of Ohio participation?" to which Mayor White replied that it was in the hands of Governor Voinovich and legislative leaders Stanley Aronoff and Jo Ann Davidson.

Goodell then turned to Howell and asked him a number of questions regarding club seats and other premium seating elements. It didn't take Goodell long to segue into personal seat licensing ("PSL's"). Howell questioned whether PSL's would sell in Cleveland, noting the region's blue-collar identity, and suggested that doubling the number of club seats—from 4,000 to 8,000—may prove to be more workable. That didn't slow Goodell down, who countered that PSL's could offer the fans "something of value." He then baited a hook for us by speculating that "if it takes $225 million to do our Stadium the right way, maybe the NFL could use PSL funding to get that last $50 million."

The meeting concluded with a discussion of the logistics regarding Cleveland's submission package that would be reviewed by the NFL owners at their January 17, 1996, meeting.

For the remainder of December, we refocused—with considerable NFL guidance—on our construction assumptions. Several of us traveled to Jacksonville to observe the recently renovated Gator Bowl. As a side trip to a family holiday trip to North Carolina, I took a day's excursion to Charlotte to see the under-construction new stadium there and walk around the stadium's environs.

In several late-December conference calls with Joe Ellis and Roger Goodell, we learned that the NFL staff had serious concerns regarding the cost and timeline of our stadium renovation project:

- Both Charlotte and Jacksonville were started with much more extensive design work than our project, yet they still came in 12-17% over their cost estimates;
- We needed to add a 15% design contingency and a 15% construction contingency; together, these items would add 25-30% to our cost estimate;
- The logistics of our plan to "construct around the fans" were too difficult: we'd probably have to find an interim site for games in 1998 and 1999;
- Our plan showed only one million square feet of programmable space (versus an average of 1.5 million square feet in a typical new NFL stadium);
- Our planned loges seemed "cramped."

Then a telling observation from an interesting source—the NFL Players Association— popped up in the Plain Dealer; it reinforced our belief that Modell's ongoing complaint about losing $21 million in the last two years was self-inflicted trauma:

> Twenty-six of the league's 30 teams spent more than the $37.1 million salary cap in 1995, according to NFL Players Association figures reported yesterday by the San Francisco Chronicle. The teams evaded the cap by paying large bonuses, but pro-rating them over the length of the player's contract, the newspaper said. Dallas spent the most money, more than $62.2 million, or 67 percent above the cap. According to the union's figures, Cowboys owner Jerry Jones paid almost $40.5 million in signing bonuses, including $13 million to Deion Sanders. *The second highest amount of signing bonus money, more than $23 million, was spent by Cleveland, which had a 5-11 record.*[44] (Emphasis added)

Writing several years later, Browns staffer Michael Poplar would make a similar point:

> In his presentation to his fellow NFL owners, Modell revealed that the Browns had lost $21 million in the previous two years. While that number was a rounded-up estimate, it was essentially due to higher player payroll costs, the result of chasing after (not-so) free agents.[45]

As the calendar turned to January, our national campaign continued to gather momentum. One unexpected ally came from, of all places, the Maryland House of Delegates. In a January 5, 1996, letter to Mayor White, Representative Dana Lee Denbrow wrote:

> This correspondence is to apologize to you and the City of Cleveland on behalf of my constituents for the manner of treatment that has been afforded the City of Cleveland, Ohio by the Maryland Stadium Authority. This office is hopeful that the National Football League will have the foresight and fairness to prohibit your football team from abandoning their city and fans in order that the franchise owner may accept a bribe from the people of Maryland.

And, amongst her legislative colleagues, Representative Denbrow was not alone in her views: several weeks earlier the Washington Post had reported that Maryland House Speaker Casper R. Taylor had summoned Modell to a meeting "to welcome him but also to caution him that the team's proposed move to Baltimore faces substantial opposition in the General Assembly which convenes Jan. 10."[46]

Baltimore Orioles owner Peter G. Angelos even jumped into the fray by issuing a January 24, 1996, press release to correct "mischaracterizations before Congress and the Maryland General Assembly" regarding the parity provision of the Orioles lease: Angelos asserted that the extremely favorable terms the Browns received "now require significant adjustment to the Orioles lease...in a number of areas such as rent, facility use, number of private suites...."

On the legal front, on January 12, 1996, our attorneys deposed John Moag of the Maryland Stadium Authority and, based on information learned in that proceeding, we moved to amend our $300 million lawsuit against the Browns and Cleveland Stadium Corp. to add Modell, the Maryland Stadium Authority, and Moag as defendants. The lawsuit claims included breach of contract, tortious interference, breach of fiduciary duty, and civil conspiracy.

On January 15, 1996, we met with our design (Dennis Wellner of HOK) and construction (Ted Wellmeyer of Huber Hunt Nichols) advisors to sort through the NFL concerns. At that meeting, taking into account the comparison construction numbers from Jacksonville and Charlotte and adding in 6,000 club seats, the advisors presented us with four new scenarios:

- A stadium renovation estimate of $191 million;
- A new open-air stadium construction estimate of $244 to $265 million;
- A new domed stadium construction estimate of $306 to $326 million; and
- A new domed multi-purpose stadium construction estimate of $318 to $340 million.

Then it was time to finalize our presentations for, and our travel to, Atlanta for the NFL owners' January 17, 1996 meeting. Initially, Mayor White had arranged for us to travel on LTV Steel CEO Dave Hoag's corporate jet. But several of our presenters approached me with concerns about this mode of travel (Cleveland was being lashed with some blizzardy weather at the time). I agreed to approach Mayor White, and in the midst of our next NFL prep discussion I inserted a question: "Are you sure you want to travel on that Buddy Holly plane in this blizzard?" The Mayor looked out the window, scratched his beard, and then returned to our NFL strategy. But later that day the Mayor's Executive Assistant called me and the other presenters with American Airlines reservation information.

All of our arguments to the NFL owners were incorporated into a 1 ½" thick document entitled "THE CLEVELAND BROWNS SHOULD STAY IN CLEVELAND: Statement of the City of Cleveland in Opposition to the Cleveland Browns' Request to the National Football League to Relocate Its Franchise to Baltimore." Several of the key sections were entitled "Cleveland Has a Sound Plan of Finance to Fund the Reconstruction Program," and "Cleveland's Proposed Lease Terms Are as Advantageous to the Browns as Any in Force Today in the NFL."

We needed to show, and did show, that our deal to the Browns was competitive with that offered by Maryland. A version of the below table, supplemented with information later learned from other sources, was included in our materials.

ITEM	CLEVELAND PROPOSAL	MARYLAND PROPOSAL
Rent	0	0
Ticket Sales	100% to team	100% to team
Advertising	100% to team	100% to team
Food, drink, other	100% to team	100% to team
Novelty	100% to team	100% to team
Private Suite $	100% to team	100% to team
Club Seat $	100% to team	100% to team
Naming Rights	100% to team	To be determined
Construction Cost	$175 million	$175-200 million
PSL/other payments to team	$14 million	$75 million
Moving cost/relocation	0	To be determined
Training Facility expense	$15 million	$15 million
NFL Relocation Fee	0	$29 million
Admissions Tax	8%	10%
Capital Repairs Committed	$57.6 million	$15 million
Annual Revenues to Team	$21.3 million	$30 million

We also responded to the two Maryland surface advantages—"Annual Revenues to Team" and "PSL/other payments to team"—by stating that while our $21.3 million annual revenue estimate was fully documented in our proposal, Maryland's $30 million estimate was far more speculative, and by stating that the much-touted Maryland $75 million payment would be offset by many expenses that would not be applicable to Cleveland's proposal.

Specifically, the $75 million would be first reduced by a $29 million relocation fee owed to the NFL owners. There would also be unknown expenses for moving, relocation, and severance payments to laid off Cleveland Stadium Corp. employees. We also referenced the activities of Maryland legislators who were questioning the Glendening/Moag proposal (we'd later learn that the legislature struck a deal under which Modell would repay $24 million to the State over time, which would cost the Browns owner $13 million in present value terms[47]). Moreover, within a month, Modell would incur an $11.15 million expense to settle Cleveland's legal claims.

ESTIMATED BROWNS RELOCATION EXPENSES

YEAR	EXPENSE ITEM	SOURCE	$ EXPENSE (MILLIONS)
1996	Payments to 29 other NFL owners	Poplar, p. 317-318	29
	Payments to City in settlement of lease litigation		11
	Retiring Cleveland Stadium Corp. debt		15
	TOTAL		55

The NFL owners meeting was set to commence at Atlanta's Stouffer Renaissance Hotel on January 17, 1996. A sizable contingent of Browns Backers was already making its views known. Two nights before, a group of 168 fans arrived on four buses that drove all-night from Cleveland. They staged an evening vigil, holding small flashlights and lining the road to the Stouffer Renaissance Hotel. At noon on the next day, the fans unrolled more than 2.2 million Save Our Browns signatures at the Georgia International Convention Center, and later had the bundles of signatures transported via a motorized caravan to the Stouffer Renaissance Hotel where Mayor White presented them to NFL staffer Harold Henderson.[48]

On Wednesday, the owners' plan was to hear from Commissioner Tagliabue and league lawyers at 10 AM, from Mayor White and his staff after lunch, and Modell and his team at 3:30 PM. The first meeting with the lawyers would be particularly important, since—going into the meeting—some league owners were considering "drawing the line" against Modell's planned move.[49]

Mayor White commenced by alerting the owners of all that was at stake locally and nationally. Finance Director Hyer presented our financing plan, Nance gave our legal arguments, I reviewed the City's history of loyalty to the franchise, and Ohio Governor Voinovich summarized the state's support for retaining the Browns. While we were speaking, our support staff was distributing copies of our 200-page statement entitled "The Cleveland Browns Franchise Should Stay in Cleveland," with chapters speaking to our construction, financing, and premium seating plans, our proposed lease terms, the Browns' bad faith in negotiations, public support, fan loyalty, strength of the TV market, tradition, and the City's lakefront plan.

Later in the afternoon, Modell and his team made their presentation in favor of their relocation plan. They distributed their 865-page statement, first delivered to league offices November 4, 1995, entitled "Notice and Statement of Reasons of the Cleveland Browns Supporting Relocation of Franchise to Baltimore." The 22-page summary statement attached six bulky exhibits: the Browns' Memorandum of Agreement with the Maryland Stadium Authority, a sampling of newspaper articles, an Osborn Engineering Report, the Lease Between the City and the Stadium Corp., the Sublease Between the Stadium Corp. and the Browns, and a Term Sheet of the Browns Lease Arrangement in Baltimore.

The owners responded to the presentations by postponing their decision on the Browns' proposed move until their next meeting in Chicago on February 8-9, 1996. More complications arose the next day, as reported by the Plain Dealer:

> Despite lengthy presentations and handouts from both sides this week, several owners said they need more information on the NFL's ability to stand up to antitrust litigation if the league tries to block Modell. Depending on who loses, either Cleveland or Modell is expected to sue the league, and Maryland officials yesterday announced their own antitrust lawsuit against the league, saying its foot-dragging is costing the state money.[50]

Probably speaking for a number of owners, New Orleans Saints owner (and chairman of the NFL's Finance Committee) Tom Benson said "If I was a judge, I'd be scratching my head on this one."[51] But league counsel Jay Moyer did acknowledge that there was some sentiment toward voting down Modell and testing the league's relocation guidelines in court.[52]

On January 23, 1996, we attended a lengthy debriefing meeting with the NFL staff. NFL attendees were Goodell, Austrian, Hawkins, and Spack; our attendees were Nance, Hawley, and me. The NFL owners, meanwhile, were in the process of reviewing the Modell and Cleveland submissions with the view of deciding the issue at their February 8 meeting in Chicago.

Austrian had the most to say. In introducing the complexities of the expansion issue, he said: "The problem with expansion is we're still assimilating the last one." Then he moved to the details: assume two expansion teams, not one; the price will be higher than the last time (the fee is designed to amortize the hit on other teams of reduced TV revenues over a 4-5 year period); don't see us agreeing to expand for Modell; it would more likely be a team swap; though an NFL February 8 expansion vote is unlikely, there might instead be an NFL guaranty of a team to Baltimore (or Cleveland) in three years with no commitment as to whether the team arrives via expansion or relocation. On the structure of a lease, he speculated that the League or a League entity would sign a lease—or a term sheet—with the League having the right to assign the lease to a team owner of its choice: "The NFL's signature on the lease ensures the team stays for the full 30 years."

He was very animated whenever he spoke of our damages claims: "No way Modell pays damages if he gives up the franchise.... Are you saying that apart from the resolution of your stadium matter, you still need damages? If so, we can't do a deal!"

Austrian also asked about an alternative playing site for the Browns, and Nance responded that initial discussions with Dick Jacobs re

Jacobs Field were inconclusive at best, but we would also be looking into Commissioner Tagliabue's suggestion of The Ohio State University Stadium. On the latter option, Austrian reminded the group that the University had previously allowed pro football there (in the form of the World Football League).

Goodell continued his previous focus on the NFL partial financing options via dedicated club seat revenues or PSL's. Hawkins and Spack explained that they were looking at a 12-15-year arrangement (12 years for renovation/15 years for new construction) in which 100% of club seat revenues would be diverted to stadium construction costs (versus the usual arrangement in which the team owner gets 2/3 and the NFL gets 1/3). To divert revenues to stadium construction costs, the owner would need to waive his 2/3 share and apply to the NFL's Finance Committee. Regardless, Goodell suggested that we all assume that the NFL pays $30 million through whatever means it can do it: club seats, PSL's, whatever.... And, as to Cleveland's stadium renovation proposal, Goodell reiterated that "the biggest concern was with the loges."

Nance addressed all points, citing Mayor White's concerns with PSL's in Cleveland (they'd assess an unfair surcharge to long time loyal season ticket holders), requesting that Cleveland retain input in the decision on what portion—if any—of the NFL financing was derived from PSL's, cautioning that Cleveland would have moral objections to getting a relocated team, and asserting that the chances of our public entities adding to our $175 million public financing were "minimal."

We regrouped after this NFL meeting and divided up the homework assignments: one of mine was to get some answers on the alternative site question. Ohio Stadium was located in Columbus on The Ohio State University campus: for Browns fans, it would be a two-hour,

142-mile, trip on game days. The Stadium, also known as "The Horseshoe," had opened in 1922 with a seating capacity of 66,210. By the time of our discussions, capacity was at 91,470 and the University was planning extensive renovations including premium seating.

My contact would be African-American lawyer/professor/administrator David Williams II, who was in the midst of a 14-year tenure at Ohio State. I called Williams on January 24 (the day after our NFL meeting). He'd been expecting my call, noting that only the University President, the Athletic Director, and he knew about our interest in the Horseshoe. He confirmed that the Ohio Glory of the World Football League had played there on a two-year contract in 1991-1992.). He promised to be very helpful to our cause.

He then cited particulars: getting permission from the Big Ten college league (permission was usually granted in two-year increments), a need to coordinate scheduling with the Columbus Crew pro soccer team, and a pending decision on loge configurations within the planned Stadium renovation. The University was planning to install 1,500 new club seats as well as 80 luxury suites seating 16 persons, at proposed annual pricing levels of $50,000/$30,000/$20,000. A day later, Williams informed us that the University had just received an inquiry from the Plain Dealer. The Athletic Director had given an initial statement— "If it comes to that, we'd be supportive"—but the reporter intended to call back.

We also had to maximize the NFL contribution toward our Stadium, so I prepared a comparison chart for team or league contributions toward sports facilities. Given Goodell's tendency to compare the Cleveland baseball and basketball facilities to our efforts to accommodate the Browns, this chart would be useful in our next meetings by showing that the discussed NFL participation amounts were very reasonable by comparison.

FACILITY	CATEGORY OF TEAM/LEAGUE CONTRIBUTION	$ AMOUNT OF TEAM/LEAGUE CONTRIBUTION	TOTAL $ COST	TEAM/LEAGUE % OF TOTAL CONTRIBUTION
Jacobs Field	Ballpark Revenue Bonds	26,740,000	180,000,000	26.0
	Prepaid Premium Seating	20,000,000		
	Total Team Contribution	46,740,000		
Gund Arena	Team Cash	9,295,000	157,200,000	8.4
	Premium Seating Deposits	3,877,257		
	Total Team Contribution	13,172,287		
NFL Stadium	NFL (low scenario)	28,000,000	220,000,000	12.7
	NFL (high scenario)	48,000,000	240,000,000	20.0

Those next meetings occurred on January 30 and on February 1, when the NFL staff members traveled to Cleveland and met with us at the Squire Sanders Dempsey offices. Major discussion topics were refining the stadium construction cost estimates, further exploring the "renovate versus new" issue, doing a "deep dive" on the PSL financing option, yet another discussion of the NFL contribution level, and an update of our Ohio State discussions

We commenced with a lengthy presentation by our construction consultants— Dennis Wellner of HOK and Ted Wellmeyer of Huber Hunt Nichols—who we had tasked with updating our cost estimates based on detailed final construction numbers from the Jacksonville ($138 million renovation) and Charlotte ($184 new construction) projects. Wellner explained their process: start with the other cities' actual costs (less site costs and training facilities), adjust for the Cleveland region's higher labor and weather-related construction costs, adjust for club seat differences, and escalate to 1997 dollars. Additionally, they were programming for a larger—1.7 million square feet—and brand-new Cleveland stadium.

Squire attorney Barbara Hawley asked Wellner what (aside from a bigger footprint) we get in the new construction that we wouldn't get in the renovation, and Wellner replied "club seats are no longer distracted by columns." Goodell quickly added that there were other problems with the renovation option, including timing and cost uncertainty. Later—in the February 1 session—he tossed in another reason for new construction: "the baseball and basketball teams just got new facilities." The NFL staffers were becoming more aggressive on this point with each new meeting. Reading the tea leaves, we could see our proposal being downgraded in the owners' final analysis if we stuck with our original renovation plan.

But, back to the Wellner/Wellmeyer presentation, their new cost estimate was landing in the $240-250 million region. That estimate prompted Goodell to ask how far away they were from determining a Guaranteed Maximum Price, to which Wellner replied: "six months." Goodell then asked the consultants how they could trim the cost to $220 million. The response: maybe under the best conditions—i.e., no owner change orders, design-build option, and minimal design review.

Nance sought NFL confirmation that we were still assuming a 30-year lease term with the NFL's backing. I took particular note of NFL attorney Frank Hawkins's reply, highlighting it in my notes for future reference. He said: "We would put it in terms similar to the (St. Louis) Rams (lease): the City keeps the facility in 'first-class' condition (not 'state-of-the-art'); and a specific performance provision (that the team play all home games in Cleveland, as in the City's present Browns lease)."I was aware of the terms in the St. Louis lease, particularly its "state of the art" clause requiring major facility upgrades at the lease's 10-year and 15- year timeframes. This issue would bear close watching in lease negotiations.

We then moved to a lengthy PSL discussion. Our construction consultants exited and were replaced by our premium seating consultant, Hamp Howell. The NFL group then plugged in—via phone—national PSL expert Max Muhleman out of Charlotte. Muhleman began sizing up the Cleveland market with basic questions re the size of our stadium (72,000 seats) and our historic season ticket holder base (48,000). The latter number became the maximum for PSL sales projections (because single game ticket purchasers couldn't be expected to deal with PSL's).

He cited Oakland as an example of how *not* to do PSL's: "*personal* seat licenses" for terms of only 10 years (versus Charlotte's *permanent* licenses) together with an annual "maintenance fee." For Cleveland, he proposed a market study but—noting Nance's comment that if we did them at all they should be capped at $500—he speculated that a sales price that low would give buyers "phenomenal apprecia-tion" and would yield $25 million (assuming you charged that price to 50,000 season ticket holders). Nance replied that "50,000 is aggressive for here." And Howell said that he'd prefer to go with fewer PSL's at a higher price. Goodell explained that the NFL exempts PSL's from revenue sharing—even though they are techni-cally ticket revenue—as long as the proceeds are going toward the construction of the facility.

Goodell opened the NFL contribution topic with a question: "What if the NFL picks up $28 million, and the City/NFL split overruns over that at 50/50?" Before anyone could answer, he posed a second question as well as a caveat: "Or the NFL does 28, and then the next 10, City does the 10 after that, and any excesses are then split? But in both scenarios, the formulas apply only to the design phase; once the construction bids are in, the City is solely responsible for over-runs from that point forward." A round-robin discussion ensued, with no immediate resolution.

Lastly, we updated the NFL staff members on our preliminary Ohio State discussions. Goodell expressed some NFL priorities for that arrangement: 1) the team retains suite revenue, 2) the team gets ticket proceeds, parking, and concessions, 3) the University can retain advertising revenues, and 4) either the University takes a percentage of the gate for game days, or the team pays game day operation and maintenance expenses. After Nance explained that Mayor White would be talking to Governor Voinovich about this historic proposal, Goodell warned: "If this number goes off the chart, it's a deal killer."

My next Ohio State conversation was on the afternoon of February 1, and Nance joined this one. Williams opened by advising that their Athletic Director was concerned that the Browns' presence might lessen Buckeye sellouts, to which Nance responded that the University could sell packages that included a Buckeyes Saturday game with a Browns Sunday game. Williams added that he had spoken with University President Gordon Gee that morning: Gee requested that we have a "further, fuller discussion."

At a follow-up call at 9 PM that evening, Williams reported that earlier that evening President Gee did present our request to the University Board of Trustees, and that several board members were concerned about pro agents hanging around their student athletes. But, initially, there were no dissenting board members: rather, there was a general consensus that this was "good for the State of Ohio."

On February 5, I discussed the Ohio State plan internally with Law Director Sobol Jordan, Chief Assistant Director of Law Rick Horvath, Assistant Director of Law Debra Rosman, and Finance Director Hyer. Rosman reviewed the impact of Columbus' 1% income tax on players' salaries. Sobol Jordan—an Ohio State law grad— noted that Columbus is already packed on Saturday nights so we have to simplify Clevelanders' travel there. She also suggested it was time to contact the City of Columbus. Hyer reviewed income tax and admission tax implications.

In my next Ohio State call—on Tuesday, February 6, the day before our departure for the NFL owners meeting in Chicago—we discussed the possibility of the University moving up its planned 1999 renovations, agreeing that the Browns' tenancy might assist in expediting that timeline. Williams cautioned me that Ohio Stadium "was not well laid-out for concessions," but there shouldn't be a great disparity between the Buckeyes' ticket prices ($28-29) and the Browns' ticket prices.

That same day I continued an ongoing discussion with Greg Sponseller, Law Director for the City of Berea. Before and during the Save the Browns campaign, Mayor White had developed a strong relationship with Berea Mayor Stanley Trupo, and in my conversation with Sponseller I previewed our NFL presentation. We talked again later that day; this time joined by Mayor Trupo. Sponseller said that "Goodell didn't lead me to believe that Berea's bonds would be paid off. He suggested that they would assume the existing obligation. Also, they asked Berea to itemize damages in the event of a three-year gap." Mayor Trupo and Sponseller then stressed that Berea's obligations didn't end with the (annual $1.55 million) bond payments: there were also annual real estate taxes ($260,000) and insurance costs ($20,000).

Later that afternoon, I joined Mayor White who initiated a conference call amongst Roman of Cleveland Tomorrow, and Dave Nolan and Lee Hawley of the Convention and Visitors Bureau. After summarizing our status with the NFL, the Mayor asked "if you three believe it makes sense" to initiate a 30-to-45-day study to determine whether the community could raise an additional $150 million (supplemental to the stadium funding) to build a new convention center (along the lines of St. Louis' domed stadium attached to its convention center). Hawley asked whether we had cost estimates for a domed stadium, and the Mayor said "Ken can share his numbers" (which were $318-340 million). Roman asked whether this work group would be similar to the Stadium Task Force, and the Mayor replied: "Yes, but much quieter." He made me the staff point person and added Planning Director Morrison.

Early the following morning—Wednesday, February 7, 1996— Nance, Barbara Hawley, Press Secretary Nancy Lesic and I boarded our Continental Airlines flight to Chicago for the pivotal NFL owners meeting. Right before the flight, Lesic told us that Mayor White—who wasn't joining us until Thursday morning—had chosen to give an exclusive updating interview to ABC affiliate WEWS TV 5 in Cleveland. As we reviewed our expectations during the short plane ride, it was clear that the NFL decision would take the form of one of two options:

(*Option 1*) ...keeping the Browns in Cleveland, to be operated by an NFL trust, while Maryland built its stadium. When the new ballpark opened, Modell would move and rename his franchise, and Cleveland would get a new team, called the Browns.[53]

(*Option 2*) Modell and his franchise would be allowed to move to Baltimore but would have to pay off Cleveland's legal bills and stadium debt and leave the Browns' name, history books, and colors behind. The NFL would promise, in writing, that a franchise would be in Cleveland by 1999. The league would also contribute tens of millions of dollars to Cleveland to help build a stadium—an unprecedented concession to one of its cities. In exchange for all this, Cleveland and Maryland would drop their lawsuits.[54]

Obviously, Option 1 was our strong preference.

Later that morning, we arrived at the long, semicircular, 860-room Hilton Chicago O'Hare Airport Hotel. Amongst those schooled in sports history, the O'Hare Hilton had since its 1973 opening become an unofficial historic landmark for pro sports owners' decisions. It was a long-time favorite haunt for Major League Baseball owners: it was there that baseball's owners—on September 3, 1992—had voted 18-9 (with one abstention) in favor of a "no confidence" resolution regarding Commissioner Fay Vincent (four days later Vincent tendered his resignation); and, more recently—on April 2, 1995—the baseball owners voted to effectively end their 8-month stalemate with the players that had vanquished the 1994 World Series.

Sensing that even greater history was in store for our gathering, we checked into our rooms, gathered at a hotel conference room, and plunged right into a 10:30 AM session with NFL representatives Goodell, Austrian, and Hawkins.

Austrian began by referencing his Saturday, Sunday and Monday discussions with Modell, and declared that:

> "I have Art's proxy. He'd like to make a deal. I suggest we jump to
> Option 2. Art won't give up the team for three years."

Austrian then said that, from the owners' perspective, there wasn't enough support for the Browns playing two seasons (1997 and 1998) in Columbus. Goodell added: "If you had some place to play in Cleveland, then the owners' concerns would be lessened." Hawkins urged us to "tie up Ohio State anyway." I then replied:

> "You need to understand that Option 2 isn't Cleveland's preference.
> But rather than reject it (as Art did on Option 1), we can talk."

So, we commenced discussing Option 2. Austrian conceded that the NFL contribution up to $240 million "is OK with us. After that is the question." Nance replied: "Then we just have a $5 million gap.

The Mayor wants to take the sharing up to $250 million, so the NFL maximum exposure would be $48 million rather than $43 million." Hawley then summarized the Indians' and Cavaliers' respective contributions to their facilities, which she summarized as being on the order of "one-third." By contrast, we were only asking the NFL to give 20%. Austrian responded: "Let's hold that and see where we come out on the other issues."

Nance confirmed that Governor Voinovich would contribute 15% of $220 million and noted that the PSL issue was still open. Austrian conceded that if the gap comes in lower, we might not sell PSL's at all. I reminded the group that any deal was subject to City Council lease approval, which prompted Goodell to stress the need for City Council deal approval prior to the NFL owners' next—March 10—meeting. Hawkins began discussing lease particulars. It could take the form of a memo with a lease attached:

> "The capital repair fund...we want it retained at the level stated in your proposal. We'll need "first-class" language re capital repair breeches: a covenant on this part of Cleveland that is the flip side of specific performance."

This sounded dangerously close to the St. Louis lease's "state of the art clause", so I responded: "No St. Louis language, particularly on stadium economics." Goodell asked: "Why not stadium economics?" to which I replied: "_No way_." Goodell said: "I realize we're not going to win this one, but...."

That was the end of the St. Louis clause's appearance in our NFL discussions. History since then has taught us that at least three other cities (Kansas City, San Diego, and Cincinnati[55]) allowed the clause to creep into their football leases. The St. Louis lease clause was primarily responsible for the Rams' departure from that city in

2015,[56] and it is perhaps no coincidence that the San Diego Chargers left for Los Angeles in 2017 after San Diego failed to procure a new stadium. We were fortunate to have a strong negotiating base with the NFL; make no mistake, it was the strength of Nance's $300 million lawsuit that empowered me to be as aggressive on this point in that day's discussions.

That said, the NFL did have a legitimate interest in ensuring that we were committing to an adequate amount of capital repairs over time; after all, the City of Cleveland did not have a spotless record of maintaining Cleveland Municipal Stadium. Moving to the timing of notifications to the City, Goodell suggested that we would be notified by November 1997, if we were getting an expansion team. If we were getting a relocated team, the notification would occur by March 1999.

On the Berea issue, Goodell began by describing the current arrangement: on the $1.55 million annual bond debt service payments, Modell annually pays Berea $1.2 million in the form of rent, and Berea annually pays $350,000. Goodell's proposal going forward was: NFL would take over payment of the entire bond debt service and would "waive" Berea's former $350,000 payment; Berea could then use those savings to take care of the annual property tax ($260,000) and insurance ($20,000) bills. The NFL would also cover the facility's operation and maintenance costs.

Nance then said: "That brings us to the last $5 million and the issue of damages," touching off an animated debate over the amount of our damages. We had previously claimed $28 million in damages, and Nance said if we relinquish that overall claim, we would need dollar for dollar recovery on our business interruption claim: i.e., the full $9.3 million. If we were to receive that amount, we would apply

$5 million of it toward the back end of any stadium construction overruns.

We were approaching lunchtime, so we broke for each side to confer with our principals. Nance developed the below list of major deal points, and we discussed them with Mayor White several hours later:

1. NFL contribution of up to $48 million toward stadium construction costs;
2. Damages paid by Modell or NFL in amount of $9.3 million or more;
3. Change order approval process;
4. The "first class" capital repair issue;
5. PSL's over $30 million go to the City (and no PSL's in Dawg Pound);
6. The NFL's March 10 deadline for City Council action;
7. Whether we are willing to waive our damages claims against Maryland;
8. The deadline dates for notifying us on an expansion or relocated team;
9. The amount of the State of Ohio capital allocation;
10. Cleveland Tomorrow's commitment deadline for its $10 million share;
11. Goodell's Berea proposal.

The Mayor listened to our summaries and indicated that he would ponder these issues that evening. He did give some preliminary reactions: "I can't explain in strong enough terms how difficult it would be to take a relocated team," he said. "Why can't we have an expansion team and be done with it?" We discussed some possible limits on the relocation option (no lease breaking, strong prohibition on NFL taking a team from a supportive city, and "no Cincinnati"). On the Cleveland Tomorrow issue, the Mayor promised to take it up with Dave Hoag and Carole Hoover in the next few hours. He needed to see the PSL language in writing. I asked him to particularly focus on the Maryland issue, and he concluded our discussion by promising that he "would be off the plane at 9:30 AM tomorrow (Thursday) ready to deal."

We resumed our NFL discussions at 2 PM. Austrian began by saying: "On damages, we're swallowing very hard and assuming your $11.5 million...." He followed with his own list of outstanding issues: the damage payment stream, Cincinnati, Cleveland Tomorrow, Maryland dismissal, City Council approval, and PSL's. The NFL folks needed to prepare for their planned 9 PM meeting with the owners, so we agreed to meet again at 8:30 AM Thursday morning in conference room 1002. But we'd end up seeing them much sooner, as noted by the Baltimore Sun's Morgan:

> At about 9 p.m., the NFL's top brass—Tagliabue, president Neil Austrian, and operations vice president Roger Goodell—reported to a joint meeting of the league's finance and stadium committee. They explained the deal that was coming together but also laid out the option of keeping the Browns in Cleveland and promising owner Art Modell and Baltimore an expansion team after Maryland built its stadium.[57]

That led to a heated debate amongst the 12 owners. Wayne Weaver of Jacksonville and Dan Rooney of Pittsburgh favored our Option 1 (making Modell wait), but Jerry Richardson of Carolina—arguing that Option 2 would yield four new NFL stadiums (in Baltimore, Cleveland, Washington, and Cincinnati)—took Modell's side. That session ended with a decision that the owners would ask Modell one more time whether he could wait for a team.[58]

That outcome brought us back to the table with the NFL staff at midnight, and there we stayed until 3 AM Thursday morning, spending most of our time reviewing the language of the NFL's draft interim contract.

In the midst of all this, I broke off from the group to buy a Snickers bar in the hotel's main lobby: there I encountered Plain Dealer reporters Tony Grossi and Steve Koff. They'd learned of our TV 5 exclusive update, and they weren't shy in pointing out our breech of media protocol. Koff was particularly volatile, saying: "You can't f--- with (Plain Dealer publisher) Alex Machaskee and get away with it!" Then, as I was making my escape to a nearby elevator, I encountered Cleveland City Council consulting attorney Craig White—who we had been ducking since we arrived (the NFL was not going to accept a new party at the negotiating table)—and told him I was returning to my room. After pushing "8" on the elevator button (my room number was 8110) and riding all the way up there for good measure, I then pushed the Lower Lobby button and returned to our group in Squire Sanders' makeshift "War Room" in Conference Room 3.

We took a minute to call Mayor White in the middle of the night and update him on the latest trajectories. He told us that he had talked to Hoag and Hoover, and we needed "bland language" on the Cleveland Tomorrow time deadline.

By mid-morning Thursday, February 8, 1996, we were back with the NFL staff. It had been a long night, everyone was edgy, and things got testy in a hurry. Austrian declared that Modell wouldn't pay $3.1 million in damages to Berea on account of its loss in income taxes over the next three years. He added that the NFL took Cleveland

Tomorrow at its word on its commitment, to which Nance responded that we're asking to make the time period and target reasonable. Austrian shot back: "Compare Jacksonville and Carolina: If Cleveland can't do it, maybe Art was right."

Nance asked whether Option 1 was gone. Austrian replied: "It's gone" with no further elaboration. Piling on, he sniped: "The Maryland litigation has to be dropped, and we want your damages pledged to the capital reserve fund."

Trading bluntness for bluntness, I snapped: "Mayor White wants to use damages to offset the hit on our general fund." Slightly changing the subject, Goodell suggested that our damages be paid over a five-year period, and he, Austrian and Fred ended up compromising on four years.

We adjourned to meet Mayor White who had just checked into his hotel room. There, sitting on the two beds, the Mayor, Nance and I sorted out all the issues. The Maryland litigation was the elephant in the room, and I'd been waiting for this moment. I recommended that we tell the NFL we were ready to accept all the Option 2 terms in the manner we had left them this morning, with one exception: we would retain our lawsuit against Glendening, Moag, and the Maryland Stadium Authority. As long as we dismissed Modell, Tagliabue, the NFL, and the Browns from our lawsuit, why should the NFL care what we did with Maryland?

But we all knew that the NFL *did* care, and that was the rub. The last thing the NFL wanted—after all the sound and fury of the last three months—was a leftover lawsuit that, while tangential to the NFL, might end up blocking Modell's funding from the Maryland legislature. A number of Maryland legislators were still grumbling about Glendening's deal, and our continued litigation wouldn't make things any easier. In short, if we stuck to our guns on the Maryland issue, it might crater our whole deal with the NFL.

But I was arguing that there was no harm standing our ground, for the rest of the day at least, in the hope that the NFL would concede that it was tired of protecting Maryland from the mess it had made. And, if we were somehow successful in getting our deal, retaining our Maryland litigation, and prevailing in court, think of the blow we could strike against "franchise free agency." No other governor, and no other state agency, would again dare to behave the brazen way Governor Glendening and the Maryland Stadium Authority behaved in this instance.

Mayor White patiently heard me out, and then he began calmly explaining to us why he was ready to accept the NFL's deal and dismiss the Maryland litigation. He reminded us of something I already knew—that he intended 1996 to be primarily focused on Cleveland's schools—and then he explained what I should have grasped earlier: if we ended this national fight with Modell and the NFL *now*, and obtained City Council approval of the deal in March, we could quickly segue to the schools and focus on passage that year of a much-needed operating levy.

If Cleveland continued its fight with Maryland, the civic agenda would remain divided and the schools issue would suffer. There was nothing more to discuss, and I knew it. It was time to bury the hatchet and accept a better deal than any other abandoned city had struck with the NFL.

Having decided the biggest issue, we moved to some of the other deal points: one of those was the NFL requirement that Cleveland Tomorrow sell a minimum percentage of premium seats by January of 1996. Looking ahead to the press conferences on the horizon, the Mayor predicted that the Cleveland Tomorrow obligation would be hard to explain to the public. In his words, "I understand this one's a skunk...we need to pretty it up as best as possible, but it will still be a black and white animal with a tail."

With our hotel room discussion concluded, we called the NFL staff and told them the Mayor was ready to meet with Commissioner Tagliabue. The meeting was arranged, and everyone began transitioning into press conference mode. Tagliabue agreed to attend the key March, 1996, Cleveland City Council meeting.

Later that evening Austrian called me to stress three deal points: the importance of the March 8 deadline for City Council approval; the NFL's concerns about City Council's desire to investigate alternate stadium sites; and the importance of the Cleveland business community's commitment on premium seating sales. Then, as to the upcoming press announcements, he urged us to stress that Cleveland's deal with the NFL was *unprecedented*. Then, per the Baltimore Sun's Morgan:

> The final handshake came at about 9 p.m. on Thursday, Feb. 8, after a long day of diplomacy by NFL officials shuttling between the Cleveland and Browns delegations, which never actually met in the same room, even after the deal was consummated.... After signing the documents at a short ceremony with Tagliabue, Mayor White struck a conciliatory tone, one that was in sharp contrast to his months of Modell-bashing.
>
> "It's time for us to let the past go and for us to look with clearer eyes, to look with kinder eyes and maybe softer eyes at the future," White said. "I'm hopeful that we can commence a period of healing and a period of building."
>
> White and Modell conducted back-to-back news conferences and left the hotel without appearing together. [59]

Cleveland City Council's Response to the NFL Deal

The next day back in Cleveland, we convened a long debriefing session with Cleveland City Council members. At this time, their desires included:

- Taking up to a year to investigate alternate stadium sites;
- Extending—by another 5 months—the March 1996 goal to resolve the "dome/no dome" question;
- Avoiding a scenario in which the new team owner would seek additional public moneys to assist him or her in paying the NFL's expansion fee;
- Procuring local ownership; and
- Procuring up to 800 free seats in the stadium.

On Sunday, February 11, from 12 PM to 2 PM, local radio talk host Rich Passan took calls from listeners reacting to our deal. The comments included:

- A caller stating that Mayor White did the best he could: now the caller could take his 4-year-old son to a Browns game when the son turns 7;
- A caller saying he couldn't wait till Modell brings his Ravens to our new stadium in 1999;
- Three consecutive callers believing that Mayor White had "sold out;"
- A caller asked what had happened to "No team, no peace." And what if we end up with (Cardinals owner) Bill Bidwell as our owner?
- Jim of Independence asked "What if the new owner doesn't want our name and colors?"

- Bruce from Seven Hills, commenting on PSL's, asked: "Can you imagine going to a store and paying ten dollars before entering? Only a monopoly like the NFL could pull this off...keep the PSL's under 10% of the total seats."
- Jack of Bainbridge said: "Voinovich/Latourette/White need to answer for this."
- Angela, a 12-year Dawg Pound season ticket holder, said: "Don't retire name/colors: we all tore the old stadium apart 'cuz we thought we were losing those;" and
- Joe of Cleveland said: "I won't miss Modell: I'm for the new stadium."

Passan then took a few minutes to interview Squire Sanders attorney George von Mehren, who confirmed that he and the other members of Fred Nance's litigation team had been "ready for trial, and knew we'd win: we'd have enforced three more years of Modell in the old stadium."

Passan asked "What's to ensure performance in 1999?" to which von Mehren responded: "Our specific performance clause, and the NFL knows that Cleveland is a good football town." Passan returned to the callers:

- Isaac in Fairlawn said: "von Mehren makes sense...nothing's guaranteed in court. We got a good deal. Owners won't tangle with Cleveland again."
- Steve of Strongsville observed that "If you go to Vegas, you can't afford to bet the mortgage on your house: the NFL's downside wasn't as big as ours."

Passan then brought in County Commissioner Lee Weingart, who started by saying that: "Without all the fan support we wouldn't have gotten this deal. No other vacated city got this." When asked how this deal will impact Mayor White's political standing, Weingart replied: "Positive. By rallying people and changing a negative to a positive. I like working with White because he's a fighter."

The next day—Monday—Nance and I met with Law Director Sobol Jordan, Finance Director Hyer, and attorney Horvath to commence work on our legislative drafting task. The remainder of that week was devoted to a series of construction meetings. We struggled with the concept of "fast-tracking" the work—City Architect Ken Nobilio was very uncomfortable with that approach—and tried to find the right balance. But we all agreed on the need to appoint a "stadium construction czar."

On Monday, February 19, 1996, Mayor White met his Chief of Staff LaVonne Sheffield Turner, Hoover, Roman, and me to discuss the dome question and the Cleveland Tomorrow premium seating obligation.

Now that we were commencing detailed negotiations of the NFL franchise agreement and the lease, three new lawyers entered the discussions. For the NFL, the first new player was Covington & Burling corporate and securities attorney Andy Jack. It was Jack—a George Washington undergrad, and honors GW law school grad, — who prepared the initial and subsequent draft franchise agreements. The second new NFL attorney was Robert Gage, a cum laude Harvard Law School graduate who headed Covington & Burling's real estate practice.

On our side, Nance brought then-Squire associate Dynda Thomas into the fray. Thomas was a 1982 Miami University grad who earned her law degree at the University of Cincinnati where she served as editor of the law review. Thomas drafted, and redrafted, the hotly-debated lease that was to consume much of our negotiating time.

The City of Cleveland would lease the Stadium to the NFL (with the expectation that the NFL would assign its rights to a team owner once one was selected). The lease was negotiated over an intense one-month period from mid-February to mid-March. The City's capital repair obligation was a key topic consuming thirteen pages of the final lease. Several key takeaways are:

- The City bore responsibility for capital repairs, but annual expenditures would be capped per an attached schedule: this" Capital Repair Fund", defined in Lease Section 14(f), was the same schedule of required City deposits that we gave the NFL owners on January 17, 1996; and
- The City bore responsibility for capital improvements maintaining the economic competitiveness of the Stadium as measured by the top half of NFL stadia (but, unlike St. Louis's "state of the art clause, *such expenditures are capped by the amount remaining in the Capital Repair Fund*).

Other key lease terms were:

- A 30-year lease term;
- The lessee's commitment to play all home games at the new stadium, enforceable by a strong specific performance clause;
- The lessee's obligation to pay stadium operation and maintenance costs; and
- The lessee's right to receive all revenues from stadium operations: ticket sales, licensing and broadcasting, advertising: scoreboard and signage, food and drinks and other concessions, novelty sales, stadium naming rights, promotion and other events, and—to the extent not pledged toward stadium construction per the

Stadium Funding Agreement—all premium seating payments.

On March 4, 1996, Cleveland City Council commenced its hearings on our proposed NFL deal. First up were the NFL leaders: Commissioner Paul Tagliabue, Roger Goodell, and Frank Hawkins.

Tagliabue summarized the factors in the agreement: The Browns' history, tradition, and fan support, the financing of a new stadium, a mutual desire to minimize the interruption of football (by committing to its return in 1999), and the dismissal of all the pending litigation. Goodell cited two concerns with the City's previous renovation proposal: the 10% contingency was low (it should have been 30%) and building around the team's schedule would have been problematic. Tagliabue stated an intention to finalize the lease—and thereby avoid a second round of negotiations with the eventual owner—by the March 11, 1996, proposed NFL owners vote at their annual meeting in Palm Beach, Florida.

Councilman Ed Rybka asked about the NFL's flexibility on the timeline, construction cost, and site, to which Tagliabue responded "Yes, we want to be as responsive as we can be. We could have done an 'agreement to agree' but instead we have specific terms. Within that framework, we can be responsive to your land use concerns."

Councilman Gary Paulenske inquired about owner expenses, and Tagliabue explained that the NFL will invest up to $48 million in our new stadium, and that a typical team's player costs average $40-50 million per year. Councilman David McGuirk expressed concern about City Council having to deal with a "floating construction number." Goodell responded that we've all done extensive analysis of a $220 million cost number. When Councilwoman Fannie Lewis raised questions regarding "the flexibility of the deal," Tagliabue warned that "major changes would require a new (NFL owners) vote: that could be tragic."

Later, the Council heard from Congressman Martin Hoke on the site selection topic. The Congressman began by opining that the City's planners "made a big mistake 62 years ago by locating Cleveland Municipal Stadium on the lakefront." He added that they made the same mistake with Burke Lakefront Airport. He envisioned Cleveland Hopkins Airport's future as a commuter airport, with a new regional airport being sited between Cleveland and Akron thirty years hence. He concluded by urging passage of the deal with the NFL, but with amendment to the site selection part.

The Council hearings resumed on March 6, 1996, with an appearance by Cleveland AFL-CIO President Frank Valenta. After briefly reviewing the history of Gateway and other major local projects, he quickly got to his point: "Though we don't always agree with Mayor White, we agree with him on this one. We're here to support what the Mayor's done, and the ball is in your court." Councilman Michael Polensek asked whether the AFL-CIO's Executive Board was aware of the document's contents. Valenta responded "no," which drew this rejoinder from Councilwoman Fannie Lewis: "I'm shocked that you voted without reading the deal. I will vote no. I would have voted yes on the renovation." Councilman Roosevelt Coats added that he hoped the AFL-CIO would work with us on minorities (participation), to which Valenta responded "that was part of the agreement."

Next were Law Director Sobol Jordan and Squire attorney Thomas, who carefully walked the Council through the negotiated lease terms. After their summary, Council President Jay Westbrook brought outside counsel Craig White to the table to articulate some

City Council concerns on property insurance, property taxes, rental amount, minority participation, and the site decision.

After extensive discussion of all these issues, Cleveland City Council ultimately voted 13-8 to approve the deal, barely meeting the NFL's imposed March 10, 1996, deadline. With the Council approval in hand, Mayor White sent Nance and me to Palm Beach, Florida to nail everything down at the NFL owners meeting at The Breakers Hotel.

This would mark our third NFL Owners meetings in the last three months: first Atlanta, then Chicago, and now in Palm Beach. The latter venue radiated the luxurious vibe of this unique gathering of thirty of the nation's richest and most egotistical corporate lions. The Breakers had been built a century earlier by one of their kind— industrialist Henry M. Flagler—and the story of The Breakers endures, "...holding fast to the ideals that put it on the map— unapologetic luxury, seaside glamour and world-class service..."[60] The owners themselves made a fascinating collage: an account describing them twenty years later would have been just as accurate in depicting our 1996 assemblage:

> There is much about the Membership that is "inadvertent," starting with who gets to join this freakish assembly. They are quite a bunch: old money and new, recovering drug addicts and born-again Christians and Orthodox Jews, sweethearts, criminals, and a fair number of Dirty Old Men.... One imagines those black felt pictures from the seventies with dogs playing poker around a table. Trails of ex-wives, litigants, estranged children, and fired coaches populate their histories.[61]

The Breakers' meal planners were more than ready for the challenge of feeding the grazing tycoons: owners balanced cocktails and plates crammed with lobster, crab, shrimp, roast beef, and an endless array of sides. And the hotel supplied each place setting with pads of note paper and pencils, all emblazoned with "The Breakers" and its logo of crashing waves.

Over the several days of owners' meetings, Nance and I met with Roger Goodell and his colleagues during the lulls between their sessions with the owners. During one of those lulls, Nance and I had three hours to kill when we walked by The Breakers' main dining room and noticed that the Modell family had commandeered a large table at the corner of the dining area. Immediately adjacent to that table—and several feet lower in elevation—were several small cocktail tables. We picked the cocktail table closest to the Modells' table and spent several hours nursing a few drinks, which had the effect—the Modells knew us and were forced to conduct their conversations in lowered voices—of annoying our adversaries with our presence.

Stadium Construction

On March 12, 1996, the NFL owners formally voted in approval of our deal, and we returned to Cleveland with the next task being the construction of a new stadium. But first we had to resolve the site issue. In their March, 1996, deliberations, the City Council had created a stadium site selection task force and given it a 60-day deadline to finalize a decision. Councilman Ed Rybka and Carole Hoover co-chaired the task force. The Committee would be staffed by Mayor White's newly-appointed Stadium Construction Manager, City Hall veteran Diane Downing.

Downing, best described as a career problem solver—not unlike (but a little less gruesome in her practices) the "Mr. Wolf" character who presided over the disposal of the hit men's blood-soaked auto in the movie Pulp Fiction—grew up in New York State and first came to Cleveland in 1977 shortly after graduation from Vassar College (where she had served as president of student government). After a three-year stint in the office of Republican County Commissioner Seth Taft, she joined newly-elected Republican Mayor George Voinovich's Community Development Department in 1980 and served there for the next decade. When Mayor Michael R. White took office in 1990, he appointed Downing his Executive Assistant for Service where she ably served until 1995 when she left for a position with the Ohio Lottery.

Though I had worked with Downing for some time, she was leaving for her Lottery position just as I was moving up to Mayor White's office in February, 1995. But she did give me some outgoing advice re problem-solving in Mayor White's office: "The issues that end up on your desk will be pretty fouled up: after all, they're the ones that a project manager tried to solve...and failed, a Commissioner tried to solve...and failed, and a Director tried to solve...and failed!"

Downing staffed the Stadium Site Selection Task Force during its six weeks of deliberations in March and April. After reviewing more than a dozen downtown sites, the Task Force settled on two finalists: the lakefront site and a Norfolk-Southern site located just south of the Gateway complex. Preliminary due diligence work indicated several challenges with the Norfolk-Southern site: it would take longer to develop (thus imperiling the tight NFL deadline), and its geotechnical character (part of the site was a deep valley) suggested extraordinary site development costs).

There was a third issue with the Norfolk Southern site. The Browns' fan base had—*both then and now*[62] --- insisted that the new stadium remain at the same lakefront location. And, though lesser known at the time, the NFL had made it very clear to us that the stadium had to be on the lakefront. By the end of April, the Task Force had voted unanimously to proceed on the lakefront site.

The rest of 1996 was devoted to design work by principal designers HOK and its subcontracting landscape architects. In December, 1996, the historic Cleveland Municipal Stadium (and the adjacent Donald Gray Gardens) was demolished.

Early 1997 was devoted to continued design work, and to the commencement of site work. In a January 31, 1997, meeting, HOK's Dennis Wellner and landscape architect Lee Behnke led a discussion of site development, building design, and interior finishes, Behnke identified the challenge of developing new landscaping to replace the Donald Gray Gardens. Mayor White asked for trees that would flower at different times throughout the year.

The building design showed openings on both sides of the "Dawg Pound" east end zone seating to set that area off from the rest of the building (though the northernmost opening would later be partially closed), and I suggested plaza tree plantings outside each opening. Mayor White told Wellner to involve me in the review of stadium seat colors. Planning Director Morrison suggested that we engage General Electric in the site lighting for the North Coast Harbor. In a February 5, 1997, follow-up meeting, Behnke reviewed a plan for consistent landscaping throughout North Coast Harbor.

On March 25, 1997, we began discussing site preparation specifics. Downing identified a contingency of up to $1 million for hazardous materials during drilling, and she described the first bid package (mass excavation and pilings). The second bid package would be structural and concrete, and there would be a total of 13 bid packages for the project with the last three (sitework, seats, and furniture, fixtures, and equipment) to be bid in April, 1998.

Mayor White (who had by then been advised by the Convention & Visitors Bureau that a dome would not yield enough additional stadium events to be cost-efficient) said he'd still love to have a dome but can't justify it in terms of money or time: it would cost $80 million more and delay the project a year. Morrison added that there was no guarantee that it would fit under the FAA flight path for Burke Lakefront Airport.

Downing noted that a new walkway to the Stadium wasn't part of the Stadium analysis: it would instead be part of a separate inter-modal study. Such a walkway would not connect to the Stadium; it would land on the front lawn of the Great Lakes Science Center.

On May 19, 1997, we had the first of what would be many discussions on wind studies. Wellner described an initial wind chamber analysis that showed problems in the east and west end zones: he proposed a ten-foot screen at the top of the north seating bowl canopy, and further review of the pedestrian bridges traversing the Stadium gaps. He advised us: "We had to fight the wind people who wanted to close the gaps." Mayor White and I had been discussing seat colors, and he informed the group that "blue and gray are out...so is green... I like the Dawg Pound as brown with the rest of the seating as orange."

Our next meeting was of a "come-to-Jesus" type I'd experienced many times during my tenue serving Mayor White. All employees in Mayor White's office were very accustomed to such meetings. But sometimes consultants had to share in them, particularly when a bid —specifically, structural and concrete—comes in $18 million over estimates, which was the subject of a lengthy June 13, 1997 session.

Mayor White first held an internal meeting: Downing Nance, construction advisor Jim Conrath, and me were there. After Downing reminded us that our owner-protective general conditions (and supplemental general conditions) for construction contracts often cause bidders to inflate their bids, Nance told us that consultant Huber Hunt Nichols ("HHN") had made several mistakes in its concrete estimates: underestimating quantity by 10%, and failing to add extra cost for wintertime installation. As a result, HHN's estimate of $390/yard was exceeded by a bid amount of $410/yard (and as high as $600/yard for the upper concourse). And it wasn't just HHN: HOK had an obligation to update us.

We then proceeded to a meeting with the whole consultant team. Mayor White stated:

> "After going to war with the NFL, we determined we were going to do this as a City project. What I want is _that_— (he pointed to the latest Stadium sketch)—Stadium, on time and within our $247 million budget. Now we have our best team (of consultants) assembled. But if it digresses to finger pointing, etc., I'll go to no lengths to see the City redressed. Now, I'm ready to hear your presentation."

The consultant team described their issues—8,000-10,000 yards of additional concrete beyond what was estimated in design drawings, 1,000 tons of additional reinforcing steel, a tunnel from the building's east side to across the street—and concluded that these issues were responsible for half of an $18 million problem. They added that they were very disappointed at the few bidders. Mayor White asked them if this situation could be repeated in each future bid package, and the reply was "We hope not. We have to identify why local contractors feel uncomfortable about bidding for the City." Mayor White replied: "You know there's no more money. This is not going to be Gateway. We're not taking the roof off; we're not cheapening the building."

On August 26, 1997, Downing convened an internal group of us to assess the project's status. She began by reporting that Independence Excavating had finished excavation, and was 2/3 complete with the installation of 3,200 pilings (with completion envisioned by Halloween). She anticipated a September 2 bid opening date for the "superstructure."

Public Utilities Director Michael Konicek reported on a $4 million cost for the Ontario Sewer—which actually runs under the football playing field—with the Northeast Ohio Regional Sewer District committing to pay $3.2 million and the City committing to pay the remaining $800,000 (which Downing confirmed was in her Stadium budget). She added that Permanent Seat License sales to the public would commence the following week (and, in a December 2, 1997, meeting, she updated that 53,000 PSLs had been sold, as well as 8,000 of the 10,000 Dawg Pound seats).

Downing convened the next internal meeting on September 12, 1997, attended by Mayor White, Nance, Conrath, and me. Mayor White started: "We're not going to cut down the east end zone (Dawg Pound)." Conrath described a seating reduction from 70,000 ADA-compliant seats to 66,000 ADA-compliant seats.

On March 30, 1998, Mayor White followed up on his persistent theme of exterior landscaping: he asked if the trees were all budgeted for the Stadium. Diane replied that everything north and south of the Stadium was budgeted.

On April 21, 1998, Downing summarized the seven remaining bid packages which would be bid out in the May through November time frame: these were three electrical packages, a signage and graphics package, a scoreboard package, a telephone and data package, and a furniture and equipment package. Turning to premium seating parking, she said that loge parking would be in the Great

Lakes Science Center Garage and club seat parking would be within the 2,200-space Port Authority lot.

By the summer of 1998, enough bids were in to allow the consultants to update their construction cost estimate. The new number was $280 million, and Mayor White announced the revised number to the public on July 28, 1998. But, given the level of contribution from the NFL, there would be no need for additional public revenue sources.

Several months later—when Al Lerner successfully bid for the Browns expansion franchise in September, 1998—the bid included an agreement to reimburse the NFL for its $54 million loan. And when the new stadium's cost eventually rose to $300 million in 1999, Lerner agreed with the City to split $10 million of the additional cost (i.e., that portion between $283 million and $293 million).

The Expansion Decision

As previously noted, Mayor White was insistent on getting an expansion team—we were not going to do to another city what Maryland had done to us—and he instructed Nance to lock this down in our NFL deal. And Nance pushed extremely hard on this issue, but we were only partially successful.

Though the NFL would not <u>guarantee</u> us an expansion team, it did agree that the owner of a team in another city would have to clear many high hurdles before relocating to Cleveland: the threshold was even higher than the NFL's own relocation standards. Though we didn't get our guarantee, in practicality we came close: and we already knew that the NFL was disinclined to preside over another team relocation. As far back as January, 1996, Commissioner Tagli-abue had discounted the possibility of Cleveland getting an existing team from another city:

> Tagliabue downplayed the likelihood of an existing team relocating to Cleveland, saying "We're trying to stabilize teams. We're not trying to encourage team moves."[63]

But in the same interview he gave expression to a longstanding sore point shared by NFL owners and the Commissioner's office: Major League Baseball's ease in procuring construction of new ballparks, while the NFL kept striking out.

> The problems of team movement and instability...are grounded by escalating salaries and competition with other sports who are building new facilities such as Jacobs Field, Gund Arena, (the Colorado Rockies') Coors Field and so forth.[64]

Over the next several years, the NFL Commissioner's Office successfully threaded a needle by pushing other cities to build new football stadia—using Cleveland as a stalking horse—but stopping just short of actually threatening team relocations to Cleveland.[65]

In that 1996-1998 time period, we received very few calls from other cities' concerned officials. For those who did call, we explained our deal terms and emphasized how the odds of Cleveland getting a relocated team were remote at best. But I suspect that most city officials who found themselves under the NFL's trained "build a new stadium or else" gun were afraid of Cleveland and thus refrained from calling us.

The end result could not have been more ironic: Cleveland, a city that despised franchise free agency and did more than anyone to fight it, unwittingly became the crowbar that the NFL successfully employed to pry loose its heretofore hopelessly stuck stadium building agenda. Or, as explained by Baltimore reporter Jon Morgan:

> Far from reassuring host cities, the NFL continued to threaten the loss of their franchise if cities didn't provide the best stadium terms possible. And the league wasn't offering to help pay for the stadiums. In this sense, the Browns' relocation to Baltimore actually upped the ante. No longer could a city like Chicago, with generations of loyal fans, hope to keep the Bears in town with just a rehab of old Soldier Field, with new, luxury structures—new gold mines to be exact—popping up in Maryland and Ohio.

> Directly or indirectly, the Browns' relocation caused new stadiums to be built for the Ravens, the Redskins, the Bengals, the Browns, the Buccaneers, the Lions, the 49ers, and the Seahawks. The impact of the Browns' move on taxpayers nationwide was thus staggering.[66]

It was not until March 23, 1998—*five months after the November, 1997 deadline set by Roger Goodell during our February 7, 1995 meeting in Chicago*—that the NFL ended Cleveland's stalking horse status by officially declaring that Cleveland's new team would come via expansion. Several months later, the league agreed to a managed bid process to set the new owner and the price he or she would pay.

On August 19, 1998, seven ownership groups made presentations to NFL owners, but the New York Times reported that the number was soon winnowed:

> For months, there were seven candidates; second bids were due at noon yesterday and were to form the basis of talks between the groups and Goldman, Sachs & Company, the N.F.L.'s financial

adviser, which will seek to negotiate still higher bids. The first round of bids last month created an informal floor estimated at $350 million. The highest bidder will not necessarily win; the league will present at least two finalists to the 30 owners next Tuesday, and a winner will have to be approved by at least 23 of them. But three groups declined to make second bids....[67]

Four groups remained:

- The Al Lerner group included former 49ers executive Carmen Policy and was endorsed by Bernie Kosar;
- The Larry Dolan and Charles Dolan group included Bill Cosby and Hall of Fame NFL coach Don Shula;
- The Howard Millstein group included two former Browns (Paul Warfield and Calvin Hill) and a virtual "Who's Who" of Cleveland business leaders (Joe Gorman, Bill Sanford, Michael Horvitz, Patrick McCartan, Mal Mixon, and David Daberko); and
- Bart Wolstein.

On September 8, 1998, the NFL owners, guided in part by an Art Modell last-minute lobbying effort to procure a unanimous vote, selected the Lerner group's $530 million bid to become the owners of the Browns expansion franchise. Lerner's bid included $54 million toward repayment of the NFL's stadium construction loans, which meant that the real franchise fee of $476 million was still almost double the previous high of $250 million paid for the Minnesota Vikings.[68]

Lerner's Cleveland franchise award left the NFL with the uneven number of 31 teams, which it needed to cure for both scheduling and division alignment reasons. The remedy came in October 1999, when the league awarded Houston the NFL's 32nd franchise for a fee of $700 million. That decision enabled the owners to vote for eight divisions of four teams each (which remains the current arrangement). The Chicago Tribune reported that Houston businessman Bob McNair's bid "beat out competing and unorganized factions from Los Angeles, leaving the nation's second-largest television market open to the next owner who wants to move."[69]

The Los Angeles stalking horse would remain in play for nearly two more decades, until the Rams returned from St. Louis for the 2016-2017 season and the Chargers relocated from San Diego to Los Angeles for the 2017-2018 season.

Assessing Mayor White's Save Our Browns Campaign

From the date of Art Modell's Baltimore press conference, Mayor White led a national campaign to reclaim Cleveland's team, its name, and its colors. He achieved unprecedented success in reclaiming the name and colors, but he had to wait three years to get the team back. Modell got to take the team to Baltimore with him, and the Maryland officials were rewarded for their subterfuge.

The Save Our Browns national campaign lasted three months—from November 6,1995, until the NFL deal was reached on February 9, 1996—and some outsiders have criticized Mayor White's relentless focus during that time: "Cleveland Mayor Michael White spent months, "observed Field of Schemes authors Cagan and DeMause, "talking of little but the Browns to local media during the fight over the Browns."[70] True? Yes, to a degree. But, as my notes during that time can confirm, we did not literally drop everything else at City Hall. Other things got done.

Mayor White stepped forward during that time for reasons far beyond football. At its core, the campaign was about fair dealing and civic respect: neither the City nor its citizens were going to play a passive victim's role to the machinations of scheming Maryland politicos and a desperate team owner. In that short but intense three months, he made our case to fellow mayors, to the U.S. Congress, to the national media, and to the NFL. And he got closure in the form of a deal that no other victimized NFL city had achieved so quickly or so favorably.

Cleveland's campaign did make history. Consider the below table of NFL team relocations since 1950 (the year the Browns joined the league).

TEAM	FROM	TO	YEAR LEFT	YEAR RETURNED OR REPLACED	GAP IN YEARS
Cardinals	Chicago	St. Louis	1960	Never	-
Chargers	Los Angeles	San Diego	1961	2017	56
Texans	Dallas	Kansas City	1963	Never	-
Raiders	Oakland	Los Angeles	1982	1995	13
Colts	Baltimore	Indianapolis	1984	1996	12
Cardinals	St. Louis	Phoenix	1988	1995	7
Rams	Los Angeles	St. Louis	1995	2016	21
Browns	Cleveland	Baltimore	1996	1999	3
Oilers	Houston	Nashville	1997	2002	5
Rams	St. Louis	Los Angeles	2016	Never	-
Raiders	Oakland	Las Vegas	2019	-	-

Cleveland had the shortest gap—three years—between a team's departure and a team's return. Houston was next at five years, then St. Louis at seven years. Most cities waited much longer, and several cities will never see a replacement team.

The short turnaround time is especially significant when viewed against the city's overall civic agendas. A lost football team remains a cloud on a city's agenda until a team is returned; the football issue ends up competing for attention with other important civic issues. Mayor White was determined to avoid such a cloud in Cleveland, particularly since he had already framed 1996 as a year for improving Cleveland schools. His strategy worked, and later that year Cleveland voters did pass a sorely needed schools operating levy.

Opening Day: September 12, 1999

On September 12, 1999, my mother, brother and I were onsite to see the expansion Cleveland Browns open their new $300 million stadium in a nationally televised Sunday Night Football game. Al Lerner declined sale of naming rights, so the new facility opened as "Cleveland Browns Stadium" (which it stayed until new owner Jimmy Haslam sold naming rights to First Energy in 2102 for an estimated price of $104 million). Pittsburgh Steelers' quarterback Kordell Stewart and his teammates spoiled the party by trouncing the Browns, 43-0.

Team Performance and Drafting Record Since 1999

Concerning on-field performance, the 2018 NFL season was the 20th year since the Browns returned to the NFL via expansion in 1999. In that time period their won/loss record stood at 88-216, by far the worst in the League. Though there are many explanations for the Browns' poor performance since their return, including constant front office and coaching turnover, one cause stands out: it's the same cause that led to the team's struggles in the early 1990's—poor player procurement practices highlighted by an abysmal drafting record.

Consider the Browns' draft record in years 1999-2018: in those 20 years they drafted 11 players who appeared in the NFL Pro Bowl. By contrast, their chief rival—the Pittsburgh Steelers—over the same time period drafted *19 Pro Bowl players* and their next biggest division rival—the Baltimore Ravens with former Brown Ozzie Newsome calling the shots—also drafted 19 Pro Bowl players.

Now it's possible that the strong coaching staffs at Pittsburgh and Baltimore played a role in turning their respective draft choices into Pro Bowl material. But it's also true that both the Steelers and Ravens fielded very good teams during most of this time period and as a result were picking much lower in each draft round than were the 88-216 Browns. With this last point in mind, let's look more closely at how the Browns performed in selecting their relatively high first-round draft picks.

In a June 27, 2018, analysis, writer Christian D'Andrea compiled for the period of 2000-2014 a list of all first-round NFL "bust" draft picks: that is, all first-rounders who spent two years or less with the teams that drafted them. His leaderboard of "Most 1st round draft busts, 2000-2014" read as follows: Cleveland Browns (7), Green Bay Packers (6), San Francisco 49ers (6), Minnesota Vikings (6), Buffalo Bills (5), Arizona Cardinals (5), and Seattle Seahawks (5).[71]

In an April, 2017, USA Today analysis of every NFL team's draft performance in the last five years, the Seattle Seahawks finished first and the Cleveland Browns finished dead last amongst the league's 32 franchises. The methodology developed player grades using Pro-Football-Reference.com's Approximate Value metric. It evaluated every player drafted from 2012 through 2016, and concluded:

> So, every time the Seahawks picked in the last five years, they got a player who produced an average AV 2.88 higher than expected

based on their draft position. The Browns, meanwhile, got a player who produced an AV 2.75 lower than expected based on their draft position.[72]

Moreover, the study found that the Browns selected the league's worst draft classes *in consecutive years*— 2013 and 2014—and never achieved a positive grade in any of the five evaluated years.

One other point stands out in the returning Browns' draft record. In the modern NFL, the quarterback's dominant role in team performance has steadily ascended. With very few exceptions, the teams that regularly appear in the post-season all have "franchise quarterbacks." Yet despite having more top ten draft picks, by a wide margin, than any other team in the past twenty years, only twice (Tim Couch in 1999, and Baker Mayfield in 2018) did the team select a quarterback with a top ten draft pick.

To address the longstanding poor draft performance (arguably, over 30 years of substandard performance dating back to the 1980s), the Haslams hired experienced NFL professional John Dorsey as General Manager on December 7, 2017, and Dorsey added veteran personnel to the front office. Initial returns were positive: his 2018 draft class received a "B" grade from The Sporting News (compared to "A- "grades for Pittsburgh and Baltimore)[73] before regressing to a "C- "in 2019.[74]

But Dorsey was replaced after two years, and a five-year look-back on the Dorsey tenure argues for harsher grades. His signature 2018 pick of Baker Mayfield at number one overall did lead to the Browns' 2020-2021 playoff season. But Mayfield has been outperformed by both Josh Allen and Lamar Jackson (later quarterback picks in that draft) and his awkward exit in 2022 as a byproduct of the Browns' controversial DeShaun Watson acquisition left everyone involved with black eyes. Although Dorsey's 2018 draft did yield star players Denzel Ward and Nick Chubb, he inherited a veritable treasure trove of picks from prior GM Sashi Brown and failed to score on the remaining picks.[75]

The Haslams' 2020 choices (Andrew Berry as General Manager and Kevin Stefanski as Head Coach) began with a 6-10 record in a 2019 transition season, and improved to an 11-5 record—and the team's first playoff appearance in nearly 20 years—in the 2020-2021 season. The slide back to an 8-9 record in 2021-2022 was largely due to Mayfield's injury-riddled season, and a further slide to 7-10 in 2022-2023 was attributable to Watson's 11-game suspension arising from his prior conduct in Houston. Their future will depend on the outcome of their huge dice roll in acquiring Watson for a slew of draft choices.

CHAPTER FIVE

MAINTAINING THE FACILITIES

At the dawn of a new century in year 2000, Cleveland and Cuyahoga County were deservedly proud of their three brand-new centrally-located sports facilities. In the new millennium, the public sector's challenge would shift from designing and building the facilities to prolonging their useful lives. It's not too different from preserving your car or house: you need to do routine maintenance to make sure that minor problems don't grow into major problems, and you need to invest more significant capital at defined intervals if you want your asset to have a long life.

The leases of all three facilities assigned routine maintenance responsibilities to the tenant sports teams. Concerning the more significant capital repair responsibilities, the approaches varied:

- The Browns lease placed most of the burden on the City (even to the point of including an annual funding schedule) and earmarked a portion of the 2006-2015 sin tax renewal proceeds ($29 million worth in years 2012-2015) toward these capital repair obligations;

- By contrast, the Gateway facilities evolved (after 2004 lease amendments described below) toward shared responsibilities, with the teams covering capital repairs costing $500,000 or less and Gateway (actually, the public sector since Gateway has minimal assets) responsible for capital repairs exceeding $500,000.

Gateway Capital Repairs History 1994-2013

As expected with two brand-new sports facilities that opened in 1994, there were minimal initial capital repair concerns for the ballpark and the arena. By 2004, Gateway and the teams had been working together for a decade. It had become apparent that the original economic relationships between Gateway and the teams needed some tweaking. Gateway's income from team rents and facility naming rights had proved insufficient to fund its operating requirements and capital repair obligations. Accordingly, Gateway commenced negotiations with the teams that led to a January 1, 2004 Memorandum of Understanding ("MOU") with the Indians and a February 3, 2004 MOU with the Cavaliers.

The Indians MOU revised the rent so that it now consisted of the funds necessary to permit Gateway to meet its obligations to the Indians under the lease and common area agreements. And Gateway would now be responsible for those capital repairs costing in excess of $500,000 (without aggregation of such capital repairs). In return, Gateway gave up all rights to future ballpark naming rights revenues.

The Cavaliers MOU similarly had the Cavaliers paying Gateway's operating and common area expenses, with the same $500,000 capital repair language. In return, Gateway gave up all rights to future arena naming rights revenues.

In considering capital repairs occurring at Quicken Loans Arena between 1994 and 2013, the bulk of the work consisted of either capital improvements (i.e, entirely new additions or alterations designed to modernize the facility). Much of this work occurred within five years of Dan Gilbert's purchase of the team in the spring of 2005. In that time period, Gilbert's ownership group funded $40 million of work, including new wine-colored seats, a state-of-the-art new ANC scoreboard including video and sound systems, new graphics and signage, security and locker room improvements, and a redesigned two-story team shop.[1]

At Progressive Field, the Indians funded over $23 million of capital improvements and renovations in the 1994-2013 timeframe. This work included suite renovations, Collection Auto Club, Heritage Park, and a 5,000 square-foot scoreboard installed before the 2004 baseball season.[2]

Concerning more routine capital repairs paid for by the teams from 2005 through 2013, Gateway shows the following records:

Repair $ in Millions	2005	2006	2007	2008	2009	2010	2011	2102	2013
Ballpark Capital	1.3	1.2	1.5	2.0	1.6	1.3	1.8	2.0	1.9
Arena Capital	8.4	7.6	4.7	3.1	3.1	0.9	0.7	0.7	1.0
TOTAL	9.7	8.8	6.2	5.1	4.7	2.2	2.5	2.7	2.9

Cleveland Browns Stadium Capital Repairs History 2000-2013

The capital repair schedule appended to the Browns lease required the City to fund capital repairs at levels of $500,000 annually in years 1999 and 2000, $650,000 annually in years 2001-2005, $850,000 annually in years 2006-2020, and multi-million-dollar annual amounts in years 2021-2028.

The Lerner family owned the Browns until their sale to the Haslams in 2012, and during their tenure the City generally performed annual capital repairs in the scheduled amounts: each year the Browns would submit an engineer's audit listing needed capital repairs, City staff would review the list and cost the line items, the parties would settle on a list of items falling within that year's budget, and the City would then obtain legislation and bid and perform the work.

There were two notable exceptions to this annual routine. The first occurred during a July 14, 2007, Kenny Chesney concert. The Stadium was flooded with 50,000 gallons due to toilet valve malfunctions, necessitating $1 million worth of repairs to make the facility usable by the date of an August preseason game against the Kansas City Chiefs. Several of the contractors for that work submitted exorbitant bills, touching off a jousting match between Browns staff (who wanted to pay the entire bills) and City lawyers and the insurer (who disputed portions); eventually, the City and the insurer prevailed.

The second exception was in late 2011. The Browns sought experience with the Stadium lease and—after our Law Department granted a conflict-of-interest waiver—hired Fred Nance as outside counsel. Nance approached the City, citing a need to cause $5.8 million of repairs—seat refurbishment and replacement, concrete repair and waterproofing, plaza repair—to be completed prior to the team's 2012 football season.

Mayor Frank G. Jackson had been in office for five years. He was an African-American resident of Cleveland's Central neighborhood and —following long stints as a City Councilman (since 1990) and City

Council President (since 2002)—he had run for mayor in 2005 and defeated incumbent Jane Campbell.

I had established a real estate law practice after Mayor White left office in 2002, and had worked on Mayor Jackson's campaign throughout 2005. A month after his November, 2005 election victory, Mayor-elect Jackson had asked me to return to City Hall as his Chief of Staff and I had accepted.

So on December 6, 2011—five years into my role as Mayor Jackson's Chief of Staff—I met with City finance officials, attorneys, engineers, and bond counsel to summarize the Browns' $5.8 million capital request: The Browns would select a design/builder and advance the entire $5.8 million for the work, and the City would pass an ordinance authorizing the City's Finance Director to reimburse the Browns from sin tax extension dollars.

Bond counsel Barbara Hawley explained that, commencing May, 2012 and continuing until the City accumulated $29 million, all sin tax extension dollars would flow to the City Finance Department. She suggested that we push the Browns toward making "Material Capital Repairs" (as defined in the lease) rather than Stadium enhancements such as "Capital Improvements."

Then, on January 20, 2012, the Browns' Brian Wiedemeir and Nance met with Mayor Jackson and me to elaborate. Nance stated that: the Browns had spent $82 million on capital repairs and maintenance since the Stadium opened in 1999; the Browns' desired bid date was February 29; and the Browns proposed to design the work, perform the construction, and seek reimbursement from the City when extended sin tax monies became available in August or September.

Mayor Jackson was receptive to this concept but stated his desire to spend the City's $29 million sin tax monies "in a way that minimizes costs down the road." He also previewed his long-term approach toward capital repairs: he would support another sin tax extension for capital repairs for all three major sports facilities. At the Mayor's request, we met later that day with City Council President Martin Sweeney to brief him on the issue and prepare for the legislative hearings.

We appeared before Cleveland City Council on February 6, 2012. I made the initial presentation, and Nance (joined by the Browns' Dave Jenkins and Osborn Engineering representatives) answered Council questions about the project. The Plain Dealer's Thomas Ott was there and wrote this summary:

> The Browns, sensitive to criticism of the team's deal with the city, came to the hearing armed with a breakdown of money it has invested in the stadium and the community.
>
> Included were $74 million contributed to the construction, another $50 million paid for features such as escalators, a restaurant and team shop and more than $30 million spent on cleaning and other everyday maintenance. The team also detailed more than $2.9 million donated to community programs and sports facilities.
>
> Ken Silliman, chief of staff to Mayor Frank Jackson, said the city reviewed the repair plans and confirmed the need. The agreement approved Monday is supposed to free the city from its repair obligations for seven years, but Silliman would not rule out tapping sin-tax money again during that time if necessary. "We own Cleveland Browns Stadium," he told the council. "When you own a building and a few years go by, it starts to develop needs. It's just like when you own a home."[3]

Though generally supportive, Council members raised concerns about funding future capital repairs.

> The so-called sin tax took effect in 1990. Voters initially approved the tax to finance Progressive Field and the Q, then extended it for 10 years, starting in 2005, to build and repair Cleveland Browns Stadium.
>
> The ballot issue required that the first $87 million from the extension pay a portion of the stadium construction costs. After the cap is reached this year, the next $29 million must be applied to repairs previously paid for out of the city's general fund.... Cleveland's obligations for stadium repairs will spike from $850,000 to $5.9 million a year in 2021. The amount will continue to rise annually, reaching $7.1 million before the lease runs out in 2025.
>
> City Council members called for working with Cuyahoga County leaders to renew the sin tax for a second time. The discussion may be complicated because there's been talk of renewing the tax for fixing The Q and Progressive Field, which opened in 1994. "We have to go back to voters for a conversation to extend that sin tax." Councilman Zack Reed said. "There's no other way around it," [4]

Ultimately, Cleveland City Council passed the ordinance authorizing the $5.8 million expenditure, and the Browns' contractors constructed the most significant capital repairs since the football stadium opened in 1999.

Other than verifying the work and processing the reimbursement payments, our main task going forward was to insure that the Browns' contractors complied with our inclusion and diversity ordinance requirements. Apart from our longstanding goals for participation by minority business enterprises and female business enterprises, City Council had, during Frank Jackson's tenure as Council President, enacted the "Fannie Lewis Law" requiring 20% employment of Cleveland residents and 4% employment of low and moderate income persons. The Browns complied with all these goals and requirements.

A Decision to Maintain the Sports Facilities From 2014-2034

On November 13, 2013, as Mayor Jackson was concluding negotiations with the Cleveland Browns on a $120 million renovation project described in Chapter 6, the City of Atlanta issued a significant announcement. As reported by NBC Sports:

> The Marietta Daily Journal reports — and the Braves have since confirmed — that they are moving to a new, suburban ballpark after the 2016 season. The new park will be in Cobb County, near the intersection of I-75 and I-285. The move is occasioned by the end of their 20-year lease agreement for Turner Field, which expires at the end of the 2016 season.
>
> This move is completely unexpected. Turner Field, which is a retrofit of the Olympic stadium from the 1996 summer games, has only housed the Braves since 1997. There is nothing about it that is obsolete or lacking for baseball. It's a bit big and the Braves don't draw as well as teams who have been as successful as they have been should draw, but that speaks to the nature and popularity of baseball in Atlanta — and a bit about Atlanta geography and demographics — not the ballpark.
>
> It is worth noting, however, that the area where this report would have a new Braves ballpark is in the prosperous and growing

northern Atlanta suburbs, where a great many Braves fans (and players) reside already. So, while such a move would be against the tide of recent history, a team actually leaving the urban center to move to the burbs would not be as an insane and antiquated notion in Atlanta as it might be in other cities.[5]

This announcement came less than a year after Atlanta had decided to replace its twenty-year-old Georgia Dome with a new $1 billion plus facility that would become known as the Mercedes-Benz Stadium. Was this the wave of the future? Would cities have to begin planning to replace their sports facilities at twenty-year intervals?

Not in Cleveland, Ohio. In a November 18, 2013 press conference held to describe the Browns' stadium renovation plan, Mayor Jackson and the Browns' Joe Banner previewed the need for an upcoming sin tax extension.

> Banner and Jackson said they would support a campaign to extend the sin tax, which expires in 2015 and is solely dedicated to the FirstEnergy Stadium's capital fund. Jackson said a new sin tax would help reduce the city's liability. The Cleveland Indians and Cavaliers also want to extend the sin tax to help pay for improvement plans for Progressive Field and Quicken Loans Arena. Any sin tax, which requires support from Cuyahoga County Council and county voters, would be split three ways.[6]

Intentionally or not, the City of Cleveland and Cuyahoga County were about to embark on a polar opposite course to that charted by the Atlanta metro area. If twenty-year life spans for sports facilities *were* the wave of the future, then the Cleveland metro area was opting *not* to surf that wave. Instead, if County voters agreed at the polls, this region would seek to *preserve* its existing sports facilities for at least another twenty years. And the extended sin tax – receding each year but still yielding $13 million annually—would provide the City and County with the funding stream to make this goal a reality.

The 2014 Sin Tax Extension Campaign

By the beginning of 2014, civic leaders had all agreed on the initiative: at a May, 2014 election date, they would ask Cuyahoga County voters to approve a twenty-year (from 2015-2034) extension of the County sin tax, with the proceeds to be allocated toward future capital repairs for all three major sports facilities.

Each sports team had designated a point person for the campaign: Dave Jenkins, the Cleveland Browns' Executive Vice President; Dennis Lehman, the Cleveland Indians' Executive Vice President, Business; and Len Komoroski, the Cleveland Cavaliers' CEO. Each had a long track record of accomplishments.

Jenkins joined the Cleveland Browns in 2004, as a financial and business analyst. He was steadily promoted: to director of finance (2006), vice president of finance (2007-10), senior vice president of finance & administration (2010-12), and executive vice president (in May 2018, he would be named Chief Operating Officer). He was also involved in most of the Browns' meetings with City Hall, and I had dealt with him extensively on some complicated capital repair issues.

Lehman was a 1973 graduate of LaSalle University with a degree in political science. He began his sports management career with the

Philadelphia Phillies, serving that organization for 18 years. In 1988, he began a long career with the Cleveland Indians when he was hired as Senior Vice President, Business. In 1992 he was promoted to his current role of Executive Vice President, Business. In that role his responsibilities included ballpark operations, merchandise, food and beverage, human resources, community outreach and finance. He was our principal point of contact for City and Gateway matters, and through the years I had grown to regard him as one the business community's most trustworthy and reliable leaders.

Komoroski had carved out an impressive career as one of America's most diversely employed sports executives. He was the Chief Executive Officer of the Cleveland Cavaliers and Quicken Loans Arena organization. The organization included the Lake Erie Monsters (AHL), Cleveland Gladiators (AFL), and Canton Charge (NBADL). He was also a Principal at Rock Gaming, LLC, which operated Cleveland's downtown casino.

He graduated cum laude in 1982 from Duquesne University in Pittsburgh and got his start in sports that year with the Pittsburgh Spirit of the Major Indoor Soccer League. Then came management roles with the Pittsburgh Penguins of the National Hockey League and the Minnesota Strikers of the MISL, and as a regional manager for the Miller Brewing Company's sports marketing arm.

From 1988-1996 he worked for the Minnesota Timberwolves of the NBA, playing a major role in the start-up of the team and the Target Center. Then, after a brief but successful stint with the Cleveland Lumberjacks of the International Hockey League, he joined the Philadelphia Eagles of the NFL. He brought many properties in-house during his 1996-2003 tenure, including the industry-leading Eagles Television Network. He also managed several major naming rights transactions, and played a leadership role in the development of Lincoln Financial Field.

He returned to Cleveland in 2003 as president of the Cavaliers. There he furthered a dramatically larger relationship with Fox SportsOhio, and expanded the Q Arena's event calendar by facilitating the acquisition of an American Hockey League franchise (now known as the Lake Erie Monsters). The Cavaliers franchise was repeatedly recognized within the pro sports team industry as one of five finalists for Sports Business Journal's prestigious "Sports Team of the Year" award.

He excelled in business settings—such as our sin tax campaign—and he was known for his well-crafted PowerPoint presentations. But he could also overdo the PowerPoints, and I thought of Komoroski when GEICO aired a 2018 commercial produced by the Martin Agency. A James Bond-ish man strapped to a chair—and confronted with a death ray machine—invites a villain to "Do your worst, Doctor." But the Doctor eschews the death ray machine and instead activates a PowerPoint presentation. After enduring a dose of slides, the victim's reaction indicated that he might have preferred the death ray.

The campaign for the initiative formally kicked off on January 6, 2014, with a meeting convened by political strategist Jeff Rusnak. Rusnak opened with a summary of the timetable, working backward from the May election date. He noted that early voting would start in 90 days, he committed to weekly meetings, he identified a need for point persons for "social media" and "contacts and outreach," he proposed Mayor Jackson and County Executive Ed Fitzgerald as campaign co-chairs, and he estimated a campaign cost of $1.2 million.

County Councilman Dan Brady then summarized the County's timeframe, with a proposed January 28 final vote date by the County Council (the Council needed to approve the initiative before it could be formally placed on the ballot by the Board of Elections, and Council passage would require a "super majority" which meant 8 of 11 votes). He listed some necessary political appearances for that voting date: a City spokesperson (that would end up being City Council President Kevin Kelley and me), and the County Executive (ideally, in person) or a representative.

County Councilman Pernell Jones, with a strong background of advocacy for equal opportunity and diversity, argued for a strong economic opportunity platform.

Councilman Brady warned the group to anticipate amendments proffered by the Council members, informed it that there would be an article tomorrow by Mark Naymik of the Plain Dealer, and urged that the sports teams come forward with lists of their respective needed future capital repairs (inclusive of specific cost estimates). Council staffer Joe Nanni advised that Gateway board chair Tim Offtermatt would represent Gateway at the hearings. Councilman Brady and Matt Carroll of the County Executive's Office each stressed that "the (financing) mechanism will be a key question for the Council."

Greater Cleveland Partnership President Joe Roman indicated that its presentation would contain four elements: a fact sheet, a communication sheet, "the case," and the overall message.

Former press secretary to Mayor White Nancy Lesic, now leading her own firm, and communications consultant/spokeswoman for the campaign, spoke to media outreach: "protocol in call-in response is key; so are the informational materials." She added that "two Plain Dealer folks have editorialized against the sin tax extension, and we'll need to attend the editorial board before January 28." Roman urged that "any media inquiry be run through Nancy: she determines where they get referred." He added that we should take full advantage of the sports teams' capacities.

My colleague Valarie McCall, Mayor Jackson's Chief of Government Affairs, had joined me at the meeting, and we later briefed Mayor Jackson on the meeting highlights. An African-American native Clevelander who oozed youthful energy, Valarie had grown up in the Glenville neighborhood and graduated from Martin Luther King Law & Public Services Magnet High School. A former licensed social worker, she earned a bachelor's degree in social work from Cleveland State University and a master's degree in public administration from Cleveland State University's Levin College of Urban Affairs. In addition, she was awarded an Honorary Doctor of Public Service Degree by Cleveland State University.

She began her career with the City under Mayor White in 1998, serving as Director of the Empowerment Zone (where she managed a $200 million budget, distributed job training and placement funds, and led direct lending programs that assisted businesses in four targeted neighborhoods). Shortly after Frank Jackson became Cleveland City Council President in 2002, he and the Council appointed her as Council's youngest City Clerk, Clerk of Council in the City's history. In that office she streamlined the legislative process, installed an effective management team and reorganized the day-to-day operations of the office to maximize efficiency.

As Chief of Government and International Affairs, she served as Mayor Jackson's primary liaison to local and state governments, and all federal and international agencies and organizations. In the next few years, she would serve a term as President of the American Public Transit Association's Executive Committee, and as Mayor

Jackson's point person in preparing for Cleveland's successful hosting of the 2016 Republican National Convention. In the latter two roles she would sometimes "break some China"— occasionally drawing resentment from some of her colleagues— but in each instance the disagreements could be traced back to her overwhelming loyalty to Mayor Jackson's agenda.

Councilman Brady kicked off our next meeting on January 13 with a warning that as of then we were not up to the eight Council votes we needed. The council's legislative budget advisor Trevor McAleer walked us through the County Council meeting schedule.

There'd be a January 21 meeting at 3 PM at which the sports teams would be expected to present their individual (capital repair) needs; there'd be continued discussions on January 23; and the (hopefully) decisive January 28 meeting with the final votes.

Roman suggested that the teams should document their facility investments over the years, and Komoroski informed the group that Tom Yablonsky (Executive Director of both the Historic Warehouse and Gateway Development Corporations) "tells an amazing story on the transformation of the Gateway District."

McCall had two key suggestions:

1. Once you get through the County Council, you should do a City Council briefing at its Monday noon Democratic Caucus meeting; and
2. When you are doing your "Frequently Asked Questions," remember that many people who have gone to Arena concerts have never gone to Arena sporting events.

Polling authority Bob Dykes observed that "propensity to vote is a function of age: 60% for 60-year-olds, 40% for 40-year-olds, 20%

for 20-year-olds. We will use information from focus groups to construct our surveys."

Dykes' reference to focus groups transitioned the discussion to our presentation materials. On the topic of economic impact data, I argued that we should use it "defensively rather than offensively" (in other words, we should not lead with this info). This was the first round in what would be an ongoing debate throughout the history of our four-month campaign. Sports team representatives in general, and Komoroski in particular, were fond of referencing economic impact statistics and projections as justifications for investments in the sports facilities.

Lesic and I always pushed back on the campaign's proactive use of this data. In our many appearances before Cleveland City Council during Mayor White's tenure, we had grown tired of City Council members' complaints about some of the Gateway economic projections that had not yet come to pass. Reminiscent of the political baggage shouldered by Herbert Hoover's 1928 presidential campaign stemming from an ad that promised "a chicken in every pot and two cars in every garage," we were constantly called to account for the 1990 Gateway ad that promised 28,000 jobs.

But our debate went deeper than our prior wounds inflicted by boisterous City Council members. Lesic and I believed then, and still believe, that putting too many numbers out there allows your opponent to kick up a fuss debating the accuracy of your numbers; a prolonged numbers debate confuses the voters and deflects their attention from the core issue you are trying to sell (which in our case was "protecting our existing assets and insuring their longevity").

On January 21, 2014, we made our respective presentations to Cuyahoga County Council: Roman began and spoke to the region's long history of partnerships with its sports teams which dated back to 1928 (Cleveland voters approving funding for Cleveland Municipal Stadium), and was renewed in the 1990s (County voters passing the original ten-year sin tax in 1990 to fund Gateway, and County voters passing a ten-year sin tax extension in 1995 to fund the football stadium). He then recited the impact of the facilities on the region's growth and prosperity and concluded with a call to maintain these assets over time.

Next was Gateway board chair Tim Offtermatt, who covered the details of the sin tax: how it was used through the years, when it runs out, and how the tax is proposed to be used in the event the 20-year extension was approved. He also provided some information on the sports team leases.

I was next, and I gave the Council members an 11-page document entitled *FirstEnergy Stadium and the Proposed Sin Tax Extension*. Since Offtermatt had already spoken to the two Gateway facilities, my job was to give the Council an overview on the future capital needs for the football stadium and answer their questions regarding same. Drawing upon the recently-completed URS Stadium audit, I detailed the improvements included within the Browns' recently approved $120 million stadium renovation and forecasted an additional $47 million in remaining capital repair needs over the next decade (of which $24 million could be funded via the existing sin tax and $23 million would be funded by the proposed sin tax extension).

I characterized our region as a leader in wise sports facility investments, contrasting us with other regions who took a Scarlett O'Hara approach— "I'll think about that tomorrow"—to their facility needs.

Roman then introduced representatives from each of the three teams, who spoke to their individual capital repair needs. That portion of the testimony was summarized by Eric Sandy of Cleveland Scene:

> Members of the public listened to impassioned pleas from Indians, Cavs and Browns' top brass today. The sports management leaders, in short, want to continue the running tap of tax dollars to rehab their stadiums. The teams' reps rattled off their respective wish lists and financial specs during a County Council hearing on Tuesday. In sum, repairs to FirstEnergy Stadium will total $80 million; repairs to Progressive Field will total $60 to $70 million; and repairs to the Q will total $55 to $65 million (all figures are over the next 10 years). The big question on the day was what, precisely, the teams were looking to buy and/or repair.[7]

Serious questioning and commenting by County Council members commenced at the next meeting held on January 23. Council member Michael Gallagher said: "It's imperative that the City at its highest level contact the County at its highest level re the appropriate split of the annual $13 million sin tax—and before the May vote." Council member Dave Greenspan immediately concurred.

I advised the Council of Mayor Jackson's firm stance that the proceeds should be divided equally amongst the facilities:1/3, 1/3, 1/3. But Council member Jack Schron suggested a different allocation: he would allocate the proceeds according to days of facility usage (which of course would place the football stadium at a major funding disadvantage).

By the time the third County Council meeting rolled around on January 28, the Council members were convinced of the need to act. Though sizable opposition had arisen by that time and expressed itself at the Council meetings, the Council members viewed their decision to be simply allowing the voters to decide this controversial issue (testimony by City Council President Kevin Kelley had zeroed in on this point). They voted unanimously to send the issue to the ballot.

Five years later, at a Great Lakes Brewing Company booth on a cold February 2019, evening, Council President Kelley looked back on the political environment that circumscribed the decision-making in the early stages of the 2014 sin tax extension campaign. "I had just been elected Council President," he recalled (succeeding former President Martin Sweeney), "and my (trusted political) advisors were telling me: 'Stay away from this issue: it's *toxic*.' But then the County Council leaders asked me to speak at their hearing, and I agreed. My message was simple: 'Put it on the ballot...because we, the public, are the owners of these sports facilities and we have to take care of them.'"

"From that point on," he added, "people came to me and asked me to speak on the issue. As I gave it more thought, I reasoned that the people had *twice* voted for this tax: first in 1990 to fund the Gateway facilities, and then doubling down in 1995 to extend the tax as part of the Browns Stadium package. It's been their will, and we owe it to them to allow them to vote on this latest proposal. So, I voluntarily took on a leadership role (Mayor Jackson was focused on the school levy at the time, and he was pleased to allow other leaders to step forward on key tax issues)."

On February 13, 2004, Roman met with Mayor Jackson and me to update us on the campaign. He opened as follows:

> No one message moves the voters enough: it's a combination. The city and county own the facilities, and without the sin tax they will have to pay anyway. Jeff Rusnak and Bob Dykes estimate a $2 million cost for a contested campaign. The teams have committed

$1 million to date, and the general business community is good for $100,000-200,000. How can we best use you?

Echoing what he had recently told Council President Kelley, Mayor Jackson replied that "it can't be a Cleveland-kind of thing...how can I speak for the benefit of County voters? I don't want to be the face of it. I will do my part."

At our next campaign meeting, pollster Dykes reported on the early results of phone surveys of County voters. On the vote itself, 19% were "definitely yes," 25% were "probably yes," 19% were probably no," 37% were "definitely no," and 4% were "not sure." When asked about the condition of the sports facilities, 36% responded "good," 36% said the facilities needed "minor repairs," 4% said they needed "major repairs," 3% said "mixed," and 22% "didn't know." If the vote were held today, Dykes projected 38% yes and 62% no; however, once the arguments in favor of the extension were explained, the yes votes increased to 44%.

On March 11, 2014, the sin tax extension opponents formalized their stance via a grassroots opposition group entitled Coalition Against the Sin Tax ("CAST") and a press release listing local attorney Peter Pattakos as the contact. They set forth their reasons for opposition:

Transparency

Proponents of the Sin Tax refer to the public's "obligations" to finance the teams' facilities, but they have never been able to explain exactly what those "obligations" are, or how the Sin Tax proceeds would satisfy them.

Control of Public Subsidies

First enacted in 1990, the Sin Tax has been combined with over a half dozen public subsidies (Parking Tax, Admissions Tax, Bed Tax, Video Game Tax, Rental Car Tax and Property Tax exemption) that have amounted to almost $1 Billion tax payer dollars to the athletic facilities, practically a bottomless pit of public funding for these hugely profitable private businesses.

Opportunity Costs:

Sin Tax proponents refer to it as a "pennies-per-purchase tax," but the truth is that it amounts to an additional hundreds of millions of dollars that Cuyahoga County residents simply can't afford. We already have the highest sales tax, the highest school property taxes, and levy after levy that fall on the shoulders of County taxpayers. Additionally, as a nation, we have suffered the deepest economic recession since the 1930s. Unemployment, prices and inequality have skyrocketed, and Cuyahoga County's population and resources are scarce.

Unfair Burden on City of Cleveland and Cuyahoga County Residents:

75% of the visitors to the sports facilities are from outside of Cuyahoga County. There is no good reason for Cleveland and Cuyahoga County to shoulder the whole burden for these facilities.

Unfair Burden on the Poor and Working Class

This is a regressive tax, which means, that disproportionately impacts low-income residents and the working class citizens of our county.[8]

The City Club of Cleveland took appropriate interest, and promptly scheduled an April 1 debate on the topic with Council President Kelley and Komoroski appearing for the proponents and attorney Peter Pattakos and Field of Schemes author Neil deMause speaking for the opponents. Cleveland Scene's Sam Allard had this to say about the debate:

> Despite the best efforts of the City Club to frame its Tuesday forum on the sin tax as "a conversation," temperatures and voices rose as the pro- and anti- Issue 7 factions traded jabs in a spirited debate. The forum capped a week of activity in the contentious Issue 7 campaigning. Both sides are now fully assembling their troops and talking points in advance of the May vote.
>
> The Coalition Against the Sin Tax (C.A.S.T) co-chairman Peter Pattakos and Neil deMause, author of *Field of Schemes,* spoke in opposition to Issue 7 on Tuesday. [Ed. Note: Pattakos is an occasional *Scene* contributing author.] They felt that that the 20-year extension of the current tax on cigarettes and alcohol, which would generate more than $260 million for the maintenance of Progressive Field, Quicken Loans Arena, and First Energy Stadium, unfairly lines the pockets of billionaire owners and continues to cripple a city already strapped for cash. Pattakos stressed that alternatives haven't been meaningfully considered and said he can't gauge the level of the sports franchises' contributions when there's a total lack of transparency from the ownership groups. DeMause argued that a sin tax disproportionately affects the poor and uneducated.
>
> City Council President Kevin Kelley and Cavaliers' CEO Len Komoroski helmed the pro-sin side, arguing that the city is contractually obligated to fund repairs at the stadiums and that the sin tax is a relatively painless way to produce the funds. They

offered possible holes in the ideas of an admission tax or a multi-county sin tax in lieu of a sin tax.[9]

In his 2019 remembrances, Kelley continued: "It took a while, but the Building Trades Unions came on board, as did the NAACP, the Cleveland Clergy Coalition, the Black Contractors Association, and (eventually) the Cuyahoga County Mayors and Managers Association. But we were very disappointed that the CPPA (Cleveland Police Patrolmen's Association) sat it out. And we were *really, reay* annoyed that the House of LaRose (which represented the region's major beer distributors, and greatly benefited from beer sales at the sports facilities) lined up in opposition to the sin tax extension."

The proponents and opponents continued to bash away at each other in the month remaining until the May 6 voting date, although —funding-wise—it wasn't a very even match. The voters did pass the tax by a 56% to 44% margin, after which Cleveland Scene's Allard observed:

> Voters in Cuyahoga County approved the twenty-year extension of the Sin Tax yesterday by a margin of roughly 56 to 44 percent. The Issue 7 opposition released a statement Wednesday morning which characterized the race as a David vs. Goliath battle in which Sin Tax backers (led by the Greater Cleveland Partnership and the sports teams themselves) outspent opponents by millions of dollars.
>
> "We challenged our elected officials, civic organizations and leaders of our business community to think differently," the CAST statement read. "We wanted a better way of approaching our obligations to the owners, and recognition that the status quo in Cleveland isn't good enough."

"In a city with more than half its children living in poverty, one of the worst public-school systems in the nation, third-world infant mortality rates, a rapidly shrinking population, and a vanishing job market and middle class, it could hardly have been a worse time to have rubber stamped the Sin Tax on terms from the 1990's with no questions asked."[10]

A document entitled "Issue 7 Campaign Debrief: 5/2/14" summarized the voting geography—the highest approval percentages were in the eastern suburbs, with the western suburbs placing a close second—and listed a number of keys to victory: the early vote effort (early media, early mail, absentee follow-up); endorsements (by public officials, businesses, labor, Cuyahoga County Mayors & Managers, NAACP); and early activity (the County Council process, and Kevin Kelley messages). And Kelley further highlighted a strategy that would drive future elections: "Where the campaign was won was in the early vote campaign."

The County's First Sin Tax Bond Issue--$60.5 Million

The Indians and Cavaliers had each submitted their ten-year wish lists for capital repairs early in 2014. Now that the sin tax extension was approved, they began discussions with Gateway on their immediate priorities. A year and a half later, County Executive Armond Budish submitted a proposed $60.5 million bond issue for County Council consideration. The Council approved the bond issue in November, 2015, and the resulting bond expenditures became the first significant public monies spent on capital repairs at the Gateway complex (all previous capital repairs having been funded by either Gateway or the teams themselves).

The below table lists the Progressive Field and Quicken Loans Arena improvements covered by the bond issue: as originally presented to the Council on October 27, 2015[11] as later amended via Gateway approvals (column 2)[12] and as completed by the time of a May, 2018, Gateway board meeting (column 3).[13]

PROGRESSIVE FIELD MAJOR CAPITAL	GATEWAY APPROVAL ($)	$ SPENT AS OF MAY 2018
Sound System	3,460,000	3,387,855
High Steel Painting	2,184,230	1,144,213
Concrete Resurfacing	1,500,000	966,857
Replacement of Food Service Equipment	1,426,757	1,427,000
Scoreboard System	15,583,560	15,570,409
Mechanical—HVAC Systems (Chilled Water Plant)	5,201,340	5,073,592
Suite & Press Box—Fire Suppression Systems	83,992	83,992
Suite & Press Box—Glass and Glazing	1,500,000	1,482,504
Suite & Balcony Floors	59,582	59,582
Glass	260,168	183,484
Access Control & Surveillance System	2,856,000	2,684,603
LED Lights	2,100,000	554,728
Elevator Project	750,000	674,087
Suite Renovation	450,000	1,200,001
Total for Progressive Field	**37,415,629**	**34,492,663**
QUICKEN LOANS ARENA MAJOR CAPITAL		
Flat and Curved Roof Replacement	7,234,445	4.310,478
Safety & Security System (CCTV Access Control)	2,571,747	2,549,483
Scoreboard & Digital Display Replacements	9,338,750	9,338,750
Video Production Control Room	4,376,545	4,376,545
Arena Bowl Sound Systems	1,663,729	1,685,993
Hoist	571,500	504,853
Hot Water Tanks	628,000	367,379
Total for Quicken Loans Arena	**26,384,716**	**23,133,480**

The public officials also had to finalize the split of the extended sin tax proceeds. Mayor Jackson had always believed it should be split 1/3, 1/3, 1/3 amongst the three sports teams, and the teams themselves had agreed to this split in the early stages of the campaign. But during the County Council hearings, County Councilman Jack Schron had argued for an allocation according to days of facility usage.

In June, 2014—barely a month after the tax's passage—County Executive Ed Fitzgerald surprised everyone with a plan to allocate the proceeds, in part, according to the teams' respective won/loss records: he called his idea the "win tax." This proposal burned up the phone lines on local talk radio and even earned some national media attention from ESPN and other sports networks.

But Fitzgerald was running for Governor of Ohio and only had six months left on his term as County Executive. With all the other issues on his plate, he failed to offer authorizing legislation prior to the expiration of his term. And his successor as County Executive, former State legislator Armond Budish, didn't share his enthusiasm for the concept.

Instead, County Executive Budish and Mayor Jackson began extensive discussions that continued into the latter part of 2016. Their respective Chiefs of Staff, Sobol Jordan and myself, kept the issue alive in our regular meetings. By the summer of 2016, the County Executive and the Mayor had reached agreement on a 1/3, 1/3, 1/3 split of the proceeds, and it was time to give formal expression to the concept.

That required some expert assistance, so we brought on a very capable team: City Chief Corporate Counsel Rick Horvath, Squire Sanders bond counsel David Goodman, County Law Director Bob Triozzi, and County financial advisor Offtermatt. Throughout the summer and fall of 2016, this group negotiated the terms of an agreement that provided "that proceeds of the Excise taxes will be allocated equally among the Sports Facilities, with the equal allocation commencing from the beginning of the collection of the Excise Taxes in August 2015."

The agreement identified a First Energy Stadium Account into which the County would monthly deposit one-third of the net sin tax proceeds (i.e., the gross amount collected minus tax collection cost deducted by the State).

In practical operation, assume that in 2018 the County accrued $13.5 million in net sin tax proceeds. Under the agreement, the County would deposit one-third of those proceeds--$4.5 million—into the First Energy Stadium Account and that amount would ultimately become available to the City for funding capital improvements to the football stadium.

That would leave a balance of $9 million available to the County for funding capital improvements to the arena and ballpark. From this $9 million, the County would first have to pay the approximate $6.9 million debt service[14] on the County's twelve-year, $60,485,000 Series 2015 Excise Tax Bonds (i.e., the above-referenced bonds issued to fund listed Gateway major capital repairs). That would leave the County with about $2.1 million in 2018 to cover year-to-year Gateway capital repairs, as well as funding a capital reserve.

In November, 2016, County Executive Budish submitted to County Council a resolution authorizing the tax split agreement, the Council approved the resolution, and the agreement was executed.

On February 14, 2018, the Gateway Board approved $1,500,000 of Indians' major capital requests ($950,000 for improvements to the players parking lot, $500,000 for Data Room HVAC, and $50,000 for Suite Balcony Flooring).

When the Q Arena Project (which is described in full in Chapter 7) commenced in February, 2018, the Q Arena's management determined that, since major interior work would be performed in 2018, it made sense to upgrade the Q's Heating, Ventilation & Air Conditioning ("HVAC") systems (which had not been replaced since the building opened in 1994) simultaneously with the Q Arena Projectt work. The cost for this HVAC work was $27,895,839, and the Gateway Board approved this item as a qualifying major capital repair item.

The Board submitted this item to County officials, and in an April, 2018, meeting with both teams' officials, County Executive Armond Budish informed the group that they should not expect a second County sin tax bond issue until 2019. So, the Cavaliers— reluctantly —appeared resigned to fronting this expense while awaiting reimbursement from the proceeds of a future bond issue.

On June 19, 2018, I appeared before County Council's Human Resources, Appointments and Equity Committee to answer questions regarding the County Executive's proposed appointment of me to the Gateway Board as a joint City/County member (Mayor Jackson and Cleveland City Council had approved my appointment in April, 2018). Committee Chair Shontel Brown (who would be elected to Congress three years later) asked me whether we should consider merging the football stadium under Gateway's management. I replied that there is already coordination via sin tax matters, but suggested that this was a policy question for city and county governments.

When Council member Michael Gallagher quizzed me about the decision on the football stadium's location, I referenced the decision by City Council's 1996 Stadium Site Selection Task Force. He opined that the stadium's lakefront location was a poor choice. Concerned about the future cost of a new football stadium, Council member Dale Miller asked about combining baseball and football in the same facility. I opined that the respective leagues would reject this notion. I suggested that we focus on preserving our existing facilities.

In late 2016 and early 2017, the Indians and Cavaliers catalogued their anticipated capital needs over the next five years. The Indians' needs stated below were based on a 2018 facility condition assessment.

Progressive Field Anticipated Needs 2019-2038[15]

CATEGORY	CAPITAL DESCRIPTION	COST ESTIMATE ($)
1-5 Years Top Ten Projects In Rank Order By Category		
Mechanical	Air Handlers (65)	7,915,000
Vertical Transportation	Escalators	3,807,200
Mechanical	Exhaust Fans (257)	1,749,437
Architectural	Seating bowl guardrails, replace	1,350,000
Mechanical	DDC Controls	1,190,467
Vertical Transportation	Passenger Elevators	1,088,725
Mechanical	Fan Coil Units (96)	945,364
Architectural	Fiberglass composite, replace	730,000
Vertical Transportation	Freight Elevators	647,350
Mechanical	Elect Cabinet Unit Heaters (250)	580,177
Subtotal of All (Not Just Top Ten) Projects in Years 1-5		*25,913,494*
6-10 Years Top Ten Projects In Rank Order By Category		
Technology	Scoreboard	13,150,000
Architectural	Bowl Seating Replace	6,120,000
Technology	Scoreboard AV	5,375,000
Vertical Transportation	Passenger Elevators	2,429,328
Mechanical	Exhaust Fans (297)	1,749,437
Architectural	Seating Bowl Guardrails, replace	1,350,000
Structural	Expansion Joint Seal	1,060,875
Mechanical	Elect Cabinet Unit Heaters (250)	580,177
Mechanical	VAV Boxes (150)	427,500
Mechanical	DDC Controls	396,822
Subtotal of All (Not Just Top Ten) Projects in Years 6-10		*37,727,165*
11-20 Years Top Ten Projects In Rank Order By Category		
Technology	Scoreboard	18,061,000
Technology	Scoreboard AV	7,225,000
Technology	Sound System	6,682,000
Architectural	Interior Finishes, Suites	5,000,000
Architectural	Interior Finishes, Terrace Club	2,000,000
Vertical Transportation	Freight Elevators	1,414,754
Vertical Transportation	Passenger Elevators	1,334,718
Architectural	Interior Finishes, Club Lounge	1,200,000
Electrical	Riser C Served from Switchboard 5	865,866
Electrical	Riser A Served from Switchboard 2	831,903
Subtotal of All (Not Just Top Ten) Projects in Years 11-20		*52,793,048*
TOTAL OF ALL PROJECTS YEARS 1-20		116,433,706

The Cavaliers identified their needs in a 2017 submission to the Gateway staff. Those needs, many of which would become part of a complete transformation of the Q Arena described in detail in Chapter 7, are detailed in the below table.

Quicken Loans Arena Anticipated Needs 2018-2022[16]

CATEGORY	CAPITAL DESCRIPTION	COST ESTIMATE ($)
Architectural	Precast Sealing/Painting	4,502,035
	Arena Curtain System	854,900
	Window Glazing System	1,038,175
Electrical	Lighting Controls	983,454
	Sport Lighting	1,957,160
Fire Protection	Fire Alarm System	597,026
Mechanical/Plumbing	Replace Ice Floor and Plant	3,095,149
Structural	Sidewalks, Stone Steps, Railing	597,026
Vertical Transportation	Refurbishing	672,027
TOTAL		14,296,952

Though the Browns were not asked to submit a request for future capital needs, a projection of material capital repairs needs through year 2024 was made in the 2014 URS study. The future needs are summarized below:

Cleveland Browns Stadium Anticipated Needs 2018-2024

CATEGORY	CAPITAL DESCRIPTION	COST ESTIMATE ($)
Architectural		8,328,400
Electrical		1,349,073
Fire Protection		4,975,349
Mechanical/Plumbing		74,952
Site/Civil/Landscape		177,966
Structural		2,356,684
Telecommunications		0
TOTAL		17,262,425

In a July 2018 article in Cleveland Scene, writer Sam Allard examined the future of the sin tax proceeds. Allard asserted—presumably based on his multiplication of annual proceeds of $13 million times a twenty-year term, and then dividing by three to account for the facilities' equal shares—that "each facility would be in line to receive $86.6 million for capital repairs over the 20-year life of the tax (2015-

2035)."[17] But, in his assessment of the 2014 sin tax extension at its four-year mark, he warned:

> The teams have been spending their sin tax allotments so quickly that funding for necessary maintenance will dry up long before the sin tax comes up for renewal.[18]

Though the sin tax issue was Allard's first foray into the realm of Cleveland sports facility deal commentary, he'd proven himself to be a formidable critic. And, as his future assaults on the Q Arena deal (see Chapter 7) and the Indians lease extension (see Chapter 8) would confirm, he was, in the memorable Al Pacino phrase from the movie Scent of a Woman, "...*just getting warmed up.*"

Still, the passage of the sin tax extension made Cuyahoga County unique in its establishment of a long-term maintenance fund for all three of its major league sports facilities. Though time would show that the sin tax alone could not ensure full maintenance of each facility, it set our region apart from those communities who were prematurely replacing their facilities.

The County's Second Sin Tax Bond Issue-- $40 Million

By the spring of 2019, the accumulating needs of the ballpark and arena caused County officials to begin discussing a sooner-than-anticipated follow-up sin tax bond issue—adding on to the County's $60.5 million December 2015 bond issue. The proceeds of that 2015 bond issue had been fully spent, yet each team had advanced significant sums for needed repairs. The Cavaliers had advanced $40 million—mainly for a complete HVAC overhaul—and the Indians had advanced $7.5 million. The Indians were willing to await reimbursement from future sin tax proceeds, but the Cavaliers needed their much larger sum immediately.

After some financial modeling, County financial advisor Bob Franz proposed a two-step approach: 1) refund the $47.5 million balance owed on the $60.5 million 2015 Excise Tax Bonds via a $40 million new taxable general obligation bond issue that would save the County almost $1.5 million in annual debt service payments (since the re-issue would be backed by the County's general fund rather than sin tax revenues); then 2) issue a separate $40.5 million general obligation bond issue to reimburse the Cavaliers for their previous advances.

Assessing Komoroski's reaction to the idea—and whether the arena would need other repairs not covered by the proposed bond sale—the Plain Dealer's Courtney Astolfi wrote:

> Komoroski said the $40 million will take care of the "preponderance" of what's needed for the foreseeable near future." Elevator and escalator repairs will be needed, but Komoroski said that's a "smaller need" compared to other projects already approved or under construction. [19]

On May 17, 2019, I met with Mayor Jackson and briefed him on the structure of the two proposed County bond issues as well as the Indians decision to decline participation in the new bonding. If these new bond issues were to pass, the annual sin tax proceeds in years 2019-2035 would average a little over $13 million; the County's annual total debt service payments in years 2020-2035 would average a little over $6 million; and the Browns annual 1/3 share would average $4.5 million. That would leave annual leftover sin tax proceeds of $2.7 million (which would mostly go to the Indians due to their nonparticipation in the second round of bond financing).

On the afternoon of June 11, 2019, a Cuyahoga County Council Committee of the Whole (chaired by Council member Dale Miller) considered the two bond issue authorizing resolutions.[20] In the audience with me were Franz, Komoroski, Indians' counsel Joe Znidarsic, and Gateway staff. Franz began by summarizing the numbers in the bond spreadsheets, emphasizing the annual $1.5 million cost savings due to the refunding.

There were a lot of Council questions re discrepancies between the Cavaliers original capital projections during the 2014 sin tax deliberations versus the numbers on the pending projects. Then Councilwoman Shontell Brown asked about some of the projects deleted since 2014, and Komoroski responded that they were covered in the Q Arena Transformation. In response to Councilman Nan Baker's questions regarding the now $28 million HVAC project, Komoroski explained that a $16 million 2014 estimate was just that—an estimate.

Gateway staff had also prepared a handout summarizing the achievement of diversity goals on the Q Arena Transformation Project, and that served to quell questions that would have normally arisen under this important topic. Councilman Miller concluded that, hearing no objections, he'd entertain a motion to refer the resolutions to the full Council for vote. Councilman Dan Brady tendered the motion, seconded by Councilwoman Cheryl Stephens: the motion passed and the full Council passed the measures that same day.

As later chapters will show, the $40 million second sin tax bond issue left us with a ticking time bomb of sorts. By my crude math, by 2019 the Cavaliers had nearly exhausted their share of sin tax proceeds for the next 15 years. The Indians had only drawn down $37 million and would be relying on nearly all—$2.5 million— of the estimated annual $2.7 million "sin tax leftovers" to catch up over time.

Cleveland Browns Stadium Capital Repairs 2014-2023

While the County was issuing bonds to fund capital repairs to the Gateway facilities, the City was steadily banking the football stadium's annual $4.5 million share of the sin tax proceeds. Still, by year 2022—eight years since the County voters passed the sin tax extension— the City had funded three rounds of capital repairs to First Energy Stadium. The first, an investment of $10 million, occurred in August, 2016 and was summarized by a NEO Sports Insiders blog:

> City Council on Wednesday night passed legislation permitting city officials to spend the money on general upkeep, including new LED lights on the upper concourse, sprinkler lines, repairing rusty metal decks, upgrading security cameras, repairing ducts, pipes, drains and water pumps, retrofitting elevators and making general repairs to the exterior of the facility.[21]

The second round occurred in December, 2020, shortly after Osborn Engineering presented a five-year facility condition audit and assessment opining, overall, that the Stadium was in good condition, considering its age and harsh climate. Again, NEO Sports Insiders summarized:

The Cleveland City Council unanimously approved the allocation of $12 million on Thursday afternoon for much-needed repairs at First Energy Stadium, including repairs to the stadium's electrical and plumbing infrastructure, as well as replacing pedestrian ramps....

The proposed repairs also include the replacement of hot water tanks; the installation of chiller lines to the south end of the stadium; the replacement of compressors in walk-in coolers and freezers; the replacement of the stadium's lighting control system; the replacement of corroded fire sprinkler lines as well as the patching and replacing of structural and non-structural concrete.[22]

The Osborn report also looked ahead to future needs:

The report also outlined future repairs that could exceed $50 million over the next 10 years. Some of the repairs include the replacement of numerous seats in the lower bowl, which engineers rated to be in fair or poor condition. Further updates are needed to the stadium's broadcast and lighting facilities as well as its technology.

According to the report, as much as $33 million needs to be invested at the stadium in the next two to five years and another $35 million will need to be invested within the next six to 10 years.[23]

The City's third round of capital repairs investments occurred in June, 2022, when Cleveland City Council approved roughly $10 million worth of work highlighted by a $3 million expenditure replacing Stadium pedestrian ramps. Other upgrades included a new heater, facility-wide concrete repairs, replacement doors, structural joints on the plaza level, and replacement lights.[24]

To address these needs, the City will continue to receive—through year 2034— approximately $4.5 million annually from County sin tax proceeds.

CHAPTER SIX

CLEVELAND BROWNS STADIUM RENOVATIONS

In October, 2012, Jimmy Haslam purchased the Cleveland Browns franchise from Randy Lerner. Haslam's family was prominent in Knoxville, Tennessee: his father Jim had founded the Pilot Oil Corporation (now Pilot Flying J) which operated convenience stores with fuel sales; his brother Bill was the Governor of Tennessee. The Haslam family was very active in community affairs: Jimmy had served on the board of the United Way of Greater Knoxville, and his wife Dee had used her strong media background to produce shows for Animal Planet, TLC, HGTV and DIY Networks. Jimmy had prior NFL experience: he had been a Pittsburgh Steeler minority shareholder since 2008.

Haslam moved quickly to assemble his front office. CEO Joe Banner came from the Philadelphia Eagles, president Alec Scheiner came from the Dallas Cowboys, and General Counsel Sashi Brown came from the Jacksonville Jaguars. Haslam elected to retain Fred Nance as the Browns' outside counsel.

The next step was to establish a relationship with Cleveland City Hall. Frank G. Jackson was mid-way through his second term as Mayor of Cleveland and had demonstrated strong financial leadership in navigating the city through the Great Recession of 2007-2010. He'd shown a sincere commitment toward education and had made a good start toward his goal of mining the strengths of each Cleveland neighborhood.

Having served under Mayors White and Jackson for roughly equal periods of time, I can say that—behind closed doors—they were remarkably similar. They were each forceful, demanding, exacting, and unwavering in their empathy for and commitment to Cleveland residents. They didn't suffer fools gladly; they didn't want to hear excuses; and they expected you to proactively solve problems.

Their motivations for seeking office were also similar: education of schoolkids was paramount; neighborhood development and revitalization were key; so were diversity and inclusion. Neither cared much about the trappings or privileges of office. And, unlike most local politicians, neither cared about or spent any time pursuing political opportunities beyond the mayor's office.

All that said, their routes to office and their public personas couldn't have been more different. White had decided at age 14 that he wanted to be Mayor of Cleveland, and his life choices between age 14 and his 1990 mayoral election can be seen as signposts along a straight-line, carefully-plotted career path. As he explained in an interview given several weeks prior to his 1990 inauguration:

> First of all, Carl Stokes (Cleveland mayor from 1967 to 1971) and Leo Jackson (a Cleveland councilman from 1967 to 1970...)...had a great effect on me. I grew up in the years of the Kennedys and King. That had a real big effect on me. And both of my parents

were givers—my father was in the union movement and my mother was a champion for animal rights—so those people closest to me were involved in the whole notion of giving back. And since I've never been interested in being rich, the next best way to make an impact is to be an elected official.[1]

Growing up in Cleveland's Central neighborhood, Jackson had no such early ambitions. Born in 1946 to an inter-racial family, he served in the U.S. Army during the Vietnam War. After his military service, he returned to Central, working factory jobs and experiencing street life. But he went on to earn a degree from Cuyahoga Community College and three degrees—including a law degree and a Master's Degree in Public Administration—from Cleveland State University. While serving as an assistant city prosecutor, he and some friends began working with promising City Councilman Lonnie Burten on neighborhood improvements.

It was Burten's untimely death from a heart attack—he was only 40 —in 1984 that indirectly propelled Jackson toward politics. When Burten successor Preston Terry came up short on neighborhood commitments, Central leaders asked Jackson to challenge Terry: Jackson won the 1989 election and began a 16-year tenure in Cleveland City Council. After progressing through Council leadership posts, he was elected City Council President in 2001 and—when once again a sitting politician (this time Mayor Jane Campbell) failed to honor neighborhood commitments—he ran for mayor in 2005 and won a decisive victory.

As Mayor, Jackson lacked White's charisma and oratorical gifts, but he compensated by being extremely careful in his public statements, steering clear of drama and rarely calling out adversaries in public; that approach went a long way toward cementing relationships with County Commissioners, suburban mayors and managers, neighborhood and business leaders, and even the Governor of Ohio.

He excelled in negotiations, aided in part by a unique understanding of people and their motives: he once observed: "What's on the table is not what's really on the table." A 2013 Cleveland Magazine article elaborated:

> Often, his witty asides and near-riddles reflect cynical insights into people's motives. A lifelong resident of Cleveland's poorest neighborhoods, Jackson has long insisted that his work should improve the lives of "the least of us." He knows not everyone shares that value, though most pretend to.... Jackson succeeds by listening, not talking, by shrewdly observing and understanding people's motivations. Skilled at strategy and dealmaking, he got his school reforms passed by thinking two or three steps ahead and applying leverage to make adversaries into allies.[2]

Or, as I added in the same article: "He is able to understand people, what makes them tick, how they are, in a way that few people I've ever met [can].... It's like he is a student of human behavior and sees things that a lot of us miss."

Thus it was that on November 12, 2012—understanding the importance of the Browns' relationship to Mayor Jackson— Nance brought Joe Banner to City Hall to introduce him to Mayor Jackson and me. Banner summarized his background and highlighted his passion for education. He intended to work with City Year, establish new programming (not just recreational) for Cleveland's kids, and upgrade the city's high school football fields. Mayor Jackson observed that: "Sometimes when our schools are torn down, their rebuilding didn't include the athletic side. If you take the lead, I'm sure our other sports teams will follow." Banner nodded assent, adding that Cavaliers CEO Len Komoroski had worked for him for seven years.

I suggested that if the Browns use the Stadium more for other events, it would go a long way toward their relationship with Cleveland City Council. Several weeks later, Banner followed up with a call to me and our Public Works Director Michael Cox, citing an NFL funding opportunity that could bring us a $250,000 grant to install artificial turf on a local field. Director Cox targeted Lonnie Burten field, which eventually led to a City/Browns/FirstEnergy partnership on a $900,000 new synthetic field at that recreation center.

Having made a fine start in community relations, Haslam and his front office turned their attention to their team—the Browns would finish 5-11 that year—and their facilities in Cleveland and Berea. Six months later they had a plan and they asked for a meeting. On May 29, 2013, we welcomed Haslam and his front office to our Red Room at City Hall. Haslam's group included Banner, Scheiner, Nance, and a Browns intern. Mayor Jackson asked Chief of Regional Development Chris Warren and me to join him.

As a City Hall veteran and a close friend, Warren brought to our team a clear strategic approach and formidable negotiating skills. Born in 1950 and raised in New England (his mother was related to Austria's famous Trapp Family singers), he graduated from Hiram College and began a twenty-year career as an organizer in Cleveland's neighborhoods. He founded the Tremont West Development Corp. and the Cleveland Housing Network and worked as a community organizer for the Welfare Rights Organization and Merrick House. Though Warren's aggressive tactics sometimes annoyed prior Cleveland mayors, Mayor White sent a strong message on his commitment to neighborhoods when he selected Warren to be his Director of Community Development in 1990.

In the ensuing 24 years, Warren had served three different Cleveland mayors—White, Campbell, and Jackson—in the roles of Director of Community Development, Director of Empowerment Zone, Director of Economic Development, and Chief of Regional Development. While he always retained his neighborhood focus, his assignments broadened to include major banking and real estate development initiatives. Under Mayor Jackson, his portfolio included stemming the tide of foreclosures, cleaning up blighted properties, spurring neighborhood reinvestment, and managing lakefront development (he was also a wiry, smooth-fielding, clutch-hitting infielder on the Mayor's Office softball team).

Haslam began the meeting with an agenda of discussion items—a holistic approach, streamlining permitting, offsite improvements, financial partnerships—and indicated that Scheiner and Banner would be contacting Warren and me for more detailed discussions.

Nance previewed as follows: "As the Stadium enters the second half of its life (it was then 15 years old), it's about to require significant capital repairs—whether they be called out by specific provisions of the lease, or whether they be capital improvements made if money is available—and we said we would come back to continue the discussion." Banner shared some details: they'd hired an architect (Genzler of L.A.), a construction company (Turner, represented by John DeWine), and an owner's representative (Weston, represented by Mark Horton). Getting more specific, he said:

> We're looking at doing a lot of work in the next two years: some of it discretionary, some of it keeping the team in the top 15. We'll add escalators and new entrances. All of it together is in the $100-

120 million range: of that, 75% might be capital repairs. We're prepared to assume some of the cost of the City's obligations. As a second part of our idea, we may be willing to pay the entire $120 million, or a major part up front, for some lease concessions: (removing the) $250,000 annual rent, doing something about the requirement that we use Cleveland Public Power (it being costlier than other facilities pay), and broadening the definition of capital repair money.

He closed by stating it was important to get into the ground by January.

I informed the group that we've considered doing a five-year capital study, and Banner said they'd support that. Warren then asked a very important question: "Is the useful life of the Stadium a structural question or an economic obsolescence question?", to which Banner replied: "Both." Then, as the meeting was breaking up, Banner asked me to stay for a minute.

When the others had left, he said that he wanted to ask a new question now that he didn't want to mix with the main presentation—as this new question was more of a long shot—but would the City instead consider building a brand-new football stadium and, if so, where might it be located? I responded that I appreciated him deferring this question until after the meeting, but I couldn't speculate on a response as it was "over my pay grade." I did promise to take it up with Mayor Jackson and get back to him within a week.

Then Banner left and I returned to my office to gather my thoughts. I had already logged several concerns during the main body of the meeting: the sheer magnitude of the project ($100-120 million worth of work), the statement that "75% of that might be capital repairs" (which under the lease were mostly the City's financial responsibility), and the offer for the Browns to fund the whole project if we were just willing to broaden the lease definition of capital repairs (presumably to a St. Louis-type term that would require us to keep the Stadium within the top one-third of NFL facilities). Then, the after-meeting trial balloon of *even considering* replacing a facility that hadn't yet reached its 15th birthday...fortunately, Mayor Jackson was still in his office and that's where I went next.

First, allow me a brief digression on the Cleveland media. Those reporters and editorialists who regularly covered City Hall were generally very perceptive when they reported on public meetings and a mayoral administration's interactions with City Council and others in those public settings. But most of them had a blind spot as to how things actually get done behind the closed doors of a mayor's office. Those of us who have served in mayoral staff positions are partly to blame for this media naivete, for we are exceedingly careful to keep all internal discussions or debates "inside the tent." Failing to do so equates to flunking the loyalty test, the result of which would be a quick exit from City Hall.

A wise mayor (and Mayor Jackson was a <u>very</u> wise mayor) will encourage his high-level staff members to express their views—and even rigorously debate their boss—so long as the staff members bury their dissent (and keep their previous dissent private) once their mayor makes his final decision. And, accordingly, neither the general public nor the sophisticated media is privy to these internal debates.

When I entered Mayor Jackson's office, I resembled the robot in the long-ago *Lost In Space* TV series, spinning my head and sounding "Danger! Danger!." I recited my concerns, but then followed one of my longstanding principles: "Never present your superior with a problem without also offering a detailed proposed solution to the problem." In this case, my recommendation was to: (1) meet with Law and develop a capital repair negotiating strategy that was firmly grounded in every lease nuance; (2) be absolutely unyielding whenever the Browns proposed to amend lease language; but (3) in all other respects maintain a courteous and dispassionate manner with the Browns' negotiators. Deferring an immediate response to my concerns and recommendations, Mayor Jackson instructed me to meet and brief our upper management and arrange a follow up meeting when those meetings were completed.

That follow-up meeting occurred on June 28, 2013: appearing before Mayor Jackson were Chief Operating Officer Darnell Brown, Warren, Finance Director Sharon Dumas, and me. The Mayor's preliminary instructions were simple and straightforward: "Determine what's in the lease; put it in simple terms; identify gray areas. I don't want what you *feel* (he briefly glanced at me). And what are the NFL's rights?"

On July 9, 2013, we (Warren, Dumas, Chief Corporate Counsel Rick Horvath, and me) met to prepare our response to the Mayor's directives. Horvath began: "Essentially, the City's obligations are taxes, capital repairs, insurance, parking, and keeping the pedestrian walkways open." He got into the weeds on the capital repair obligations (see pages 146 above) and characterized the scoreboard as probably the largest pending cost item.

Two days later our same group met with Mayor Jackson. Horvath recapped his summary of lease terms, with special emphasis on the capital repair section; he said we were most exposed on what the lease called "Major Capital Repairs." The Browns were most exposed on "Maintenance." Dumas summarized our capital repair resources, which consisted of our take from the tail end of the 2006-2015 sin tax extension: we had collected $15.9 million to date, paid $5 million of it for repairs to date, expected to collect another $3 million in August, and $10 million more until the tax's expiration in 2015.

Mayor Jackson said: "Let's start at the beginning on who's responsible for what, given the available information. Then determine what we're going to say we're going to do and gather all the supporting information." He listed five action steps:

1. Respond to their ask—"we need to review it" (don't *disagree* with anything);
2. Do the capital repair audit (which would need authorizing legislation);
3. Do a maintenance audit;
4. Do our own traffic control plan for the changed downtown; and
5. Fix the deteriorated pedestrian bridge over the railroad tracks.

These were our marching orders which I would of course follow. But in the back of my mind I was thinking: "The wolf is at our door, and he has very sharp teeth."

So directed, we (Warren, Horvath, and myself) proceeded to meet with the Browns (Banner, Scheiner, Sashi Brown, and Nance) on August 15, 2013. Banner led off:

> We'll borrow $60 million from the League and $60 million from a bank. We seek a dollar value out of the things we've asked for. Those things are fungible: we look to fill the gap between new revenue (e.g., from a new scoreboard and ribbon boards) and our costs. *Perhaps this could be done with you paying $2 million per year plus getting us utility savings* (my emphasis). We are worried about

your capital repair audit needing to be done before a deal is made.

I politely explained that the Mayor needs the audit before he signs off on the deal. Changing topics, Banner said that we need to take the "gray" out of the capital repair definition, to which I cringed but —having in mind our Mayoral directive not to argue—I remained silent.

A week later, in a conference call with Nance, Horvath asked: "How much of the $120 million project consists of Material Capital Repairs;" Nance replied that they'd get back with us.

There were hints of an answer—actually, just some needed detail on project elements given by the Browns contractor, Turner Construction Company—in an August 26, 2013, meeting. Turner's John DeWine said they would be rebuilding each end zone, with a goal of putting the Browns in the top 5-10 ranking of NFL stadia re video presentation. They would double the escalators (from 2 to 4), which would improve capacity from 9,600 persons per hour to 22,000 persons per hour. By the time they were done with all work, they would be touching 700,000 square feet of the 1.6 million-square-foot Stadium.

They'd set an October 8 deadline for approval of all plans by Cleveland's City Planning Commission. In response to my question of what they needed from us to reach that target, DeWine replied: "Multi-department meetings as soon as possible." This was Warren's bailiwick, and he promised to set things in motion. I added: "Then we'll need to brief City Council leadership at least a day before the Planning Commission meeting."

Several weeks later, we (Warren, Horvath, and I) met with the Browns negotiators (Scheiner, Sashi Brown and Nance) and Scheiner asked us to pursue parallel tracks: on one track, the $120 million with a $2 million-plus City annual payment plus a repaired pedestrian bridge plus permit fee waivers, and on the other track, a continuing examination of long-term capital repairs. Then, on September 16, 2013, we confidentially briefed Council President Martin Sweeney who suggested that November 18 might be a good ordinance introduction date.

By this time Banner was fairly regularly calling Mayor Jackson to offer his own version of the progress of our discussions. Following up on one of those phone conversations, we all got together to try to make headway on the dollar amount of the City's capital repair responsibilities.

Horvath began by summarizing a two-page handout we'd prepared to outline the capital repair processes. Nance said: "We envision that $80-90 million of the $120 million would be required City investment." I just couldn't let this stand, even if it meant disobeying the Mayor's instructions not to argue with the Browns reps. So, I replied "We envisioned $30 million." The meeting ended a few minutes later.

In a follow-up meeting three days later, on September 27, 2013, it quickly became apparent that my cost estimate had been remembered. Scheiner had this to say:

> We could give the City (legal) notice and it would be a whole lot more than $30 million—more like $90 million—I can't think of any other team in the NFL that would fund $120 million with the lease we have... Most cities have made continuous investments. So, there is some catch-up here.

Then, in an October 7 phone call, Nance cited to us "a fundamental disagreement over City responsibilities ($30+ million versus $80-90 million)." And in our next large group meeting on October 10, Scheiner said that we either need to reach agreement today or determine the best we can do. In the ensuing discussion, we all sidestepped the $30 versus $90 million disparity and instead focused on the $2 million a year City contribution: by now the Mayor had given us authority to commit to this payment over a 15-year term, and we did so (subject, of course, to approval by Cleveland City Council).

Our willingness to commit to a $30 million contribution (i.e., $2 million per year for fifteen years coming directly from the City's general fund) was a major step in resolving what Scheiner called "track one" of his two parallel tracks. But we were no closer to resolving the Browns' future expectations of capital repair moneys beyond the $120 million project. In an October 14 meeting, the Browns sought both lease amendments and a controlling say in the $24 million of sin tax moneys that the City either had on hand or was expecting by 2015. We were willing to give them say on $10 million of those moneys and no more.

Meanwhile, Warren had been meeting with Turner Construction to further clarify the scope of the $120 million of repairs and improvements. In an October 18 meeting with Mayor Jackson, Warren described Phase One as the "big, bold stuff." Phase Two would be painting, carpeting, surfacing, and lighting: of concourses, hospitality suites, concessions; it also included scoreboards, ribbon boards and back of the house stuff.

But there was suddenly a major new stumbling block: The Browns' contractors were asking for a building code foundation variance to allow them to place the massive, heavy new scoreboard on the east end zone (i., e., the Dawg Pound) structure. Mayor Jackson didn't hesitate: "We won't do a variance," he said. A week later, when advised that the Browns were looking more deeply into the engineer's soil report, he remined firm in opposing a variance.

All of these issues came to a head in a "make or break" negotiating session in the Red Room of the Mayor's Office on November 4, 2013. Browns attendees were Banner, Scheiner, Nance, and Sashi Brown. City attendees were Mayor Jackson, me, Chief Operating Officer Brown, Dumas, Warren, and Horvath. Banner, beginning by asserting that it was in everyone's interest to work this out, identified five major issues: 1) the $2 million per year from the City, which he deemed acceptable, 2) the City's design review of proposed exterior signage, 3) an admissions tax question, 4) the Cleveland Public Power issue, and 5) the City's funding of future capital repairs. On the latter point, he proposed that the City's previous $10 million commitment "become $12 million, which we won't seek till 2016."

Mayor Jackson added the structural variance issue to Banner's list, and asked Warren to summarize the current status (the main takeaway being that "there was a key meeting with the structural engineers tomorrow").

We then adjourned the meeting for 30 minutes to allow us to discuss Banner's future capital repairs proposal. In the meeting the Browns had given us a list of categories from which they would select the future repairs. Horvath and I reviewed that list and advised the Mayor that it was mainly structural repairs (with no whimsical enhancements to the Stadium on the list). The Mayor concurred this was acceptable, and we reconvened in the Red Room. After Horvath summarized our position on this issue—and got the Browns to confirm that these $12 million of repairs would all be credited against our future annual investment schedule that was attached to the lease—we ended the meeting with both sides agreeing that progress had been made.

And things got better two days later when Warren reported to the Mayor that our capital repair audit consultant (the URS firm was on board and working hard on its report to us) had reviewed and confirmed Browns' engineer Osborn's structural analysis of the east end zone (a variance would not be needed). On November 22, URS then gave us an initial summary of its overall capital repair audit findings, which confirmed that the $30 million commitment we had made was in the ballpark of what we would be responsible for under our lease in the next several years.

But as we began drafting legislation authorizing our $30 million contribution ($2 million a year for 15 years), we were surprised to receive a Saturday morning, November 16, 2013, email proposal sent by Haslam to Mayor Jackson care of my colleague, Valarie McCall. He suggested that the City cede to the Browns game-day control of the City's Municipal Lot and Burke Lakefront Airport parking spaces and reduce the Browns' annual rent from $250,000 to $1,000; in return for these and other City commitments re CPP power and admissions tax collections, the Browns would agree to fund the whole $120 million.

Though Mayor Jackson, Haslam, and their respective staffs spent much of the weekend fleshing out this proposal, there were enough disconnects to cause it to fall apart on Sunday evening. By Monday morning, we were back to the previous deal.

We then finalized our authorizing legislation, and it was now time to present our proposed deal to Cleveland City Council. Mayor Jackson and Banner conducted a press conference on November 18, 2013, and the Plain Dealer's Mark Naymik reported:

Cleveland taxpayers will be kicking in $2 million in each of the next 15 years toward the $120 million cost of improvements at FirstEnergy Stadium under a tentative agreement reached Tuesday between the city and the Cleveland Browns. Cleveland City Council will consider legislation to confirm the deal Monday under its fast-track procedures.

The Browns are paying up front the entire cost of the renovations the team announced last week. The true cost of the city's contribution is estimated at $22 million, not $30 million, because the money is being committed at the present-day value of the dollar.

Cleveland Mayor Frank Jackson and Browns CEO Joe Banner announced the deal Tuesday afternoon from City Hall.

Jackson said the city would not sacrifice any services to residents to make the payments.... City and Browns officials spent the day briefing individual council members.

Councilman Jeffrey Johnson said in an interview after the news conference that siphoning $2 million from the city's general fund each year unquestionably would hurt the neighborhoods....

As part of the deal, the city will give the Browns organization more input on how to spend about $12 million of the $24 million already in the stadium's existing capital improvement fund set by the stadium lease and fed by the existing Cuyahoga County tax on alcohol and cigarette sales, known as a sin tax. In exchange for having input on the capital repairs fund, the Browns will allow the city to reduce its payments to the capital repairs fund in the final years of the lease.

Banner said the deal is a modest investment by the city based on its lease obligations....

Ask how he would characterize Jackson as a negotiator, Banner said, "he kicked our ass."

Councilman Zack Reed said he supports the deal and hopes the investment will stem further deterioration at the stadium. "We are either going to make the improvements now or we will have to do them later," Reed said. "You cannot defer these improvements down the line or we'll be looking at even greater expenses."

Councilmen Michael Polensek and Brian Cummins, who also attended the news conference, said they are concerned that city services would suffer on account of the city's contribution. But they said they would reserve their judgments until they see the legislation presented on Monday.[3]

The above article was not only accurate on the deal terms, but it was unique in its willingness to recite our present value calculations: more on that issue later. In the same press conference, Mayor Jackson and Banner also spoke to the need for an upcoming sin tax extension.[4] On that point, Naymik said:

The Cleveland Indians and Cavaliers also want to extend the sin tax to help pay for improvement plans for Progressive Field and Quicken Loans Arena. Any sin tax, which requires support from Cuyahoga County Council and county voters, would be split three ways.

The deal announced Tuesday avoids a drawn out and potentially costly legal battle over the stadium lease, which spells out repairs and improvements that must be made by the city and the team. But the lease language leaves room for debate over some improvements. Banner said the city would owe the team millions more if it were held to the lease and deal shows the team's good will. The city believes the deal is fair and reflects its lease obligations.[5]

A day later several other Council members weighed in.

"I've got residents calling me, saying, 'Please don't support the stadium,'" said Councilman Kevin Conwell. "That stadium is modern enough right now, in my opinion. They've got to break out budgets to show me that putting up that money toward improvements won't affect city services." ....

"I'd much rather deal with the sin tax renewal first," said Councilman Tony Brancatelli. "It's only a year away. And if we make this significant commitment up front, I'd like to see the lease extended.... At the end of the day, for us to kick in a couple million dollars out of our own operating budget will cause me to look at this much harder." Brancatelli also criticized the Browns' assertion that the upgrades are primarily to improve the "fan experience," when the expensive scoreboards will boost advertising revenue for the team, he said.

Council President-elect Kevin Kelley said he is inclined to support the deal but wants to see evidence that the improvements are necessary and fall under the city's obligations. He said he has asked the administration for a preliminary report from URS Corporation, a firm hired by the city in September to conduct an audit of repairs that must be made to the stadium. The report is not expected to be complete until January, but Kelley said he would like to see the firm's findings before he casts his vote. "I don't intend to authorize any funds above and beyond our obligations that are contained in that lease," Kelley said. "That's my guiding principle. Based on what I've seen so far, it seems we won't be asked to do that. But there are many details that need to be learned between now and Monday."[6]

The Council hearings on our Ordinance No. 1578-13 commenced on November 23, and we set about our tasks of proving two points: that our deal did not obligate the City any further than what would have been required under the lease, and that the unprecedented commitment of $2 million per year of general fund monies would not unduly harm City services.

Councilman Polensek had asked for sin tax information, so Director Dumas submitted a three-page memo answering questions such as: the amount of our outstanding Stadium debt ($128,245,000), and the amount of the sin tax we had collected—and would collect—to fund Stadium capital repairs (to date, we'd collected $23,138,727 of an eventual total of $29 million).

Councilman Jeff Johnson had asked for a legal opinion whether the City would be obligated under the lease to pay for some of the capital repairs proposed to be made as part of the Stadium project. Horvath submitted a six-page opinion that stated "...there is no question that the City is obligated to make Capital Repairs under the Lease and that the City would be obligated under the Lease to pay for some of the Capital Repairs proposed to be made as part of (the) Stadium repair and improvement program proposed by the Cleveland Browns."

It would be my job to flesh this capital repairs responsibility out further. Comparing the early results from the URS capital audit with what Warren had learned about project scope from the Turner Construction meetings, I prepared a handout that summarized the two phases of Stadium improvements. As to the $70 million in Phase One in 2014:

> The most significant Browns repairs and improvements, in rank order of their cost estimates, are the scoreboard and related audio/control rooms ($30 million), end zone improvements ($28 million), lower bowl improvements including American Disabilities Act changes ($6 million), and escalators ($4 million). Of the Phase One repairs and improvements, City staff believes the City would be responsible for $23 million under the lease terms. The Browns believe the City would be responsible for a higher number.

As to the $50 million in Phase Two in 2015:

> The most significant Browns repairs and improvements, in rank order of their cost estimates, are club seating repairs and improvements including painting and carpeting ($13 million), suite repairs and improvements including painting and carpeting ($10 million), concessions ($7 million), concourse and surface lighting ($6 million), increased hospitality ($5 million), new south side entry ($3 million), field lighting ($3 million), infrastructure ($2 million), and back of house sound ($1 million). Of the Phase Two repairs and improvements, City staff believes that the City would be responsible for $10 million under the lease terms. The Browns believe the City would be responsible for a higher number.

In describing the annual $2 million appropriations we were seeking, I explained that although the City would pay the Browns $2 million per year for 15 years—a gross total of $30 million—the present value of our total payments is $22 million (because the Browns are allowing us to pay over time rather than upfront). And that number was much less than the $33 million we believed we were responsible for under the lease.

In describing our $12 million future capital repairs commitment, I explained that, commencing in 2015, the Browns would be able to pick from a list of nine categories of repairs (all of which deal with basic structural and building systems) and propose repairs to be made by the City from the proceeds of a $12 million deposit of sin tax monies.

Cleveland.com reporter Leila Atassi attended the Council hearings and blogged several of the Council comments:

> Council President Martin Sweeney: This could have gone many different ways if we didn't have a team committed to a city and a city committed to a team. I am comfortable and supportive because I think it boils down to the best interests of the city. I think this is a step toward a championship team.
>
> Councilwoman Dona Brady: It seems to me that an extension of the sin tax would take care of this issue. $22 million is not a lot of money for a team that is making hundreds of millions of dollars in revenue with billionaire owners. The residents of the city of cleveland are struggling and most are not going to the browns games and could care less. I acknowledge how important the browns are to the city of cleveland. But $2 million a year to us, struggling out here -- and having to pay for waste collection to ask them to pay for this is something that i cannot support.
>
> Councilman Tony Brancatelli: You say these resources are needed to improve the fan experience. Do you also anticipate increasing your revenue stream on account of the new scoreboards?
>
> Banner: yes.

Councilman Eugene Miller: Are the Browns going to renew their commitment to staying in the city? Will they guaranteed that they won't move?

Silliman: There are still 15 yrs remaining on the lease. The lease that is in place has a specific clause to require the team to play all home games in that stadium. So we have a lease that will ensure they will play here until 2029.

Miller: When the contract is up, will the Browns stay in the city of Cleveland?

Banner: We value the fact that the franchise is here and the passion of the fans. But I can't speak to what will be in 15 yrs.[7]

Councilman Michael Polensek: Many of my citizens can't paint their houses and live week to week trying to provide for their families, and here we are being asked to support the Cleveland Browns above and beyond the terms of the lease, Just once I'd like to see the Browns say 'We understand the economic reality that the men and women of this city have to contend with everyday.'[8]

Summing up: "The ordinance needed at least 12 votes to pass as an emergency measure, and it scraped by with 13 – an unusual occurrence for a council typically known for its compliance with the wishes of Mayor Frank Jackson's administration. Council members Dona Brady, Jeffrey Johnson, Kevin Conwell, Michael Polensek and Brian Cummins voted no. Councilman Zack Reed was absent."[9]

It had been a tough, tough six-month negotiation with the Browns to get to the deal we reached with them in mid-November. But, as with many of our other major City deals, we closed ranks with Banner and the other Browns staff members once we proceeded to the table in Cleveland City Council. We worked there as a team, and when Council approved the deal, we all—City officials and Browns officials— felt a strong sense of accomplishment.

Early in 2014, Haslam called Mayor Jackson and expressed a desire to have a more cordial day-to-day working relationship with City Hall. And in February, 2014, the Browns announced that CEO Banner and General Manager Mike Lombardi would be leaving the Browns within two months.

Sure enough, from that point forward we saw a less demanding manner from the Browns leaders: though they continued to aggressively engage us on such issues as traffic control, parking and capital repairs, their engagements now took on more of a mutual problem-solving approach. Gone were the demands to amend the lease which, in turn, made it easier for us to accommodate their requests.

In August 2015, Horvath and I received an invitation from Scheiner to tour the Stadium and observe the completion of the $120 million renovation project. It was a splendid day and the Stadium was awash with sunshine that displayed all the changes in the most striking fashion. As I told Scheiner at the conclusion of the tour, if I was visiting the Stadium for the first time I would have thought I was seeing a newly opened facility.

FirstEnergy Stadium was the first of Cleveland's downtown sports facilities to receive a mid-life facelift, updating, and repurposing. As with a home, if longevity is your goal, it is not enough to replace the major building elements—roof, furnace, windows—when wear and tear requires action. You also need to take a fresh look at your property every 15-20 years and make some changes that allow your investment to remain competitive with the new product that is just now coming on the market. Though we didn't fully appreciate it when we were immersed in negotiations, that's what we were able to achieve with our football stadium.

Future Browns Lease Extension

The Browns lease expires on December 31, 2028, and there is much media speculation on what the team will seek as a condition for a long-term lease extension. I have some initial thoughts on the Browns' possible requests and the appropriate public response to same. But first, some caveats. Unlike other local topics I've discussed in this book, on this matter I have no firsthand knowledge. Like the rest of the public, I base what I know primarily on what's printed in the media. If those media reports prove inaccurate, my conclusions will be flawed.

The drum roll began in May, 2018, with Dee Haslam's statement to ESPN that the team was exploring lakefront development options "...that may include substantially renovating FirstEnergy Stadium or building a new facility somewhere downtown.[10]" On the land development question, the Haslam's' interest in development around the Stadium meshes with the City's lakefront planning efforts. Both parties seek to solve the long-term puzzle of bridging the gap between the City's Mall C and the North Coast Harbor neighborhood.

The "new versus renovated" stadium part of the equation has been murkier.

There are those in Cleveland who never got over the 1996 decision to keep the football stadium on the lakefront. So once Ms. Haslam tossed in the "new stadium" ingredient in 2018, the local media stirred the pot until the Haslam's appeared to settle it via a March 26, 2019, quote at the NFL owners annual meeting.

"We think the best thing for Cleveland is to stay where we are," said Dee. "We feel like this is the best place for us." She said the important thing is to make the stadium more pedestrian-friendly with a walkway. The Browns are also committed to making the stadium "the best it can possibly be for fans."[11]

The Haslam's have since reaffirmed their renovation plans, consistently denying "new stadium to the east" rumors.[12] Hopefully they stay this course. The public can't afford, nor does it need, a new covered football stadium. Proponents argue that "we can get a Super Bowl and an NCAA Final Four." But cold-weather Super Bowl hosts risk media backlash (Detroit's 1982 Silverdome Super Bowl backfired when early-arriving sports writers endured blizzard conditions that spilled into their critiques of the city), and the NCAA Final Four is booked elsewhere through 2031. Rocket Mortgage Fieldhouse is a superb concert venue, and the public would be foolish to subsidize a dome adding few events while cannibalizing the Fieldhouse.

As the Browns discussions move forward, City and County officials need to learn from— and steer well clear of – the path taken by Nashville in what is shaping up as one of the worst public sports deals ever made. Nashville Mayor John Cooper's advocacy for an exorbitant $1.26 billion public price tag for a new domed football stadium was fueled by his—and the Tennessee Titans'—contention that the public renovation tab for 23-year-old Nissan Stadium under the existing lease would cost as much or more.[13] But Councilperson Ginny Welsch and other opponents on Nashville's Metro Council[14] have argued that the administration and team were using inflated renovation figures that wildly exceeded the public's real obligations.

Enough on the new stadium possibility. Turning to the Browns' expressed desire for a renovated stadium, what kinds of renovations are they contemplating? They are rumored to be seeking more of a rebuild than a renovation (including costly widened concourses), with total costs approaching one billion dollars. And the rumored public share approaches a half billion dollars. If true, that's nearly as bad a public outcome as a new stadium

Why? To begin with, as a 24-year Browns season ticket holder, I visited the Stadium 8-10 times annually. The facility is in fine shape, perfectly suited to hosting fans for 3-4 hours a game. Concession lines aren't overly long, and there are TVs to follow the action while standing in line. Rest rooms can get ugly, but that's due to the habits of some of the users rather than any inherent property defects.

Given that the Stadium is in use no more than 15 dates a year, its economic impact pales next to Rocket Mortgage Fieldhouse's 200 dates and Progressive Field's 81 dates (with the latter side-by-side venues collectively comprising a nearly full calendar year). While it's true that the same disparity in facility usage existed in 1995-1996 when we were making the case for a new football stadium, then we were dealing with a 63-year-old existing stadium that had suffered deferred maintenance over the years. That's certainly not the case today.

But what about the case for a major rebuild of Cleveland Browns Stadium that serves as a linchpin in driving lakefront redevelopment? Nice try, but the true driver of lakefront development will be the proposed $600+/- million land bridge that would span the railroad tracks and Shoreway. If designed properly—with the land bridge's northern terminus touching down at ground level at North Coast Harbor and its underpinnings including not just parking but new and improved train and bus terminals—a predominantly public investment in the land bridge can achieve catalytic impact on lakefront development.

And that huge public investment will greatly enhance the property values and accessibility of the three recipient institutions: Cleveland Browns Stadium, Great Lakes Science Center, and the Rock and Roll Hall of Fame and Museum. That, in turn, should motivate each institution to invest its own dollars in any significant remodel/rebuild activities—either directly via their own funds or indirectly via private capital funds collected through a North Coast Development Authority.[15] Viewed in this context, coincidentally or not, it was good to hear Mayor Justin Bibb's statement during Q&A after his April 19, 2023, State of the City Address:

> My vision right now is making sure we finally see real inclusive development on the lakefront. While we begin early conversations with the Haslams about the stadium, we want to be creative with how we address this issue because I'm no longer going to risk general revenue fund dollars for maintenance of a privately-owned football franchise.[16]

CHAPTER SEVEN

THE QUICKEN LOANS ARENA RENOVATION

In December, 2013, the Quickens Loan Arena was approaching its 20th anniversary. Compared to other NBA arenas, the Q Arena had aged gracefully: Cavaliers owners had invested $69 million in ongoing improvements (with much of that investment occurring since Dan Gilbert purchased the team in 2005). The building also had "good bones" in that the concourse layouts and seating arrangements remained good when measured by contemporary standards.

Finally, many of the costly investments (such as the terrazzo floors) that were heavily criticized when Gateway was struggling with cost overruns were wearing well twenty years later. In 2014 the Chicago Tribune would rank our arena as the 11th best NBA arena.[1] Yet the Q Arena was then the second oldest NBA arena that had not benefitted from a major renovation since its opening.

Thus, we at City Hall were not greatly surprised when Cavaliers leadership asked for a meeting to discuss the need for new Q Arena investments. On December 17, 2013, Dan Gibert's leadership team for the Cavaliers and the Horseshoe Casino (Len Komoroski, Nate

Forbes, and Jeff Cohen) convened a meeting at the Q Arena to present its vision. Mayor Jackson, Chris Warren and I represented the City. Forbes led off by saying that they had spent the past year and a half focused on private development in the Gateway District; Komoroski added that Gateway was Cleveland's "front door" and that—to date— Dan Gilbert had invested over a billion dollars in the Gateway neighborhood.

Komoroski also referenced an upcoming meeting we were having with car dealer Bernie Moreno regarding a potential investment in a Ferrari headquarters building and dealership with 65 jobs, as well as adjacent planned housing investments by developers such as T.J. Asher and David Goldberg.

He asked us to envision an exciting Gateway District where the building interiors opened up to show the energy inside and engage the sidewalk pedestrians, with a renovated Q Arena at the center of it all. He cited comparable areas including the Columbus Arena District, the Kansas City Power and Light District, and San Diego's Ballpark District, and he cited a total of 11 million Gateway visitors in 2013 distributed amongst the Casino (5.3 million), the Arena (2 million), and the Ballpark (1.7 million).

He then described their plans for the Q Arena. Though its attendance in 2011 had ranked 31st in the world and 11th in the U.S., the renovations would make the building more competitive in the next several decades by:

- Extending its footprint out to the Huron Road sidewalk and using glass facades to link inside activities to the outside pedestrians;
- Eliminating 1,500 of the worst seats to expand the concourses and create milling areas for fans; and

- Creating a rooftop deck looking back on the City.

And to do all this he had a "fair financial plan" (which, after our meeting, he intended to share with County Executive Ed Fitzgerald). The project would cost $195 million and it would require no new taxes. The ingredients were an extended sin tax, a 10-year extension of the City's pledged admissions taxes (kicking in when the City's Gateway pledge expired in 2023), and additional team rent.

After the presentation concluded, Mayor Jackson replied that his biggest question was: "Who's on the hook to cover debt service?"

Mayor Jackson, Warren and I sure had a lot to discuss as we rode back to City Hall and reassembled in the Mayor's office. First, the political timing couldn't have been worse. We were less than a month removed from City Council's passage of the controversial $130 million renovation package for FirstEnergy Stadium. Though it was the right thing to do, we took a real shellacking in both City Council and the media to get that passed. Though I could sense the Cavaliers proposal was fundamentally sound (many basketball teams were seeking brand new arenas, including the Bucks in Milwaukee with an arena barely older than ours: the Cavaliers proposal of public/private cost sharing on a $195 million renovation project looked darned good by comparison), we had used up a lot of good will in pushing for passage of the Browns deal.

Second, I was questioning whether the structural changes to the Q Arena (i.e., moving the new glass wall footprint all the way to the Huron sidewalk) weren't a little bit extreme. It seemed to me that some significant value engineering on this element of the proposal could save us all a great deal of money.

Third, I knew that the 1996 Browns deal had resulted in the City pledging *all* of its 8% admissions tax proceeds as security for our bond issue that funded the new football stadium. How, then, could we commit a portion of our admissions tax to this new Q Arena proposal?

Fourth, and most importantly (as Mayor Jackson regularly reminded us during the entire history of our Cavaliers discussions), the Q Arena was primarily the County's financial responsibility (just as the Ballpark was primarily the City's responsibility). This arrangement was embedded not only in the public parties' respective Gateway financing agreements, but also in the deed under which Gateway took title to its property: that deed contained clauses that provided that the Q Arena would eventually revert to the County and the Ballpark would eventually revert to the City.

Given these understandings, did we even want to be in the room when the particulars of Q Arena renovation financing were being discussed? For the time being, Mayor Jackson told us we should continue to attend briefings as long as we always issued a polite disclaimer of financial responsibility.

Subject to those rules of engagement, I accompanied Finance Director Sharon Dumas and Chief Corporate Counsel Rick Horvath in attendance at the next briefing session which was intended to flesh out the financing particulars. The Cavaliers presenters were Komoroski, VP and Chief Financial Officer Mozelle Jackson, VP and General Counsel Jason Hillman, and financial advisors Michael Zeiti and Paul Komlosi. County Attorney Bob Triozzi also attended. Zeiti began by breaking down the $195 million project's major funding streams:

- $71 million in County-issued bonds backed solely by Cavaliers rent (at $5.7 million per year from 2016 until 2032);
- $64 million from City admissions tax payments to the County from 2023 until 2032 (which payments would replicate a Gateway arrangement expiring in 2023 under which the City made these payments to the County); and
- $60 million from sin tax bonds ($44 million in new monies assuming a 20-year extension of the sin tax, coupled with $16 million due to the County from the previous 2005-2015 sin tax extension.

These sources would go towards the following uses:

ITEM	DESCRIPTION	COST ESTIMATE ($)
Structural Changes	Extending the Huron façade to the sidewalk with new glass wall, concourse widenings, seat removals, new gathering areas	110,000,000
Seating bowl	LED	9,000,000
	Sound	1,800,000
Video	In-house production	4,900,000
CATV	Replace	2,600,000
Interior/Exterior	LED	4,400,000
Lease-Obligated Capital Repairs	Total roof replacement, HVAC replacement, building control systems, fire and security replacements	35,300,000
Soft Costs	Architectural, engineering, testing	27,000,000
TOTAL		195,000,000

Wrapping up this financially-focused presentation, Komoroski asked: "Next steps?" Dumas spoke well for the City attendees when she replied: "We need to resolve the admissions tax question." The next day, after we updated Mayor Jackson, the Mayor said that he would discuss this with County Executive Fitzgerald at their next regular meeting.

Over the next six months we were able to stay out of the Cavaliers line of fire: our next meeting was not until July 23, 2014. Komoroski began by asking: "What part of the project—possibly the new glass frontage—can be done before the July, 2016 Republican Convention?" (The Q Arena was to be the focal point of Convention activities). I warned that the admissions tax extension sought by the Cavaliers was probably precluded by the bond documents associated with our 1996 football stadium deal.

Komoroski responded that he didn't see why the City couldn't just continue to pay something it was already paying. He added that his staff was continuing to work through the Gateway capital repair approval process, with requests for the Q Arena's roof, security system, scoreboard and control system all awaiting approval; he also clarified that the Gateway/sin tax portion of the $195 project comprised $55 million of the total. Since Cuyahoga County voters had approved the County's 20-year sin tax extension in May, that portion of the project funding was in place, leaving a balance of $140 million needed for the remaining project elements.

Deputy County Chief of Staff Matt Carroll then advised us that County Executive Ed Fitzgerald was holding regular discussions on the Q Arena project with County Council member Dan Brady. "That's good," I replied, "since this is a County deal." But I added that we would remain at the table. A month later Komoroski called me to report that: 1) he had talked with Brady who "will work with (City Council President) Kevin Kelley", and 2) that County Council President Ellen Connally had "somewhat" passed the torch to Brady.

On December 18, 2014—one year after the first meeting—Komoroski and his VP/Chief Financial Officer Mozelle Jackson invited us to an update meeting. Public sector attendees were Mayor Jackson, new Chief of Development (and former City Councilman) Ed Rybka, me, and County Attorney Triozzi. Komoroski summarized the current status:

We're at a point where we understand the County needs to take a leadership role. There's been a lot of discussions and engagement there by (County Councilman) Dan Brady. We've met with incoming County Executive Armond Budish and his transition team: he asked "Why should *this* be a priority over other projects?"

We were then treated to (yet another) Power Point update (Komoroski and his staff always made high quality presentations, but the economic impact parts were by this time, as well as in future renditions, a little repetitious). We paid closer attention when he reached the financial slides:

- Total project cost was $140 million;
- The first $70 million would come via bonds paid by the Cavs' additional rent;
- The second tronch of $70 million would consist of $17 million up front from the County, coupled with extended County debt service of $8 million a year from 2023-2032 (knowing our continuing concerns about an extension of our admissions tax payments to the County, he did not call out a source for the debt service payments).

He said they were spending money now—at their risk—on soft costs, and he characterized the project as "renovation" rather than "repair." When the PowerPoint concluded, Mayor Jackson asked: "So you're suggesting the City and County should meet?" Komoroski nodded, and the Mayor said he would start the conversation with County Executive Budish.

At the staff level, the next meeting was a City/County brainstorming session. On March 3, 2015, I met with old friends County Chief of

Staff Sharon Sobol Jordan, Deputy Chief Matt Carroll, and County financial advisor Tim Offtermatt.

Offtermatt began by minimizing the economic spinoff benefits of the Q Arena deal that we were used to seeing in the early slides of the Komoroski PowerPoints; instead, he focused on the Cavaliers lease extension as the term that brought real value. He reminded us that the Indians lease would expire in eight years and that they had recently submitted $50 million of capital needs to the Gateway board (which Tim chaired), led by a $20 million scoreboard.

He then walked us through the current Gateway/City/County admissions tax deal that was struck in the early 1990s to help fund the Q Arena and which expired in 2023. Under that agreement, the County made annual Q Arena debt service payments of $8.8 million aided by annual contributions of $3.5 million from the City and $1.4 million from the Convention and Visitor's Bureau (since renamed "Destination Cleveland"). These were the payments that the Cavaliers sought to extend- from 2024 to 2032—to help pay for the Q Arena renovation.

Since Offtermatt had also worked on our 1996 Browns stadium deal, he was able to answer my question about the City's pledge of its 8% admissions tax as security for that Browns deal: because the City's pledge of admissions taxes to the County predated the Browns deal, it was not part of that deal's security and thus was available to use for the Arena deal if we chose to do so.

On March 16, 2015, we all reconvened with Komoroski and his Q Arena team to assess the deal status. Komoroski restated their request that we "continue County flat debt service payments of $8.8 million per year from 2024 through 2032." Offtermatt confirmed that the County payments were funded through its general fund, with assistance from the City and Destination Cleveland. I issued what by now had come to be the standard City disclaimers: 1) that we had to check the legal and financial do-ability of committing the admissions taxes, and even then, there was a policy issue; and 2) does the Arena façade really need to extend all the way to the Huron sidewalk: can't the proposal be "value-engineered?"

Speaking to Republican National Convention timing, Jeff Cohen warned that we needed to make a decision in the next two weeks. Komoroski added that the Convention would require the $140 million project to be phased. Sobol Jordan commented that this was a tough time for the County to be having this kind of conversation.

After the Komoroski meeting, City and County staff debriefed. Construction attorney Jeff Appelbaum confirmed that the Cavaliers needed to put their steel order in "right now." He added that, as a rule of thumb, public entities average paying $20 million per year of lease extensions—at a minimum, we should seek an extension to 2034. I then emphasized the importance to the City of saving some of the admissions tax monies for a day when the Indians come calling for Ballpark improvements.

A week later we all came to better understand Sobol Jordan's remark about bad timing for the County: in a press conference summarizing current County bond indebtedness, County Executive Budish announced that the County had in effect "maxed out its credit card."

Nevertheless, on April 10, 2015, the County Executive convened a strategy session at his offices. He was joined by staff members Sobol Jordan and Carroll, and by financial advisor Offtermatt, construction attorney Appelbaum, and Gateway attorney Dennis Wilcox. I was the lone City invitee. Offtermatt summarized a March 31 meeting that he and Wilcox had attended with Komoroski and his General Counsel Jason Hillman.

The Q Arena officials had been willing to share information on the staging of the $140 million project: Phase One would be the 70,000 square-foot space expansion highlighted by an exterior curtain wall and a carved wooden interior wall; Phase Two would be food and concession improvements, new gathering spaces, and seating removals replaced by a new socializing space. They continued to believe that at least the façade work could be complete by the July 2016 Republican National Convention, and they sought the County's guaranty of principal and interest on the $70 million bonds based on lease payments (which County guaranty would cost the County $20 million). Offtermatt added that the $17 million up-front payment from a prior sin tax extension was not available for this deal (it had already been included in the County's 2015 budget).

Noting that the Indians' lease expired in 2023, Appelbaum characterized that franchise as "more vulnerable," given recent poor attendance coupled with a number of growing Sunbelt cities attempting to attract baseball teams. He concluded: "You can't develop a comprehensive plan without dealing with the Indians," adding that the Indians' Lehman envisioned $60 million worth of Ballpark work needed in the next decade (of which Gateway could only afford $30 million).

Offtermatt then presented some options:

- Cut the Q Arena public contribution in half—to $35 million —and contribute the other $35 million toward Indians' future capital needs;
- Grow the leveraging ability of the sin tax;
- Guarantee the private $70 million bonds (at a County cost of $20 million);
- "Clean up" the Cavaliers lease.

The County Executive then added a fifth term (as more of a *require-ment* than an *option*): he needed Dan Gilbert to commit to $500 million of riverfront development (via either construction of a new Phase Two Casino Project, or other equivalent development). Offtermatt concluded by stating that the next step was to arrange separate meetings with the Indians and the Cavaliers.

Later that week I updated Mayor Jackson, who was not enthusiastic about me attending the meetings with the Indians and Cavaliers. I was able to change the Mayor's mind by stressing the importance of me being there to *directly state* the City's position: that we cannot completely drain our future admissions tax monies and leave nothing left for Ballpark needs (which, after all, remained the City's prime obligation). But in making my argument to Mayor Jackson, I erred by "burying a lead item," and that would be the cause of some future stress in our relationship with the Cavaliers.

Throughout my career in City Hall, I had stressed to our staff the importance of highlighting major issues in their written and oral reports to me and the Mayor. Over and over again I admonished them: "Don't bury the lead!" Once, when a City director buried a several-million-dollar cost overrun in the middle of page 8 of a 15-page biweekly report, I sent her back the highlighted page from her report, attaching to it a copy of a back-of-a-cereal-box puzzle that challenged the customer to "find the hidden leprechaun" in a pictured maze.

But in my Q Arena briefing to Mayor Jackson, I violated my own rule. Though I did tell him about the County Executive's desire for a $500 riverfront development, I did not highlight it as a "make or break issue" in the Executive's frame of mind and I failed to forecast that this would become a sharp bone in the throats of the Cavaliers leadership team.

On August 26, 2015, we devoted the entire day to two separate meetings with Indians and Cavaliers leadership. The Indians were represented by Lehman and VP/General Counsel Joe Znidarsic; our public-sector attendees were Offtermatt, Wilcox, Sobol Jordan, Carroll, and myself. We let Offtermatt walk through the Cavaliers request and our proposed response, which was to split the admissions tax proceeds in the manner Offtermatt had proposed several months ago: the Cavaliers would get $30 million conditioned on a lease extension to 2034 and they would also derive a $20 million benefit from the County's guaranty of the $70 million private bonds secured by the Cavaliers' additional rent; the Indians would get $30 conditioned on a matching contribution by the team and a lease extension to 2034,

The Indians' reaction was guarded: Lehman asked if they could borrow the team's $30 million match from us. He then noted that by Opening Day 2016 the Indians would have spent $33 million on their own renovations. He concluded by asking if Gateway could activate sin tax bonds prior to the Indians agreeing to a lease extension. Knowing that the sin tax bonds were already in the works, Offtermatt promised to get back to them on this point.

Our presentation to the Cavaliers was a lot dicier. Their attendees were Komoroski, Cohen, Mozelle Jackson and Jason Hillman. Offtermatt made a similar presentation, but this time he added the piece sought by the County Executive: that Dan Gilbert would commit to $500 million worth of riverfront development. Cohen was unimpressed with the value we assigned to the County guaranty, growling that "You can't buy a cup of coffee with what the County incurs regarding the guaranty." Komoroski chimed in that it was typical across the country to have the public entity guaranty bond issues like this. He added that "We're doing more than any private player in our League."

It quickly became apparent that the $500 million riverfront ask was a major irritant. Komoroski called it "punitive," reminding us that since the time that the State had approved four casinos in Ohio it had flooded the market by approving seven more. Lauding the new Brooklyn arena and its surrounding development, Cohen lectured us that "You don't get to where Brooklyn is by cutting budgets.... for us to do a deal like this would take $200 million off the value of our franchise."

The meeting continued to deteriorate. If there was any redeeming feature from the County Executive's $500 million riverfront ask, it at least drew away some heat from our proposal to make room for the Indians by cutting the Cavaliers public allocation to $30 million. Everyone departed with somber faces.

Two days later, the public-sector participants (Offtermatt, Sobol Jordan, Carroll, and myself) hooked up on a conference call to debrief from the Cavaliers meeting. I told the group that the meeting reminded me of the spring of 1995 when Art Modell set his moratorium on stadium renovation discussions: in both cases the public sector's stance at the time was reasonable, but what matters down the road is the perception of the team...and its league. I shared my concern that the Cavaliers might now shift from a renovation request to a demand for a new arena, and that before that occurs, we should consider removing the riverfront development condition.

Meanwhile, back at City Hall, I had briefed Mayor Jackson on the meeting outcomes and he was less than pleased. And it didn't take Komoroski very long to call the Mayor and give his own report. After that, the Mayor gave me a stern and well-deserved lecture on how hard he had worked to maintain a courteous and businesslike relationship with Cleveland's sports teams and how this last meeting

—which he had allowed me to attend against his better judgment—had thrown that in peril. As a result, I would be attending no more of these meetings for the foreseeable future.

But Dan Gilbert's team acted quickly to set all the public-sector players straight on the current market conditions regarding Ohio casinos. In an October 15, 2015 meeting convened in Mayor Jackson's Red Room, Keybank Capital Markets expert Jake Massanqui walked us through present-day realities: Keybank had 20 years' experience of casino lending; the suburban Hard Rock Casino had a number of competitive advantages over downtown's Horseshoe Casino; and a bank loan to finance a Phase Two downtown riverfront casino was not in the offing. County Executive Budish asked: "If the Horseshoe built Phase Two (with entertainment), would that help its competitiveness? Massanqui replied: "Minimally. Making downtown more walkable would be more productive."

By then the County officials had hired attorney Fred Nance to assist in the Arena negotiations, and they attempted —without success for a several months period—to arrange meetings with Destination Cleveland's leadership to seek its financing help on the deal. On November 15, 2015, Komoroski called me with several updates:

> "While Nance has explained to us the City's "unplugging" from the discussions, the City is in a position to ensure the longevity of three downtown sports facilities with 'good bones.' All the leases need not be extended at once. The County Executive recently told our Dan Rinehart that he may be willing to decouple the Phase Two Casino from the negotiations. Your participation would help keep the discussions 'practical.'"

I promised him that I would relay his updates to Mayor Jackson.

Very little occurred during the next nine months. The community as a whole was focused on preparations for the July, 2016, Republican National Convention. That was particularly true for Destination Cleveland president David Gilbert and his board chairman Dan Walsh, so they continued to avoid meeting with the County's Q Arena deal team. The Convention was the tourism magnet of the decade, and though no one knew it at the time, it would be preceded in June by a downtown crowd of 1.4 million people turning out to celebrate the Cavaliers' NBA Championship. For Gilbert and Walsh, tourism was their business and they had never seen a year like 2016.

The year 2016 was a rousing success for Cleveland tourism, as confirmed by a Forbes article:

> Notwithstanding the possibility of the second largest city in Ohio winning two of America's four major professional sports titles in less than five months, Cleveland's recent rebirth is far less linear and simplistic than the sports-only logic would suggest. It's the result of years of forward-thinking investments in community revitalization, tourism infrastructure, and creating an identity that's distinctly "Cleveland," explains David Gilbert, Director of Destination Cleveland and the Greater Cleveland Sports Commission.[2]

It was easy to understand the tourism officials' lack of enthusiasm for contributing to the Q Arena deal: it would reduce their tourism promotion dollars at a time when they were poised to capitalize on the City's positive national coverage. But the parties finally got together in the late summer and began wrestling over the amount of the contribution.

On November 7, 2016, I joined a conference call with Sobol Jordan and Offtermatt. Sobol Jordan began: "We're at a turning point in our discussions." Offtermatt explained that the County team (counsel Nance and Greater Cleveland Partnership's Joe Roman) was asking Destination Cleveland to contribute $2 million per year to the Arena deal. Gilbert was reluctant to reduce his revenue stream (most of which came from County bed taxes) even though that stream had dramatically increased due to downtown hotel construction (Destination Cleveland had netted tax revenues of $6.3 million in 2011, and those net revenues increased to $10 million in 2016 and were projected to grow to $11.6 million in 2017). The Cavaliers were becoming very impatient, and something needed to be done soon. After the call, I updated Mayor Jackson and he agreed to invite all the parties to a negotiating session in our Red Room.

The meeting occurred on November 23, 2016. Destination Cleveland attendees were Dave Gilbert, Dan Walsh, and Destination Cleveland's attorney Jon Pinney. County attendees were County Executive Budish, Sobol Jordan, and Offtermatt. City attendees were Mayor Jackson, Finance Director Dumas, and myself. Mayor Jackson started the meeting by asking that we start with the finance issues and defer the legal issues to later. Accordingly, Offtermatt reviewed the proposed public contributions. When he got to the admissions tax proceeds from 2024 to 2034, he explained that his projected amounts assume "substantial" increases in Cavaliers season ticket prices. The total public revenues would generate debt service for two County bond issues: $35 million taxable, and $35 million nontaxable. From annual debt service payments of $8.65 million, the Cavaliers would get $70 million and the Indians would get $30 million.

When Offtermatt completed his summary, Mayor Jackson asked: "What is Destination Cleveland offering?" Walsh replied: "Take out the Indians contribution and the gap reduces from $62 million to $15 million." The Mayor countered: "Why would I do this deal for the City if the Indians are not in it? I can't give up a revenue stream and not have a stream for the Indians in the future."

Gilbert explained Destination Cleveland's annual budget in which bed taxes were a major—but not the only—source of the agency's revenue. And the annual gross bed taxes received by the agency (from respective 3% and 1.5% County bed taxes) were reduced by a number of capital contributions the agency had agreed to over the years on various civic projects: Gateway, the convention center, a wayfinding signage system, the Hilton convention hotel, and the semi-annual Rock and Roll Hall of Fame Induction ceremonies. "Our budget after capital obligations is $16 million per year," he said, "and that places us in the middle of the pack of our peers."

The County Executive responded: "When the 1.5% bed tax was extended in 2014, everyone assumed it would raise $4 million a year and it now raises $6 million a year. That's the increment we seek."

To that, Walsh rejoined: "Arena financing is not a needle mover for us." The Mayor suggested we look at what each party is providing. The County Executive said that he didn't view Destination Cleveland as an equal partner, and I could see Walsh, Gilbert and Pinney all recoil—and then stiffen— at the other side of the table. After a pause, Pinney was the first of their group to respond: "The whole 1.5% bed tax is being taken back from Destination Cleveland after it added 12 people to its sales staff."

The County Executive volleyed that the County had asked for $2 million a year from Destination Cleveland to make this work: a year ago the answer was "raise the bed tax" and now the answer is "remove the Indians."

Seeking a pause in this heated ping pong match between Destination Cleveland and the County Executive, I began to explain the

Indians part of the deal: the City was already sending a slice from its Q Arena admissions taxes to the County under the Gateway agreements until 2023; this new deal asks us to extend this slice for another ten years; but if we don't reserve some of that slice for the Indians' future needs, we would have nothing available if they come calling; remember, the Indians lease expires in 2023 and—as between the City and County—the City is primarily responsible for the Ballpark's capital needs. Walsh interjected that it was Destination Cleveland's goal to grow from 17 million annual visitors to 20 million annual visitors.

In my nearly 40 years of experience in government negotiations, Mayor Jackson had proven again and again to be one of the best judges of personalities—and the best at knowing how to diffuse a tense situation—that I have ever encountered. At this point, he again demonstrated those traits by: 1) asking the group how we could make this work without taking the Indians out of the deal, and 2) suggesting that we take a 30-45-minute break for the sides to gather their thoughts. Everyone agreed, and when we reconvened, there was still a gap—Walsh offered a $1.5 million annual flat payment (i.e., no inflation adjustments) over 20 years which he characterized as a $30 million contribution. Offtermatt said that still left a $25 million hole in the $70 million public share of the deal—, but at least the tension in the room had been diffused. The meeting adjourned.

The next day the Mayor received separate phone calls from the County Executive and Walsh, each expressing frustration at the recent turn of events. The Mayor listened patiently to each caller, recognizing that there was benefit in allowing each party to fully vent his concerns. With the County Executive's consent, he enlisted Nance to take the next steps and, several weeks later, the gap was closed and the deal was ready for submission to the County Council and the City Council.

On December 13, 2016, County, City, Cavaliers and Destination Cleveland officials announced agreement on a deal that was conditional on County Council and City Council approvals. The criticism began, with Cleveland Scene writer Sam Allard leading the charge (accepting the baton from a less-active Roldo Bartimole).

> Roughly $140 million will be bonded by the County — the very same county with a "maxed-out credit card" — and repaid over 18 years using a variety of revenue streams. The final repayment costs will be roughly double the initial price tag, which is why you might have seen the $282-million figure at Cleveland.com. Tim Offtermatt, recent Chairman of the Gateway Board, advised during a Q&A that the final costs are at this point unknown. They could be even higher than $282 million and will depend on "market conditions."

> (If it helps, when the County talks about "bonds," just substitute the word "loans." They're taking out massive loans.) ....

> We'd be remiss if we didn't note that the energy and creativity expended to scrape every last available dollar for renovations at the Q might have been expended on worthier causes. Where is the county's innovation and creativity in helping solve the financial perils of public transit? Where is the city's creativity on infant mortality and lead poisoning? What if leaders bent over backwards to find money to solve, you know, actual problems?[3]

In our booth at Great Lakes Brewing Company in February 2019, City Council President Kevin Kelley explained some of the differences between his role on the 2014 sin tax extension campaign and his role on the Q Arena deal. "All the arguments against the sin tax extension pale when it comes to the admissions tax extension in the Q Arena deal: the admissions tax is a true user fee (the only ones paying it are the ones actually using the Q Arena). And the proposal before us is to just extend what we were already doing."

"Nevertheless," he continued, "I intentionally stayed away from the Mayor/County Executive/Cavs press conference announcing the deal in order to preserve City Council's free hand in taking up the authorizing legislation."

On January 12, 2017, several formal opposition groups joined the fray.

> Outside the Quicken Loans Arena on this rainy Thursday morning, representatives from the Greater Cleveland Congregations announced their opposition to using public dollars on arena renovations without public input or benefit. The GCC, said several speakers, is "NOT all in."....
>
> "We're asking for a dollar-for-dollar match," said the Rev. Jawanza Colvin, of Olivet Institutional Baptist Church and a member of GCC's strategy team. "We're talking about *matching* dollars. It is amazing how we have the ingenuity and creativity to find the dollars to invest in a world-class arena. We are supposed to be 'cash-strapped.' The credit card is supposed to be 'maxed.' But yet, we can find, when we put our minds together, 160 million dollars [sic]. We want that same ingenuity, that same creativity, that same ability to look under the same rock that you found this money under." [4]

"I thought the 'Not All In' opposition by the Greater Cleveland Congregation and the Progressive Caucus was 'embarrassingly disingenuous,' Kelley continued, "but it caused me problems: several City Council members latched on to the opposition's populist argument, and the issue went from a 'no-brainer' to a real challenge."

"The groups' demands were extensive," he continued, "since they were asking for a dollar-for-dollar match for their social programs and—though they later backtracked—at the start *they* were seeking to become the recipients of this match money. Their tangible programs were initially undefined, but later they settled on two new mental health facilities—one on the east side and one on the west side—that would allow for redirection of defendants who would otherwise be sentenced to jail time. But they hadn't talked to mental health professionals, and their concepts were naïve."

On February 21, 2017, the Cuyahoga County Council commenced its deliberations on the Q Arena Renovation authorizing resolution. Cleveland Scene's Allard wrote:

County Executive Armond Budish has seldom appeared more exercised than he did yesterday when he addressed Cuyahoga County Council about the proposed Quicken Loans Arena renovation plan. After more than 30 public comments, passionately delineating familiar notes of opposition and support, Budish took to the podium to present a doomsday scenario in which the county was all but guaranteed to lose the Cavaliers' franchise and the arena itself if council did not authorize the deal.

For background: The so-called Q Transformation has an advertised all-in price of $140 million, and has been billed — and *continues* to be billed, by Budish and Cleveland.com — as an even split between the Cavs and the public. But as has been reported extensively, the total cost of the project, after interest and the creation of a rainy-day fund, will be ~$282 million, of which the public will pay an estimated $160 million.

The largest share of those funds (~$88 million) will be borne by the city, via an admissions tax on ticketed events at the Q from 2024-2034. The reason why it won't be activated until 2024 is because until 2023, this portion of the admissions tax will be used to pay off existing Gateway bonds — from the *nineties*. ....

Final note and theme: For observers like Scene, one of the most challenging elements of this debate to countenance in good faith is the fervid support for the deal by the construction trades. Outside the tradespeople, virtually every public commenter in support of the deal was a CEO, a downtown nonprofit executive, a suburban Mayor, or — oddly enough — a chef.[5]

Nevertheless, after much consternation and deliberation, the County Council passed the deal in March, 2017. City Council was next, and we began our preparations. It is customary to prepare a short legislative summary for the benefit of the Council members, and my summary for Arena Ordinance No. 305-17 read as follows:

Since the early 1990's, the City of Cleveland has contributed to the original Arena project by annually sending to Cuyahoga County a portion of Arena admissions taxes (in recent years $5-7 million a year) calculated as follows:

- 5/8 of the 8% admissions taxes on Cavaliers games; and
- 2/8 of the 8% admissions taxes on all other Arena events.

This arrangement ends in 2023. Ordinance No. 305-17 would extend the current arrangement for another 11 years—from 2024 to 2034—as the City's share toward $70 million of County bonds. The

Q would fund the remaining $70 million of a $140 million Arena renovation project.

The Q's financial projections show these annual City payments averaging $8 million for the 11-year term. But the City is only responsible for paying its percentages; if actual receipts fall short, it is up to the County or the Q to cover any shortfalls.

The extension of the current admissions tax arrangement would mean that Q ticket purchasers would contribute to the costs of the $140 million Arena enhancements. The City's contribution to the Arena Bonds requires no new taxes; it simply extends the duration of an annual admissions tax payment that the City already makes to Cuyahoga County.

In exchange, the Arena lease would be extended seven years to 2034. We can continue to use the existing Arena—and avoid the half billion to a billion-dollar cost for a new arena—for almost twenty more years.

I also prepared a Power Point that more fully explained the flow of funds, described the Indians' share of our contribution, and demonstrated how the $88 million we contributed over time had a present value of $47 million ($26.4 million toward the Arena and $20.6 million toward the Ballpark). Lastly, I prepared (but did not end up using) the following chart:

ARENAS RECENTLY BUILT OR RENOVATED[6]

CITY	ORIGINAL YEAR BUILT	RECENT STATUS	YEAR BUILT OR RENOVATED	TOTAL COST IN MILLIONS	PUBLIC SHARE IN MILLIONS	PUBLIC % OF COST
San Francisco	2016	New	2016	1 Billion	0	0
New York	1966	Renovated	2013	1 Billion	0	0
Salt Lake City	1991	Renovated	2016	110	22	20
Cleveland	1994	Renovated	2017	140	70	50
Charlotte	2005	Renovated	2014	40	33.5	83.7
New Orleans	1999	Renovated	2016	54	54	100
Minnesota	1990	Renovated	2013	128.9	74	57.4
Oklahoma City	2008	Renovated	2012	95	95	100
Atlanta	1999	Renovated	2016	192.5	142.5	74
Milwaukee	2015	New	2015	500	250	50
Sacramento	2015	New	2015	507	272.9	54
Brooklyn	2012	New	2012	1 Billion	511	51.1

Our first appearance occurred on March 28, 2017, before City Council's Development, Planning and Sustainability Committee, chaired by Councilman Tony Brancatelli. Nance gave a superb opening statement:

"Are we going to keep all three teams? If so, we compete in a national market. Cleveland is the smallest U.S. city with baseball, football and basketball. The TV market is key. In small markets, the public has to pay a higher percentage (for its sports facilities) because of TV market differentials. The existing (Cavaliers) lease expires June, 2027. It has a specific performance clause. The team is likely to be sold in 2027. The new owner will expect a new arena at a cost of $500-700 million. The Cavaliers pay cost overruns on this deal. And the Indians lease will come due and there's a fund set aside for that. Their lease expires 2023. The Arena has generated $180 million in tax revenues for Cleveland. If we are going to be in the business, this is a good deal."

Then it was on. Komoroski and Offtermatt each gave presentations, and I passed out a Power Point overview. Chairman Brancatelli invited deal opponents to the table, including Greater Cleveland Congregation Representatives Reverend Jawanza Colvin of Olivet Institutional Baptist Church and Pastor Richard Gibson of the Elizabet Baptist Church.

Pastor Gibson analogized our Q Arena deal to Milwaukee's recent negotiations of an arena deal that led to a substantial community benefits agreement (however, he failed to mention that the Milwaukee deal was for a brand-new $500 million new arena; that the public share of that project was $250 million compared to our $70 million public share; and that the community benefits agreement negotiated by Milwaukee's Common Ground community group was largely fueled by the alleged predatory lending practices pursued in Milwaukee neighborhoods by Nationstar Mortgage, which was controlled by the owner of the Milwaukee Bucks).

Chairman Brancatelli also invited to the table some project supporters, including Norman Edwards of the Black Contractors Group and Dave Wondolowski of the Cleveland Building and Construction Trades Council.

Then it was time for questioning by Council members, and Cleveland Scene's Allard summarized the most vocal Council member deal opponents.

> The City Council objections arose from familiar quarters — from Jeff Johnson and Zack Reed, both of whom objected to "mortgaging the general fund" of the future. Johnson said we'd be encumbering "a future mayor, a future city council, future residents" with this burden. Reed told *Scene* after the meeting that he does not oppose a Q deal. He opposes *this* deal, because he's anxious to find ways to pay for the upgrade that don't impact general fund dollars.

The most forceful opposition, though, came from Councilman Polensek. After Phyllis Cleveland, Kerry McCormack, Kevin Kelley and Terrell Pruitt asked a series of softball questions, all sort of designed (it seemed) to countervail against the perception of corporate welfare — "We're investing in a facility, not a franchise, right?" McCormack asked — Polensek spoiled the party.

"I want to divert from the political love-fest that's taking place here," Polensek said. "I'm surprised you don't have the Cavaliers' cheerleaders here in the audience. When I look at Ken and Tim and Fred here, it reminds of that movie *Poltergeist*: They're back."

Polensek leaned on his considerable experience. He is the only member of council who served during the initial conception of the Gateway neighborhood. And he cited the region's perilous economic situation to urge not only patience, but an outright rejection of the subsidy. He also spoke to the vile threats that the Cavs, Budish and Cleveland.com have all made — threats of the franchise's departure if the upgrade isn't immediately ratified.

"I can't speak for anyone else around this table, but I don't wanna hear your threats," Polensek said. "I didn't believe it then and I don't believe it now. As a young man growing up, there were people who were very good at making threats. It was called The Outfit. I resented that group then and I resent any group that comes in and threatens this legislative body."

"We've paid dearly already," Polensek continued. "As an elected official, I was elected to serve. And I gotta tell ya, it aint happening here. You can't keep talking about all this prosperity and then drive 10 minutes where there's poverty and despair and lack of opportunity... We're being asked to commit $88 million for a whooping seven-year extension? Come on. Get serious."[7]

Councilman Polensek lamented "a $282 million public giveaway" (he —as well as Plain Dealer reporter Robert Higgs—arrived at the $282 million number by adding together all the principal and interest payments made over time). I countered that the public contribution was a $70 million bond issue and no more. I explained that when you go to your bank to refinance your $50,000 mortgage and the bank asks how much you currently owe on your home, you reply "$50,000;" you don't give them the much higher number that would be the total of each of your remaining principal and interest payments.

While I was explaining these basic financial points at the City Council table, I kept reminding myself of Mayor Jackson's advice on testifying before Council: "Remember, what's the truth got to do with it?"—because I knew, as did every Council person at the table, how a basic mortgage worked—since Councilman Polensek was pretending ignorance to dramatize the amount of the public investment. What was important now was the Council President's vote-counting.

"We needed 12 votes" (out of the total of 17 Council members), Kelley recalled, "in order to pass the ordinance as an emergency measure" (the significance of this emergency passage will be explained below). "I was certain of 11 votes, so I was looking to one of four council members for that 12th vote. After some initial discussions, I eliminated Councilmen Kevin Conwell and Jeff Johnson as nonstarters: that left Councilmen Zack Reed and Brian Cummins. Though Dan Gilbert and others placed calls to Councilmen Reed, in the end Zack couldn't get past the political consequences" (Reed would run an unsuccessful mayoral campaign later that year).

"That left Brian Cummins, who was the most principled of the dissenters," Kelley continued, "and I knew that he had a thorough understanding of the financials and the comparisons with deals in other cities. I started thinking: 'How do we make this deal better?' I knew that, historically, our admissions tax deal with the County had worked out to annual 50/50 splits between contributions to the County and the City's general fund. And I knew that the Cavaliers' family of companies were very good at filling the Arena 200 nights a year. So, I proposed to the Cavaliers' Len Komoroski—and he agreed to—two new conditions:

- That for every admissions tax dollar that goes toward Arena debt service, the Cavaliers would agree that at least one dollar goes to the City general fund; and
- That the Cavaliers would pay for the refurbishment of gym floors in every City recreation center and every CMSD high school."

"Then," he continued, "I talked to Councilman Cummins re these new terms and the hard-core financials. He got comfortable with it and, on the very last day, that sealed his vote. It took a lot of courage on his part, as he was under tremendous pressure and his 'yes' vote would mean going against his (populist) base." As a result, on April 24, 2017, Kelley finally had mustered his 12 votes for passage of the ordinance as an emergency measure. The Plain Dealer's Robert Higgs described the decision:

> Cleveland City Council on Monday approved committing an esti-
> mated $88 million for upgrades to Quicken Loans Arena. Council's
> vote approved the ordinance 12-5, meaning that it passed with
> emergency status. It takes effect immediately. The deal was the last
> piece of a package involving the city, Cuyahoga County, Destina-

tion Cleveland and the Cavaliers that will finance $140 million in improvements to the arena.

Debate over the issue, was at times contentious. A group of six councilman -- Zack Reed from Ward 2, TJ Dow from Ward 7, Mike Polensek from Ward 8, Kevin Conwell from Ward 9, Jeff Johnson from Ward 10 and Brian Cummins from Ward 14 -- blocked the issue from being approved two weeks ago.

Monday was no different right up to the final vote. City Council chambers was filled with several hundred people, many vocal opponents of the deal. Cummins sided with the majority Monday evening, becoming the 12th vote needed to make the ordinance effective immediately. ...

What happened Monday afternoon?

At a news conference Monday afternoon on the steps of City Hall, Council President Kevin Kelley, County Executive Armond Budish and Cavaliers President and CEO Len Komoroski announced a series of commitments the Cavaliers made to sweeten the deal.

Those commitments were:

- The Cavaliers pledged to match dollar for dollar the amount of money that was committed to debt service on the project from the admissions tax if that exceeds the remaining amount that goes to the city. If that happens, the Cavaliers will write the city a check for the difference.
- The Cavaliers agreed to refurbish the basketball floors in city recreation centers, more than 20 in total. After the announcement, the city confirmed that the Cavs will also refurbish high school basketball courts in Cleveland public high schools.

- Additionally, the Cavaliers announced it will donate all admissions revenues from its road-game watch parties at The Q during the NBA playoffs to benefit Habitat for Humanity. Over the last two seasons, those watch parties have raised more than $1 million from admissions that was donated to several charities. It will now be directed to Habitat for Humanity to help renovate 100 homes over three years.

What changed with Monday's votes?

"My [initial] no vote was principally with the overall issue of sports stadium funding," Cummins said in an interview after the meeting. But he said his position softened some over the last week or so as he heard presentations from Mayor Frank Jackson's administration and listened to their arguments in favor of the agreement. And the sweeteners announced Monday also helped. He estimates that over the last five cash-strapped years Cleveland would have had as much as $4 million more in its general fund had there been a guarantee like the one the Cavaliers made on the admissions tax....

What remains to be seen is whether groups opposing the deal will seek a referendum to repeal it. The Greater Cleveland Congregations and Cuyahoga County Progressive Caucus, two social advocacy groups, have panned the deal, saying that the city has much more serious needs in its neighborhoods - crime, poverty and unemployment - and that they must be addressed first.

The caucus and Greater Cleveland Congregations could work with the Service Employees International Union on a referendum campaign.... If they decide to seek a repeal, they will have to collect about 6,000 valid signatures from registered voters in Cleveland on petitions they file with the clerk of council within 30 days of Monday's vote.[8]

GCC dismissed the Cavaliers' 11th-hour additional commitments (including refurbished gym floors at City recreation centers and CMSD high schools) as insufficient when compared to GCC's requested dollar-for-dollar match. Then, within a week of City Council's action, GCC declared that a group of entities— GCC, Service Employees International Union Local 1199 ("SEIU 1199"), the Cuyahoga County Progressive Caucus, AFSCME Ohio Council 8, and Amalgamated Transit Union Local 268—would begin gathering signatures for a voter referendum in an effort to repeal the legislation known as Ordinance No. 305-17. By terms in Cleveland's Charter, they would have 30 days to submit a total of 6,000 valid signatures.

It was Council President Kelley's anticipation of this this referendum possibility that had driven him to achieve passage of the ordinance as an emergency measure. Section 33 of the Cleveland City Charter provides, in relevant part:

All ordinances and resolutions shall be in effect from and after thirty (30) days from the date of their passage by the Council except as otherwise provided in this Charter. The Council may by a two-thirds vote of the members elected to the Council, pass emergency measures to take effect at the time indicated in the emergency measure.

Thus, via passage as an emergency ordinance, the Q deal became effective upon Mayor Jackson's signature and allowed immediate actions such as the County's bond issuance to commence before the time period—30 days within the ordinance passage date—within which challengers to an ordinance must submit the required number of petition signatures for a referendum. As a practicing attorney, Council President Kelley had carefully studied the City Charter sections and believed that the emergency passage, coupled with prompt implementing actions, could preclude a referendum on the ordinance.

In the ensuing 30-day petition drive, SEIU 1199 performed the brunt of the work. Over the past year, the Union—which represents health care and social service workers in Ohio, Kentucky, and West Virginia—had already staked out a strong political stance opposing Mayor Jackson, Council President Kelley, and many other members of Cleveland City Council.

The bad blood had started with a May 17, 2016, meeting of City Council's Workforce and Community Benefits Committee chaired by Phyllis Cleveland. The Committee was considering an ordinance that would have established a $15 minimum wage in Cleveland: the ordinance's introduction was propelled via a petition drive from local entity Raise Up Cleveland which received significant assistance from SEIU.

I was present at the Committee hearing to hear SEIU Local 1199 President Becky Williams threaten Council members in a manner I hadn't heard from any other guest in the nearly-30 years I'd attended Council meetings. Among her remarks: "If you don't stand with the working people of the City of Cleveland, mark our words, you are standing against them..." and "If...you do nothing, shame on you."

Though they were sympathetic to a federal—or possibly even a state —$15 minimum wage, Mayor Jackson and Council President Kelley announced their opposition to the Cleveland-only $15 minimum wage ordinance, and eventually the State of Ohio determined that a

Cleveland-only ordinance on this topic would run afoul of the Ohio Constitution. Thus, the question never reached Cleveland voters, and the SEIU officials were furious. In 2017, they responded politically:

> The Service Employees International Union, which has endorsed City Councilman Jeff Johnson for Cleveland mayor, also is getting involved in City Council races. The union, with 6,000 Cleve-landers in its membership, already is backing three challengers with SEIU ties, and plans on helping others take on an unspecified number of incumbents, all of whom are Democrats. The union remains sore over Mayor Frank Jackson and council leaders opposing a union initiative to establish a $15-an-hour minimum wage in Cleveland and supporting the use of tax dollars to help pay for upgrades to Quicken Loans Arena. Both illustrate that City Council and Mayor Frank Jackson are not putting the people and the plight of the neighborhoods in the forefront, said SEIU spokesman Anthony Caldwell.[9]

Thus, the embittered union, with its distinct political agenda that partially overlapped the interests of those opposing the Q deal, turned loose its dollars and manpower in the 30-day petition drive.

Not surprisingly, prior to its May, 2017, deadline, the coalition collected over 20,000 signatures on petitions calling for a referendum on the ordinance. However, when the group attempted to deliver the signed petitions, Council Clerk Patricia Britt, through one of her deputies, refused to accept the petitions, asserting that the referendum would unconstitutionally interfere with an already executed legal contract. That led to a case before the Ohio Supreme Court, filed initially by Cleveland Law Director Barbara Langhenry. Langhenry and outside parties—including Local 310 of the Building and Laborers Union, Downtown Cleveland Alliance and Greater Cleveland Sports Commission –argued that Britt exceeded her authority in determining that the referendum would unconstitution-ally interfere with a contract.

Petitioning groups' attorneys, Subodh Chandra and Peter Pattakos, argued that Clerk Britt's job was limited to accepting the petitions and starting a process to validate signatures to see if there were enough for the issue to qualify as a ballot issue. Additionally, they argued that impairment of contract obligations was a non-issue because the ordinance did not involve a change in city law that would interrupt the reasonable expectations of people involved in a contract.

For the next three months the Cleveland City Charter—and the City's Director of Law—were often front-page news: "Why was the City suing itself?" reporters asked. But Barbara Langhenry was well prepared for this fish bowl. Born in 1957 and raised in suburban Chicago, she first glimpsed the legal world by seeing her father John become a fine litigator. As early as elementary school, she was demonstrating both a gift for advocacy and an attention to detail, exacting more time from her teachers so as to not turn in her art project assignments until they met her own exacting standards.

She earned a bachelor's degree in Government and Philosophy from the University of Notre Dame in 1979 and then moved to Cleveland as a Jesuit Volunteer where she taught fifth graders in the Glenville neighborhood and worked alongside Chris Warren as a community organizer in the Tremont neighborhood.

She decided to attend law school, and earned a law degree from Case Western Reserve University in 1987. After a stint at the Arter & Hadden law firm, she answered newly-elected Mayor White's call for public servants by joining the Cleveland Law Department in

1990 in our Real Estate and Development Section. She steadily advanced, becoming Chief of Code Enforcement in 1994, Chief of the Contracts, Legislation and Municipal Law Section in 1998, and Chief Counsel in 2006.

In 2011, Mayor Jackson appointed her Director of Law. Though a director of law must display many qualities—among them intelligence, toughness, practicality, political savvy, work ethic—and Langhenry displayed all of them, she truly excelled in appellate advocacy: given a deadline to file a first-class appellate brief, she always rose to the challenge. Her role in the Q Arena litigation would test all these qualities, as she—along with City Council Clerk Patricia Britt and City Council President Kevin Kelley—became the center of a media firestorm.

On the surface, the combatants were clearly aligned (much like a highly promoted boxing match): in one corner were the City, the County, and the Cavaliers, and in the opposing corner were the Greater Cleveland Congregation. The Progressive Caucus, and SEIU 1199. But things were less settled beneath the surface. "In the lead up (to the Ohio Supreme Court's decision on the referendum issue)," remembered Kelley, "at least four major congregations left the Greater Cleveland Congregation. And Carole Hoover, former Cleveland Law Director Teresa Beasley, and Congresswoman Marcia Fudge were very involved in brokering a settlement."

On August 10, 2017, the Ohio Supreme Court ruled.

The Ohio Supreme Court has ordered Cleveland City Council Clerk Pat Britt to accept referendum petitions submitted by a coalition that opposes Cleveland's use of tax dollars on upgrades at Quicken Loans Arena. The 4-3 ruling on Thursday leaves the project in limbo, at least in the short term. Cuyahoga County delayed selling bonds to finance the project while Cleveland's role was being contested. The Cavaliers had hoped to begin work right after the playoffs ended in June.

The decision also likely scuttles Cleveland's hopes of hosting the NBA All-Star Game in either 2020 or 2021. The NBA recently warned Cleveland that if work on the upgrades did not start by Sept. 15, the city's bid would not be considered.[10]

As a result of the court decision, both Q opponents and Q supporters recognized that the referendum would now have to be placed before Cleveland voters, and that vote would probably not occur until 2018. "Once the Ohio Supreme Court issued its ruling," Kelley observed, "*I really got to see what happens when a barking dog catches the car.*"

After pondering the deal's status over a several-week period, on Monday, August 28, 2017, Cavaliers owner Daniel Gilbert issued a statement killing the Q Arena deal, citing delays in construction "which pushes the overall price tag of the project higher due to rising construction costs. In addition, a time sensitive financing package that included historically low interest rates would be nega-tively impacted by further delay due to a prospective referendum exposing the project to an expected higher interest rate envi-ronment."

Sports radio talk shows—and presumably church phone lines—immediately lit up with angry callers who were furious at the groups responsible for derailing the project. Three days later—on August 31, 2017— GCC issued a statement:

Today, Greater Cleveland Congregations (GCC) has reached an agreement that will benefit both downtown and Cleveland's neighborhoods, and has agreed to withdraw petitions challenging the Quicken Loans Arena deal. GCC applauds the expressed commitment from County Executive Armond Budish, through mediators, to mental health and substance abuse crisis centers, which GCC has sought throughout its current campaign. This commitment represents a dramatic shift toward decriminalizing mental illness and drug and alcohol addiction. Research and evidence suggest that the construction or rehab costs for at least two centers to be $10 million, with annual costs of roughly $1.4 million per center. We recognize the county's intent to further research these investment costs and search for best practices. These centers in other cities have been shown to save municipalities tens of millions of dollars over the life of the centers. Even more importantly, coupled with the ADAHMS Board and the county's continued commitment to Crisis Intervention Training for law enforcement officers, these centers can contribute to a dramatic reduction of our jail population, as it has in other cities around the country. THIS WILL BE OF SIGNIFICANT BENEFIT TO OUR ENTIRE COMMUNITY.

GCC also acknowledges with esteem the bridge building efforts by Bishop Larry Macon and Dr. C. J. Matthews of United Pastors in Mission (UPM) for bringing parties to mutual agreement for the benefit and betterment of our entire community. This agreement represents a shift toward truly connecting downtown development with community investments which prioritize our most urgent community needs.[11]

Cleveland Scene's Allard had this to say about GCC's latest action:

The Greater Cleveland Congregations, a regional faith-based coalition, is now scrambling to put an adequate spin on the latest news:

that they intend to withdraw their petitions seeking a referendum on the Q Deal; that in doing so, Dan Gilbert will return to the negotiating table; and that the renovation will now resume exactly as planned, without the intervention of voters. (This the current assumption anyway.)

The death of the deal, announced Monday — which marked the first time nationwide that activist groups had triumphed over a sports owner seeking public subsidies — was fleeting. It now seems almost fake.

Shortly after the Cavs issued their statement declaring the deal dead, County representatives got in touch with GCC, advising that a window still existed. They thought they could get the Cavs back to the table and still get construction underway before a Sep. 15 deadline imposed by the NBA. Construction on the arena upgrades had to start by that date, the NBA said, if Cleveland were to remain in contention as a host city for an All-Star Game in 2020 or 2021.

Armond Budish's "intermediaries" negotiated with GCC and affirmed their commitment to mental health crisis centers. The crisis centers — one on the west side, one on the east — had been central to GCC's proposed community equity fund from the beginning. GCC also sought workforce training pipelines and capital investments in neighborhoods.[12]

The GCC's preemptive action did not sit well with its fellow entities SEIU Local 1199 and the Cuyahoga County Progressive Caucus. Phrases like "betrayal" and "sell-out" were tossed around. But within a week, Dan Gilbert confirmed that the deal was revived.

Taking account of these latest developments, the Plain Dealer editorialized that it was time to move on and made several observations in the process:

- That the Greater Cleveland Congregation and other community groups should generally refrain from using referendum threats to stall public-private investments;
- That rather than engaging in "cat-and-mouse political games (i.e., rejecting the petitions signed by 22,000 Clevelanders), the Cleveland officials should have confined their efforts to selling the deal on its merits;
- Those merits included an equal public-private partnership (at a time when many pro teams were demanding "full public underwriting for sports arenas"), prolonging the life of an aging arena, the Cavaliers' agreement to extend their lease of the Arena until 2034, and providing both construction jobs and 700 new jobs;
- That those irresponsible politicians who persisted in "demagoguing the deal as 'downtown versus the neighborhoods'" would pay a political price for their actions.[13]

The compromise enabled the County to go forward with its bond closing. Construction commenced in February, 2018, and the transformation project was scheduled for completion in October, 2019. On September 18, 2018—roughly the halfway point of the construction project—the Cavaliers issued a press release announcing that owner Dan Gilbert would spend an extra $45 million for additional Arena upgrades including the home team locker room, AV equipment, and LED lighting. As a result, the Cavaliers would now be contributing $115 million toward the now-increased-to $185 million project.[14]

Komoroski elaborated in a phone conversation with a Crain's Cleveland reporter:

> Every area of the building is being touched and as you go into this type of project there are opportunities to enhance even further.... We're blessed to have ownership that looks at from the perspective of what's the right thing to do for the long term.[15]

Moreover, the press release indicated that, as of July 2018, the project was exceeding diversity goals:

- 19% Minority Business Enterprise participation (versus 15% goal);
- 23% Female Business Enterprise participation (versus 7% goal); and
- 36% diverse workforce (versus 16% goal).

The renovations reduced the Q Arena's seating capacity by about 1,000 seats (from a previous number of 20,917 to a new number in the mid-19,000s), which puts the Q Arena in the range of Denver's Pepsi Center (19,520) and Portland's Media Center (19,441): the latter two venues now rank as the NBA's 11th and 12th largest capacity arenas.[16] And the renovations increased Q Arena public space from 95,380 square feet to 152,970 square feet: this new total exceeds public space totals for many newer arenas (e.g., Sacramento's Golden 1 Center has 131,560 square feet).[17]

On September 28, 2019, an estimated 2,500 people attended a 30-minute confetti and streamer-populated grand opening ceremony in front of the new glass exterior that included speakers Komoroski, Mayor Jackson, County Executive Budish, U.S. Representative Marcia Fudge, and Quicken Loans CEO Jay Farmer. Then the doors opened to give attendees a first-hand look at the $185 million of improvements.

> Updates visitors were able to enjoy Saturday include a 77,110 square foot illuminated aluminum curtain, more than 42,000 square feet of new space in the atrium, a power portal entryway featuring LED panels and Soundscape technology and extensive displays of art, including pieces from local artists. Some of the most popular upgrades were the new dining and beverage options, which include the Overlook Bar and the Budweiser Brewhouse.[18]

Komoroski did not appear to be exaggerating when he claimed that the venue, renamed the Rocket Mortgage FieldHouse, was now the world's premier arena. And the new glass walls and the curtain behind them gives the venue "...an iconic look suitable for the front of postcards...(that) will become one of Cleveland's well-recognized features."[19]

The Plain Dealer's Saturday Forum Section, by contrast, came down squarely in the middle in assessing the Q deal's impact. To ostensibly reclaim objectivity after a week's worth of laudatory articles on the project, the newspaper published an Editorial Board Roundtable on the topic "Is public financing of our sports venues worth the cost?"[20] With some degree of hedging by both supporters and detractors, the final verdict was 4-4.

Cleveland Scene's Allard remains on the other end of the spectrum, and his dislike for the project seems to increase over time. In 2018 he wrote:

> The Q Deal, on the other hand, was not required in any lease. And its blind support from the vast majority of our local elected leaders

was a scandal of recklessness and shortsightedness long before it became an abortion of democracy.[21]

But that was mild compared to his 2020 lament:

The public must never forget or let local elected leaders forget: The Q Deal was one of the ugliest and most dispiriting episodes in recent Cleveland history. With shocking clarity over multiple months, it demonstrated the lengths to which elected leaders would go to crush the will of the electorate at the behest of their private masters. For the privilege of mortgaging their constituents' future, leaders ultimately sabotaged the most energizing grassroots coalition Cleveland had seen in decades.[22]

A final assessment of the Q Arena deal's impact must include a reminder of its least-publicized and most overlooked aspect: that was its provision for a reserve account—the "Sports Facility Reserve"—that allocated separate monies in years 2024-2034 for improvements/capital repairs to a separate "sports facility" (read Progressive Field). That Reserve would end up playing an important role in our Cleveland Indians lease extension negotiations described in Chapter 8 of this book.

The New Base Ball Park, Cleveland, Ohio.

Predecessor baseball and football sports facilities were League Park (above photo, from Walter C. Reedy, Michael Schwartz Library, Cleveland State University) and Cleveland Municipal Stadium in 1966 (bottom photo, from Clay Herrick Slide Collection, Michael Schwartz Library, Cleveland State University)

Predecessor arenas were the Cleveland Arena (above photo, by Bill Nehez, Cleveland Press Collection, Michael Shwartz Library, Cleveland State University) and the Richfield Coliseum (bottom photo, by Gus Chan, Plain Dealer photographer)

*Art Model displays his model of a proposed renovation of Cleveland
Municipal Stadium at the Stadium infield on August 16, 1989
(Plain Dealer Archives)*

Gateway Project under construction in 1993 (Jacobs Field foreground; Gund Arena background (Author photo)

Jacobs Field under construction in 1993 (Author photo)

A June 1994 night game in Jacob Field's inaugural season (Author photo)

Gund Arena viewed from Cuyahoga River in 1994 (Author photo)

Frederick R. Nance, Mayor Michael R. White's lawyer, testifies before Cleveland City Council re NFL negotiations (Dale Omori, Plain Dealer photographer)

Mayors of several cities with NFL teams talk at a December 16, 1995 news conference. From left, the mayors are Walter Moore (Pontiac, Michigan), Michael R. White (Cleveland), Bob Lanier (Houston), Norman Rice at podium (Seattle), Roxanne Quas (Cincinnati), and Paul Juda (Green Bay) (Chuck Crow, Plain Dealer photographer)

Cleveland Mayor Michael R. White holds a sign during a November 29, 1995, pep rally on Capitol Hill (Associated Press)

Exiting Cuyahoga County Common Pleas Judge Kenneth Cal'ahan's courtroom on November 6, 1995, with an order restraining the Browns from moving to Baltimore, are Squire Sanders and Dempsey lawyers Damon Mace (center) and George von Mehrin (right). On the left is Mayor White's executive assistant Ken Sil'iman (Mike Levi, Plain Dealer photographer).

Browns fans protest the Baltimore move at a November, 1995 ral'y (David Anderson, Plain Dealer photographer)

Browns owner Art Model waits on the witness stand on November 21, 1995, in Cuyahoga County Common Pleas Court as lawyers huddle in a conference with Judge Kenneth R. Callahan (Gus Chan, Plain Dealer photographer)

Cleveland finance director Kathryn Hyer briefs council on the city's proposed NFL agreement (Scott Shaw, Plain Dealer photographer)

Michael R. White confers with Fred Nance, left, the city's lawyer on NFL matters, and Ken Si'liman, White's executive assistant (Phaedra Singelis, Plain Dealer photographer)

Ba'lpark 2016 renovations created concourse field views (Author photo)

Ball'park 2015 renovations enhanced the southeast plaza (Author photo)

Q Transformation Project as of June 30, 2018 (Author photo)

Gateway site viewed from Cleveland's Terminal Tower (Author photo)

Progressive Field: still beautiful at age 25 in 2019 (Author photo)

Cleveland Browns Stadium as of July 21, 2012 (Author photo)

Cleveland Cavaliers Victory Parade, June 22, 2016 Author photo)

Extra Innings: Chicago Cubs at Cleveland Indians, Game 7 of the 2016 World Series, November 3, 2016 (Author photo)

CHAPTER EIGHT

PROGRESSIVE FIELD BALLPARK RENOVATIONS

On January 8, 2014, I met with Indians' President Mark Shapiro and business manager Dennis Lehman at their ballpark offices for what was described as a "preview." With the sin tax extension campaign beginning to accelerate toward a May, 2014, County vote date, the Indians' officials confidentially described their plans for over $100 million of ballpark improvements.

The more conventional improvements--$80 million worth of "nuts and bolts" work managed over the course of the next decade— would be paid for via team-funded capital repairs ($20 million) and the Indians' share of the proposed 20-year sin tax extension ($60 million) assuming passage of same by County voters in May, 2014.

The more avant-garde improvements—estimated at over $30 million, all to be paid for by the team—would include changing the right-center field upper decks by eliminating 3,500-7,500 seats and replacing them with a standing-room only deck (the Colorado Rockies were making a similar change), a completely revised entrance area in the ballpark's Gate C northeast plaza, and relocated bullpens that would bring them closer to centerfield seating areas.

Acting on my suggestion that they promptly brief Mayor Jackson on their proposals, President Shapiro—joined by Lehman and strategist Andrew Miller— met with the Mayor and I at Cleveland City Hall on April 14, 2014. Before starting in on the main topic, we chatted on the possibilities of the team's improving upon its 2013 wild card playoff appearance. Shapiro then described the team's extensive fan surveys and studies which in turn guided the front office's plans to "repurpose Progressive Field for the next generation."

Shapiro contrasted their renovation-focused plan with the Atlanta Braves' recent "demolition-focused" decision to replace its 20-year-old downtown ballpark with an expensive suburban facility. Lehman explained that one factor in their thinking was the ballpark's "over-capacity in luxury areas." Miller then summarized the changes that were previewed to me in January, tying many of them together with their marketing insight that "people want to periodically leave their seats." He added that average capacities in new ballparks was down 13% (hence their plans for eliminating some distant seats).

Shapiro spoke to changes that would draw people to the park even when the team wasn't winning; opening part of Gate C to the City when no game is on; moving the bullpens closer to the fans, losing the first six rows in the mezzanine to open up lighting to the concourse; and taking out the right-centerfield upper deck and replacing it with a party deck. Given the wide range in seat removals (3,500-7,500) in our January discussion, I asked about the new seating capacity, Miller said they'd remove 7,500 seats and add 1,500 new seats, yielding a new capacity of 37,500 (compared to the existing capacity of 42,404).

The Mayor asked how this plan would impact the lease with Gateway (Lehman's answer: "No financial impact") and how it would extend the useful life of the ballpark (Shapiro's answer: "You'll be updating the structure in the centerfield area and you'll get new fixtures features there"). He added:

- On maintenance, we will continue to perform it at the same top-quality level;
- On infrastructure, we continue to spend $3-4 million per year; and
- Our model is shifting away from its previous premium-seating focus.

Mayor Jackson concluded by indicating that he understood the concept, and that "Ken and I will discuss this." After our ensuing discussions (we had similar views), Mayor Jackson decided to support the Indians' proposal.

Consequently, in August, 2014, the Cleveland Indians announced a two-year plan to renovate Progressive Field to make it more competitive for the next generation of ballpark attendees. The Plain Dealer's Michelle Jarboe described Phase One of the renovation plan for the 21-year-old ballpark (the plan tracked our Indians' discussions, with the exception that a closing off of the right-centerfield upper deck was substituted for the previously proposed costly demolition of same):

> The renovations, which will stretch from center field to right field, could be finished by opening day of 2015. "We're really adapting the building to the current sports landscape and the size of the market," Shapiro said. The plans include:

- Capping off a section of the upper deck, which sits empty on all but the busiest days, with a platform that will conceal unused seats and create new game-viewing areas.
- Remaking the Gate C entrance off East Ninth Street by pulling out concrete and opening up views of the ballpark from the street. The gate makeover will eliminate a pavilion and a bar, but the Indians plan to build a two-story, indoor-outdoor bar in right field. To open up the gate, the Indians will move the Bob Feller and Jim Thome statues to another site in the Gate C area. Shapiro said the team also plans to add a statue of Larry Doby, who was the first black player in the American League.
- Moving the bullpens up into the seating area in center field to give fans a better view of the players during warm-ups. This shift will create a section of exclusive seats in front of the new bullpens and will open up the existing bullpen space to fans who want to stand closer to the field.
- Expanding the Kids Clubhouse, which opened in 2012, to two levels and renovating the mezzanine. The expansion will eliminate 16 or so suites, continuing the team's ongoing efforts to replace higher-priced, poorly used private areas with spaces that all ticketholders can access. After the renovations, the ballpark still will have upwards of 80 suites - far more than the Indians can fill, and more than many other parks offer.
- Incorporating five neighborhood-themed areas with food from Ohio City, Tremont and other popular area.[1]

Almost a year later—on July 17, 2015, — I visited the Cleveland Indians' offices at Progressive Field to listen to a presentation on Phase Two of the team's renovations. The Indians' presenters were led by Lehman and included strategist Andrew Miller, Alex King from

Marketing and Chief Information Officer Neil Weiss. Besides me, invited guests were Tim Offtermatt and Todd Greathouse of Gateway, and Matt Carroll from the County.

The Indians' presenters assigned a $33 million price tag for both stages of improvements. Phase Two of the project would be completed by Opening Day of the 2016 baseball season. The Indians were self-financing nearly all of the alterations, having executed a long-term contract with concessionaire Delaware North Cos. which would contract for the work and recover its capital expenditures from the Indians over time. The construction would be performed by Gilbane Building Company. Miller then described Phase Two:

- Opening the lower concourse to allow field views;
- Renovate concessions and add Cleveland-based food and drink operators;
- Construct a new season ticket holder lounge behind home plate;
- Convert ten suites to double-wide suites;
- Remove right-field upper decks seating (new capacity would be 36,500).

There were several companion capital repair asks from Gateway: $701,000 for suite alterations, and $1,330,625 for concessions. And the Indians had previously submitted a request for a $20 million new scoreboard which would, if approved by Gateway, make it the largest scoreboard in the Major Leagues. The "Waiting for Next Year" blog described the project in the three passages quoted below:

> While the scoreboard addition is the most obvious.... The right field and infield Districts ('The Corner' in right field and 'The Home Run Porch' in left field) have created a party atmosphere....

Local food and beer delicacies rule concessions, with Great Lakes Brewing, Ohio City Burrito, Fat Head's Brewery, and The Brew Kettle just a few of the neighborhood favorites....Added to the mix are a much more open concourse, a fantastic walk-around view of the stadium *and* the city that still gives it that retro-feel, and a true fan-and-kid-friendly experience that seems to incorporate the incredible diversity that Cleveland has to offer.[2]

When they launched their renovation project in 2014, Shapiro and Antonetti had clearly targeted millennial—and future generations— as key customers. In the opinion of one online reviewer, the changes more than achieved their goal:

... "The Corner" represents the team's ongoing efforts to cater to the way individuals take in sporting events in the year 2015 where the social elements become increasingly more important.... team president Mark Shapiro unveiled the new addition along with the new field-level bullpens, the expanded Kids Clubhouse and various other items new to Progressive Field for 2015.[3]

And then, after the completion of Phase Two one year later:

... the Indians were beyond satisfied with the reception given to The Corner by today's baseball fan.... Looking to replicate this success on the other side of the field, the team has opened up space between the concourse and the field, allowing for better flow, and brighter, more open-air views. Where right field had been renovated to bring fans menu items from Melt Bar and Grilled, Barrio and Sweet Moses, left field is now giving The Corner a run for it's high-calorie money... here are...food options like Westlake's Fathead's Brewery, Ohio City's Momocho and Strongsville's The Brew Kettle.[4]

Though the team's initial cost estimate for the two renovation stages was $33 million, when the dust settled the final tally was $44 million: all of it paid by the team. That was significant, particularly when weighed against far more costly—to the public—renovation plans that would soon follow.

At the August 8, 2018, meeting of the Gateway Economic Development Corporation of Greater Cleveland, I was admitted to the board and voted Chairman of the Board (as the joint appointee of Mayor Jackson and County Executive Budish, I assumed the chairmanship by prior board custom). I had a working knowledge of the board's responsibilities, having served previous terms in the 1990s and having attended several meetings in 2017 and 2018 in anticipation of my appointment. I had also discussed board operating practices with Executive Director Todd Greathouse and his staff, board attorney Dennis Wilcox, and prior board chairman Matt Carroll.

Apart from overseeing these ongoing operations, I rejoined the board knowing that we needed to get the Cleveland Indians signed to a long-term lease extension (the existing lease being due to expire in 2023). At that time, I knew from several conversations with the Indians' Dennis Lehman that the team was studying the "Gateway Neighborhood" as a first step prior to discussing the lease.

My Preparation for the Lease Discussions

The 2023 expiration date gave the Indians lease the shortest duration of Cleveland's three major league sports franchises. Historically, owner Paul Dolan had worked very well with local governments; impending lease extension discussions would hopefully continue along this track. However, unexpected events could cause a

KEN SILLIMAN

change in ownership, and new owners might be less accommodating to the history of baseball in Cleveland.

Certainly, a city and county that lost the Cleveland Browns in 1995 had learned to take nothing for granted in lease negotiations. A cynical view of what calamities might occur—however remote they may have appeared—was an essential beginning point for all the public sector players. Accordingly, in the spring of 2019 I commenced a quiet study of potential lease issues. My first step was to determine those cities that then lacked MLB franchises but may become serious competitors—either via expansion or relocation—for a franchise in the future. There were several sources of this intelligence, including demographic factors, media reports, and strong existing minor league franchises.

Demographic Factors

On September 16, 2016, the Barrett Sports Group, LLC prepared a preliminary report entitled "City of San Antonio Minor League Baseball Due Diligence Report." The authors of the study focused on San Antonio's potential for attracting a Triple-A minor league baseball franchise by locating and funding a new $70+ million ballpark. However, in Appendix C, the authors also examined San Antonio's case for attracting a Major League Baseball franchise. Although the Report ultimately recommended that—for then at least—the city focus on the Triple-A minor league path, the study contains some very useful demographic comparisons.

The Report made comparisons with a number of potential MLB expansion markets, and from that section[5] I drafted the below comparison chart:

294

CATEGORY	Cleveland	San Ant	Montreal	Charlotte	Las Vegs	Portland	Ok City
2016 Population	3,494,400	2,394,200	4,061,000	2,593,800	2,366,700	3,109,100	1,437,700
2016 Households	1,443,100	858,800	1,757,900	994,300	873,600	1,207,100	560,500
High Income HH's	305,900	194,100	254,500	228,900	155,700	302,600	118,400
TV Market	3,521,000	2,429,400	4,856,600	2,925,000	1,995,900	2,818,500	1,708,100
Radio Market	1,775,000	1,990,600	3,536,000	2,205,400	1,785,800	2,257,300	1,230,400
# Cos >$20 million/yr.	1,707	684	2,370	1,024	540	1,175	531

The Cleveland market area—for then at least—appeared to hold its own when compared with the hottest potential new MLB markets. But the competition was close enough that Cleveland's civic leaders could not become complacent.

Media Speculation

In the last three years there had been considerable media discussion of potential MLB expansion cities. In 2018, Major League Baseball Commissioner Rob Manfred listed Montreal, Nashville and Charlotte as targets, along with Portland, Las Vegas, Vancouver and even Mexico.[6]

Strong Minor League Cities

In considering cities that may become candidates for either an expansion or relocated franchise, I also examined existing minor league franchises that had demonstrated strong recent performance records.

In 2016, a Forbes article listed the top ten minor league franchises ranked by market value: 1) Sacramento @ $49 million, 2) Charlotte @ $47.5 million, 3) Dayton @ $45 million, 4) Lehigh Valley, PA @$43 million, 5) Columbus @$41 million, 6) Round Rock TX @$40 million, 7) Durham @$39 million, 8) El Paso @$38.5 million, 9) Indianapolis @$37.5 million, and 10) Frisco, TX @$37 million.[7]

Not surprisingly, these cities were also leaders in minor league attendance: with the exception of Durham and Frisco, each had averaged over 8,000 fans per game. Buffalo, Nashville, and Albuquerque were additional minor league leaders.

Relevance of Data from Other Cities

To be clear, Indians officials had not expressed a desire to relocate their franchise; nor had they previewed an intent to leverage other markets' availability as a wedge in lease discussions. But the memory of the Browns' relocation was still fresh, and my legal training always drove me to examine worst-case scenarios. The data from the other markets would be there if we needed it.

Preliminary Lease Discussions

Armed with my research on comparable markets, I was eager to get the Indians in a room to see what they needed to justify a lease extension. But Indians' attorney Joe Znidarsic was more concerned with how Gateway was interpreting its major capital repair responsibilities on recent projects such as the modernization of the ballpark's club seating area. His concerns eventually led to a meeting hosted by Indians officials at their offices.

Indians' officials showed up in force at the September 17, 2018, meeting; attendees included Znidarsic, President of Business Operations Brian Barren, VP of Business Operations Dennis Lehman, Chief Information Officer Neil Weiss, and VP of Ballpark Operations Jim Folk. Joining me in representing Gateway were Todd Greathouse, Dennis Wilcox, and Matt Carroll.

Using an 18-page PowerPoint presentation, Znidarsic opened the meeting— which he labelled as a "moderate bitch session"—by itemizing $390 million of Indians ballpark investments since the 1994 opening date, under the subheadings of initial build commitment ($47 million), lease operating costs ($127 million), and other payments such as bond debt service and taxes ($216 million).

Then he compared private and public capital investments since the ballpark's 1994 opening date. The Indians invested $94 million— including the $44 million for renovations in the 2014-2016 timeframe—, while the public had invested $38 million via proceeds from the County's $60 million sin tax bond issue in 2015.

The next slides cited Gateway's 2014 analysis by Barrett Sports Group which concluded that the Indians lease was "one of the least team favorable leases among Major League Baseball peers." After citing examples of peer markets—Pittsburgh, Cincinnati, Kansas City, Minnesota, and Baltimore—he offered this punch line:

> While the small size of the market relative to other MLB teams would normally suggest a competitive Lease for the Indians would have lower occupancy costs, the BSG report concluded that the occupancy costs for the Indians under their lease, were higher than their peers and in some cases substantially higher, particularly when compared to markets of similar size.

He added an increasing concern about shrinking suite demand, and recited recent team actions—conversion of suites into the "Kid-zone," conversion of another ten suites to the Infinity Club, making suites more flexible day-to-day as opposed to 81-date rentals— to reduce the surplus of suites. Then came Znidarsic's objections—not necessarily shared by all the Indians officials—to Gateway's recent interpretations of capital repair responsibilities on projects such as the club seating area.

Turning to the future, he predicted that the next 20 years of ballpark capital expenses will be more expensive than the first 24 years. He based this projection on the recently completed Gateway Facility Condition Assessment that allocated $116 million in estimated costs for repairs and replacements over the next 20 years. In anticipation of such a need, the City and County had built in a "Sports Facility Reserve" into the Q Transformation Deal that was projected to yield $8 million by 2023 and $3.5 million annually from 2024-2034.

Znidarsic closed by asking about the process for resolving capital repair disputes, the process for accessing the Sports Facility Reserve, and the potential new public revenue sources that might be available to fund a lease extension. After the meeting, we knew we needed to update our elected officials.

I had already scheduled a meeting with former Gateway board chair Tim Offtermatt, and we met on September 27. We began with a discussion of potential sources for future sports facility needs, and Tim offered several options:

- The City's parking revenue bonds expire in 2022 (the City's parking tax was expected to raise $13 million in 2018);

- The County's ¼ % sales tax for the convention center was up in 2027;
- The Stadium bonds mature in 2029; and
- The City could consider using some of its admissions tax.

We then discussed the status of the 2014 sin tax extension, and Offtermatt projected that the County could still support another $50-60 million bond issue above and beyond its original 2015 bond issue of $60 million.

On November 12, 2018, a Gateway group—Carroll, Wilcox, and I—met with Mayor Jackson and County Executive Budish in the Mayor's Red Room to update them on recent Gateway issues (with a particular emphasis on the Indians' September PowerPoint presentation). Speaking to what these recent developments portended re a ballpark lease extension, we concluded:

- Gateway's lease to the Indians expires in 2023;
- The Indians want to see a presently undefined public contribution toward the $116 million basic repair needs for the next twenty years;
- Though they haven't specifically stated this, they are implying that the number of years of lease extension will be linked to the amount of public dollars invested toward the $116 million repair needs.

After first noting that I was not at this time recommending any additional ballpark public dollars beyond those produced by the extended sin tax and the Sports Facility Reserve, I speculated that we could roughly match Seattle's recent contribution toward a Safeco Field lease extension by finding an additional $2 million per year ($1 million from the City; $1 million from the County).

For a number of years, I had been joining the Indians' Lehman for lunch at Johnny Mango's in my Ohio City neighborhood, and we met again on December 12. Lehman told me to expect a call from Znidarsic, and that call came on December 14. Znidarsic asked whether Gateway's would amend the lease to make it more competitive with comparable markets, such as broadening the definition of "Major Capital." I replied that the "Major Capital" definition was a red herring, and the core issue was the resources of the public sector to contribute to the ballpark. I summarized those resources as they currently existed:

- An additional $14-19 million for the ballpark (on top of the $37 million already contributed) from the extended sin tax); and
- A potential 2023 bond issue from the Sports Facility Reserve that might yield $30 million.

When we then discussed a lease extension. Znidarsic conceded that the 2023 lease expiration date limited the Indians' flexibility; for example, there was their deal with food and beverage concessionaire Delaware North. That company had financed much of the Indians' $44 million 2015-2016 ballpark renovation cost (with the Indians agreeing to surrender their 2014-2023 concession revenues in exchange for Delaware North's capital investment), and the Indians couldn't revisit this financing tool without a lease extension.

I added that lease extension talks were very timely because City and County elected officials were both knowledgeable of and understanding of the dynamics of sports facility funding (as evidenced by their foresight in creating the Sports Facility Reserve as part of the Q Transformation funding package). I asked whether we had a shared vision in extending the useful life of Progressive Field over the long term, and Znidarsic answered "Yes." We then agreed to update our dialogue after the Indians progressed in their study of "a Progressive Field for the future" in the context of the Gateway neighborhood.

Meanwhile, a once-promising on-the-field scenario (the team won the Central Division for the third year in a row in 2018, the MLB All-Star Game was coming to Cleveland in 2019) had soured. The team's journey to Game 7 of the 2016 World Series had yielded rich post-season revenues for both team and City, and ownership had responded by aggressive spending prior to the 2017 season (most notably on a three-year, $60 million free-agent contract to Toronto slugger Edwin Encarnacion).

But despite the 2017 team's superb regular season (which included an American League record 22-game win streak), it exited the playoffs via a first-round upset by the New York Yankees. Then, just two months ago in 2018, the Houston Astros had swept the Indians out of the playoffs, and as a byproduct of that sweep some financial chickens came home to roost.

The cumulative effect of those lost playoff revenue opportunities in both 2017 and 2018 was to create a huge projected 2019 payroll deficit. The team's 2018 payroll had approached $140 million, and anticipated 2019 arbitration awards could have pushed the 2019 payroll to well over $150 million. But break-even in 2019 was $120 million—or even less—and ownership was not prepared to incur this level of deficit.

While not specifying to the public the exact dimensions of the deficit spending problem, team management did announce a need for cost-cutting in 2019 and indicated a willingness to listen to trade offers for its most expensive players (including outstanding pitchers Corey Kluber and Trevor Bauer).

Much to fans' consternation, Indians' management effected major surgery to its roster over the offseason: gone were Encarnacion (saving the team $20 million), outfielder Michael Brantley (who signed a two-year, $32 million contract with Houston), catcher Yan Gomes (saving $7 million), and third-baseman Yandy Diaz. In their places were returning favorite Carlos Santana (adding a salary of $20 million), and a number of young players earning league-minimum salaries. The net effect of these moves was to reduce the 2019 payroll to approximately $120 million.

In our next Johnny Mango's discussion on January 16, 2019. Znidarsic began by explaining the increasing role of minority investor John Sherman from Kansas City. Sherman had a 25% interest that would annually increase, and the Dolan family was "absolutely comfortable" with Sherman as a potential successor. Znidarsic added that the Indians were potentially interested in purchasing a small Gateway-owned development parcel that fronted on East Ninth Street, as well as the L-shaped Gateway East Garage (once the City parking revenue bonds are retired).

Turning to public contributions toward a lease extension, he identified total capital needs of $240 million comprised of three elements: the $116 million projected over the next 20 years by the Gateway Facility Condition Assessment, the team's annual $2-3 million share of Gateway operating costs, and the remainder for ballpark modernization. Given the $240 million need, he asked what new public sources—separate and apart from sin tax monies and the Sports Facility Reserve—could be added to address that need. I replied that only the public officials could answer that question, but that approving a major new source would be "extremely challenging."

In the meantime, Cleveland was hosting the Major-League All-Star Game from Saturday, July 6 through Tuesday, July 9. Much like the

2016 Republican National Convention three years earlier, the weather was splendid throughout and the activities played out flawlessly to an international audience. Play Ball Park, an interactive fan festival held Saturday through Tuesday at the Huntington Convention Center, attracted 149,513 visitors, which an MLB press release noted was the highest total in the past ten years.[8]

Monday night's Home Run Derby was the most-watched Derby in seven years and the second-most watched in the network's history.[9] All those viewers—including over 30,000 ticket holders at Progressive Field— were treated to quite a show: a dramatic second-round three-tiebreaker battle between Blue Jays rookie Vladimir Guerrero, Jr. and the Dodgers' Joc Pederson, Guerrero's record total of 91 home runs, and Mets rookie Pete Alonso's ultimate triumph.

The game itself was equally dramatic, featuring a 4-3 American League victory with the Indians' Shane Bieber named MVP, Indians All Stars and Manager Terry Francona coordinating an emotional mid-game tribute from the third-base coaching box to Indians pitcher Carlos Carrasco and his stand against cancer, and loud and long fan applauses for former Indians Michael Brantley and C.C. Sabathia.

During the long weekend, MLB and the Indians cut ribbons on two brand new turf ball diamonds for Cleveland kids: one at Luke Easter Park on the city's east side, and another at Brookside Reservation on the city's west side. MLB Commissioner Rob Manfred praised Cleveland's hosting of the All-Star events, especially noting the city's compact downtown which made travel to and from events extremely convenient for attendees.

Shortly after the All-Star weekend—on July 17, 2019— Znidarsic called me to meet for lunch the following day at Johnny Mango's. He began by stating that the team needed lease changes to enable the owner—or any succeeding owner—to justify staying in Cleveland for 20 years after 2023. I replied that lease changes alone, devoid of funding capacity, would simply "kick the can down the road," with Gateway approving more major capital projects—under a presumably broadened definition of same—without benefit of the public dollars to fund the projects.

I compared the Q Transformation deal, where the team spelled out: 1) the exact elements and cost of a $190 million project; and 2) the new public dollars that they were requesting to enable the project. I opined that, lacking that specificity, the project would never have obtained the requested County and City legislative approvals. He distinguished the Q deal by noting that—unlike the Cavaliers—the Indians could not presently identify all the ballpark's modernization needs. Instead, they sought flexibility over time. I then asked about three other points:

- Would the impact study separately track city/county/state revenues?
- Were the Indians still interested in the Gateway Development Parcel? and
- Were the Indians still interested in the East Parking Garage?

He replied "Yes" to all three questions, and added a departing remark: "We can all agree the first 25 years of Cleveland Municipal Stadium was a good experience, the next 25 years were not, and we can't replicate the latter at Progressive Field.

The Negotiations Begin

Several months later—in a September 10, 2019, meeting held at a Progressive Field suite—a six-member team of Indians executives delivered a one-hour PowerPoint display on the team's needs for a long-term lease extension. Joining me as listeners were City Finance Director/Chief of Staff Sharon Dumas, County Chief of Staff Bill Mason and Deputy Chief Matt Carroll, and Gateway counsel Dennis Wilcox.

Znidarsic's opening statement conveyed the Indians' theme: that "meaningful changes were needed for the public's operational and financial support." Having initially studied the option of adding a retractable roof, but rejecting it due to cost and responsibility concerns, the Indians were now focused on ballpark improvements staged over time. This was the opposite approach to the front-loaded plan launched by the Cavaliers in 2013 (i.e., "Here's a $190 million design for improving the arena that will add twenty years to its useful life").

In reviewing the ballpark's history from 1994 to 2019, he characterized the 2004 lease amendment as a watershed event: but rather than acknowledging the amendment as a fairly-negotiated agreement, he asserted that the teams had rescued the public sector from an impending default. Later slides presented by President of Business Operations Brian Barren and Senior VP of Marketing & Strategy Alex King listed the owners' investments since 1994 ($179 million on rent and ballpark maintenance/operations, and $68 million in community donations), the declining population of the city and its metro area, and the harsh lease terms.

Next was Assistant Director of Strategy & Business Analytics Christy Corfias, who compared the team's lease to those of comparable markets (San Diego, Minnesota, Baltimore, Pittsburgh, Kansas City, Cincinnati, Tampa Bay and Denver) and concluded that, over the past three years, the Indians had incurred annual operating costs of $8.6 million more than the average of the other markets.

CFO Rich Dorffer then projected annual future needs (routine maintenance of $1.7 million eventually growing to $4 million, minor capital repairs of $2.8 million eventually growing to $6.6 million) and a heavily backloaded 30-year facility assessment showing $284 million of needed investments. All told, the future investments totaled $500 million, *exclusive* of modernization improvements. Znidarsic concluded the presentation with a statement of the Indians proposed new lease terms, which he divided into five categories:

1. Rent/Routine Maintenance— the Indians would continue to perform routine maintenance ($1.7 million annually escalating) as a proxy for rent, and would no longer split with the Cavaliers Gateway's annual $4.6 million budget;
2. Capital Repairs— the team would no longer fund capital repairs costing less than $500,000, under the new lease, Gateway would fund _a_ capital repairs;
3. Ballpark Improvements—based on modernization costs of $15 million per year, the team would fund $4 million annually, the City would fund $5 million annually, and the County would fund $6.5 million annually.
4. Financial Responsibility—the City and County would guaranty Gateway's performance of all lease terms; and

5. Community Development—the team would partner with the public sector in developing the neighborhood surrounding the ballpark.

I asked about TV revenues (the Indians founded Sports Time Ohio in 2006 and sold it to Fox in 2012, and it is now owned by Sinclair Broadcasting; the Indians have considered repurchase but the obstacle is filling programming when the team is not playing), and about suite rentals (renovations were now done suite by suite per contracts with individual renters). I posited sticker shock by elected officials,since the Indians' proposal would have the public paying almost twice the $10.6 million annual amount paid by the public for the Seattle Mariners' T-Mobile Field.

The next day, the team sent us a PowerPoint listing $289,654,413 of improvements:

- $40,447,430 for Terrace Club renovations;
- $10,328,374 for Dugout Club;
- $75,161,653 for Service Level (and Clubhouses);
- $12,336,807 for Upper Deck Concourse;
- $64,891,407 for Upper Deck Right Field;
- $17,952,581 for Social Suites and Press Box;
- $30,728,170 for Office Renovations; and
- $37,807,991 for Bleacher Cutout at Eagle Avenue.

I then prepared the following summary page:

ENTITY PAYING	ANNUAL COST ITEM	INDIANS LEASE 1994-2019* IN $	INDIANS 9/10/19 PROPOSED LEASE** IN $	T-MOBILE SEATTLE 2019-2044*** IN $
Team	Rent	2,600,000	0	1,500,000
	Routine Maintenance	1,200,000	1,700,000	10,000,000
	Operations	unknown	unknown	
	Capital Repairs	2,200,000	0	10,000,000
	Improvements	1,700,000	4,000,000	6,400,000
	Naming Rights****	(3,600,000)	TBD	(3,500,000)
Public Sector	Capital Repairs	1,360,000	5,160,000	10,650,000
	Improvements	0	11,500,000	
	Gateway Op Expense	0	2,700,000	N/A
TOTAL ANNUAL PUBLIC SECTOR $		1,360,000	19,360,000	10,650,000

NOTES *The annual amounts for the team's Routine Maintenance, Capital Repairs, and Improvements are based on the respective Indians' Power Point totals ($32 million, $57 million, $44 million) divided by the 26 expired lease years. The annual amounts for Public Sector Capital Repairs and Improvements are based on the respective Indians' Power Point totals ($38 million, 0 dollars) divided by the 26 expired lease years.

**The annual amount for Public Sector Capital Repairs is derived by dividing the $93,000,000 cumulative total for year 2037 of the Gateway Facility Condition Assessment (derived by deducting double counting with Indians' planned Improvements) by an assumed eighteen years of an extended lease. All other entries are derived from the Indians' Power Point and a subsequent Indians Power Point detailing $289 million of planned Improvements.

***The $10 million annual amounts for combined Routine Maintenance/Operations and for Capital Repairs are derived from respective $250 million totals—divided by 25 lease years—referenced in Zach Spedden, "County Gives Final Approval to Safeco Field Funding," ballparkdigest.com, September 18, 2018. The $6.4 million annual amount for Improvements is derived from a $160 million total—divided by 25 lease years—referenced in the Spedden article. The $10.65 million annual Public Sector contribution for Capital Repairs and Improvements is drawn from four sources: 1) an annual $5.4 million from a lodging tax (see Mike Rosenberg, "King County Council approves $135 million in taxpayer funds for Mariners ballpark," THE SEATTLE TIMES, September 5, 2018), 2) an annual $4.5 million from an admissions tax, 3) an annual $500,000 from a parking tax, and 4) an annual $250,000 from the Mariners rent payment (see Kevin Schofield, "Safeco Field and the lodging tax," https://scinsight. com/2018/07/31/safeco-field-and-the-lodging-tax/).

****Progressive Field's annual $3.6 million naming rights is derived from "Progressive Buys Naming Rights to Cleveland Indians Ballpark," INSURANCE JOURNAL, January 11, 2008. T-Mobile Field's annual $3.5 million naming rights is derived from Ryan Divish, "Goodbye Safeco Field: The Mariners Stadium is now called T-Mobile Park, THE SEATTLE TIMES, December 19, 2018.

INDIANS ANNUAL ATTENDANCE				INDIANS ANNUAL TV MARKET			
	Rank	Average	Total	Rank	Rating	Mkt Size	Size Rank
2016	28	19,650	1,591,667	5	7.12	128,000	5
2017	22	25,285	2,048,138	1	9.22	128,000	5
2018	21	24,083	1,926,701	3	6.85	99,000	8
2019	22	21,676	1,517,332	1	7.18	99,000	8

NOTES: Attendance data is from espn.com. TV data is from annual reports issued in October of each year by FORBES (see, e.g., Maury Brown, "2018 MLB Regional TV Ratings in Prime Time Shows Continued Strong Popularity," https://www.forbes.com/ sites/maurybrown/2018/10/04/18-mlb-regional-tv-ratings-in=primetime-shows-contin ued-strong-popularity#4b84).

As stated in the notes to the first table, we assumed that the Indians' lease would be extended to year 2037 (one year prior to incursion of over $35 million of projected facility expenses in year 2038).

The Public Sector Formulates Its $10.5 Million Initial Offer

On October 21, Chief Dumas and I met with Mayor Jackson to review the Indians' ask and present a proposed public sector response with the following components:

PUBLIC SECTOR SOURCE	ANNUAL REVENUE IN $ 2020-2037	PRESENT VALUE OF REVENUES IN $ @5% DISCOUNT RATE
Extended Sin Tax*	2,300,000	26,886,050
Sports Facility Reserve Fund*	3,500,000	36,328,803
County 1% bed tax increase	3,000,000	35,068,761
City sale of E Gateway Garage	1,666,666	25,000,000
TOTAL	10,466,666	123,283,614

*Expires in 2034, so present values in last column are adjusted accordingly.

After listening to the proposed public sources, Mayor Jackson nodded and then observed: "We need a backup source: something to add to what we initially put on the table." I responded that the State of Ohio—via JobsOhio, State Capital Budget, or some other source —was worth considering, and he authorized me to contact JobsOhio chairperson Bob Smith.

I contacted Smith's office, which arranged a 7:45 AM time for me to call him on October 24 (during a break in his Dallas conference). After listening to my summary of the Mayor Jackson meeting, Smith put me in touch with Dana Saucier of JobsOhio. Later that morning, Mr. Saucier and I did talk, and he agreed to meet me in Cleveland at a future date, I then sent him my contact info along with a preliminary summary of Cleveland State University's economic impact study.

On November 8, 2019—nearly two months after the Indians' Power-Point presentation of their ask— Znidarsic sent me an email reading: "Some time has passed and I thought it might be appropriate for you and I to get together for lunch and get caught up a bit..." We arranged lunch at Johnny Mango's on Monday, November 11. After a brief discussion of off-season baseball, I gave him a timeline of our activities since the Indians' PowerPoint meeting. I then reviewed each meeting, omitting the particulars of our potential financial responses.

As we were leaving, he added that Paul Dolan had asked him whether "he had done anything wrong" to cause the two-month delay in our response to the Indians' ask. I replied "No." He speculated that the Sherwin Williams headquarters issue might have been a distraction.

A month later—on December 9, 2019—we were able to gather City and County leadership together in Mayor Jackson's Red Room. The City was represented by Mayor Jackson and his Chief of Staff Sharon Dumas; the County by County Executive Budish, his Chief of Staff Bill Mason, Matt Carroll, and financial advisor Bob Franz; and Gateway by me and attorney Dennis Wilcox.

Several hours prior to the Red Room meeting, Chief Dumas and I updated Mayor Jackson on recent developments: I covered my negligible progress with the State's JobsOhio staff, and Chief Dumas noted that—although the City's $4 million annual parking bond debt service would cease in 2022—those same monies would be needed from year 2023 forward to fund payments to the Sports Facility Fund that would be one of our contributors to the Indians' lease extension requests.

In the Red Room meeting, Mayor Jackson asked me to walk through the numbers on my one-page table. Taking 20 minutes to do so, I reviewed the elements of the Indians' $20 million annual ask, the public sector's responsive $10.5 million annual offer, and the City of Seattle's comparable $10.6 million annual contribution toward a 25-year lease extension by the Seattle Mariners.

Our $10.5 million proposed annual offer had four components: $2.3 million from the County's 2014-2034 sin tax extension, $3 million from the County's 2019 bed tax increase, $3.5 million from City contributions to the Sports Facility Fund, and $1.67 million from an annuity formed from the City's $25 million proceeds from a presumed 2022 sale to the teams of the 2200-space Gateway East Parking Garage. Franz reminded us that any Sports Facility Fund payments to the Indians were dependent upon an agreement between the team and the County.

County Executive Budish made an interesting observation: if we were to divide the $70 million public sector contribution toward the Arena deal by the seven years of lease extension we earned thereby, it worked out to a similar $10 million annual public contribution. I added that—although the Indians sought a 20-year lease extension —my chart showed only an extension through year 2037: Wilcox then explained that the years 2038 and 2039 of the capital repairs facility plan were very heavy on major expenditures.

Budish stated that he would need to discuss the $3 million annual bed tax contribution with County Council leadership. Then he asked about the possibility of State assistance, and I relayed my JobsOhio conversations. Summarizing, we speculated on how the Indians would respond to our $10.5 million annual offer after they had requested a nearly $20 million annual amount. Mayor Jackson predicted that "if they come back seeking 12 or 13, we should be able to make a deal."

So, armed with the direction of the elected officials, we proceeded to meet with the six Indians' officials on Friday, December 13. I took the first 20 minutes to review my one-page summary which compared the Indians' $20 million annual ask, our proposed $10.5 million response, and Seattle's $10.65 million lease extension deal with the Mariners. The initial response from the Indians was neither positive nor negative.

They asked questions regarding our capital repairs estimates, our proposal for the extension to go only to 2037, and our retention of annual team rent payments. We knew the last item would be a bone down the Indians' throats, and we explained how politically awkward it would be for the public sector to undertake payment of Gateway's annual operating expenses. We agreed to meet on Thursday, December 19, at which time the Indians would give their thoughts on our proposal.

A Step Backward

On Thursday, December 19, we reconvened with the Indians at the offices of Gateway attorney Dennis Wilcox. Znidarsic commenced the meeting as we expected, noting that the Indians had studied our numbers from the last meeting and would give a response. Indians' Chief Information Officer Neil Weiss then presented a chart that tracked annual dollar amounts from each of our public contributions over our proposed lease extension through year 2037.

But the handout had no entry for the parking garage sales proceeds and I interrupted Weiss's presentation to ask about this omission. He replied that those proceeds were "private money." Wilcox and I quickly disagreed, explaining that the City was legally required to obtain a fair market price for the garage and that we were proposing to allocate the entirety of those proceeds toward Indians' capital repair and improvement projects.

Znidarsic asked if the same would hold true if we sold the garage to another entity. When we replied "yes," Weiss nodded and offered to correct his sheet to add garage proceeds. Carroll added a further clarification that our proposal was a $10.5 million annual contribution, and that if our indicated sources didn't yet total to that amount, we would backfill to achieve the $10.5 million.

So far, so good. But the meeting really turned sour when Brian Barren began presenting his own one-page summary. It didn't take long for us to grasp the essence of Barren's approach: it was an item-by-item summary of how our proposal fell short of the Indians' original $20 million per year ask. And the notations on each item—"unsatisfactory" "insufficient" and the like—struck us as offensive and insulting given the lengths our public sector leaders had gone to in essentially matching Seattle's deal with the Mariners.

I tossed Brian's one pager back to the Indians' side of the table and asked the Indians' group this question: "Are you simply going through the motions with us to lay the groundwork for the MLB Commissioner's approval of a relocation of your team to someplace like Montreal or Nashville? I've been through that process with the Browns in the 90s and don't care to go through it again." Chief Dumas added some observations regarding the City's political process, and Chief Mason urged the Indians to "tell us what you really need, because if you think we're going to give you $20 million a year that's just not going to happen."

No one from the Indians directly responded to these remarks. Instead, they discussed a January vetting process where Indians' capital repairs experts would meet with Gateway capital repair experts to get a better handle on the numbers for minor and major capital repairs projected over the next 20 years. We agreed to this process, noting that it was the public sector's intent to cover both kinds of repairs throughout the lease extension.

The Indians' Counter Offer

On January 17, 2020, the negotiating teams—six Indians officials and six public representatives—reconvened to hear the team's counter-offer to our proposal. But first, Znidarsic took a few minutes to summarize, to date, the areas of agreement and disagreement; then he asked Weiss to review the outcome of a recent staff-to-staff meeting that sought to better catalogue future minor and major capital repairs. Eventually, all agreed to get staff together in the future and dive into the numbers. That freed up Znidarsic to lay out the four elements of the team's latest negotiating stance:

- A lease extension until only 2037 could work, as long as everyone understood that the assumed $15 million annual funding for ballpark improvements would only yield $270 million by the end of the term (as opposed to the Indians' desired $300 million);
- The Indians would up their annual ballpark improvement contribution by $500,000—from $4 million to $4.5 million —and would reduce their requested public contribution by $2.9 million (from $11.4 million to $8.5 million);
- The Indians would annually contribute $1.7 million toward the Gateway operating budget; and
- The public would pay all (minor and major) capital repairs and there would be a rolling three-year re-assessment of capital repair needs.

Doing quick math (and assuming for then no increase in the public's projected $5.16 million capital repair contribution, which we knew the Indians weren't close to accepting), I translated the Indians' stance into a $14.6 million annual public ask and asked Znidarsic whether the Indians were prepared to partner with us in seeking State assistance. He replied "Absolutely." And could that include the assistance of Paul Dolan's brother, State Senator Matt Dolan? The reply: "Yes, but within reason" (Senator Dolan led the Senate's capital committee, and would steer clear of a conflict of interest). After speculating on how much the State might come up with, we adjourned to a lunch served up by our meeting hosts.

Routine Maintenance Versus Minor Capital Repairs

Late in the afternoon after our morning meeting, Matt Carroll—who had to leave before the meeting concluded—called me seeking the outcome of the final twenty minutes. After my recap, I asked him when he thought we could get the elected officials together to review the Indians' counter-proposal. His reply was insightful: "I think we first need to get a better handle on the capital repair numbers, and on the distinction between routine maintenance (which would remain the Indians' responsibility) and minor capital repairs (which we were now proposing to assume)."

He was right. If the Indians interpreted capital repairs broadly, and routine maintenance narrowly, the result would be to add an annual $2 million or more to the public sector obligations. We were already facing *at least* a $4 million gap between the public sector offer ($10.5 million a year) and the Indians' counter offer that I had characterized as a $14.6 million annual ask. Adding another $2 million a year from a more expansive interpretation of capital repairs would grow the gap to *$6 million a year*.

Carroll's recommendation also triggered my recollection of a related key point: Znidarsic had wanted to meet with Wilcox to discuss "lease language." All things considered, I agreed with Carroll that it was best to await the outcome of the Znidarsic/Wilcox discussion—and another staff-to-staff review of the Gateway Facility Condition Assessment numbers—prior to scheduling a meeting with the elected officials.

On January 28, Wilcox met with Znidarsic to discuss the lease. Sure enough, Znidarsic submitted a long list of proposed revisions, some of which clarified previous language but most of which expanded the scope of "Minor Capital Repairs" while reducing the scope of "Routine Maintenance." Wilcox called me the next day to summarize the meeting, and I concurred with his assessment of the likely negative response of the elected officials.

Meanwhile, Todd Greathouse and Gateway consultant Dave Faller of Osborn Engineering were studying the Gateway Facilities Condition Assessment to identify minor capital needs that may have been excluded from the original plan. They found cumulative capital needs from 2020 through 2037 of $103.7 million, or $5.76 million a year. After they shared their findings with me, Carroll and Wilcox, I asked them to forward their work product to Indians' staff.

The Indians were not happy with the results, believing that our staff had improperly labelled $1.4 million worth of annual capital repairs as "routine maintenance." Znidarsic asked for a meeting, and we met at Wilcox's office on February 13. Znidarsic and Weiss argued that items such as structural steel painting and concrete repairs—amongst many other items—met the lease definition of capital repairs.

Wilcox and I followed up with a February 19 meeting with Greathouse and Faller, and agreed to reclassify about $400,000 worth of items from "Routine Maintenance" to "Minor Capital

Repairs." That outcome translated to a new eighteen-year total of $110 million of capital repairs, or about $6.1 million a year.

Media Inquiries

As far back as December, 2019, TV 3 reporter Mark Naymik had contacted the Indians' Alex King seeking to confirm that "the Indians had made a $15 million annual public ask." The Indians had declined comment and Naymik did not pursue his inquiry at the time. Two months later, at the conclusion of the February 19 Gateway board meeting, Naymik asked me to comment on whether there was a request for the Indians in the pending State of Ohio biennial capital budget. I replied that I was unaware of such a request. But on February 26, Naymik extracted the following quote from Mark Englehart of JobsOhio:

> While this is not a project that aligns with JobsOhio's financial assistance or strategy, we have had limited contact with representatives of Gateway and Cuyahoga County to advise on other possible funding solutions.

Having sought comment from the Indians and County, Naymik was directed to me and called me in North Carolina. After discussing my response with County, City and Indians officials, I called Naymik and confirmed that I had contacted JobsOhio seeking State assistance—not unprecedented in stadium funding matters—but to date we were still in discussions with no conclusions. I confirmed that we were in discussions with the Indians, but unable to comment on the substance of those talks. Naymik had some detailed questions regarding the operation of the sin tax, and I did answer those inquiries.

Our State of Ohio Request

Late in the afternoon of February 26, JobsOhio's Dana Saucier coordinated a conference call including himself, Assistant Director of Development Matt Peters, County Executive Armond Budish, County Chief of Staff Bill Mason, County Deputy Chief of Staff Matt Carroll, and me. Saucier asked me to summarize the current state of negotiations with the Indians, and I described the $5.5 million gap between the Indians' estimated public annual ask of $16 million (allowing for their view of capital improvements) and the public response of $10.5 million.

Peters offered that he had discussed our call with his director and that they had identified two recent State investments in sports facilities: a $25 million loan for Cincinnati's soccer stadium, and a pending decision on Columbus' soccer stadium in which the State participation would be "equitable" to the Cincinnati deal. Also, back in 2011, the State had done an $11 million loan (part of which was forgivable) towards Columbus/ Nationwide Arena. Clearly surprised by the magnitude of our request, Peters warned us that grant assistance would be "a real reach," particularly with State legislators.

Then, in early May, Mayor Jackson coordinated a May 8 conference call with Bob Smith and County Executive Budish. Smith admitted that there was no State appetite for sports team financing. But he promised to take another run at it, which he hoped to do within a week. The County Executive acknowledged that, to Dolan's credit, he'd not threatened to move the team (though I inserted that the threat of a team sale was a possibility).

Smith was good to his word: he called each of us on the evening of Monday, May 11, with a response. JobsOhio would not be able to help on the Indians. Nor could the Governor's office. I responded that I hoped the State officials realized the impact of their decision if Cleveland loses its team (especially since other states have helped in these situations).

The Coronavirus Stoppage

By the beginning of March, 2020, the spread of coronavirus cases worldwide had begun supplanting business and social interactions. Ohio Governor Mike DeWine and his public health expert Dr. Amy Acton became national leaders in responding to the emerging crisis. They boldly canceled the Arnold Sports Festival USA (slated to host 22,000 athletes from 80 nations) that had been scheduled March 5-8 at the Columbus Convention Center. They banned live spectators at NCAA basketball tournaments sites in Ohio (eventually the NCAA's canceled the entire tournament). Then Dr. Acton issued an order postponing Ohio's scheduled March 17 Primary.

Major League Baseball responded in mid-March by suspending all baseball operations, including the remainder of spring training and the start of the 2020 regular season. As virus infections continued to accelerate in late March and early April, the league began reviewing numerous options that included playing regular season games at Arizona and Florida spring training locations (eventually, MLB and its players association would agree on a shortened 60-game 2020 schedule, including an expanded playoff pool).

The Indians' Emergency Request

Meanwhile, as with other leisure and hospitality businesses, the Indians were particularly hard-hit by the global pandemic. Citing the impacts to the team in a March 26 email, Znidarsic proposed that the County withdraw $3 million from its Sports Facility Reserve ("SFR") to reimburse the team for its previous advances for Major Capital Repairs.

Znidarsic's proposal gave me several concerns. As one of the architects of the SFR during the Q deal, I knew that it was intended to be a partial funding stream to support a ballpark lease extension, and at present we weren't close to an extension. I also knew that the bond indenture required "an agreement" prior to the release of funds. Such an agreement would require authorizing legislation that would be politically difficult to procure from the County Council without some assurance that we were at least getting close to agreement on a lease extension.

Accordingly, my response email suggested that we first try to close the gap in our respective lease extension proposals and that the key to that would be the Indians' joining us in our request for State assistance. That suggestion went over like a wet balloon: Znidarsic viewed our request for State assistance as a remote delaying tactic, opined that the City and County were capable of closing the gap with their own resources, and appeared to take offense to my reluctance to endorse immediate SFR relief for the team under this state of emergency. We were at stalemate, although I did offer to talk the issues through at any time.

After more than a week passed, Znidarsic emailed me on Good Friday—April 10—that he had discussed our email dialogues with

Paul Dolan and that Paul Dolan "would like to reach out to Armond Budish to explain personally why he feels it is appropriate for the County to consider releasing Sports Facility Reserve funds now." Further, as attachments to his email, he included a County economic impact report, a City economic impact report, and a one-page fiscal impact report that demonstrated the County and City achieved annual total direct tax payments[10] of $12.44 million deriving from the Indians' operations.

On May 4, 2020, we arranged a conference call amongst Mayor Jackson, County Executive Budish, and their respective staffs. This was the first time we'd all talked since the onset of the coronavirus. The County Executive commenced by summarizing his recent call with Paul Dolan. The Indians owner had described the team's dire financial position due to the virus and the challenge of repaying departed minority investor John Sherman's approximate 25% share of the franchise's ownership (Sherman had left to purchase the Kansas City Royals). Dolan had then asked the County to pay the $3+ million owed by Gateway.

I then reminded everyone of the big gap on the larger deal: a difference of $5.5 million between our $10.5 million December 2019 proposal and the Indians' $16 million counter offer. Mayor Jackson responded that "even with the $10.5 million we don't have the revenue to pay for that now." Chief Dumas added that the virus shutdown has adversely impacted the sin tax, the bed tax, and the funding sources for the Sports Facility Reserve.

Several days later, Znidarsic called Wilcox to advise that the Indians had decided to pursue a $100 million credit facility from PNC Bank. As partial security for the credit facility, the bank would require the Indians and Gateway to execute a leasehold mortgage on the ballpark parcel. By late May Wilcox had received draft documents from the bank's attorneys.

We Propose to Cap Public Capital Repair Obligations

Znidarsic was working on a proposal that he believed would save money on future capital repair projects, and on May 13, 2020, he emailed me a proposed "rolling review concept" which included the following elements:

- Gateway's engineering consultant—Osborn—would be replaced by "an engineering firm selected through a competitive bid process by (the Indians) subject to the review and approval of Gateway;"
- The consultant would annually prepare a facility assessment report that would guide capital repair projects in the upcoming budget year and provide updated projections of projects required in the next two years;
- Guided by the report, the Indians would perform all capital repair work;
- The consultant would resolve all disputes between Gateway and the Indians as to whether a work item constituted Routine Maintenance or a Capital Repair.
- Gateway and the Indians would engage an escrow agent to establish a capital repairs fund into which the County, City and Gateway would deposit funds necessary to fund capital repairs in the current budget year and the next two Gateway operating years beyond the current year.

After forwarding Znidarsic's terms to Wilcox and discussing them over the next several days, we agreed that Wilcox would send Znidarsic a reply—accomplished on May 19— encompassing the following responses:

- The engineering consultant would be selected by Gateway and the Indians through a RFP&Q process which included as the principal selection criteria someone/firm with significant institutional knowledge of the Ballpark;
- The consultant would work with both Gateway and the Indians in the preparation of facility assessment reports;
- The Indians would only perform work on capital repair items costing less than $250,000;
- The amount provided annually by Gateway for capital repairs would be limited to a maximum of $6 million annually; and
- We would not agree to the consultant arbitrating interpretation differences.

The following day Znidarsic sent a tart email reply that stated "... there is an issue posed here that is far greater than the concept of introducing a three-year review.... that the Gateway Capital Repairs responsibility be limited to no more than $6 million on an annual basis." The tone of the email was such that I sought an immediate phone conversation, and that was achieved later that day.

Znidarsic began the call with a strong statement: "Your sudden introduction of a <u>cap</u> on the public's capital repair responsibility is an act of bad faith, and the team will never accept it." He was basically accusing us of throwing a dead cat into (the deal's) punchbowl.

He wasn't necessarily out of line with his assertion. We'd been negotiating for over eight months and Wilcox's May 19, 2020, letter was the first time we'd put this notion in writing. One of the unwritten rules of negotiations is that you don't surprise your adversary with controversial new deal terms late in the game.

Since this would end up being one of the most troublesome issues in a long negotiation—and will likely be a recurring topic in lease discussions in other cities—some context is needed.

Our existing lease held Gateway responsible for "Major Capital Repairs" and placed no upper limit on our responsibility. Nor did our initial $10.5 million annual offer to the team in our early days of negotiations. But as we kept climbing in our annual dollar offers— while the team refused to budge from its $20+ million annual demand—we sought some means of limiting the public's future exposure. And the team's recent proposal for an annual "rolling capital review" reinforced our concerns that we were shooting at a constantly moving target. Accordingly, we chose an annual capital repair cap—of $6 million—that was grounded in the projections in Gateway's Facility Condition Assessment.

Moreover, we knew that public capital repair obligations *were* capped in recent baseball lease extensions in Seattle, Denver and Houston. As it became apparent that the Indians were asking for much higher public dollar commitments than in these other cities, we sought to offset our higher costs with an upper limit on our exposure.

Given all that was at stake for both parties on this issue, I suggested a follow-up three-way call with Znidarsic, Wilcox and me. That call took place on May 22. Wilcox began by explaining that the main point of his email was to move toward deal closure. A shared under-standing of the magnitude of long-term capital repairs was essential, and Wilcox referenced three occasions—in January, February, and in May—when we had sought staff-to-staff work sessions on this topic.

He added that his email "wasn't intended to send you off the rails." Znidarsic replied "Well, there is a problem. Let's see what we can do. I get a sense that we've been talking to each other but not listening to each other. I take some responsibility there...we assumed you had capital repair responsibility"

Znidarsic recalled that the Indians' original 20-year lease proposal contemplated a $510 million public contribution. But he did acknowledge that shrinking the lease term to 18 years would reduce the capital repairs number down from $212 million to $148 million, and he added that a 15-year lease term might be worth considering. Wilcox and I concurred, and we ended the call by asking Znidarsic to respond to Wilcox's February email on capital repair estimates.

We Ask for More Time to Respond to the Indians' Counter Offer

Several days after our phone call, Znidarsic sent an official request that the public sector respond to the Indians' counter offer by June 12. Before arranging a Mayor Jackson/County Executive Budish conference call, I knew we would need to update our tax estimates to account for the coronavirus impacts. To this end, Carroll, Franz and I participated on a call which resulted in Franz' submission of updated projections on the morning of Monday, June 8. Essentially, to achieve an annual public contribution of $10.5 million for a 15-year lease term from 2021 through 2035, we would need to fill a gap of about $8 million of one-time monies.

On June 12, Wilcox sent a letter which sought three months to respond (considering the risk of the State trimming local monies, together with other pandemic-related impacts). Several days later Znidarsic advised us that the Indians' negotiating team was meeting to review our letter, and asked whether the letter had been cleared by the elected officials. We confirmed that we had read it to them several times.

On July 28, Znidarsic finally responded to our June 12 letter via an 8-page email to Wilcox. He recapped the Indians' original September, 2019, session with us: their ask translated to an annual public ask of $25.5 million (an amount I knew to be comparable to Arlington's contribution to that city's new $1.2 billion ballpark and greater than Cobb County, Georgia's payments for the Atlanta Braves' two-year old ballpark). He cited the team's significant concessions in its January, 2020, counter-offer. Finally, he asserted without proof that the Cavaliers' Q deal was better than our offer. We knew we had to refute these assertions and conclusions, but deferred response until we could communicate an enhanced public offer.

A Bad Moon Rising[11]

By now we knew we were in for stormy weather. The historically cooperative Indians' management—most recently evidenced by the team's $44 million private financing of the 2015-2016 Progressive Field enhancements—had turned blunt and aggressive. We were learning that there is nothing harder than a baseball lease negotiation with a small-market franchise. That's because these franchises face unique national and local revenue challenges.

Nationally, baseball TV revenues are skewed toward large market teams. MLB's 162-game schedule means that weekly or bi-weekly national telecasts (in which revenues are equally shared by the 30 franchises) comprise a small percentage of total MLB TV revenues.

The vast majority of TV revenues are captured by powerful regional sports networks serving the coastal large-market teams.

By contrast, NFL owners in the 1960s agreed to divide all TV revenues equally amongst the franchises. Structurally, this was doable with games being scheduled once a week. Over time, the NBA made similar arrangements. Hence small-market franchises in these leagues (e.g., Green Bay in the NFL; Oklahoma City in the NBA) suffer no TV revenue disparities.

Second, the NFL and NBA have salary caps; MLB does not. Though MLB does penalize its highest-spending franchises, its players' union has limited the thresholds and magnitudes of those penalties (believing that the expensive free-agent contracts awarded by the high-dollar spenders will "lift all boats" for the rank-and-file players).

Third, the higher populations in the big-market cities generally—with some exceptions—lead to higher attendance and concession revenues there (and, given MLB TV revenue disparities, those attendance and concession dollars are more important to MLB teams than for their NFL and NBA counterparts). Over time, the small market MLB franchises did try to reduce these three disparities via the collective bargaining process—most notably during the 1994/1995 lockout—with little to show for their efforts.

Turning to local and timing-related club revenue issues, the pandemic cast a huge shadow and, as noted below, would cost the team $77 million by the end of 2020. And it quickly became apparent that the team officials believed that they had made a bad deal with Gateway in 2004, and they were determined to recover lost ground.

Finally, a self-fulfilling prophecy played out in the 2020-2021 baseball seasons. The team trimmed payroll in both seasons, but that very act dampened fan interest and attendance and—ultimately—weakened the team's on-field performance which further depressed attendance, concession sales, and other game-day revenues.

These factors considered, the team's hardline negotiating stance was more understandable and was a harbinger for what lay ahead for us in Cleveland as well as our counterparts in Oakland, Tampa, Baltimore and other MLB towns who would soon face their own lease extension challenges.

There was, and is, one compensating factor: unlike the NFL and NBA, the MLB retains its antitrust immunity and has historically been more resistant than the other leagues to "franchise free agency." There were thirteen franchise relocations in MLB's history, but only two in the last 50 years: the Washington Senators' 1972 move to Arlington, Texas and the Montreal Expo's 2005 move to Washington, D.C. .

What did all this mean if the Indians presented a relocation case before MLB Commissioner Rob Manfred? They would cite weak attendance—a decade of ranking in the bottom third of MLB clubs, while fielding clubs that won the seventh most games (855) amongst MLB franchises in the 2010s decade—, the metro area's decline in population and Fortune 500 companies, and the negative vibe from the "Dolans are cheap" segment of the fan base. They would certainly cite the more team-friendly leases enjoyed by many of their comparable middle market franchises.

And our potential responses? First, despite the metro area's decline, it was still large enough—as shown by comparison charts earlier in this chapter—to stand its ground against all likely Sunbelt relocation candidates. Second, though Cleveland's baseball fan base is less trusting than that of the football Browns, it has responded to teams such as the 1948 World Series champions and the 455-straight-sellout teams of the 90s (and though the Browns were absent for three years of that streak, that leaves almost another three years when the Browns *were* in town). As for the ballpark, we had Stadium Journey's #1 ranking from September 2019.

As for our proposed lease terms, our $10.5 million annual public offer matched Seattle's contribution deemed sufficient by the Mariners. Moreover, the Indians had a TV gold mine they could tap when their existing deal expired: first amongst the 30 MLB franchises in 2019 Nielsen ratings, within MLB's *eighth* largest TV market. And the team ranked 5th, 1st, and 3rd in ratings in the prior three years.

Probing further, I prepared a lease comparison between Cleveland and the other 29 MLB franchises. Drawing heavily from lease summaries prepared by the Marquette University School of Law, I prepared a chart based on leases for 19 of the MLB franchises. As to the remaining 11 teams, I lacked information for four (New York Yankees, New York Mets, Toronto Blue Jays and Texas Rangers), excluded two that are under MLB relocation watch (Oakland A's and Tampa Bay Rays), and excluded five teams that own their own stadia (Los Angeles Dodgers, Los Angeles Angels, San Francisco Giants, Chicago Cubs, and Boston Red Sox).

Ballpark Lease Comparisons[12]

BALLPARK LEASE COMPARISONS[207] (WITH RECENT EXTENSIONS SHADED)

TEAM	LAST YEAR	ANNUAL RENT $	ROUTINE MAINT.	PUBLIC PAYS	ANNUAL PUBLIC $ FOR CAPITAL REPAIRS/IMPROVE	
Kansas City	2031	2,818,267[1]	Public pays for cleaning & maintain	See last column	50% Truman debt serv: 50% State of Missouri: 50% Jackson County: 50% Kansas City: REFI interest savings (Team rent offset) TOTAL	15,000.000 1,500,000 1,750,000 1,000,000 4,000,000 4,067,280 19,183,780
Seattle	2043	1,500,000	Team	Tax proceeds	From rent: Parking tax : Admissions tax: Bed tax: TOTAL	250,000 500,000 4,500,000 5,400,000 10,650,000
Cleveland	2035	2,700,000	Team	Capital Repairs	County bed tax: Sports facility reserve: Sin tax: Garage annuity: TOTAL	3,000,000 3,500,000 2,300,000 2,070,000 10,460,000
Cincinnati	2037	1	Team, less insurance	Capital Repairs	Annual deposit:	1,000,000
San Diego	2030	500,000	Team	Capital Repairs	Team submits annual amount for City's annual budget	
Milwaukee	2031	1,200,000	District pays roof, Team rest	Major Capital Repairs	Annual deposit:	2,500,000
Baltimore	2022	% Rent	Public (less clean/field)	Capital Fund	Annual deposit:	600,000
Houston	2050	3,400,000	Team	Fixed annual amount	Annual deposit:	2,500,000
Chicago	2029	2,000,000	Team	Major Capital Repairs	Authority must also pay for those items "in use in at least 75% of MLB stadia"	
Minnesota	2037	900,000	Team	CapEx Reserve Fund	From rent: Additional deposit: TOTAL	900,000 1,100,000 2,000,000
Washington	2038	5,500,000	Team	Fund	Annual deposit:	1,500,000
Pittsburgh	2030	100,000 +	Team	Fund	Annual deposit:	650,000
Miami	2047	2,300,000	Team	Fund		
Atlanta	2046	6,100,000	Team	50/50	Annual deposits by each	
Colorado	2047	2,500,000	Team	None	Team pays	
Detroit	2035	1	Team	Fund	Annual deposit:	250,000
Arizona	2023	1,000,000+	Team	Fund		
Philadelph	2031	30	Team	None	Team pays	
St. Louis	2041	% Rent	Team	None	Team pays	

---

[1] 2017 Royals revenues pledged to bond debt service included the lease payment of $2,818,267 plus parking fees of $480,793 plus ticket fees of $768,220 for total pledged Royals-related revenues of $4,067,280. See page 87 of 2018 Jackson County Comprehensive Annual Financial Statement.

A Sin Tax Increase Proposal

Meanwhile, County Executive Budish and Mayor Jackson were not sitting on their hands. They were discussing a concept that Budish had asked his financial advisor Bob Franz to work up: this was an increase in sin tax rates (which had remained static since the original 1990 countywide vote). Franz noted that the Consumer Price Index has increased 100% since 1990. If we applied the same increase to the sin tax, the additional annual yield would approach $14 million. In consumer terms, the 100% increase would add 3 cents to the cost of a beer and 1 cent to the cost of a glass of wine. In any sin tax increase scenario, there would be two required steps: passage by the Ohio legislature, and passage by County voters.

They also discussed a dual-purpose initiative, in which the new proceeds would be equally split between the Indians and performing arts groups. Since 2007, County arts groups had received annual grants from a cigarette tax. County voters approved a ten-year extension of the tax in 2015, but annual awards dipped below $12 million in 2020 and arts leaders sought a supplemental funding source.

I updated Mayor Jackson and Council President Kelley, and they each had concerns. So, I called the County Executive to relay those concerns and he said he would be conversing with County Council President Dan Brady. On Monday, August 24, the County Executive called me to advise that Brady had reacted similarly to City Hall and accordingly the sin tax scenario had run out of steam.

Nine Tense Months

The nine months of negotiations between August, 2020 and May, 2021 were contentious and challenged: contentious because of the wide gulf between the public sector's $10.5 million annual offer and the team's desired $20+ million; and challenging because the enduring global pandemic virtually precluded face-to-face meetings (the phone and Zoom sessions were not ideally suited for delicate negotiations).

The debates during this time period centered on four major topics:

1. *Ballpark Improvements.* The team eventually settled on a sum of $202.5 million for its Ballpark improvements, of which the team's share would be $67.5 million. However, that concept would require the County to issue bonds to fund the $135 million balance. After accounting for $2 million in annual bond interest payments, the public sector would end up paying $11 million annually to retire these bonds;
2. *Capital Repairs.* The heated debate over capital repairs continued unabated. The two main issues were whether the public's annual obligation would be capped (in April, 2021, the public officials would agree to rescind our previously proposed cap), and the amount of the public's annual contribution (which we proposed at $8 million in April, 2021);
3. *The 2/3, 1/3 Formula.* In a November, 2020 meeting of the principals, Paul Dolan proposed that the parties adhere to a "2/3 public contribution, 1/3 private contribution model;
4. *The Garage.* As part of the public annual $8 million capital repair contribution, we were depending on Garage revenues

to annually generate $2 million. In our thinking, this could occur in one of two ways: either the team would buy the Garage for our $25 million asking price and the City would place the sales proceeds in an annuity, or the City would retain the Garage and send its annual net revenues therefrom to a capital repair fund.

Meanwhile, late July of 2020 had brought sports product to an entertainment-starved populace. Though the late-starting MLB season was trimmed to 60 games, the Indians made the most of it, earning a 21-14 record through the end of August. Their TV ratings stayed strong: through Labor Day, September 7, they again led all 30 MLB franchises in Nielsen ratings, this time with a 7.07 rating.[13] National ratings were also up, with the games attracting higher percentages of younger and women viewers than in prior years.[14] These new viewers joined Cleveland's nursing home and retirement home residents who welcomed sports viewing after a spring and early summer devoid of other forms of entertainment.

On August 24, 2020, I called Chief Dumas to preview with her a proposal I intended to make to Mayor Jackson the next day: this was to route another $2 million annually into our deal via tapping 40% of the Indians' admissions tax. Chief Dumas summarized the budgetary challenges to this approach: a 50% drop—from $40 million to $19 million—in 2020 city entertainment taxes, a 10% drop in city income taxes yielding an additional $40 million budgetary hit, and continuing challenges ahead in 2021. She also noted that the Indians had just requested a $2 million refund on their already deposited admission taxes.

I called Mayor Jackson the next morning to propose the 40% Indians admission tax contribution, and he was willing to consider it (subject to input from Chief Dumas and Council President Kelley).

I followed that call with an update to Kelley, who observed: "I'm interested in going down that path to see where it can take us. Conceptually, I'm comfortable. But it won't be easy getting 12 (City Council) votes."

A flurry of calls ensued that afternoon amongst the Mayor, Council President, and Chief Dumas. Late in the afternoon Chief Dumas called me with the outcome: the City would proceed with the 60/40 split of Indians admissions taxes, with the hope that the County could come up with an additional annual $2.5 million to make our total annual offer add up to $15 million.

Several days later I updated the County Executive, who balked at the $2.5 million amount and made two points: 1) up till then the City and County had maintained a 50/50 participation ratio, and diverting from that formula was problematic for him and his council; and 2) the *City* was the owner of the ballpark. Nevertheless, he promised to review our proposal with County Council President Dan Brady the following week. It went without saying that we were running out of time.

But on a sunny Thursday afternoon—September 3—the County Executive called me to advise that he had talked to County Council President Dan Brady and they were agreed to add $2 million annually from the County. The next day Wilcox and I updated Mayor Jackson in the midst of a tragic day for the City: Thursday evening an undercover police officer had perished in the line of duty at Storer Avenue and West 65th Street, and then another officer committed suicide at his residence.

The Mayor kept his phone appointment with us despite an impending 3 PM media briefing on the tragedies. He agreed with the County Executive that it was now time to update the Indians, and suggested that Wilcox and I do this by phone. After listening to a half dozen clarifications and corrections we wanted to make to the Znidarsic July letter prior to revealing our enhanced offer, the Mayor concurred with our points but urged us:

> "...not to dwell on them. Stress how much we want to get this deal done. And point out that our new proposal splits the $6 million gap equally: City $2 million more, County $2 million more, and team sacrificing $2 million."

We then briefed Chief Mason and Matt Carroll of the County and their financial advisor Bob Franz and they all concurred. We commenced as planned in our call to Znidarsic, quickly ticking off our corrections and clarifications to Joe's last letter. Then we laid out our new $4 million annual payments from the City and County, with a caveat on the still uncertain 2021 year. This new money, we noted, upped our offer to an annual—capped—total of $14.5 million. While thanking us for our response on the economics, he cautioned that our offer still fell short of the Q deal and that our capital repairs cap was still a nonstarter for the team.

Wilcox and I then set about compiling a four-page summary of our terms that answered the team's questions in the form of an overall narrative. We knew we would need to review our draft with the Mayor and County Executive, and were able to arrange a Thursday, September 24, conference call. The elected officials were generally satisfied after our first read and, after some fine tuning of a section dealing with possible bonding of our $14.5 million annual payments, were able to approve the form of the letter the following day.

Clevelanders woke up feeling good about the world on Monday, September 28, 2020. The splendid summer weather was extending through the first week of fall. Over the weekend, the Browns had defeated Washington to move above .500 for the first time since

2014. The Indians had rallied from a four-run deficit in their last game of the season to win 8-6 and capture the 4th playoff seed (and home park status in their first playoff series against the New York Yankees). The following evening the eyes of the nation would be focused on Cleveland, first for the 7 PM Yankees-Indians game, and then for the 9 PM Presidential Debate hosted by Cleveland Clinic and Case Western Reserve University. In the midst of these optimistic vibes, Dennis confidently emailed our written response to Znidarsic at 10:30 AM.

Coincidentally, our letter was sent the day after the Indians closed the financial books on the end of the truncated 60-game regular season. We knew from Znidarsic's prior emails that the team was incurring significant financial losses. And an article describing the Miami Marlins' financial losses included the following guesstimate:

> Like the San Diego Padres, Arizona Diamondbacks and Texas Rangers, the Marlins will probably lose in the $100 million range.[15]

Given that background, a recent statement by Indians' CFO Rich Dorffer to our Gateway staff seemed plausible: "that the team had lost $77 million this year." But it didn't seem that the team was recognizing a corresponding virus hit on local government finances. In assessing the outlook for a new Tampa stadium back in the spring, Florida political commentator Joe Henderson cryptically observed:

> It's starting to look like the Tampa Bay Rays badly overplayed their hand in their quest for a new stadium.... When the pandemic eases, the first priority for Florida communities is rebuilding a shattered workforce. Spending money on a baseball team would likely be met with pitchforks and flaming torches.[16]

Meanwhile, end of the season 2020 tallies confirmed that—despite their mid-September eight-game losing streak—the Indians again led all 30 MLB franchises with a 6.61 Nielsen rating.[17] But in their highly viewed wild-card playoff matchup with the New York Yankees, the Indians' vaunted pitching staff collapsed in the course of a two-game Yankees sweep, leaving the team's fans resigned to confronting offseason rumors of further payroll cuts and a potential trade of star shortstop Francisco Lindor.

On Friday, October 23, 2020, I sat in my Kia rental car in its space at Wilmington International Airport while participating in a conference call with Znidarsic and Wilcox. Znidarsic started the discussion by stating that the Indians and the public sector were "misaligned in our positions" and the positions were "hard to reconcile." He then enumerated four "concepts and elements" that they had elicited through several sessions that included owner Paul Dolan:

1. The public must pay for all capital repairs absent of any cap and without resort to other monies (e.g., Ballpark Improvement Fund contributions from the public);
2. The public's Ballpark Improvement Fund contributions must be fixed and must allow for acceleration of payments in the year 2028, allowing the team to tap into the whole anticipated $200 million by that date;
3. The Indians are declining to purchase the Gateway East Garage and Gateway Development Parcel, but want a Right of First Refusal on each; and
4. As a guiding principle, the Indians envision a 2/3 public, 1/3 private division of financial responsibility over time.

The elected officials compared notes and decided it was time for them to meet face-to-face with Indians' owner Paul Dolan. Wilcox and I promised to convey this simple message in our next call to Znidarsic. We did so, and arranged a three-party meeting—Jackson, Budish, and Dolan—for the morning of Tuesday, November 10.

I called Mayor Jackson afterwards and obtained a meeting summary. At the outset, Dolan had appeared sincere in wanting to make a deal. And he seemed appreciative when the elected officials told him they were OK with negotiating a lease that was attractive enough to allow Dolan to obtain a good sales price (so long as the lease committed the team to Cleveland).

The discussion then proceeded to three separate themes. First, and probably most significant, was the elected officials' desire for a "cap" on capital repairs. When Dolan objected to a cap, the Mayor replied that:

> "If you disagree with a cap, you have to come back with something that says what you're talking about...there has to be a process to determine what items you need...you can't just come up with something and expect us to pay for it. If there are things you need that you can identify, provide them to us."

Second, regarding the Indians' desired "2/3, 1/3" contribution formula, the elected officials told Dolan that (mainly due to the capital repair uncertainty), they couldn't determine how their $14.5 million proposal fared under the team's formula.

Third, the Mayor addressed the Gateway East Garage: "First you wanted it, now you don't." Dolan replied that the team lacked the bonding capacity to pay for the Garage and the development parcel. "Then what if we sell the Garage to the Cavaliers?" the Mayor rejoined. Dolan seemed willing to consider that possibility.

The County Executive asked: "What's the real story regarding the John Sherman minority share?" Dolan clarified that Sherman himself —and not the Indians—was responsible for selling that share. And, in describing City finances, Mayor Jackson admitted that federal CARE funds had provided some short-term relief; however, going forward, the City faced an annual $70 million budget gap.

Two weeks later—on November 24— Znidarsic emailed to Wilcox and me a "club counteroffer" which he stated "reflects Paul's view of areas of potential consensus with Mayor Jackson and County Executive Budish." The document began with a key—and in our view— overly broad assertion:

> Paul believed that there was a general consensus of understanding that a new Lease Agreement could be structured in its overall economic terms consistent with the idea of a 2/3 (City and County), 1/3 (Club) understanding between the parties.

It then applied this formula to yield an annual public investment of $16.47 million (comprised of $2.8 million minor capital repairs, $4.67 million major capital repairs, and $9 million Ballpark Improvement Fund). The Club's proposed investment was $8.6 million (comprised of $1.6 million routine maintenance, $2.5 million Gateway contribution, and $4.5 million Ballpark Improvement Fund). Wilcox and I concluded that the team was continuing to demand a public open-ended capital repairs commitment that could swell the public share above $16.47 million.

In late November, 2020, I worked up a funding table under which the public would increase its offer to a capped amount of $15.8 million annually: of that, $9 million would go toward ballpark improvements and $6.8 million would go toward capital repairs. The sources of the $15.8 million would be:

	FUNDING SOURCE	NATURE: FIXED OR	ANNUAL $
ENTITY	TYPE	VARIABLE	CONTRIBUTED
City	Sports Facility Reserve	Fixed	3,200,000
City	Parking Garage Annuity	Fixed	2,000,000
City	50% of Indians Admission Tax	Variable	2,650,000
County	Bed Tax Increment	Variable	3,000,000
County	Sin Tax	Variable	2,300,000
County	General Fund	Fixed	2,650,000
ANNUAL PUBLIC SECTOR CONTRIBUTION			15,800,000

After brief conversations with each elected official, Wilcox and I joined them in a December 10 phone conference in which we read to them talking points based on these numbers. They agreed to set up another meeting with Paul Dolan to offer this approach, but first they asked us to update City Council President Kevin Kelley and County Council President Dan Brady. We achieved those briefings within a week.

On Sunday, December 13, the New York Times reported that Indians' ownership had decided to rename the team. The next day the team issued a press release confirming the decision and citing team dialogues with Native American groups in the past six months. As name suggestions poured in to sports reporters, I cynically speculated to Wilcox that "Nashville Stars" might be one of the candidates.

So, on Monday, December 21, Mayor Jackson, County Executive Budish and Paul Dolan had their second face-to-face meeting at Cleveland City Hall. Later that morning, each elected official called me to advise that Mr. Dolan had listened to our latest offer, opined that the Browns and Cavaliers leases assigned all major capital repairs to the public sector, and asked for a written version of our $15.8 million offer. Wilcox's letter, emailed the next day, led off with the following paragraph:

Before citing the terms, I have a brief response to Mr. Dolan's assertion today that "the public is solely responsible for major

341

capital repairs in the Browns and Cavaliers deals." The Browns lease includes a schedule that sets annual caps on the City's capital repair obligations, and the Cavaliers lease still holds the team responsible for minor capital repairs. Moreover, neither the Browns nor the Cavaliers require the public to fund $9 million annually for stadium improvements.

Nearly a month went by until we got Znidarsic's letter on February 5, 2021. The team's main complaints were the capping of public capital repair contributions and the failure to provide for a significant bond issuance. Our $25 million Gateway East Garage selling price was a secondary concern: the team's consultant estimated the Garage value in a range of $16-20 million. The letter did offer a team contribution of one-third of (our estimated $2 million annual) bond interest costs, and did renew interest in purchasing the Gateway Development Parcel.

A week later we conferenced with the elected officials and County financial advisor Bob Franz. Wilcox and I recited the team's February 5 letter. Knowing that there was no appetite for increasing public funding, I recommended a twofold response:

1. Working with Franz on the math for a potential bond issue; and
2. Asking the State for $15 million to fund a capital repair reserve.

The elected officials concurred, with County Executive Budish noting that "when the State said 'no' a year ago, we weren't as far along in our negotiations."

On February 17, 2021, Franz arranged a Zoom meeting at which Wilcox, Carroll and I watched Franz walk through a spreadsheet for the team's desired tax-exempt $135 million bond issue funded from our existing sources (there'd be a separate $67.5 million taxable bond issue backed by the team's annual $4.5 million payment). But our existing sources fell short on annual contributions. Carroll solved this gap via a shortened lease term of 13 years that yielded $18 million a year.

Franz ran iterations of Carroll's model over the next several days, arriving at a version that funded a $122 million bond issue while leaving $100 million for capital repairs. Carroll checked with the County Executive and I called the Mayor: each of them agreed on the 13-year lease term. Wilcox and I crafted a letter to the team summarizing our new model and offering to walk through it via a Zoom meeting.

That Zoom meeting occurred on Monday, March 1, 2021, at 11;30 A.M. Over an hour and a half session, Franz meticulously explained his spreadsheet. The left side of his ledger detailed the funding sources for the $122 million bonds. The right side showed capital repair funding. I added that the $100 million more than covered the capital repairs set forth on Gateway's Facility Condition Assessment, even before counting the hoped-for State Capital grant of $15 million.

Several days later, the hope we had after the Zoom call was shattered by an accusatory March 4 Znidarsic letter, barbs from which included: "no meaningful progress on critical issues... significant challenges to finalizing a deal... untenable and worse than our current lease... not at all in the spirit of what we proposed... The public remains unwilling to properly recognize their financial commitment."

Znidarsic's letter had concluded with a request that we join a March 10 Zoom call with the team *plus* MLB CFO Bob Starkey. After bouncing this off Carroll and Franz, Wilcox and I called Znidarsic to advise that we'd participate but if the tone of the session matched that of his letter—which letter the elected officials had yet to hear about—it would be a very short meeting. Znidarsic understood. Wilcox then relayed Carroll's request that the meeting include the team's specific dollar ask.

The team's Zoom presentation had two major revelations. The first, aided by Mr. Starkey, consisted of several bar charts showing the Indians' annual operating costs were the highest in the American League Central Division, and among the highest of MLB's small market franchises. The second—a reminder to be careful what you wish for—was a table showing that the team's financial ask to be an uncapped $21.7 million annually *plus* an annual $3 million capital repair reserve fund.

The following week, Paul Dolan called each elected official. He identified three core issues: the 2/3-1/3 split, the cap on capital repairs, and the need for a 15-year lease term. Then, on March 18, Znidarsic sent us an updated counter-proposal for a "blended" 2/3-1/3 split that allocated costs—in millions— as follows:

EXPENSE ITEM	TEAM	GATEWAY
Routine Maintenance	0.6	1.3
Capital Repairs < $500,000	1.1	2.2
Capital Repairs > $500,000	1.7	3.5
Ballpark Improvement Fund		
Principal	4.5	9.0
Interest on tax-exempt bonds	0.6	1.3
Interest on taxable bonds	0.2	0.5
Gateway Operations	0.8	1.5
Gateway Property Taxes	0.5	1.1
TOTAL	10.1	20.2

Additionally, Znidarsic's letter included the following conditions:

- A minimum 15-year lease with Club options beyond the initial term;
- A capital repair reserve fund of unspecified amount;
- Forecasting capital repairs on a rolling three-year basis;
- New definitional lease terms; and
- Provisions for the Club's acquisition of the Gateway East Garage and the Development Parcel.

On Friday, March 19, we conferenced with the elected officials and their advisors. Wilcox read them the March 4 and March 18 Znidarsic letters and, as expected, both public officials were displeased with the tone. They decided "Before responding on the merits, we have to set the record straight on these accusations of theirs." They directed Wilcox and me to draft such a letter. We did so, and on the following Tuesday we read our "set the record straight" letter to the elected officials. After some minor edits, Wilcox emailed our letter before our March 24 Zoom session.

At that meeting, Brian Barren and Znidarsic elaborated on the team's most recent counter-proposal, stressing the shared risk inherent in their "blended" cost-sharing approach (e.g., share capital repair responsibility, but continue to reject any notion of a capital repairs cap).

After the Zoom meeting, I called Franz to discuss our next response. I knew we could neither achieve a 2/3-1/3 split, nor get back to a 15-year term, without putting several million more dollars into the deal. As expected, in our April 1 elected officials discussion, they pledged no additional local monies. Thus, we'd need to "rearrange deck chairs on the Titanic" via two approaches: doubling our State ask from $15 million to $30 million, and pursuing a Garage naming rights deal.

The Garage component was tricky: our financial model required the City to receive at least $25 million from the Garage sale, but the team was only valuing the Garage at $16-20 million. To close that gap, I posited that the team buy the Garage for $25 million and then supplement its operating revenue with a sale of naming rights which, pursuant to a Gateway common areas agreement, would have to be split equally amongst the two teams and Gateway. If the naming rights could reach the $1 million yearly sum derived by an Orlando arena garage deal, that would yield $667,000 annually for the teams' joint entity and $333,000 for Gateway.

With those tweaks, coupled with a 2/3-1/3 table we devised as an alternative to the team's "blended approach," Dennis read to the officials a letter we had drafted that incorporated language addressed directly to MLB and its CFO, Bob Starkey re Cleveland's history with baseball. Our proposed table read as follows:

EXPENSE ITEM	TEAM	GATEWAY
Routine Maintenance	2.2	0
Capital Repairs < $500,000	0	2.0
Capital Repairs > $500,000	0	4.67
Reserve fund for minor capital repairs	0	1.0
Reserve fund for major capital repairs	0	0.33
Ballpark Improvement Fund		
Principal	4.0	9.0
Interest on tax-exempt bonds	0.6	1.4
Interest on taxable bonds	0.7	0
Gateway Operations	1.4	0
Gateway Property Taxes	1.1	0
TOTAL	10.1	18.4

Though the Mayor and County Executive were satisfied with both table and letter, we knew that the team would balk at agreeing. Carroll noted: "Our streamlined capital reserve will be viewed as a step backward." So Chief Mason suggested that we revisit our cap on capital repairs. Wilcox replied that—if we did drop the cap—we should insist on retaining lease definitional language as a condition of that concession. The public officials concurred, and we added this trade-off to our letter.

We sent our letter to the team on the eve of our April 7 Zoom meeting, stressing that our terms were responsive to all three of Mr. Dolan's core issues: the 15-year term, the 2/3-1/3 split, and the removal of the capital repairs cap.

At the April 7 Zoom meeting the team expressed three major concerns:

- Why won't the City/County backstop the $30 million if the State fails to act?
- The parties still disagree on the dividing line between routine maintenance and minor capital repairs; and
- The Indians need to be a sole purchaser of the Garage—not a joint purchaser with the Cavs—and we are still apart on a purchase price.

On April 20, 2021, Znidarsic sent us a "memorandum" and the following morning we had our fourth Zoom call with the team. Both the memo and the Zoom meeting came down to the same three team demands: 1) a local government "backstop" if the State $30 million never arrived; 2) an increase from our proposed $190 million Ballpark Improvement Fund to the team's desired $202.5 million (i.e., $135 million from a tax-exempt issue plus $67.5 million from a taxable issue); and 3) our embrace of the team's historic interpretation of "routine maintenance."

The team reps were most animated on the need for a local backstop. Weiss asked about a 100% abatement of team admission taxes, but I replied that Mayor Jackson "would never go above our 50% offer." Znidarsic declared that the team couldn't push for State funding without first having a backstop in place (we knew this approach was flawed—why would the State act at all if it knew there was already a local backstop in place? —but we deferred that response, instead reassuring the team that we would accurately state their position to the elected officials).

Franz stressed the short timeline to get a bond issue in place by the end of the year. Working backwards from an aggressive August completion date, he identified the need for a subgroup to develop Ballpark Improvement Fund projects and cost estimates by June. Weiss opined that this might be possible if the cost estimates could be something short of fully engineered drawings and specifications.

On the Garage issue, Weiss said that the team was hiring a consultant to evaluate the structural condition of the building. I asked them to check with Chief Dumas, since the City had performed an assessment in 2020. Chief Dumas indicated that she would contact Weiss to arrange for the delivery of the City report.

Round 2 With the State of Ohio

We did a conference call with Mayor Jackson and County Executive Budish that same day. Virtually the whole call was devoted to the State funding issue. The County Executive had spoken to newly appointed Greater Cleveland Partnership ("GCP") CEO Baiju Shah, who was eager to assist with the State funding effort. Budish identified at least four State funding options: State Capital, State Budget, State COVID funding, and JobsOhio. Mayor Jackson offered to coordinate a call amongst Governor DeWine, County Executive Budish, Baiju Shah, and himself.

Shortly after the conference call, the Mayor called me to tell me to expect a call from the Governor's Chief of Staff Laurel Dawson: when the call came, I was to concisely brief her on the deal. A call did come at 6 PM from Ohio Director of Development Services Agency Lydia Mihalik: I recounted to her the history of our offers culminating in the current $16+ million local offer, and said that the Mayor and County Executive were calling the Governor to request the $30 million—1/9 of the overall proposed public deal—to complete our offer to the team. Ms. Mihalik asked if a forgivable loan format might do the trick, and I told her I thought it could work.

Two days later, I met at Great Lakes Brewery with GCP's Marty McGann and its lobbyist, Squire Patton & Boggs attorney Tim Cosgrove (Cosgrove had worked on Gateway during his employment by Governor George Voinovich, and I'd worked with him on our Save Our Browns effort). I began by characterizing our $30 million State ask: we didn't need all the money at once, but we did need certainty in 2021. McGann was working on a deal summary for Shah and GCP's chairman, Eric Schnur of Lubrizol. I explained to him that I couldn't detail our negotiations, but could help him avoid misstatements as he prepared his advice.

Cosgrove noted that Governor DeWine was "good friends" with Paul Dolan, and advised that the elected officials tell the Governor that they had honored their pledge to Dolan to keep the discussions out of the media, and that without this last $30 million piece the community was at risk of losing the team. I passed the advice on to Mayor Jackson the following morning.

I finally got a follow-up call from Lydia Mihalik on May 6. She had briefed Governor DeWine on the status of our negotiations and, after an unsuccessful attempt to arrange a face-to-face meeting, the Governor's office was going to call Mayor Jackson. Later that afternoon, Mayor Jackson used one of his town hall phone sessions—a thoughtful choice in lieu of a more conventional press conference—

to announce to Cleveland residents that he would not seek a fifth term as Mayor.

The following evening, TV 5's Joe Pagonakis led off that station's 11 PM news show with a "tip" that Music City Baseball of Nashville was "...extremely interested in obtaining the Cleveland Indians with the Indians lease at Progressive Field expiring in 2023." He interviewed County Executive Budish (who cited our year-plus of discussions), but the team would only say: "The lease expires in 2023."

As the Nashville story germinated over the weekend, the GCP's McGann and Cosgrove sought a follow-up session with me and we met at GCP's offices on Huron Road on Monday, May 10 at 11:30 AM. On the Nashville "tip," I summarized my knowledge of the Music City Baseball entity: strong group with lots of high-profile participants, marginal public support for stadium building (the sitting mayor had run on an anti-corporate- welfare platform), a challenge of $100 million outstanding bonds on a new Triple-A ballpark, a tourist economy challenged by the pandemic: but, all that said, much could be overcome if they had a billionaire capable of writing a $2.5 billion check ($1 billion for a new ballpark, $1.2 billion to buy the Indians, and $300 million for a MLB team relocation fee).

They sought a lot of Gateway history, particularly focused on prior State aid (after the meeting, I checked my records and sent the following: $39.5 million State funding toward original Gateway project; $26 million 1996 State Capital toward the Browns Stadium; Cosgrove later suggested that there was a later $14 million allocation to the football stadium). I reiterated that if we could procure the $30 million State piece towards our ballpark, the other outstanding negotiations—Ballpark Improvement Fund amount, parking garage — were solvable.

A few days later—on Thursday, May 12, 2021—Governor DeWine connected with the Mayor and County Executive by phone. As Mayor Jackson's explained to me the next morning, the Governor appeared to view $15 million as an upper limit based on his soccer stadium experiences. But he committed to have discussions with State legislators and Paul Dolan and then update the local officials in the near future.

Knowing that GCP was having parallel discussions with the State, I relayed this update to GCP's McGann and Cosgrove over the weekend. They had already compiled info showing that the State awards to the Cincinnati and Columbus soccer stadiums each exceeded $20 million, and Cosgrove was talking with the Governor's Chief of Staff Laurel Dawson on a regular basis.

McGann and Cosgrove joined our May 19 Zoom meeting and updated the group on the State lobbying effort. The highlight was the Governor's invitation to Paul Dolan to travel to Columbus on May 28 and meet in the Governor's mansion. On the lesser issues, we learned that we would soon receive the team's latest Garage sale analysis. Subgroups would soon meet on that issue, the scope and timeline for Ballpark Improvement Projects, and (optimistically) an initial assessment of our post-deal communications approach.

As we approached the end of May, the DeWine-Dolan meeting was key: our ability to strike a deal hinged on the Governor's decision, and even a favorable outcome would still require quick work to start our legislative approval processes in June. Knowing that, I sent Wilcox an early draft of a deal term sheet.

As for the team itself, it hit the quarter-season mark with a 23-18 record, not bad for its MLB-low $50 million payroll. The first three starters were carrying the rest of the rotation, the bullpen was exceeding expectations, but the hitting was just as bad as anticipated. Effective June 2, the State was allowing the ballpark to go to 100% capacity, and it would be interesting to see how the fans responded.

On Tuesday, June 1, Znidarsic called Wilcox and me to describe Paul Dolan's meeting with Governor DeWine. They met for an hour in the Governor's mansion, with the Governor devoting 40 minutes to two themes: the importance of the Dolan family continuing ownership of the team, and the importance of the team remaining in Northeast Ohio. In the remaining 20 minutes Dolan expressed the need for $30 million and the importance of 2021 certainty on that sum. But Dolan also made clear that there were ancillary issues and the "total public gap was $50 million."

The next morning was our biweekly Zoom call, and all participants agreed that there seemed to be progress on the $30 million State ask. Once that update was given, the team's next slide attempted to link MLB's minimum requirements for lease approval with the Indians' outstanding demands. When both Chief Mason and Chief Dumas asked for more specificity on the team's annual ask, the team moved to a slide that showed an annual ask of $20.5 million, including capital repairs at $8.5 million and a reserve fund at $1.3 million.

Weiss used Chief Mason and Chief Dumas's questions to pivot to an assertion that the negotiating process was "broken"—too many memos, too many letters, too many disjointed discussions with too much time between them—to which I responded that "nothing was broken" and that the subgroups on the garage and the bonding were reducing the financial gaps. Weiss responded that trouble lay ahead if the State denied the $30 million request, because the City and County were not backstopping it with local resources (such as a 100% admissions tax abatement).

The next day, WKYC's Mark Naymik did a story on the pending lease discussions, quoting me that negotiations were "well along."[18] Then, at noon on Friday, June 4, Governor DeWine aide Laurel Dawson called me on what was basically a fact-finding mission. In the course of a 50-minute discussion she sought, and I provided, specifics on Gateway history, the three City and three County primary funding sources comprising our $16+ million local offer to the team, and the timelines for renewing expiring sources such as the sin tax.

She asked if we'd contacted any State legislators, and I replied: "No, we wanted to start with the Governor." She asked if our region could coordinate financial asks from the State, and I cited our State Capital process in which GCP plays a quarterbacking role. Finally, she expressed the Governor's desire for a 20-year extension and asked why we were settling for 15 years. I responded that we'd all prefer 20, but two of our major funding streams—sin tax and Sports Facility Reserve—expire in 2034.

Lastly, in justifying our $30 million funding request, I distinguished baseball from other pro franchises by citing the 81 home dates as well as Wilcox's point re the three Ohio-based minor league franchises (Columbus, Akron, Lake County) associated with the Indians that would be jeopardized if the Indians moved. Though MLB's recent minor league agreement did grant 10-year licenses to each minor league franchise,[19] what would happen to these franchises in year 11 if the Indians move to, say, Nashville?

Three days later, I joined GCP's McGann and Cosgrove at Town Hall to compare notes on our State ask. I learned that my minor league franchise point had registered, and that whatever decision the Governor made would depend on our prior resolution of ancillary financial gaps.

On Tuesday, June 8, the entire public sector negotiating team—Chief Mason, Carroll, Franz, Chief Dumas, Wilcox, Climaco attorney Scott Simpkins, and myself—assembled at Wilcox's conference room to review the slew of documents that had accumulated over the last several months. One of our challenges had been the need for Wilcox and I to read, rather than deliver, key documents to the City and County employees to avoid application of the public records law.

The most recent document we reviewed was an Indians sheet that asserted we were $18 million apart on our capital repairs estimates for the 15-year term. Since we had already accepted uncapped liability for capital repairs, we agreed that our next response would stress this point. On the Garage, we agreed that—if the team failed to meet our $25 million sales price—the City would retain the Garage and use net proceeds plus naming rights to deliver an annual $2.3 million to the team.

Meanwhile, we learned from GCP that the State's Dawson would be in Cleveland on Thursday, June 17, with plans to meet with both government and team representatives and further explore options to achieve a 20-year lease term. She was also telling GCP that the ancillary lease issues had to be resolved prior to the Governor's consideration of our $30 million ask.

We had a full public sector slate for that Thursday meeting at GCP on a sunny blue-sky day while the Indians played Baltimore in a day game one-quarter mile to the southwest. Dawson and Josh Rubin were there from the State; GCP hosts were Shah, McGann, and Cosgrove; Chief Mason and Carroll were there from the County; Jim Gentile represented the City, and Wilcox and I were the Gateway reps. After hearing our updates, Dawson stated the State's case:

From where we sit, this is a political lift: there's lots of stadiums and teams around the State. Come with an ask once everyone— City, County, business community, other local "askers"—is on board,

On the Governor's preference for a 20-year term, I reiterated the expiration of three of our funding sources—sin tax, Sports Facility Reserve, and Garage annuity—at the end of year 15, and Wilcox suggested a five-year "contingent option."

Chief Mason asked Dawson: "If we can get our part done, what's the timeline for the State?" She responded: "We can't do this by ourselves...we need to figure the legislature out. Your plan needs to be done, then come to the State." As the meeting wrapped, Rubin stated: "It will be important for Laurel and the Governor to understand the five-year contingent option. And the State's share of the deal needs to come in less than 15%."

Taking the State's message to heart, the public sector and Gateway staffers met the following Monday via Zoom to hear Osborn Engineering's Dave Faller walk through his latest update of the Gateway Facilities Condition Assessment. Faller's work supported our capital repairs projections of $6.67 million annually in years 1-15, but showed $9 million annually in years 16-20 and $14 million annually in years 21-25. Per Wilcox, we'd label options based on these latter ten years as "vesting options."

After the Zoom meeting, Chief Dumas and I updated Mayor Jackson, and Chief Mason and Carroll updated County Executive Budish. Chief Dumas and I talked with the Mayor again on Tuesday and he agreed to backstop $2.33 million annually from the Garage assuming the City continued owning it. The Mayor and County Executive talked later that day and patched me into to the tail end of their discussion. The elected officials stressed the importance of getting from the team a full Ballpark Improvement Fund project list with cost and schedules. Once they saw that, they'd be able to decide a $10 million private bond interest ask from the team.

Meanwhile, Brian Barren offered to host a meeting at the team's offices on Wednesday, June 23 at 11:30 AM. So, fifteen of us—GCP, Indians, City, County, and Gateway—met the following day at a suite overlooking the field (the sun-splashed field and ballpark looked much newer than its 27-year age would suggest). GCP's Shah and McGann, and Chief Mason, began by citing the Governor's stance: the need for resolution of ancillary issues by July 1, the preference for a 20-year term, and an openness to diverse State funding options including COVID monies.

I then stated the latest from the elected officials: the Mayor's willingness to guarantee the Garage-related revenues, the immediate need for a Ballpark Improvement schedule (after which the public officials would render their private bond interest decision), our proposal for a vested five-year extension option based on estimated capital repair needs of $9 million annually in those extension years), and our decision to hold firm on our $8 million annual capital repair contributions (and not the team's desired $10 million).

On the last point, I reminded the team reps that the public was on the hook for capital repairs, whatever they might be, and that we'd work with Gateway on an early notice protocol to the City and County when deficits loomed. When Znidarsic asked for language recognizing the City and County's responsibility to fund Gateway's uncapped capital repair duties, I replied that—while we would not do a lease change (the public officials had been very clear with me on that point)—we could consider another vehicle (such as recital clauses in authorizing legislation).

After the meeting, I conveyed cautious optimism to Mayor Jackson and suggested he might be able to review a Ballpark project schedule as soon as Friday. Several days later I talked with the schedulers for the public officials to pin down a time—12 noon in the Mayor's Red Room on Tuesday, June 29—and worked with Climaco attorneys Wilcox and Scott Simpkins to fine tune our Term Sheet.

And, once we finalized the Term Sheet, I arranged a briefing of the elected officials on same in the Red Room immediately after the Indians reps departed from their presentation. The night before the Red Room meetings, the Climaco attorneys sent Osborn Engineering's latest draft of the Gateway Facilities Condition Assessment to the team. As predicted by the elected officials, the team reps detonated after they saw this document, but it would be a delayed fuse.

The Indians' Red Room briefing on the Ballpark Improvements went well. The team's community development briefing was more problematic, particularly when Weiss attempted, with little success, to justify a need for a new development entity with oversight over the efforts. The meeting concluded cordially with the three principals—Jackson, Budish and Dolan—discussing City Council and County Council timelines for action on the potential deal.

The Indians officials exited the Red Room at 1:15 PM and were replaced by Climaco attorney Simpkins, the City's Jim Gentile, and myself. During my Term Sheet review, the County Executive voiced concern that the County total dollars were $18 million higher than the City's: he warned that County Councilman Michael Gallagher would object to this. I replied that I could show that the City's Q deal contribution was higher than the County's. On the $10 million interest cost on the private bonds, the public officials agreed that the team's Ballpark Improvement case was sound enough to cause them to agree to split the annual $700,000 cost.

The next morning was our regular bi-weekly session with the team, but this time it was hosted in-person at GCP's offices. GCP's Shah, McGann, and Cosgrove commenced with updates on conversations with State officials, the upshot of which was the importance of resolving our deal by the end of the week so we could communicate that news to the State. Then we discussed yesterday's Red Room meeting, and I delivered the good news on the interest cost on the private bonds.

Using a PowerPoint to identify outstanding issues, Barren remarked on the number of green checks representing closure, and turned to what appeared to be the one outstanding issue: the team believed that Osborn Engineering had undercounted the amounts required for minor capital repairs, citing a real annual number of $2-2.5 million versus an Osborn number of $1.67 million. I responded that, regardless of the Osborn sheet, the public was pledging $2 million annually for minor capital repairs plus a healthy reserve and our decision to dispense with a cap.

That wasn't enough for the team: Znidarsic sought a "contractually binding understanding" of some sort, while Weiss took it one step further by insisting that the language be inserted in the lease. I replied that we could discuss language and protocols, but not in the lease. Weiss asked "Why not?" and I explained that the elected officials had instructed us to make no lease amendments regarding this matter. Acting more boldly with us than he would have with the elected officials, Weiss asked me to explain their reasoning. I referred him back to our April letter's statement that the cap removal was conditioned on no new lease amendments.

Undaunted, Weiss lit my fuse by again demanding lease amendments because Gateway's processes "were broken." I tossed my pen aside and very nearly left the room at that point. Fortunately, Chief

Dumas restored order with a very convincing statement on the Mayor's position and a reminder that the public was ultimately responsible for capital repairs.

Filling the brief ensuing vacuum, the team's Alex King asked that the City and County designate media contacts as soon as possible. Shah arranged for everyone reconvene at GCP on Friday at 10 AM. Franz, Carroll and I stayed for another half hour to draft a new paragraph referencing the longstanding Gateway/City/County Three Party Agreement and describing Gateway's existing capital repair resolution.

From there Carroll and I trekked over to the County Administration Building where we were able to meet with County Executive Budish and brief him on the amendments we'd made to the Term Sheet since yesterday. He agreed to the changes and also agreed to add the new paragraph. Then I hiked over to the Climaco offices where I met with Scott Simpkins and summarized all the changes.

Now I had to get City Hall's approval, so I called Chief Dumas and reviewed the changes. But then, as I was preparing to read the new paragraph, Mayor Jackson called my cell phone and I merged his call with Chief Dumas's. I covered the changes from yesterday and started to recite the new paragraph. But the Mayor interjected that he wasn't going to provide the Indians with a new peg to hang their future capital repairs arguments on. So Simpkins struck the new paragraph from our document. I called Carroll to update him on the Mayor's direction and headed home. Later that afternoon Simpkins sent the Term Sheet to the team.

That evening I walked a few blocks west to the home of Tony and Rochelle Coyne. An accomplished real estate lawyer, Coyne was best known for his long tenure as Chairman of Cleveland's City Planning Commission: tonight, the Coyne's were hosting a backyard neighborhood meet-and greet for Council President/Mayoral candidate Kevin Kelley. When I saw Kelley, we chatted politically but—not wanting to be the skunk at the garden party— I didn't mention the Indians lease. Then my cell phone rang: Mayor Jackson was calling. Once I found a quiet spot, I listened while the Mayor described the end of the Red Room meeting with Paul Dolan in which all three principals appeared to acknowledge an impending deal and moved to a discussion of legislative authorization. In that spirit, the Mayor and County Executive approved paying the interest on the private bonds.

The Mayor contrasted that positive Red Room spirit with the nitpicking that Dolan's minions were doing on "the morning after," and he had no tolerance for the latter activity. From years of taking direction from Mayor Jackson, I knew that venting sessions such as this were a constructive part of his coping process, and I did a lot of listening on that call. When the call ended, I knew I now had some solid talking points for the team's inevitable critique of our Term Sheet at our end-of-week morning meeting.

In the early morning hours prior to our Friday meeting, GCP's Shah played some helpful shuttle diplomacy in attempting to resolve our capital repairs language issue. Then, at the commencement of the meeting, Shah gave the proceedings an appropriate sense of urgency by stressing the importance of resolving our local differences so we could signal "full steam ahead" to the State.

But the team representatives, having read our Term Sheet and not found much to their liking, took a surly approach. They calmed down a little when we corrected one misunderstanding, but on the critical issue of "public assurances to fill capital repair shortfalls" Brian Barren asked Znidarsic what he needed and Joe responded that he needed a provision in the enabling legislation.

That was my cue to quote Mayor Jackson—with a particularity I'd never given before—and recite the Mayor's orders to Chief Dumas and me "to not add one word of language re capital repairs." When I finished, the team quieted down a bit but continued to push for enabling legislation that would confirm that the public would respond to deficiencies. While Chief Dumas and I cautioned that even a simple addition was outside our authority, we suggested that any such provision not be additive; rather, it should just state what already exists. Meanwhile, in the adjacent GCP conference room, a splinter group was discussing communications strategy.

After the meeting, Chief Dumas and I called Mayor Jackson and he rebuffed us for even allowing the notion of new language of any kind to be referred back to him. Back home, I rang Znidarsic and left a voice mail message. I made similar calls and voice mails to Shah and Carroll. An hour later, Znidarsic called back and I added Chief Dumas. As I was stating our "hard no," both Shah and Carroll called and I hooked them in. Due to the wonders of cell phone technology, there were now three listeners when Chief Dumas and I followed the Mayor's instructions.

When Znidarsic responded predictably— "This is real bad"—Shah asked Carroll if he'd briefed the County Executive. Carroll responded that he didn't think the County would have a problem adding a clause. Znidarsic then asked me how the Mayor would respond to a deficiency; I replied that the Mayor knows there's no cap on the public's capital repair responsibility and he'd seek authorization to fund the deficiency. The retort: "That's nice, but he's only Mayor for six more months."

When Chief Dumas explained that the obligation the team was seeking to create already exists in previous agreements, Znidarsic replied: "All right, then, I'll give you a homework assignment: find such a provision and I'll consider it." After that five-person call concluded, Chief Dumas and I reported back to the Mayor who wondered what gave Znidarsic the right to assign us homework.

Over the Fourth of July weekend—suspecting we were losing credibility with the State for each day past July 1 that we failed to resolve our local differences—I undertook Znidarsic's homework assignment. I reread the 1992 Three Party Agreement (Gateway/City/County) and found phrases that linked the City and County to the Ballpark lease: these included recognition of Gateway's operating responsibilities, the City and County's express recognition of the Indians' rights in the Ground Lease, Gateway's authorization to enter into leases for operation of (the Ballpark), the City's authorization of Gateway's "contemplated plan to finance, construct and operate (the Ballpark), and the parties' mutual covenants "to take no action, inconsistent with this Agreement, that would prejudice the rights...(of) the major league professional athletic teams...." After reviewing the provisions with the Climaco attorneys, I sent them to Joe on Saturday evening.

After a quiet day on July 5, the next two days were a flurry of activity: the Team finally marked up our Term Sheet, Shah moderated the Team's comments via some shuttle diplomacy, and a call with the State offered hope for an impending Governor action. When the dust settled Wednesday night, we had a County side letter re capital repairs deficiencies, an agreed public contribution of $19 million annually, a substantially agreed Term Sheet, and early County Council member briefings.

The Governor's office contacted all the principals the next day to arrange a conference call for Friday, July 9, at 12:45 PM. That Friday morning, Shah continued playing a facilitating role, preparing all parties for the call and ensuring that the choir was singing from the same hymnal book. Meanwhile, a number of media outlets—Mark Naymik of TV 3, Cleveland Scene, The Athletic—were beginning to hype the big summer story.

So now it came down to the Friday Governor call: participants included Governor DeWine, Laurel Dawson, Paul Dolan, Baiju Shah, Tim Cosgrove, Mayor Jackson, County Executive Budish, and myself. The dialogue went something like this:

DeWine: We will be working on our end to get the additional funding.

Budish: The City and County have worked for almost two years... the City and County have financial constraints, but want to keep the team...our only hole is $30 million from the State.

Jackson: Unless something specific came up in the last week, the City has a deal with the County and the team.

Dolan: This morning we reached agreement on a term sheet, subject to memorializing.

DeWine: We're going to do everything we can to get that 30. We think we can do it. The option of a term longer than 15 years was very important to me. It may never be used, but it might be used: a potential 5 years with a potential 5 years after that.

Budish: Without your help we wouldn't be able to reach agreement.

DeWine: I haven't conversed with the Speaker... my next step... several ways we can get this done...I hope to give you a better assessment in the next few days. We're in...going to do everything to get it done.

Dawson: Agreed.

DeWine: I'll have a better idea after talking to the two leaders: the Speaker and the Senate President,

Shah: We don't want to get in front of you. We'd welcome your guidance in communicating to City Council and County Council.

DeWine: Wait until I've at least talked to the Speaker and Senate President—probably tomorrow— we'll get it done.

Jackson: If anyone asks: "It's our intention to work a deal."

DeWine; Agree.

Jackson: Negotiating in public is always a bad thing.

DeWine: Announce when we have a deal?

Jackson: Announce a deal when we have it. But deal authorization and the contract are up to the Council President.

Budish: We've all kept this under wraps for a long time. Usually, the media wants to know when I've sneezed.

Jackson: When they ask me, I just say "bless you."

DeWine: Thanks, everyone.

On Thursday, July 22, 2021, I met GCP's McGann and Cosgrove at Market Garden Brewery for one of our catch-up sessions. Cosgrove advised that the reason the State had been quiet lately—except for a few generalized Governor radio interviews—was that Governor point person Laurel Dawson was just concluding a ten-day vacation. He also confirmed that the Governor would be able to draw the $30 million from the State's Facilities Establishment Fund after going to the Controlling Board. I updated Mayor Jackson the next morning, who told me it was time for Chief Dumas and me to update the Council President on our deal.

Later that morning—via a tweet of a superb video narrated by Cleveland Playhouse alumni Tom Hanks and musically backed by the Akron-based Black Keys—the team announced its decision to change its name to the "Cleveland Guardians." Apart from the name itself, the announcement was one more step (supplementing our Governor DeWine phone call earlier in the month and the Governor's recent interviews) in putting the "Nashville Stars" in our rear-view mirror.

On August 4, GCP coordinated a conference call with State officials to address last minute questions in anticipation of an August 5 announcement and press conference. Representing the State were Governor DeWine's Chief of Staff Michael Hall, Laurel Dawson, and Deputy Director of Legislative Affairs Aaron Crooks. Representing our deal team were Shah, McGann, Cosgrove, Carroll, Barren and me. Shah, Barren, Carroll and I reviewed the Term Sheet and affirmed there was local agreement. Hall cited the need for "interested party outreach" at the State level, but Crooks did note that legislative leaders had been briefed and were on board.

Dawson asked whether we'd briefed our local State legislators, to which Shah replied "we didn't want to get out in front of the Governor." Hall asked if there'd be a problem if the State picked one source today and undefined sources in the future. Cosgrove answered "maybe," referring to Barren. Citing an upcoming call with MLB's Bob Starkey that would include Dawson, Barren said MLB will require "no contingencies," and will ask Dawson whether the State's "figured it out."

During the State conference call my cell phone rang twice: when I retrieved it, I returned the County Executive's call. He'd read the proposed talking points and was concerned there wasn't enough economic impact justification. I proposed to enlist Tom Yablonsky of the Historic Warehouse and Historic Gateway community development corporations. Yablonsky could tell the impact story like no one, and he could do it with an appropriate historic preservation emphasis.

By the second week in July, Governor DeWine and Mayor Jackson offices had approved participation of their media personnel in the Team/GCP's proactive communications group. Meanwhile, County Law Director Greg Huth and Team representatives worked on potential enabling legislation language.

A Cavaliers Issue Pops Up

Meanwhile, while we were engaged with the State, a number of side issues had cropped up. Early July had brought forth a goulash of media speculation. It kicked off with a lengthy article in *The Athletic* with the principal takeaways being that the Dolans were committed to Cleveland, the Dolans still had financial and attendance challenges, there was a potential minority investor (aptly-named New Jersey-based Freedom Mortgage CEO Stanley Middleman).

Speaking to Nashville rumors, the *Athletic* said that Nashville Music City Baseball CEO John Loar had not conversed with anyone in Cleveland and a Nashville ballpark wouldn't be ready till 2025 at the earliest (Note: Loar's statement wasn't necessarily dispositive: what he *didn't* say was whether one or more Nashville billionaires had expressed interest in Cleveland's team, which confidential sources had told me *did occur*). Spurred on by The Athletic story, other media sources jumped on the speculating bandwagon: WKYC TV 3, Fox 8, Cleveland.com, and the Field of Schemes blog.

Then, on Thursday, July 15, 2021, I received a 45-minute phone call from Cavaliers CEO Len Komoroski, allegedly in response to my previous inquiry about the Cavaliers' comfort level with our proposed sale of the Gateway Development Parcel to the Indians. But Komoroski spent most of the call on two other Gateway issues. First was the Cavaliers' desire for a full financial engagement on expected future sin tax revenues and the Cavaliers' share of same. I pledged our full cooperation going forward: we'd meet with Cavaliers legal counsel Meg Murray and Cavaliers financial officer Stephanie Meade.

The second issue was far more complicated. Komoroski was asserting that the County had illegally tapped the County portion of the Sports Facility Reserve when it made its $3.5 million reimbursement to the Indians in 2020. His theory was that the Cavaliers' lease and the Q deal bond indentures required an "agreement with a pro sports team prior to December 31, 2020" as a condition of releasing Sports Facility Reserve funds and that no such agreement existed. Though I knew that the County *had* formed an agreement, I did not debate the point at the time.

Moreover, he seemed to be arguing a broader point that the *entire* County portion of the Sports Facility Reserve was intended as a firewall in the Q deal that could not be breached by routing proceeds to the Indians. To do so was in his mind a breach of the Cavaliers lease. Though I had real doubts about that argument, I again chose not to engage: I simply committed to raise his points with Gateway's legal counsel.

The Climaco attorneys reviewed the documents over the weekend and called me Monday noon with a draft letter reciting the County's executed sports agreement and denying Komoroski's claim while still offering to meet on the sin tax projections. I approved the draft and asked them to review it with Huth. Later that day I merged a cell phone call and updated County Executive Budish and Mayor Jackson. The next day Huth approved the letter and the Climaco attorneys sent it to the Cavaliers. As I mentioned to Chief Dumas that morning, these discussions were getting "curiouser and curiouser."

Franz and I followed up on the second Komoroski issue by doing a Zoom meeting with Cavaliers attorney Meg Murray and Cavaliers CFO Stefanie Meade to discuss sin tax projections and the Field-house's share of same. Franz started by reviewing a spreadsheet he had prepared re sin tax projections. During questioning by Meade, the two of them established that: slightly increasing revenues were predicting that each of the teams' shares of total revenues would be $92 million (as compared to 2015 estimates of $86 million); the Cavaliers had received $82 million to date and should expect another $10 million over time, and the Indians had received $54 million to date and should expect another $38 million over time. When Meade argued for the Cavaliers getting about $700,000 annually, I suggested that the Indians needed a few years to catch up.

A couple days later Murray sent the Climaco attorneys a letter reaffirming the team's claims. I could no longer delay notifying the Indians that there was trouble brewing: so I forwarded Murray's letter to Znidarsic. We agreed that we all needed a refresher course on the bond indenture from the Q deal. That refresher course took the form of a conference call—amongst Znidarsic, Simpkins, Franz and me—on the morning of Tuesday, August 3, 2021. Franz commenced with this summary.

> The Q bond deal had three different series: a $35 million tax-exempt issue primarily backed by the County's bed tax and sales tax; a $35 million taxable issue primarily backed by the City's Q

arena admissions tax; and a Cooperative Reserve intended to fund shortfalls in the second series. If there's no money in the Cooperative Reserve, and no money to pay debt service, then the Cavaliers have to make the payments in the form of "contingent rent." The County Sports Facility Reserve account was funded from the first series and had raised $5.7 million by the end of 2020, but no money flowed into the City Sports Facility Reserve account until 2024. Finally, there was a County Reserve account, initially funded at closing and now having a balance of $1 million. This latter account buffers the Cavaliers from paying contingent rent, hence the team's interest in bulking up that account with proceeds from the County Sports Facility Reserve (as opposed to having said proceeds flow to the Indians). On this latter point, the payments to the Indians were proper if there was an "agreement with a pro sports team" prior to a stated deadline (the Cavaliers lease said 12/31/20 while the indenture said 12/31/21): the Cavaliers believed the answer was "no;" Gateway/ County believed the answer was "yes."

Simpkins then described his Friday phone call with Murray, in which she observed that damages to the Cavaliers may never occur: if the Cooperative Reserve remains flush, there is no threat of the Cavaliers having to pay contingent rent and the balance of the County Reserve becomes moot. Simpkins now suggested that we execute a "tolling agreement" with the Cavaliers in which all parties would preserve their rights. I liked the idea, but asked Simpkins to brief County Law Director Huth; Znidarsic agreed, adding that Huth's bond counsel should also be consulted. Our call concluded. Simpkins followed up with Huth, and Huth concurred.

The Deal Is Announced to the Public

On a brisk sunny Thursday morning, August 5, 2021, our large group of presenters assembled at the discount Drug Mart Club section of Progressive Field. The Indians' Curtis Danberg moderated a 10:30 AM virtual press conference with the following order of speakers, all of whom were seated on chairs with the Field as a backdrop: Mayor Frank Jackson, County Executive Armond Budish, County Council President Pernel Jones, Jr., Governor Mike DeWine, and team owner Paul Dolan. After the press conference, Barren and I took chairs joining the principals as we conducted successive editorial board sessions with the Plain Dealer and Crain's Cleveland Business. The local media was quick to respond. First, the Plain Dealer led with a general overview:

> The Cleveland Indians have struck a proposed $435 million deal with the city of Cleveland, Cuyahoga County and the state of Ohio to renovate Progressive Field and extend the team's lease in Cleveland for at least 15 years.... Local and state taxpayers would be footing roughly two-thirds of the cost, with the soon-to-be-renamed Cleveland Guardians contributing the rest. Over the life of the 15-year deal, the city will pay roughly $117 million, the county will pay about $138 million, the state would pay $30 million, and the team would pay $150 million.... The deal, which must win approval from both city and county council, calls for no new taxes or tax increases. All public funding would come from existing revenue sources.[20]

Then, quickly doing its homework, The Plain Dealer followed up early the next morning with a political take:

On the heels of an announced $435 million deal with the city, county, state and owners of the Cleveland Indians for renovations to Progressive Field, the Cleveland mayoral candidates for this year's election were generally receptive despite its heavy reliance on public money. The issue has a chance to become a flashpoint in the race to succeed four-term Mayor Frank Jackson, who is retiring and helped broker the agreement as one of his final acts in office. It's similar to that of the publicly funded deal for The Q − now Rocket Mortgage Fieldhouse − four years ago when opponents argued it amounted to a giveaway for wealthy sports owners as residents faced dire needs.[21]

Expressing degrees of support for the deal were candidates Kevin Kelley, Zack Reed, Sandra Williams, and Justin Bibb. Candidate Basheer Jones was neutral—he first needed to speak with community members—but he did cite potential benefits for small businesses. Candidates Dennis Kucinich and Ross DiBello declined to comment.[22] Placing the deal in an overall political context, the article went on to note:

> The Progressive Field deal comes at a precarious time in Cleveland politics. The city has not yet emerged from the coronavirus pandemic with businesses and people across the city still struggling from its effects.....The 2016 announcement that the public would pay for upgrades to now-Rocket Mortgage Fieldhouse set off a political firestorm in the city in the run-up to the 2017 municipal elections, with community members and activists infuriated at the thought of using city dollars to pay for arena upgrades instead of other pressing matters. The deal almost fell through as groups like Greater Cleveland Congregations forced the issue to a ballot referendum when Cleveland Cavaliers owner Dan Gilbert pulled out. The county stepped in and said it would address some of GCC's

concerns, such as opening mental health and substance abuse crisis centers, leading GCC to pull its opposition. Though opposition might arise, GCC is <u>unlikely to be a part of it</u> after a spokesman said it would not get involved in the debate this time around.[23]

Predictably, Cleveland Scene's Sam Allard accused the deal sponsors of "hatching" a scheme devoid of public input. negotiated entirely without public input[24] Nationally, Neil deMause had this to say in his <u>Field of Schemes</u> blog:

> Assuming a 15-year extension, and $285 million in costs, that'd pay the team owners exactly $19 million a year to stick around until at least 2036. This pay-to-play model has become <u>increasingly popular over the years</u>, but Dolan's deal would be the <u>second-highest per-year cost of all time</u>, ahead of the **Carolina Panthers'** $14.6 <u>million a year</u> but still behind **Indiana Pacers** owner Herb Simon's deal to get $600 million in exchange for a 25-year lease extension, which still boggles the mind.[25]

Preparing for Council Testimony

A public-financed sports facility deal goes through three distinct stages, each of which demands different skills from its advocates. First, you must *negotiate* the deal with the team, which requires a blend of legal and numerical command. Second, you must *explain* the deal to the media and the public in layman's terms. Third, you must *justify* the deal to public bodies in terms that they find most relevant. We had now reached the second and third stages.

In stadium deals, the same people you cross swords with during negotiations become your partners and collaborators during Council deliberations. And so it was that Znidarsic and I bonded during our preparations for City Council testimony. As the most politically seasoned of the Indians front office crew, Joe frequently called me for my take on various Council scenarios. Our ensuing discussions were useful to both of us, and probably enhanced our input to the larger group prep sessions.

Mayor Jackson had made it clear to me that he would defer to the Council President's judgment on when authorizing legislation would be introduced. And, as a courtesy, he instructed Chief Dumas and me to brief Council President Kelley: given that the issue was already swirling in the media, our briefing would insulate him against a surprise attack by the media or one of his opponents.

So, the three of us met in his Council office on the afternoon of Tuesday, July 27, 2021, and we covered the particulars in a half-hour session. Council President Kelley quickly assimilated the info, simplifying the deal in a way that experienced politicians are able to do: "So the new City money comes from half of the tax people pay on Indians tickets, and instead of the debt service payments we now make on the Garage, that money will instead go towards this deal."

We knew that diversity and equity would be big concerns for both Councils. So, at Carroll's request, I joined an August 26 Zoom meeting with members of the Cuyahoga County Citizens' Committee on Equity. Energized by the County Council's July, 2020 resolution declaring racism to be a public health crisis, the Committee had already advanced a number of initiatives addressing inequities in the County. Facilitated by the County's Laura Black, participants included Nailah Byrd, Danielle Snyder, Glen Shumate, Yanela Sims and Stephen Caviness. Several Committee members suggested new ways for Gateway and the team to expand their equitable agendas: these included team non-construction procurement activities and payment of prevailing wages. Several days later, I summarized the discussion to Znidarsic and asked him to follow up with Laura Black to arrange a discussion.

The $202.5 million worth of ballpark improvements would be a key part of our presentations to the City and County Councils: they'd give the Council members tangible outcomes from the large public investments. But these investments would have to be timed to comply with federal tax laws. Accordingly, on September 9, 2021, Bob Franz coordinated a Zoom conference amongst County bond counsel Tucker & Ellis, County officials, Indians reps, and Gateway reps.

The Tucker & Ellis attorneys began by giving a layman's view of the tax laws: that the IRS views tax-exempt debt as a burden on the Treasury, and its regulations were drafted to prevent speculative investing. Then they summarized the spend-down requirements for the tax-exempt bonds—essentially 85% of the tax-exempt bond proceeds within three years of issuance date—and spoke to the 5% of such proceeds that could be spent prior to issuance.

The Communications Group

Since mid-July, GCP had coordinated weekly Tuesday morning communications meetings amongst GCP, the team and its consultants. The group included media professional Nancy Lesic, GCP's Shah, McGann, and Olivia Ortega, the Indians' Alex King, Curtis Danberg, Neil Weiss, and Christy Corfias, and the County's Joe Nanni, Trevor McAleer, and Mary Louise Madigan.

Lesic's work product drove most meeting agendas, and her documents charted roadmaps for the group's defense of a major sports facility transaction:

- Early draft of press release announcing lease extension (July 2, 2021);
- Indians' questions and answers (July 8, 2021);
- Response to media accusations of a secretive process (August 11, 2021);
- Cleveland Building & Construction Trades press release (August 26, 2021);
- Indians' executive summary for Council presentation (October 5, 2021);
- Tom Yablonsky op-ed (October 8, 2021).

This group would have to explain a very complex agreement in simple terms. It had to refine "quick-strike" tactics to respond to criticisms levelled by media, opposition groups, and politicians seeking "wedge" issues. In a broad sense, it would need to preempt and counter the messaging of the Progressive Caucus and similar groups.

In mid-August, McGann had asked me to join the sessions (he had conversed with City Council President Kevin Kelley, asking him who should represent the Council in these meetings, and the Council President had replied "either myself or Ken Silliman:" hence the request for me to join). The group was predicting legislative introduction dates—September 14 for the County Council and September 20 for the City Council (these dates would later be revised to September 28 and September 27)—as well as likely committee assignments in each body. Team officials began preparing outlines for speakers at the Council hearings.

City and County Council Deliberations

Cleveland City Council got the first crack at the Term Sheet via a stripped-down presentation we made to the Finance Committee on October 5, 2021. Earlier that day five disgruntled Council members had forced a special meeting to air out concerns on the use of Phase 1 (approximately $250 million) of the City's federal pandemic recovery award, so those members who participated in that session as well as our session were already limbered up.

Chairman Kelley began the discussion on our Ordinance No. 844-21, explaining that this would be the first of many Council sessions on this topic. Jim Gentile and I summarized the provisions of the Term Sheet, and then it was time for Council questions. Blaine Griffin led off with a well-developed line of questions, starting with competition from other cities (Nashville, Indianapolis, and San Antonio), moving to lease comparisons (Seattle) and concluding with the importance of community benefits.

There were no surprises from Mike Polensek: I could have written his talking points, which included Cleveland's poverty rate and the failed 1990 Gateway promise of 28,000 jobs. Knowing that our economic arguments would be given at a future session, he warned us that he demand real, hard, verifiable numbers (since the Council had been misled in the past). Brian Kazy accused the team of exorbitant ticket prices (I could hear Barren's and Znidarsic's teeth grinding in the COVID-limited audience, but per the Council President's direction we deferred a response). Kazy also suggested that owner Paul Dolan should be at the next meeting.

Two days later we gathered at a suite at Progressive Field to present to the Cuyahoga County Mayors and Managers Association. In what was essentially a dry run for our Cuyahoga County Council meeting the following day, we summarized the Term Sheet (me) and the ballpark improvements (Weiss) and then took questions from our audience of about 20 suburban mayors. One mayor (everyone was masked so I didn't know which one) asked whether we'd considered a retractable roof, and Weiss said that the cost was prohibitive for an existing structure such as ours. I added that it would harm our attractive ballpark, and its cost couldn't be recovered from the few extra convention-type events it would allow.

The next day—Thursday, October 7—was our full presentation to Cuyahoga County Council's Committee of the Whole. Prior to the Council Clerk's reading of our resolution (No. 2021-0219), GCP's Shah and a half dozen other business owners and workers spoke in favor of the lease extension. Then Council President Pernel Jones, Jr. introduced Armond Budish as the first speaker, and the County Executive urged the Council to preserve baseball in Cleveland. His call to action creatively—almost poetically— used baseball cliches and he then introduced me as the "utility infielder"of our team. I spent 20 minutes on the Term Sheet and 20 minutes fielding Council inquiries: sin tax allocations amongst the three teams (Nan Baker), which City and County funding sources were capped and which were not (Martin Sweeney), and the nature of the second five-year extension option (Dale Miller).

Next came County Budget Director Mike Chambers and Franz, who displayed a number of diagrams depicting the proposed money flows and the role of the trustee (Huntington Bank) in managing the proceeds for both ballpark improvements and capital repairs. Responding to Councilman Sweeney's capping question, Chambers replied that the dollar estimates were conservative but the County General Fund would cover any shortages.

Christy Corfias led off the team's presentation with annual economic impact numbers: the Indians spend $108 million, visitors spend $215 million, the team pays $12.5 million in taxes to the City and County and provides over 4,800 jobs in the community. Her colleagues Penny Forster and Raphael Collins described the team's efforts in the community: MLB's RBI program, Boys & Girls Club, and activity centers in the City and County. Councilwoman Nan Baker asked about reasonably-priced ticket packages for families of four, and Councilwoman Cheryl Stephens revived a 1960s-era concept of free tickets for high academic achievers.

Weiss then presented the ballpark improvements: reimagining the Terrace Club @ $33 million, the upper concourse @ $40 million, the press box @ $20 million, and the dugout suites @$9 million; redesigning and upgrading the clubhouse and service level @$40 million, and office renovation/connection to Gateway Plaza @ $42 million. Councilman Scott Tuma asked whether the team would commit to player payroll increases corresponding to the public's investments in the ballpark. Councilman Yvonne Conwell wanted complete and timely notice to minority contractors on all bid packages, and Councilman Sweeney sought more non-baseball events at the ballpark. We were now well past the Council's lunch break, so further discussion was deferred to the next Committee of the Whole on the afternoon of October 12.

We'd now appeared before City and County Councils and hadn't heard a discordant voice from the audience. But opposition was gathering in the form of the Cuyahoga County Progressive Caucus, which grew out of Bernie Sanders' failed 2016 bid for President, had challenged the 2017 Q deal, and had invited the Indians to speak at the Caucus's October 19 meeting. Though the invitation promised "a rigorous look" at our terms, it declined to offer the team a presenting role; instead, it urged the team to pose questions to a stacked panel moderated by Cleveland Scene's Sam Allard and comprised of West Virginia University's Brad Humphreys (a renowned critic of the spin-off economic benefits naively attributed to sports facilities), local attorney Paul Patakos, and regular Gateway meeting attendee Will Tarter.

County Council's second Committee of the Whole met on Tuesday, October 12. Weiss reprised his Ballpark Improvements presentation. Nan Baker renewed her "family of four" ticket request and asked why the City didn't do the bonds: Franz replied by citing the City's overall payments. Cheryl Stephens asked for a Gateway community benefits report. Finally, Michael Gallagher asked why we didn't negotiate the team buying the ballpark, and I responded that the national environment—including MLB's imbalance in local TV revenues—and the lack of Congressional action denied us the leverage.

The next day the Indians hosted City Council members Blaine Griffin and Tony Brancatelli at Progressive Field. Brancatelli previewed four major points: decisions delayed into November, a Council proposal to cap the admission tax payments at $2.55 million, the importance of ticket price-points, and "progressive" Council members' idea to fund community benefits by slapping a $1.00 surcharge on tickets. He also suggested that Council leadership—rather than the team—could subtly raise the threat of team relocation if Council disapproves the proposed agreement.

The following week—on Tuesday, October 19 at 2 PM—the County Council held its third Committee of the Whole on our project. Half a dozen Progressive Caucus members expressed their concerns about the size of the public subsidy. Then Gateway Chief of Staff Daniella Nunnally presented diversity reports on Gateway major projects, focusing on the Q Transformation. In response to several

Council questions concerning how we set our targets, I referenced our ongoing collaboration with City and County diversity directors and urged Council members to pass their latest thinking on to their director.

Council President Jones then took up other questions from the Council, and the Plain Dealer's Kaitlin Durbin gave this account:

> On the county side, annual funding is expected to come primarily from collections from the bed tax and sin tax, in addition to general fund contributions. But council members during a Committee of the Whole meeting Tuesday wondered what would happen if those tax streams don't produce to expectations or if capital repairs exceed their budget. Ken Silliman, chair of Gateway, offered little comfort when he told them that the public, through Gateway, would still be responsible for making up the difference, or risk being in default of the lease. "The only way it gets out of default is if money comes from somewhere, someone to make it up," Silliman said, noting that the non-profit has no independent funding sources.
>
> Gateway did attempt to negotiate for the team to cover or contribute to capital repairs, as required in their current lease for projects up to $500,000, Silliman said, but they were not successful. In these deals, sports leagues have most of the power, he said. "The fact is that, under the present legal environment, the leverage of cities and counties is minimal, unless you're willing to lose your team," Silliman said.
>
> The resolution will now go before council for a second reading next week before a final vote. The deal also must be approved by City Council, which is currently reviewing it. While County Council appears in favor of the deal -- with Councilman Dale

Miller on Tuesday calling it "in the best interest of greater Cleveland" -- public reaction during the three committee meetings on the topic has been mixed.[26]

Later that evening I joined a Zoom conference arranged by the Progressive Caucus that was attended by about 25 participants. Caucus political director Steve Holecko kicked off the meeting and introduced moderator Sam Allard of Cleveland Scene and panelists Brad Humphries of West Virginia University, local activist attorney Pete Pattakos, and regular Gateway monitor/attendee Will Tarter.

Humphries' points, were: replacements of facilities were more common than renovations, but he'd monitored 16 renovation projects for which the average investment was $200 million; his extensive research on economic impact of sports facilities was that they added no net benefits: they just transferred impacts that would otherwise go to other economic actors; that said, there are intangible benefits (e.g., civic pride) but these values were in the $50 million range (versus the hundreds of millions sought by the team in our deal).

Pattakos referenced the teams' refusal to release their financials, which he labelled "untenable behavior" given the teams' huge public dollar demands. He questioned Gateway's claim that the facilities were public, because—if so—where were the public revenues from this ownership? He saw the stadium debate as an issue that transcended "red versus blue" politics where average citizen could see the "corrupt politics" in action. He coined a catchphrase of "Art Modell Hostage Economics."

In his mediator role, Allard lamented the lack of an opposition force as energized as that in the Q deal, and speculated that the squelching of voices at the end of the Q deal probably had a lasting effect. While acknowledging his reluctance to lose a sports team to another city, he asserted that we needed to be willing "to call a team's bluff" in seeking more favorable community terms.

Several audience questions focused on remedies and coalitions of mid-sized cities, and Humphries cited antitrust claims as a remedy that wasn't used as effectively as it could be. As the meeting wrapped up, the leaders reminded the participants that talking points and Council contact info would be distributed, and the next morning I summarized the meeting in our regular communications group meeting.

Several weeks passed. On November 2, 2022, Cleveland voters issued a strong mandate for change by electing 34-year-old Justin Bibb as their next mayor. And key committee chair Tony Brancatelli lost his Council seat to attorney Rebecca Maurer. Though neither new electee would take office prior to 2022, there was much speculation within our Council prep sessions as to impact on City Council hearings in November.

On Tuesday evening, November 9, 2021, Cuyahoga County Council held its third reading of our resolutions and passed them by 9-1 votes (Councilman Michael Gallagher was the only "no" vote). Among the Council statements: given a national template that disfavors cities, it's better to invest in an existing building rather than build new (Dale Miller; Scott Tuma); the baseball team forms community ties (Cheryl Stevens); though sports facility public subsidy concerns continue to grow, there's enough here now to support a "yes" vote (Sunny Simon); the team's response on family ticket packages--$60 for three, $80 for four, $100 for five—is appreciated (Nan Baker); thanks to Council President Jones for a full committee vetting process (Martin Sweeney). It didn't take long for Cleveland Scene's Sam Allard to respond:

This whole charade is merely the latest in an ongoing series of massive public subsidies to Cleveland's pro teams.... The teams have all the power in this system, hold all the leverage, because elected officials are so terrified of the teams' departure that they'll agree to anything.... As such, no "negotiations" of any kind occurred on the current deal. The Guardians are getting precisely what they demanded, with only minimal, and largely symbolic, concessions....[27]

A week later, City Councilman Tony Brancatelli's Development, Planning and Sustainability Committee commenced at 9:30 AM and heard four hours of testimony on the lease extension terms. Council members rolled out nearly a dozen requests for follow up information on matters including attendance breakdowns, parking garage revenues, naming rights, facility costs inclusive of bond interest, and team activities in wards. Recently retired Historic Gateway Executive Director Tom Yablonsky delivered a history of investments in the Gateway neighborhood, and sparred with Councilman Mike Polensek on this investment.

When the dust settled, the Committee moved the legislation on to the following Monday's Finance Committee with the caveat that two large questions remained: 1) as argued by Councilmen Basheer Jones and Anthony Hairston, what would the team do on diversity re all procurement activities (not just construction)? and 2) what are the proposed agreement's risks to the general fund? After highlighting the risk issue, Councilwoman Jenny Spencer transitioned to some troubling timing inquiries: "Why do we need to act now when the lease doesn't expire until 2023?" and "How far in advance are these deals negotiated in other cities?"

Chairman Brancatelli offered several responses to the first question: bond interest rates/inflation, and construction timelines. On the second question, I volunteered that we still had three years remaining on the Browns lease when the team bolted in 1995. The Committee finally wrapped at 2:00 PM. Later that week, Cleveland Scene's Sam Allard had an overview and ten takeaways' points:

Cleveland City Council's Development, Planning and Sustainability Committee met Tuesday for a mammoth all-day session that included in-depth hearings on both the Progressive Field Deal and the city's allocation of American Rescue Plan Act dollars.

Though council had held a preliminary hearing on the deal—a 15-year lease extension with the Cleveland Guardians that includes roughly $285 million in public subsidies for ballpark maintenance and improvements—it had yet to receive detailed information from team representatives. / 00:21

Tuesday's meeting occurred after Cuyahoga County Council had already authorized its portion of the deal. The county agreed to pay $9 million per year over 15 years, which includes substantial annual contributions from the general fund, and has greenlit a $202.5 million bond issue to finance what are referred to as "ballpark improvements." These are the proposed dramatic upgrades at the stadium like the re-imagined Terrace Club and upper deck; not the humdrum capital repairs on escalators, HVAC and plumbing, which the public will also pay for now.

Despite the buoyant, demented rhetoric from a few county council members last week — Marty Sweeney said he thought the deal should be considered the "prototype" for negotiations with pro teams moving forward — most voted in favor of the legislation more reluctantly. The impression was that they were doing so on pain of death, imprisoned by an economic reality in which the teams made all the rules and called all the shots. Councilman Dale

Miller said the national system of stadium financing was broken, but that paying $200 million for upgrades seemed more prudent than paying a billion or more for a new stadium down the road.

(The fact that the public, not the team, issues the bonds for these mega deals, and must therefore service the debt on them, is one of the big reasons why they're so lopsided, by the way. Remember that the Q Deal was billed as a 50/50 split between the public and the Cavs at the outset, and in fact it's now customary for leaders to say that owner Dan Gilbert paid much *more* than the public because he elected to fund additional upgrades in 2018. Once you account for the interest payments, though, the public is paying far more. The enormous debt load the county took on to finance the Q Deal was one reason why Moody's downgraded its bond rating, leading to higher interest rates and higher costs for taxpayers.)

The City of Cleveland's portion of the Progressive Field Deal will include $8 million per year over 15 years, sourced from admissions tax revenue at the ballpark, (revenue that would otherwise go to the city's general fund), a sports facility reserve fund created as part of the Q Deal, revenues from the Gateway East parking garage, and about $350,000 per year that remains unsourced and will, in all likelihood, simply be taken out of the city's general fund.

For four-and-a-half hours Tuesday, members of city council questioned Ken Silliman of the Gateway Economic Development Corporation, (formerly Mayor Frank Jackson's Chief of Staff), and reps from the Guardians legal, strategy and community impact teams to determine whether or not it was in the city's financial interest to vote yes....

Though a number of questions lingered by meeting's end, the committee voted unanimously to move the legislation (Ord. No. 844-2021) along. It will next appear before City Council's Finance

Committee and will surely be passed with minimal friction immediately thereafter.

Here are 10 key takeaways from the proceedings.

1. The deal was done long before it arrived at City Council.
   No further "negotiating" will occur....
2. An awful lot depends on the Gateway East parking garage....
3. The Gateway East parking garage could soon have a
   corporate sponsor. In fact it better....
4. Speaking of naming rights ....
5. The deal includes $42 million to renovate the team's
   administrative offices....
6. West Park Councilman Charles Slife is still "salty" about the
   Flats East Bank 60-year TIF....
7. Bad arithmetic leads to bad logic....
8. The team intends to create a "peer review equity group" to
   ensure that the team adheres to minority hiring targets
   throughout the process....
9. Demolition for ballpark improvements could start within a
   year.
10. Tom Yablonsky got got.[28]

On Monday afternoon, November 22, 2021, we appeared before City
Council's Finance Committee and endured another four-hour
session. It began with a discussion of proffered amendments, the
most significant of which was clarified to state that the team's
option to purchase the Garage would be subject to Council review
and approval. Then, after our truncated re-presentation, Chairman
Kevin Kelley summarized the previous week's Committee meeting
and asked us to respond to the Council information requests arising
from that meeting. The Guardians' Weiss did so, reciting from

responses developed by me and team representatives. During the ensuing Council questionings, Councilman Charles Slife suggested that the Council cap General Fund exposure on the Garage and promptly pass increased parking rates.

Next Councilman Joe Jones launched a long diatribe complaining (incorrectly) that: Council was not receiving responses to its information requests, Chief Dumas was not at the table (her deputy Jim Gentile was), there was no Law Department attorney imbedded in the negotiations (true), the Garage was undervalued, and the lease extension was too short. Councilman Polensek then delivered his customary litany of citywide woes: poverty rate, backlog of 4,000 houses awaiting demolition, Gateway overpromises.

When Councilman Jones sought a second round of questioning, Chairman Kelley quickly inserted a Committee vote—"hearing no objections other than Councilman Jones"—concurring on passage out of the Finance Committee. Then he granted the Councilman 6 more minutes of questions and the Committee adjourned. A week later, on the evening of Monday, November 29, 2021, the City Council passed our Ordinance No. 844-2021 by a 13-3 voting margin, with Council members Mike Polensek, Brian Moodie, and Janny Spencer comprising the "no" votes. Our dual-tracked legislative journey was finally complete.

Two months of lease language fine tuning ensued, and on January 26, 2022, Climaco attorney Simpkins sent the Gateway board members an email confirming the execution of the Amended and Restated Lease between Gateway and the Guardians, as well as the impending closure on the County's bond sale.

Assessing Our Indians Lease Negotiations

Several times during my Council appearances, I stated that "At no time during our two years of negotiations did owner Paul Dolan threaten to relocate the club to another city." And that was true. But there is in this sports franchise business what writer Neil DeMause calls a "non-threat threat," and that did cloud our discussions. Though we never thought that Dolan himself would relocate his team, we were very concerned that he might sell the team and leave us at the mercy of a new owner who, like A's executive Dave Kaval's pitting of Las Vegas against Oakland, might place us in a whipsaw new stadium building fight with Nashville or another city.

And there was some evidence of this non-threat threat. In 2020, Znidarsic had warned that the team needed to know whether it had a deal at least three years prior to lease expiration: if no deal was forthcoming, the team needed at least that much time to plan for a new stadium in another city. Then, in our Zoom sessions in the spring of 2021, the team officials inserted MLB CFO Bob Starkey into our biweekly discussions. Mr. Starkey was very professional and never uttered any warnings, but by his very presence he acted as an unofficial "enforcer."

In November, 2021, when several City Council members began asking why they had to act now, Znidarsic warned me: "If the Council decision spills into the new year, the team will have to start talking to parties you don't want them talking to." Though he didn't elaborate, I recalled a rumor from several months back that a lawyer for several Nashville billionaires was targeting our baseball team. Finally, as I reminded City Council, the Browns had left town in 1995 with three years remaining on their lease.

So how did we fare as public sector bargainers? The word "bitter-sweet" comes to mind. Starting with the bitter, I viewed King County, Oregon's annual $10.5 million contribution to the Seattle Mariners as a good comparable. I thought we were more than fair when we increased our annual offer to $14.5 million, and was shocked when that offer was rejected in October, 2020. Had we stopped there, with the team plowing an additional $4.5 million into the agreement, I would have felt good about our outcome. But we had to go all the way to $17 million locally (with an additional $2 million from the State), which was a heavy burden for County Executive Budish and Mayor Jackson during an election year and a pandemic.

Nevertheless, we did achieve 15 more years—with a doable five-year extension—of useful life on an existing 27-year-old ballpark. If we add in the Indians $44 million private investment in 2015-2016 ballpark improvements, the overall tally is closer to a 50/50 public/private funding outcome. We assessed no new taxes for our agreement. We didn't give up on State assistance after an initial rejection, and Governor DeWine delivered the critically-needed $2 million annual commitment.

Most importantly, I have to credit team owner Paul Dolan for his willingness to embrace a renovation of Progressive Field rather than follow the growing parade of owners who demand new stadiums— witness Atlanta, Arlington, Oakland, Buffalo, Nashville, and (most recently) Kansas City— when an existing facility is perfectly adequate. In our locale, at least, our debate was over tens of millions rather than hundreds of millions or even billions.

CHAPTER NINE

WHAT'S BEEN HAPPENING NATIONALLY

In subsequent Chapters 10 and 11 I will assess Cleveland's sports facility outcomes. But to place that assessment in proper context, this chapter will first review what's been happening in other American cities over the course of the last decade. Though the pace of new facility construction has slowed from the frantic years of the late 1990s and early 2000s, sports facility debates have not subsided. The main trending topics have been major renovations of existing sports facilities, new construction projects coupled with adjacent real estate development, and cities facing new stadium ultimatums.

For a number of reasons—including Camden Yards' opening of the floodgates for new baseball-only ballparks and the NFL's leveraging of the Cleveland Browns franchise relocation to trigger multiple new football stadia—the decade of the 1990s was the most aggressive sports facility construction period in American history. Of the 92 major league baseball, basketball, and football franchises, about one-third received new buildings in the 1990s. Now, 20 years later, team owners are lining up to seek major renovations of these 1990s facilities. Since the price tags of these projects often approach the facilities' original costs, the public reviews can be very lively. Seattle, Phoenix, Philadelphia, and Indianapolis illustrate the range of approaches to—and reactions to—these major renovation projects.

Safeco Field and Key Arena Renovations in Seattle

In the fall of 2018, King County, Washington and its largest city—Seattle—packed in enough sports facility drama to equal a decade of activity in most regions. The first issue was baseball: The Metropolitan King County Council presided over a heated debate over the appropriate level of public funding for long-term capital needs for the Seattle Mariners' Safeco Field ballpark.

The County Council had long ago established the Washington Baseball Public Facilities District (the "WBPFD") to manage the ballpark and its adjacent garage in much the same manner as that performed by Gateway in Cleveland. The sports facilities were leased to the Seattle Mariners in 1999 for a twenty-year term under which the Mariners pay for ballpark operating expenses, routine maintenance, an annual rent of $1 million, and most necessary capital repairs.

In the spring of 2018, the Mariners and the WBPFD announced their agreement on a 25-year lease extension under which the Mariners' annual rent will increase to $1.5 million. However, the Mariners later issued a significant clarification: their agreement was conditioned upon King County's annual contribution of $8.3 million from its 2% lodging tax proceeds. The $8.3 million would be applied toward long-term Safeco Field capital repairs (a 2015 assessment had estimated total capital needs of $297 million over the next twenty years). This new annual payment would supplement three previously existing annual public contributions:

- $4.5 million from admissions tax proceeds;
- $0.5 million from parking tax proceeds; and
- $0.25 million from Mariners rent payments.

When this proposed use of lodging tax proceeds went public in the summer of 2018, it touched off a heated debate and polarized the King County Council. Opponents argued that the annual $8.3 million lodging tax payment should be used for affordable housing or tourism promotion.

Following several months of acrimony which included reversal of positions amongst Council members, a committee of the Metropolitan King County Council voted 5-4 on September 5, 2018, in favor of a reduced annual ballpark contribution of $5.4 million.[1] The full Council vote was set for September 17, and on that date a Seattle TV station summarized the Council's decision:

> The King County Council approved a controversial package which will allow the Mariners to use $135 million in lodging taxes for Safeco Field improvements. The 5-4 council approval came after a nearly three-hour meeting which included last-minute amendments to reduce the funding package or redirect funds towards tourism promotion or homeless services. The compromise agreed upon was hammered out earlier this month after the Mariners initially asked for $180 million in funding as part of a long-term, 25-year lease extension....[2]"

After the Council's approval, the public's total annual contribution to Safeco Field (now renamed "T-Mobile Park") capital needs are:

PUBLIC FUNDING SOURCE	ANNUAL AMOUNT IN $
Admission Tax	4,500,000
Parking Tax	500,000
Mariners Rent	250,000
Lodging Tax	5,400,000
TOTAL	10,650,000

Later that month, the Seattle City Council took up the KeyArena facility:

> The Seattle City Council unanimously approved plans for a privately funded $700 million renovation of KeyArena on Monday, clearing one of the last major hurdles in the city's bid to land an expansion NHL franchise. The 8-0 vote was the final step needed to strengthen Seattle's expansion application, and it means a team could be playing in the building during the 2020-21 season....
>
> The vote ended a debate that began in the mid-2000s when Howard Schultz, then the owner of the Seattle SuperSonics, said the city-owned KeyArena needed renovations. The lack of luxury amenities and a challenging lease agreement ultimately led to the Sonics leaving following the 2008 season and moving to Oklahoma City, where the franchise was rebranded as the Thunder.[3]

Two months later—on December 4, 2018—the NHL's board of governors approved a new Seattle hockey franchise: the new team paid a $650 million league entry fee (up from the $500 million paid by the Las Vegas Golden Knights) and began play as the "Seattle Kraken" in the 2021-22 season as a member of the Pacific Division.[4]

Meanwhile, and ironically on Halloween of 2018, the last cloud had been removed from the Safeco Field deal:

> Back in late September, a referendum—formally titled Referendum 25—was filed by a mysterious group calling itself "Citizens Against

Sports Stadium Subsidies." The move came a little over a week after the King County Council narrowly approved a controversial plan Sept. 18 to spend roughly $135 million in public funds over two decades on Safeco Field maintenance. Critics had argued that the money would be better spent on affordable housing and social services, given the regional homelessness crisis. If the referendum's backers had been able to gather around 40,000 signatures by Nov. 2, the initiative would have qualified for the Feb. 2019 special election ballot. But according to a letter sent Oct. 31 to the King County Council clerk by Dmitri Iglitzin, an attorney representing the initiative's backers, the group is now withdrawing the referendum.[5]

Talking Stick Resort Arena Renovation in Phoenix

The City of Phoenix' Talking Stick Resort Arena opened as America West Arena in June, 1992 at a construction cost of $89 million. In 1998, it was joined by a new neighbor: Chase Field, home of the Arizona Diamondbacks baseball team. Former Phoenix Suns basketball team owner Jerry Colangelo orchestrated the first renovation of the arena in 2003 at a cost of $67 million; the defining improvement then was a 16,000-square-foot air-conditioned glass-enclosed atrium.

By the time the Arena turned 25-years-old in 2017, current team owner Robert Sarver had commenced quiet negotiations with City of Phoenix officials on a second major renovation deal: this time the cost would be $230 million. When the particulars emerged in December, 2018—after 21 executive sessions over the preceding several years—both the owner and city officials quickly found themselves on the defensive. Among the pointed charges: Why was the deal negotiated behind closed doors? Did the team owner threaten to move the team if the renovation isn't approved? And what was the hurry in getting a city council vote in December?

As for the specific proposed deal elements, the Arizona Republic summarized them as follows in a December 12, 2018, news story:

Phoenix pays $150 million for arena renovations.

- Suns pay $80 million for renovations.
- After the renovation, Phoenix will pay $2 million annually for 12½ years into a new renewal and replacement fund, which will be used for future renovation needs.
- Suns will pay $1 million into the new fund for 12½ years.
- Suns will continue to operate and maintain the building, including booking concerts and other events.
- Suns will continue to pay rent to the city (calculated as a percentage of annual proceeds). Currently, those payments average about $1.5 million per year, but the city expects the rent to increase to $4 million after the renovation is completed.
- Suns will build a new practice facility (estimated to cost $25-$50 million) somewhere in Phoenix.
- Suns commit to staying in downtown through 2037 with an option to extend the lease to 2042. If they leave before 2037, they will face up to a $200 million fine.[6]

On the alleged owner threat of team relocation, the Republic had this to say:

The Suns committed to a 40-year lease in 1992, but the agreement includes a provision for the Suns to opt out at 30 years if the building — one of the oldest in the NBA — is considered obsolete. That could allow the Suns to leave downtown Phoenix in 2022 if there's no new agreement. Suns owner Robert Sarver has hinted for years that he could move the team to another location in the Valley, or possibly out of state. It's unclear whether any other market has expressed serious interest in the team. If the Suns leave, Phoenix would have to take over operations and maintenance of the building, and would still have to invest in significant infrastructure repairs if it wants to attract concerts and other events, according to the city.[7]

Facing a substantial citizen and media uproar, the city council voted to postpone its vote until January 23, 2019; in the interim five weeks, the council set up a series of briefings and public hearings, team owner Sarver publicly disavowed making team relocation threats, and the Arizona Republic published an article entitled "Is the Phoenix Suns arena deal worse than other cities' deals? You decide." The article examined seven recent deals involving negligible public dollars and seven recent deals that used a lot of public money, concluding that "...the Suns' $230 million proposal requires a greater share of taxpayers' money than any city except Atlanta."[8]

The data from the article[9] is summarized in the following table.

CITY	YEAR ARENA COMPLETED	NEW OR RENOVATION?	PUBLIC $ IN MILLIONS	PRIVATE $ IN MILLIONS
Boston	2020	Renovate	0	100
Las Vegas	2016	New	0	375
Philadelphia	2022	Renovate	0	250
Washington	2018	Renovate	0	40
Seattle	2020	Renovate	3.5	700
Inglewood	2024	New	30	1.2 billion
San Francisco	2019	New	0	1.0 billion
Salt Lake City	2017	Renovate	23	102
Cleveland	2019	Renovate	70	115
Detroit	2017	New	324	539
Sacramento	2016	New	255	335
Minneapolis	2017	Renovate	74	76
Milwaukie	2018	New	250	250
Phoenix	2021	Renovate	150	80

An early December poll had shown strong disapproval of the issue. But during the several public hearings conducted in late December and early January, city staff made some points that seemed to resonate with the attendees: that the city—not the Suns—owned the arena, and that no new taxes were needed to fund the renovation (the contributing hotel and rental car taxes were already in place). By January 10, Arizona Business Magazine was reporting:

> A new poll, commissioned by the Greater Phoenix Chamber and conducted by OH Predictive Insights, showed a 53-point shift in favorability for the renovations to Talking Stick Resort Arena. Once the public had complete information on the funding mechanism along with the benefits to downtown Phoenix, our city's economy, and the community, the poll showed a near 2-to-1 ratio of support (49%) versus opposition (25%).[10]

On January 23, 2019, Mayor Thelda Williams and the Phoenix City Council presided over three hours of testimony for and against the project. The comments aligned similarly to the recent poll, with 2/3 of the speakers expressing support. Proponents included not only the predictable chamber of commerce type entities, but also an impressive number of nonprofit leaders who cited the Suns' charitable contributions. Opponents criticized the project's "corporate welfare," the "secret negotiations," the financial impact of annual debt service payments of $13.7 million, and the favoring of downtown over the city's neighborhoods. One opponent—Larry Namen—demanded a public vote and reminded the audience that he had *shot* former Maricopa County Supervisor Mary Rose Wilcox after her 1997 vote in favor of public financial support for the Arizona Diamondbacks baseball franchise.

After attaching several amendments to the legislation—one by Councilperson Vania Guevera requiring the Suns to commit at least $10 million toward community endeavors (including a minimum of $2.6 million toward the city's Head Start preschool program, to which team owner Robert Sarver voiced his consent), and a second "friendly amendment" by Councilman Michael Nowakowski that the deal's $1.5 million annual new revenues would go towards general fund public safety and homelessness needs—the Council voted 6-2 in favor of the $230 million deal. Vice Mayor Jim Waring and Councilman Sal DiCiccio comprised the "no" votes.

But the Council decision was not the last word on the issue: Donn Chavez of Petition Partners claimed that a group calling itself "Common Sense Phoenix" was poised to gather 27,000 petition signatures (17,000 more than the legally required 10,000) within 30 days to cause a referendum on the issue. If that effort had been successful, the arena issue would have joined two other topics—light rail transit and pension changes—already teed up for referenda.[11] But, in an action reminiscent of the Clerk to Cleveland City Council's action on the Q referendum, attorneys for Phoenix wrote the group advising that the city clerk would not accept the petitions (because "only legislative acts" were subject to referenda); shortly thereafter, the attorney for Common Sense Phoenix called off the referendum on behalf of his client.[12]

Wells Fargo Center Renovation in Philadelphia

Comcast Spectator opened its privately-financed Wells Fargo Center in 1996 at a cost of $210 million. When newly-installed Comcast president Dave Scott toured the arena in 2014, he concluded it was "tired."[13] After briefly considering a "demolish and build new" option, Scott chose to follow the "renovate" path blazed by many of the other owners of arenas built in the 1990s. But, unlike most other franchise owners, he did not approach his host city seeking public monies: the whole $250 million Wells Fargo upgrade was privately financed.

But, as in other cities, the nature of the arena changes was driven by demographics:

> Throughout the 1990s, sports arenas deemed antiquated were simply demolished, replaced with structures more than double their size. Phrases like *premium seating, luxury boxes,* and *VIP club* were the engines that drove that construction. Those offerings created revenue opportunities for owners and leagues that did not exist before, and radically changed the fan experience — especially for the larger corporations that could afford to lease those luxury boxes.

> Now, it is those concepts that have become antiquated as fans, particularly millennials, seek a more festival-oriented fan experience. But rather than tearing down the old, improvements in technology are allowing buildings to "gut as they go," remodeling the insides to reflect those changes.[14]

The Wells Fargo makeover shared many of the features of Cleveland's Q Arena renovation: extensive glass treatments replacing most of the existing opaque exterior walls, widened concourses, and socially interactive fan areas replacing some of the 120 private luxury boxes. The renovation was completed in 2020.

Bankers Life Fieldhouse Renovation in Indianapolis

A major renovation of Indianapolis' Bankers Life Fieldhouse was approved in a political environment that has always been receptive to downtown sports facilities. For over 50 years, Indianapolis has used amateur and professional sports facilities to drive its downtown planning agenda. As the Fieldhouse neared its twentieth birthday in 2017, owner Herb Simon stated his desire for a major overhaul:

> "For me to sign a long-term lease, which is what I really want to do for the city, we're going to have to plan it for the 21st century," he said. "Things have changed. People's viewing habits are different with more social environments. It takes a major redo because the bones are great and we want to keep it here.[15]

By the spring of 2019, Simon and the City's Capital Improvement Board had agreed on a renovation plan coupled with a lease extension. The deal required state funding approval, and the legislature complied:

> The Pacers agreed to stay in Indianapolis for 25 more years as part of a deal directing $270 million to the Bankers Life Fieldhouse project from the state and local income and sales taxes generated by several nearby hotels — diverting that money from the state, city and local schools. As part of the funding plan, Pacers Sports & Entertainment would contribute $65 million of a $360-million

public-private partnership to pay for capital improvements at the arena. City funding in the form of $25 million for public infrastructure would also be part of that mix, though it requires its own approval process. The lease extension would commit the Pacers to Bankers Life Fieldhouse through the 2043-44 NBA season, with options that could extend their agreement an additional three years.[16]

But national sports facility critic Neil deMause took a dim view of the proceedings:

> In exchange for agreeing to have his team play where it always has, Pacers owner Herb Simon—aka the billionaire developer who turned failing downtown department stores into a failing downtown mall—will accept $295 million in immediate taxpayer cash to upgrade the arena, plus a $12 million check every year for 10 years for "technology upgrades," plus 25 years' worth of $14.5 million annual operating subsidies. Total value of Simon's subsidy windfall, in 2019 dollars: about $600 million.[17]

New Sports Facilities Driving Real Estate Development

Sports facility major renovations have made a lot of news in the last decade. But there's been a second major trend. In a prophetic 2011 law review article, Martin J. Greenberg and Dennis Hughes, Jr. observed that:

> Real estate development has become a central component of sports facility development, and the results thereof—urban revitalization and transformation—may be as important as the building of the sports facility itself.[18]

They recognized—and anticipated—a widening scope of sports facility construction projects, in which the development of surrounding real estate is envisioned as a key component of the defined project *from the start* (as opposed to the *desired after-effect* it comprised in 1990s stadium projects).

> Team owners and real estate developers realize the potential bene-
> fits of constructing a new facility and from developing the
> surrounding land. Because of developed and redeveloped sports
> facilities, blighted and inner-city areas have turned into attractive
> gathering places for tourists and local citizens alike. A sports
> facility is created, and over time, the area around the facility
> develops into a popular destination place and entertainment
> district.[19]

In their view, the more successful sports facility projects from the 1990s—Camden Yards in Baltimore, Jacobs Field (now Progressive Field) in Cleveland, Coors Field in Denver, and Staples Center in Los Angeles— "...provided the perfect testing ground.... (to spur) the trend of neighborhood economic development and revitalization through the development of a sports venue."[20]

In their discussion of the Cleveland project, they particularly high-lighted the impact on neighborhood property values:

- In 1997, when the assessed value of the total downtown property of Cleveland dropped 1.7% from 1996, the assessed value of properties within the three-block radius surrounding Progressive Field *increased*;[21]
- In the years 1998-2000, assessed property value throughout downtown Cleveland rose: by 2.3% in 1998, by 3.2% in 1999, and by 38.8% in 2000. But there was an even greater

increase in the three-block radius surrounding Progressive Field.[22]

- In years 2001-2003, when downtown Cleveland suffered dramatic decreases in assessed value, the properties surrounding Progressive Field continued to increase;[23]
- From 2003 through 2007, the assessed value for the commercial businesses, residential properties, entertainment properties, and hotel properties adjoining the ballpark and arena all increased;[24] and
- Even during the great recession, the sports facilities positively impacted the area: "Although the hotel and residential properties decreased slightly, in the three-block radius surrounding the stadium, the commercial business properties increased 8.5% and the entertainment properties increased 2%".[25]

In transitioning from their discussion of the exemplary 1990s projects to the sports facility projects they were seeing in the 2000s, Greenberg and Hughes coined a new phrase: "sports. comm":

> The basic goal of a sports.comm is to transform a sports venue that attracts millions of people, but is only used on a limited basis, into a year-round entertainment destination for an entire region.... Examples of successfully completed sports.comms include Patriot Place, home of the New England Patriots; Nationwide Arena, home of the Columbus Blue Jackets; and Ballpark Village, home of the San Diego Padres.[26]

Bridging the 1990s and the 2000s, Los Angeles' Staple Center Arena project was the first project in the 2000s to seek to build upon the successful 1990s initiatives.

While the Staples Center provides a shining example on how a sports facility can create momentum for urban development, L.A. Live has helped make this area of Los Angeles one of the foremost destination places for sports and entertainment. Adjacent to the Staples Center, L.A. Live is the premier entertainment complex in downtown Los Angeles. At a cost of approximately $2.5 billion, L.A. Live was developed by Anschutz Entertainment Group, Wachovia Group, and McFarland Partners. Its 27-acre site features 5.6 million square feet of apartments, ballrooms, bars, concerts, theaters, restaurants, movie theaters, and a 54-story hotel and condominium tower.[27]

Staples Center was also noteworthy as one of the first major sports facility projects to adopt an extensive community benefits agreement ("CBA").

Some of the provisions contained in the Staples Center CBA include: $1,000,000 for the creation or improvement of parks and recreational facilities; $25,000 per year for a term of five years for the creation of a residential parking permit program; agreement to comply with the city's living wage ordinance and to make all reasonable efforts to reach the goal of ensuring that 70% of the jobs created by the project pay a living wage; priority hiring to persons displaced by the project and to low income individuals residing within three miles of the project; job training programs; a requirement that 20% of the residential units in the project be affordable; and an agreement to cooperate with the coalition to establish an advisory committee to assist with the implementation and enforcement of the agreement.[28]

In the Nationwide Arena district in Columbus, the taxpayers invested $44 million in bond funds (to be repaid from proceeds of a tax increment financing district) and Nationwide Insurance invested $150 million in a new arena. These initial investments attracted "... restaurants, bars, office space, a movie theater, a concert pavilion, a baseball stadium, hotels, and apartments and condominiums."[29]

> Beyond Nationwide's initial $350 million investment in the arena district, over $1 billion has been committed to the final project. Since the beginning of the arena district project in 1999, the average property value in the district has increased by 267%, and property values in all of Columbus have increased a total of 22%. The arena district was extremely profitable and also well planned, considering that the one million square feet of available office space has a 95% occupancy rate.[30]

San Diego's Petco Park took a very long time to bring to fruition, but the end results were impressive:

> In 1998, 60% of voters approved Proposition C, which allocated $411 million toward building a ballpark and redeveloping a twenty-six-block area of downtown San Diego now known as Ballpark Village. In return, the Padres pledged to spend $115 million on the new ballpark, to invest at least $300 million in the surrounding developments, and to be responsible for all construction cost overruns. Ultimately, the Padres contributed over $200 million to Petco Park and nearly $600 million to the surrounding redevelopment.[31]

Moreover, much like the developers of the nearby Staples Center project in Los Angeles, the developers of Petco Park were early pioneers in the use of community benefit agreements.

More recently, there is the astonishing privately-financed Hollywood Park 238-acre real estate project in Inglewood, California, in which SoFi Stadium opened in 2021 seating 100,240 at a cost exceeding $4 billion: when fully developed, the real estate project will include 2,500 dwelling units, 800,000 square-feet of offices, 600,000 square-feet of retail (including a multiplex movie theater, a 300-room luxury hotel, and a casino), 200,000 square feet for NFL Media operations relocated from Culver City, a 6,000-seat performing venue, and a large public gathering space.

An interesting question to ponder: if there *was* substantial public funding for the Los Angeles project, would the Inglewood tract still be the site of choice? On the plus side, there is the productive reuse of an abandoned tract—the former Hollywood Park racetrack—that will be thoroughly revitalized. On the other hand, does an already decentralized and sprawling Los Angeles metro area really need another entirely new center of economic activity?

To that question, Inglewood Mayor James Butts—and his entire city council— answered a declarative "yes.": in June, 2017, they authorized the start of negotiations with the Los Angeles Clippers to relocate their basketball team from the Staples Arena to a proposed new Inglewood arena to be located across the street from the new football stadium. In Mayor Butts' words" "this, to me, changes the center of gravity in Los Angeles County to Inglewood."[32]

Most of the successful sports-facility-anchored real estate projects have occurred in core urban areas. Apart from the constructed improvements, these projects delivered a critical byproduct by reclaiming prior depressed urban environments (and often spawning community benefit agreements to ensure that local residents shared in the projects' economic output). However, several sports facility developments targeted a different goal: that's the provision of entertainment and retail options to previously underserved rural areas. Two notable examples are Foxborough, Massachusetts and Green Bay, Wisconsin.

In 1999, after first exploring relocation of his New England Patriots to Boston and Hartford, owner Robert Kraft settled on a Foxborough project that would become the largest development concentration between Boston and Providence, Rhode Island. He assigned the name of "Patriot Place" to this stadium-driven, 350-acre, 1.3 million square-foot recreational/retail real estate development.

The new $325 million privately-financed Gillette Stadium anchored the *entertainment* venues (other entertainment options included an upscale cinema, a two-story concert venue, and interactive games).[33] New England's first Bass Pro Shops—a destination-retailer boasting indoor waterfalls, fish ponds, and indoor shooting ranges—anchored the *retail* venues (other retailers included Hollister, Old Navy, Bath and Body Works, Victoria's Secret, and Tech Superpowers). Patriot Place also incorporated destination restaurants, a football museum, a hotel, a spa, a health care center, condominiums, and apartments.[34]

The second notable rural stadium-based real estate project is Green Bay's Lambeau Field and its adjacent Titletown District.

> Lambeau Field has the unique distinction of being located in a cold, rural area of the country. Therefore, the success or failure of the Titletown District will be the ultimate test of whether the staged sports.comm is a viable tool for economic development regardless of market size, climate, or location.[35]

Work commenced in 2002 on the project anchor: this was the $295 million renovation of Lambeau Field:

...that caused the stadium to more than double in size to nearly 1.7 million square feet. The crown jewel of the development was the five-story Lambeau Field Atrium. The facility is home to the Green Bay Packers Hall of Fame, the Packers' team shop, interactive fan zones, event facilities, seven new restaurants, and multiple new outlets for concessions. The developer of the project, Hammes Co., strategically positioned the atrium to "open up the building to the potential of bringing people to the stadium year-round."[36]

The Packers have developed Titletown on a 45-acre parcel of land that was once an eyesore. Phase I included retailers (Hinterland Brewery and the Lodge Kohler Hotel), entertainment venues (bocce ball, table tennis, shuffleboard, bean bag toss), and a sports medicine and orthopedic clinic. Phase II included apartments, condominiums, town homes, and office buildings.[37]

In their prescient 2011 article, Greenberg and Hughes listed four "staged" projects: the New Orleans Superdome, Titletown District in Green Bay, Wisconsin, the Bricktown District in Oklahoma City, and the Platinum Triangle in Anaheim, California.[38] Then they listed six "delayed" projects—most of which have progressed to completion since 2011—in Glendale, Arizona (Westgate City Center), St. Louis (Ballpark Village), Arlington, Texas (Glorypark), Dallas (Victory Park), New Jersey (the New Meadowlands), and Brooklyn (Atlantic Yards).[39]

Cities Facing a "New Stadium or Else" Ultimatum

Baseball Commissioner Rob Manfred has often stated his intention to resolve the Tampa Bay and Oakland stadium issues prior to picking MLB expansion cities. In his December, 2018, reply to a letter from Tampa officials, he complained that—among other deficiencies—the officials' plan for a new $892 million stadium in Tampa's Ybor City neighborhood lacked "a firm proposal to arrange for at least $475 million of funding." But Tampa's 2020 business organization *had* arranged private commitments of $16 million annually over a ten-year period (exclusive of naming rights, which could yield an additional $8-10 million annually).[40] Still, a Tampa editorial writer opined those amounts weren't enough:

> The unsecured financing from the opportunity zone plan was a problem, but not the biggest hurdle. The deal-killer was Hillsborough only planning on coming up with $450 million of the $900 million cost. That meant the Rays were going to have to spend $450 million. And that was never going to happen. Why? Because it doesn't make business sense to them. They'll likely get a better deal elsewhere.[41]

Then the Tampa officials failed to meet a December, 2018, owner-imposed deadline to finalize the Ybor City site:

> Rays owner Stuart Sternberg, who made a new stadium his No. 1 priority since gaining control of the club in 2005, said the team will not be able to clear the funding and logistical hurdles to make their proposed $900 million ballpark in Tampa a reality.... Despite the potential will to try again, the reality is the club once again is back to square one: No site, and no permission - for now - to seek one in perhaps the region's most viable area. That may not force them out by 2027 – but it certainly gives a more ominous tick to their stadium clock.[42]

In January, 2019, —less than a month after the Rays announced that they'd abandoned their plans to build a stadium in Ybor City—the team announced its intent to reduce the seating at Tropicana Field to about 25,000 to 26,000 under a renovation plan aimed at improving fans' experience.[43] Later that month, the Rays decided to "improve the ballpark experience for fans" by becoming the first North American sports team to go cashless at their stadium. The Rays failed to explain why a franchise with MLB's second lowest 2018 attendance total would make things more difficult for low-income fans who may lack access to credit cards.[44]

But Rays owner Sternberg saved the most dramatic announcement for a June 25, 2019, press conference at the Dali Museum: he asked the Tampa/St. Petersburg community to consider sharing the Rays with Montreal. Each city would construct a new open-air stadium, with spring games played in Florida, and summer games played in Montreal. MLB Commissioner Rob Manfred warmed to the concept, and eight months later stated:

> "If it preserved baseball in Tampa Bay and quite frankly gave us another international market, I see that as kind of a two for one. It would be a good thing all the way around.".[45]

A negotiation that already involved two cities—Tampa and St. Petersburg—had now added a third city located in another country. But in January 2022, MLB's owners voted to kill the two-city proposal, returning owner Sternberg back to the starting gates.[46]

On the opposite coast, the City of Oakland has played punching bag for all three major sports leagues. In 1996, the Raiders football team returned to its rabid Oakland fan base after a 13-year absence, but only after owner Al Davis demanded $200 million of improvements to Oakland Coliseum (including 20,000 additional seats dubbed as

"Mount Davis" which bastardized a formerly beautiful ballpark and obliterated the former center field view of the Oakland hills). Then, in 2017—when $83 million in principal and interest on Mount Davis bond payments remained, and after several years of "negotiations" amongst the city, the Raiders, and the NFL—the league owners voted to approve the franchise's relocation to Las Vegas.

Not to be outdone, in 2018 the Golden State Warriors compounded their earlier decision to relocate from Oakland to San Francisco by challenging their liability for over $40 million in remaining debt payments attributable to 1996 improvements to the now-abandoned Oracle Arena. The Warriors at least agreed to submit the dispute to arbitration, and in October, 2018, the arbitrator ruled that the Warriors—and not Oakland or Alameda County—were responsible for the $40 million debt payments.[47]

Lest one think that the City of Oakland was passively accepting all these challenges, the NFL and its 31 other franchises learned otherwise when the city filed an antitrust lawsuit entitled City of Oakland vs. Oakland Raiders, et. al. The City trumpeted its claims via a December 11, 2018 press release:

> Recently, the NFL has allowed NFL clubs to move even when the relocation is a clear violation of its relocation policies. Threats of relocation are a central part of the NFL's practice of demanding public financing for new stadiums, which significantly increase team revenues and ticket prices. Further, each time an NFL club moves, all NFL teams share in a "relocation fee." In the last several years, the NFL defendants have shared approximately $1.47 billion in these fees.

The complaint itself elaborated on these themes:

In a competitive marketplace, NFL Clubs could not demand billion-dollar stadia with premium seating and amenities; instead, they could only seek the repairs and renovations necessary to the maintenance of the NFL brand and each NFL Club. But the NFL is anything but a competitive market. Once again, in a country with over 325 million citizens, the NFL currently limits its product to 32 clubs, and courts have repeatedly found that professional football is its own market. For a fan of professional football, the NFL is the only game in town.[48]

The NFL earned a magistrate's decision dismissing the action. But, regardless of outcome, one has to admire the City of Oakland's perseverance through adversity. That pluckiness is now being tested yet again, as Oakland remains on Baseball Commissioner Rob Manfred's watch list due to the challenged baseball environment existing at Oakland Coliseum. In late 2018. the A's announced a plan to build a new privately-financed 34,000-seat ballpark in the Jack London Square neighborhood on a 55-acre waterfront Howard Terminal site. They also plan to retain Oracle Arena and reduce the Coliseum to a scaled-down sports park reminiscent of San Francisco's treatment of Kezar Stadium.[49]

As the team's ownership proceeded toward a July 20, 2021, make-or-break Oakland City Council vote on $855 million worth of publicly-funded infrastructure at the Howard Terminal site, A's president Dave Kaval visited Las Vegas to explore relocation there. In demanding action on the Howard Terminal location—as opposed to a less costly redevelopment of the existing BART-served Coliseum site—the team cited "Petco Park in San Diego, Progressive Field in Cleveland and Oracle Park in San Francisco (as) ballparks the A's often point to as examples of their downtown, urban vision..."[50].

At the July 20, 2021 Oakland City Council meeting, broadcast via Zoom and watched in its entirety by the author, Council President Nikki Fortunato Bas commenced the proceedings at 9:00 AM PST with an hour and a half of public comments strictly limited to one minute each. By my rough assessment, the overall tally was 60% in opposition to the Howard Terminals financing plan (supporters were generally either Coliseum concession workers or union leaders, with a few civic supporters mixed in).

Then Bas called upon several members of Oakland Mayor Libby Schaff's administration. First was Assistant City Administrator Elizabeth Lake who reviewed the A's original financing plan from April, 2021, which called for the $855 million public investment via two separate tax increment financing ("TIF") districts: a $495 million district confined to the immediate 55-acre project site, and a much broader $360 million district. She explained how a July 7, 2021 City Council Community Development/Economic Development meeting had excised the wider district.

She was followed by Real Estate and Major Projects Director Molly Maybrun, who summarized the Term Sheet the administration and Council leadership had been negotiating with the A's over the last several months. The latest version proposed 35% affordable housing (15% within the immediate project site), and a 25-year non-relocation term. All project construction would be subject to the Port's Project Labor Agreement. There'd be construction deadlines for the ballpark and some parks in the immediate environs, but the rest of the supposed $12 billion project (so-called "ancillary development") could be built out at the developer's discretion.

Combined community benefit funding by the City, County, Port, and A's would yield a $10 million Port Social Justice Trust Fund and a $50 million set-aside from the Infrastructure Financing District

("IFD"). And condominium transfer fees (diverted from the city treasury to the project's community benefits stack) would add $340 million over 66 years.

The team would pay the city's game day costs for police, parking, and traffic enforcement. Wrapping the administration's summary, Vice Mayor/Council member Rebecca Kaplan listed significant amendments to the proposed Council resolution:

- Though the proposal denied the developer's requested $360 million broader TIF district, it compromised by pledging that the $351.9 million estimated offsite transportation infrastructure cost would *not* be borne by the developer: instead, regional, state and federal dollars would be sought;
- The affordable housing requirements; and
- A non-displacement requirement.

City staff believed that these compromises—particularly the offsite infrastructure one—could close the gap between the public and the team. But that hope was dashed when Bas called upon A's President Dave Kaval for his reaction. After stating a caveat that he was just today seeing the city staff's amendments, he spent the rest of his time allotment warning the Council members that there wasn't a consensus, and it would be futile to vote on that date. When pressed by Councilwoman Carroll Fife to specify what he disagreed with, Kaval's nonspecific and solution-avoiding response was "this is not a term sheet that works for the A's.""

It was now time for Council members to comment, and Council-woman Fife— clearly frustrated by her exchange with Kaval—suggested that a vote now would be meaningless and moot. Bas herself, who represented Chinatown, cited the need for fairness to that neighborhood as well as the importance of the community benefits. Councilmen Noel Gallo and Dan Kalb each voiced strong preferences for the Coliseum site.

The remaining three Council members were all conditionally supportive of the amended resolution. Councilwoman Loren Taylor was focused on community benefits and protection of the general fund: she was annoyed at the A's tactic of "bullying" via social media, but willing to overlook that conduct and "put Oakland first." Councilwoman Sheng Tao sounded a similar note, and Councilman Treva Reid cited the "disappointing feedback from Mr. Kaval" but still viewed the amended term sheet as creating a "legacy development." Council President Bas then asked for a motion. Councilwoman Tao moved approval of the amended resolution, and Bas seconded. The motion passed 6-1, with Fife abstaining and Gallo voting "no" presumably due to his preference for the Coliseum site.

Three months passed. Dave Kaval kept exploring Las Vegas sites, and kept harping on a misfit between the A's plan and the City of Oakland vote. Then, on October 26, 2021, the Alameda County Supervisors took "nonbinding action" and voted 4-1 in favor of the city proposal. In the words of Field of Schemes blogger Neil deMause:

> Right, so now all that has to happen is for Oakland and Alameda County and A's owner John Fisher to finalize a deal, including where the missing $360 million will come from, and then vote on it, at a time TBD. If the county had voted against the deal .... the plan would have been seen to have lost momentum or something, so last night's vote was definitely important, binding or not.[51]

A year and a half passed, and though there was progress on environmental approvals, neither the City of Oakland nor the Alameda County Supervisors were able to raise the "missing $360 million."

But Vice Mayor/Councilmember Rebecca Kaplan 's July 20, 2021 pledge—that the City would look to regional, state, and federal sources, and not the developer, to fill that gap—remained intact.

That proved too little and too late for A's President Dave Kaval. On April 19, 2023, he announced (prematurely, as it turned out) that the A's had closed on the purchase of 49 acres in Las Vegas. Kaval told the San Francisco Chronicle:

> For a long time we were on parallel paths and right now, at this moment, and with this transaction that we just entered into, we are really focusing our efforts on Las Vegas and on bringing the 20-year saga of the A's stadium venue efforts to kind of a final positive conclusion.[52]

Moreover, the Las Vegas Review-Journal reported that same day that the heretofore noncommittal Nevada legislature was suddenly considering a half-billion dollar public investment toward a $1.5 billion retractable roof stadium on the site purchased by the A's.[53] Several weeks later, the A's appeared to pivot to a different Las Vegas site: nine acres owned by casino operator Bally's Corp.

Rubbing salt in Oakland's newly-opened wound, MLB Commissioner Rob Manfred chimed in: "We support the A's turning their focus on Las Vegas and look forward to them bringing finality to this process by the end of the year," Manfred said in a statement provided to the Review-Journal.[54] Assessing the direct and collateral damage, former Councilwoman and newly-inaugurated Oakland Mayor Sheng Tao slammed the door on the City's negotiations, declaring that she was:

> "... deeply disappointed that the A's have chosen not to negotiate with the City of Oakland as a true partner... in the last three

months, we've made significant strides to close the deal. Yet, it is clear to me that the A's have no intention of staying in Oakland and have simply been using this process to try to extract a better deal out of Las Vegas. I am not interested in continuing to play that game — the fans and our residents deserve better."[55]

As MLB moves to join the NBA and NFL in abandoning the Oakland market, who can blame current A's fans for staying away from games at Oakland Coliseum?

On November 28, 2018, it was time for two Buffalo facilities to get some study:

> Bad audio. Inadequate video displays. Not enough high-end seating. All of this and other limitations stand out at New Era Field in Orchard Park and at KeyBank Center in downtown Buffalo amid a constant race by other sports teams across the nation to offer more to their fans. These are among the factors that drove Pegula Sports & Entertainment to hire a consultant to look into stadium options for both the Buffalo Bills and the Buffalo Sabres....[56]

The Pegulas had made significant recent investments in each facility: $26 million at KeyBank Center[57], and approximately $150 million[58] at the football stadium. At an NFL owner's meeting in May, 2018, Kim Pegula downplayed the new stadium option, citing fan concerns (not wanting to pay higher ticket prices nor personal seat licenses) as well as remote chances of attracting funding from the state or city.[59]

But that stance didn't last. By late summer of 2021: the Associated Press was reporting that the Pegulas were seeking a new $1.4 billion, 60,000-seat, 60-suite stadium to be completed no later than 2027 and located on a team-controlled parking lot across the street from the current stadium.[60] And expectations of the public funding percentage began—but didn't end at—fifty percent.[61]

Newly appointed Governor Kathy Hochul led the public side of the discussions. Not content to await the terms from Albany, NFL Commissioner Roger Goodell added the league's clout to the issue in an August, 2021, appearance in Buffalo:

> ...Goodell said the league wants to keep the Bills in Buffalo -- but in a new stadium. ... We're certainly beyond (a renovation option)," he said. "I think a new stadium is what's needed. I think it's going to require a public, private partnership. I think the Bills, the community and the NFL are all going to have to come together and do that in a smart way."[62]

Eight months later. Goodell and the Pegulas got their wish. As summarized in Neil deMause's April 8, 2022 Field of Schemes blog:

> The New York state legislature and Gov. Kathy Hochul came to a "conceptual agreement" on a state budget last night, and it will include $1 billion in state and county money for a new **Buffalo Bills** stadium.... This is very good news for Bills owners Terry and Kim Pegula.... And it's very bad news for residents of NFL cities nationwide, as the bar has now been raised for expectations of what states will do to keep their football team owners happy, something that the owners of the **Tennessee Titans** and **Washington Commanders** and **Chicago Bears** and **Baltimore Ravens** and **Jacksonville Jaguars** and eventually every other team in the league will no doubt be pressing in their own state legislatures in months and years to come.[63]

Lastly, let us not forget the forsaken football cities of St. Louis and San Diego.

In 2017, the City of St. Louis and the St. Louis Regional Convention and Sports Complex Authority sued the NFL and all of its teams in St. Louis Circuit Court. alleging that the defendants ignored their own relocation criteria. Though the lawsuit did not include the scary antitrust claims—with the threat of triple damages—asserted in the Oakland litigation, its state court jurisdiction derived the political advantage of having the case decided by judges answerable to the Missouri electorate.

The plaintiffs prevailed in virtually all pretrial legal skirmishes. The US Supreme Court delivered its own blow to the NFL defendants in April, 2020, when it denied Rams owner Stan Kroenke's request for the case to be settled through arbitration. Previously that Court had denied the Rams request to stay plaintiff's request to provide multiple years of phone records and emails for discovery.

Then, in a November, 2021, NFL owners meeting, Kroenke's 31 other owner defendants were shocked to learn that Kroenke was trying to extract himself from the indemnification agreement he had signed to protect the other owners from legal costs stemming from the owners' approval of Kroenke's move to Los Angeles. With the January 10, 2022, trial date looming as an ugly cloud over the Los Angeles-hosted Super Bowl, Kroenke and the other owners rushed to a costly settlement:

> Lawyers on Wednesday clinched a deal to settle the Rams reloca-tion lawsuit for $790 million, ending a 4-year-old legal saga and avoiding a high-stakes civil trial that could have overshadowed Super Bowl LVI in the very stadium billionaire Stan Kroenke built after leaving St. Louis. NFL Commissioner Roger Goodell

approved the settlement before noon Wednesday. The agreement binds the league to pay St. Louis, St. Louis County and the public agency that owns The Dome at America's Center within 30 days.... And it sends a message to the NFL and its owners that they must pay attention to their rules — and to local markets.[64]

In San Diego, on November 6, 2018—a little less than two years removed from the San Diego Chargers' last home football game—a majority (54%) of city voters approved a plan to redevelop the former football stadium site into a $300 million mixed-use project including a new 35,000-seat football stadium for San Diego State University. But a preservation group hasn't given up on an alternative that would adaptively reuse the existing stadium for the University.

CHAPTER TEN

HOW CLEVELAND DID: CRITICS' PERSPECTIVES

For a long time, sports teams generally built and paid for their own sports facilities.[1] That began to change in the 1950s and 1960s, but even then, the trend was to conserve municipal treasuries by building multi-purpose facilities to accommodate both baseball and football. In the 1990s, beginning with Baltimore's opening of Camden Yards, baseball teams began demanding baseball-only ballparks, and football teams—frustrated for a time that cities were not building new football stadiums with the same vigor—responded with a series of controversial franchise relocations. It reached a boiling point with the Browns move, but once the NFL settled with Cleveland and began leveraging that case with other cities, the immediate aftermath brought new football stadiums in Baltimore, Washington, Cincinnati, Tampa, Detroit, and Seattle.

Cities building new ballparks at least knew that they would be used 81 dates a year. By contrast, cities building new football stadiums contented themselves with guaranteed usage only ten dates a year. Moreover, the sports leagues themselves began using their franchise awarding powers to compel cities to fund a *greater percentage* of the costs of the new facilities. For those mayors —like Houston's Robert Lanier— who "just said no," hoping the football team owner would recant and pay up, they instead saw their teams depart for cities that *would* freight the costs of a new facility. These trends, combined with accelerating construction costs and teams' desire to incorporate premium seating and other new facility options, placed greater and greater burdens on cities' finances.

In response to these financing trends, over the last twenty years a national cadre of sports facility critics have sprouted up: among them are Brooklyn journalists Neil deMause and Joanna Cagan, professor Robert A. Baade of Illinois' Lake Forest College, Professor Judith Grant Long of the University of Michigan, professor Heywood Sanders of the University of Texas at San Antonio, and Professor Brad Humphreys of West Virginia University. Locally, Cleveland has journalists Roldo Bartimole and Sam Allard, attorneys Peter Pattakos and Subodh Chandra, and pastors Jawanza Colvin and Richard M. Gibson.

For example, in their book Field of Schemes, Joanna Cagan and Neil deMause listed six tactics that sports team owners use "to coerce elected officials, media reporters, and taxpayers into accepting the necessity of a multibillion-dollar subsidy...";[2] specifically, an owner is liable to cite or use some or all of the following: 1) facility obsolescence; 2) a potential relocation city or cities; 3) noncompetitive stadium economics; 4) economic impact studies; 5) false deadlines; and 6) shifting goalposts.[3]

How would these various critics respond to the accounts of the preceding nine chapters? Though I can't speak for them, I can review their common threads of argument and apply them to Cleveland's history in the last thirty years.

Sports Facility Investments Do Not Generate Significant Economic Returns

As noted in Chapter 5, it is common for sports teams and their advocates to prepare extensive economic impact analyses to demonstrate the benefits of public investments in their proposed facilities. The Baltimore Sun's Jon Morgan stated:

> Leaders championing stadium projects inevitably produce studies, performed by government analysts under their employ or by friendly economists for hire, to prove that taxpayers get a big return. But their ciphering is inexact at best and highly misleading at worst. During the 1993 expansion race, Maryland estimated that a Baltimore football team would bring $86 million a year and the equivalent of 1,170 full-time jobs to the local economy. A closer look suggests some mathematical hocus-pocus.[4]

Attempting to dispense with the need for city-by-city debates over economic impact, Professor Baade prepared a comprehensive study in 1996.

> A frequent critic of public-stadium building, Baade did an overview of municipal economic performance for 47 U.S. cities between 1958 and 1988. Because cities don't have "gross national products," he charted each city's economy using federal estimates of its personal income; that is, all wages and salaries paid. He then looked for some evidence of an upswing when a city acquired a sports team, or a downswing when it lost one. He found no meaningful impact or correlation. In fact, he found that Baltimore's economy actually *improved* after the Colts left in 1984, for reasons that had nothing to do with the team.[5]

There are competing economic studies on sports facility impacts, and this is not the place to sort all of them out. Suffice to say that Baade was not alone in his views, as noted by city planner Timothy S. Chapin:

> Almost every systematic study of the economic impacts of sports facilities has concluded that at face value these facilities promise a great deal for a city but deliver very little in economic returns (Baade,1996b; Baade & Dye, 1990; Coates & Humphries, 1999; Hudson, 1999; Johnson, 1995; Noll & Zimbalist, 1997; Rosentraub, 1997a; Rosentraub & Swindell, 1991; Rosentraub, Swindell, et al., 1994). Economists argue that these projects simply redirect spending from one activity to another, producing only a very small increase in economic activity, and that any jobs they create are low paying, service sector jobs (Baade, 1996). Others argue that there is no evidence that sports facilities and sports teams contribute to economic growth at the metropolitan level, and in fact, they may actually generate a negative impact on real income per capita (Coates & Humphries, 1999).[6]

Intuitively, Baade's study rings true if you assume that consumers will respond to the loss of a sports team by spending their money elsewhere in the local economy. There are many reasons—team performance and a new stadium loom large among them— for the Cleveland Indians' record of 455 straight sellouts in the 1990s, but the Browns' departure in years 1996-1998 was certainly a factor. Clevelanders who were accustomed to budgeting for Browns season tickets and game day purchases probably spent more money on Indians tickets in those years.

So, the "overall economic impact" argument was probably a losing argument with local voters (apart from the study conclusions, a "numbers-based approach" invites opponents to muddy the waters—and confuse the voters—by debating your numbers). Planner Chapin observed cities changing their emphasis in the 1990s:

> A major shift in the focus of the economic development rationale used to justify these investments has occurred in the past decade. While previous decades saw stadium proponents emphasize the indirect economic benefits of a new facility, using terms such as spinoffs, multipliers, and job creation, the current economic development rationale for almost all of these projects rests upon the idea of district redevelopment (Chapin, 2000; Rosentraub, 1997b). Since 1980, 34 cities in North America have invested in new sports facilities in downtown or near downtown areas, in part to drive (re)development of urban districts. Proponents for new sports facilities in Detroit, Seattle, San Diego, and Phoenix have centered their pro-facility argument not on the concept that a new facility is a metropolitan economic development tool (in terms of jobs and taxes), but that the facility is a catalyst for the physical redevelopment of portions of the city's core.[7]

This argument for sports facility investment is far more city-specific, and it will be discussed in more detail in Chapter 11.

Corporate Welfare

The notion that public investment in sports facilities amounts to corporate welfare is present in virtually every critic's argument. This criticism, like the economic impact skepticism, rings true. With rare exceptions (e.g., Art Modell's highly-leveraged purchase of the Cleveland Browns in in 1961), purchasers of major sports teams are almost universally wealthy. When governments absorb facility costs that would otherwise be borne by the team owners, the owners' investments become even more profitable.

Making things worse is that some of the taxes used to finance these facility investments are regressive in nature: for example, Cuyahoga County's sin tax is disproportionately paid by the County's poorer residents.

That said, the critics rarely focus on the national playing field— owners buttressed by their respective sports leagues acting with relative impunity from federal regulation—that enables wealthy owners to cause cities to bid against each other (and, often, themselves) to retain or procure a franchise. Instead, they usually naively focus their critiques on the local elected officials— "Let X owner pay!"—as though the team would stay regardless and the local official has a simple choice of making the owner pay or making the public pay.

Lack of Transparency

When sports facility deals are cooked up in back rooms outside of the public purview, critics respond by attacking the involved public officials for their lack of transparency. The new Atlanta Braves ballpark has become the gold standard for this type of critique.

> First, let's keep in mind that none of this would be possible without Cobb County, Georgia, taxpayers kicking in more than $400 million. More accurately, none of this would have been possible without one of Cobb County's former top government officials negotiating a secret deal with the Atlanta Braves to have

taxpayers pay that amount for a new stadium, and without the rest of the Cobb County commission voting to approve the stadium deal at a supposedly public hearing where members of the public were prevented from voicing their opposition to the secretly crafted deal.[8]

When it comes to a lack of transparency, there is no Cleveland sports facility decision that ranks remotely close to the Cobb County, Georgia experience. But sports facility negotiations by their nature are highly complex and are almost always performed by team and public staffers outside of public scrutiny, at least until the point at which the mayor or county executive announces the proposed deal and requests legislative authorization. Accordingly, the "lack of transparency" charge is usually levelled at the time the deal is announced, and the legislators then bear the burden of evening the playing field via their legislative hearings.

Sweetheart Deals

Critics often lament "sweetheart deals" reached between public officials and sports team owners. But the key question here—one that I previewed in the Preface to this book—is "Compared to What?"

If the deal is compared to an ideal world in which wealthy team owners always paid for their own sports facilities, leaving the public coffers free to conquer poverty, unemployment, education, public transportation, elderly care, and other charitable causes, then the deal will certainly fall short.

But American cities don't live in that kind of world. A small market city that "just says no" to a sports team owner will eventually lose its team to a city that *is* willing to pay (unless the city is blessed with an owner who, quoting County Commissioner Tim Hagan, displays Mother Teresa qualities). That's why the only fair answer to the "sweetheart deal" question is one—see Chapter 11— based on a comparison of what other similarly-situated cities are doing.

In the rare cases that sports facility critics do spend time on these comparisons, they either give flawed analogies (e.g., pastor Richard Gibson's comparison of the Milwaukee Bucks' elaborate community benefits package to the Cavaliers' proposed package for Cleveland, while failing to note the vast difference in public support dollars—$250 million in Wisconsin versus $70 million in Cleveland—between the respective communities), or they fail to account for the huge disparity in negotiating leverages between large coastal cities with huge TV markets versus smaller Midwestern cities with less extensive TV markets.

Opportunity Costs

Let's go back to the statement of the sin tax opponents in March, 2014: here's what they had to say about "Opportunity Costs":

Opportunity Costs:

Sin Tax proponents refer to it as a "pennies-per-purchase tax," but the truth is that it amounts to additional hundreds of millions of dollars that Cuyahoga County residents simply can't afford. We already have the highest sales tax, the highest school property taxes, and levy after levy that fall on the shoulders of County taxpayers. Additionally, as a nation, we have suffered the deepest economic recession since the 1930s. Unemployment, prices and inequality have skyrocketed, and Cuyahoga County's population and resources are scarce.

Of all the critics' arguments against public financing of sports facilities, this one is the most compelling. Urban education, public health, safe and affordable housing, equitable public transportation *are* more deserving of scarce public dollars.

This is why congressional action is needed to minimize the bidding wars—often encouraged by the respective sports leagues— that allow one city to steal another city's sports franchise by offering exorbitant public incentives. Maryland's secret dealings with the Browns, fueled by a once-in-a-lifetime state legislative handout, is exactly the kind of conduct that Congress should outlaw.

Unfortunately, Congress has shown no appetite for taking on the professional sports leagues. Writing in 1998, the authors of Field of Schemes were not optimistic about future legislative solutions:

> But what *are* concerned citizens supposed to do if their sports team is threatening to leave town unless it gets a publicly funded new stadium? Sympathetic to the plight of sports fans who don't want to lose their team or shell out large amounts of tax dollars, some legislators have tried to find a solution through the law. Unfortunately, those approaches do not offer a readily apparent way out of the problem.[9]

Those authors also considered public ownership of franchises, but resistance from the leagues—the NFL's constitution even specifically limits this approach—seems to ensure that the Green Bay

Packers' community ownership model will remain an isolated exception.

Also writing in the late 1990s, Baltimore writer Jon Morgan reached similar conclusions:

> With the chance for reform so remote, fans may just have to make their own calculations about whether to continue supporting professional sports.[10]

The passage of twenty years has done nothing to change these prognoses. Until Congressional action does occur—and don't hold your breath waiting— local critics of sports facility deals can and should demand a full public debate on opportunity costs prior to their local legislative body's action on a proposed public investment.

CHAPTER ELEVEN

HOW CLEVELAND DID: COMPARED TO OTHER CITIES

In preceding chapters, we've reviewed the history of Cleveland's major sports facilities: how they were planned and built, how they've been maintained, and how they were renovated on or near their respective 15-20-year anniversary dates. Though I've hinted at how each facility is doing, it's time to answer some key questions regarding: "How did Cleveland do compared to other cities who were building when we did?"

I will answer these questions by examining eight performance indicators (the first three of which were put forth in Timothy Chapin's previously referenced article in the Journal of the American Planning Association which compared Baltimore's Camden Yards to Cleveland's Gateway in terms of stimulating urban development). At the conclusion of my discussion of Cleveland's performance on each indicator, I will assign an A through F letter grade.

1.Reuse of Existing Buildings or Spaces

We can begin with Chapin's findings as of 2004:

> For the first indicator of urban redevelopment-the reuse of existing underutilized buildings-the Gateway district has experienced remarkable success. Formerly vacant buildings have been renovated as market rate housing, bringing upper-middle-class residents to this portion of the city for the first time in decades.... A total of seven residential projects, with a combined total of over 800 units, have opened in the district since 1994, with almost an equal number of units currently in the planning stages (Historic Gateway Neighborhood, 2002). Included in these renovations are a number of historic and architecturally significant structures (including the old Statler Hotel and the Osborn Building). Buildings have been reused for retail spaces as well.... Although not illustrated on the map, new restaurants have been carved out of other formerly vacant properties.... Additionally, several large new hotels have found homes in the district in historic, underutilized buildings. A new upscale hotel in The Arcade has helped to catalyze the redevelopment of downtown's earliest indoor shopping space.... Another major hotel chain anchors the ongoing redevelopment of the Colonial and Euclid arcades, two historic shopping arcades that connect Prospect and Euclid Avenues.... The Colonial Marketplace project includes not only the hotel but also retail and office space across seven buildings. Additionally, new hotels have gone into an old warehouse building immediately adjacent to Gateway and into the historic National City Bank Building....[1]

Though all that activity had occurred as of 2004, there's an even fuller story to tell in 2021. Over the last decade, the East 4th Street restaurant and entertainment district has evolved into one of the

City's favorite attractions for both residents and tourists. The Euclid Avenue storefronts from Public Square to Playhouse Square have been reborn. The Kimpton Hotel—located in the renovated Schofield Building at the corner of East 9th and Euclid—opened in 2016 and was recently rated as the City's highest quality hotel. And, across the street from the Kimpton, a Heinen's grocery store now occupies the renovated Cleveland Trust Rotunda.

There's been no significant building rehabilitation near the FirstEnergy Stadium..

Letter Grade: B+.

2. New Construction Within the Surrounding District

There have been three significant new construction projects near the Gateway District: the Hilton Garden Inn opened on Carnegie Avenue in 2000, and two Euclid Avenue apartment towers (the 19 story, 187 unit Beacon and the 34 story, 318 unit Lumen) opened in 2020. A major addition would come if Dan Gilbert's Bedrock Construction proceeds to construction of a major project on a parking lot immediately north of the Gateway site.

There has been some new lakefront construction near FirstEnergy Stadium—Cumberland Development constructed a new restaurant and a small office building in North Coast Harbor—but these projects were due more to the Lake's proximity than to Stadium spinoff. On the drawing boards, there is a proposal to build a $600 million land bridge over the Shoreway and railroad tracks to connect Mall C next to City Hall to the lakefront and Stadium.[2]

Letter Grade: C

3. Emergence of a New Entertainment or Sports Complex

Again, quoting Chapin from 2004:

> Gateway fares equally well on the final indicator of urban redevel-
> opment-the establishment of an entertainment district. Prior to
> Gateway's opening, this district was best described as a large
> parking area for downtown office workers. Since the project
> opened, the district has been given a new name, "The Gateway
> District," and it has emerged as a very healthy and successful "place
> for play" (Fainstein & Stokes, 1998). The district has experienced a
> revival through the combined investments of the public and private
> sectors in hotel, commercial, and residential projects (Bullard,
> 1998; Hirzel, 1996; "Sports Complex," 2000). To date, the value of
> redevelopment projects in the district comes in at well over $250
> million since Gateway's opening in 1994, excluding the $467
> million invested in the complex itself.[3]

Gateway belongs on a list of a dozen significant urban sports/enter-
tainment districts, including Sacramento's $1 billion Downtown
Commons (basketball arena), San Francisco's $1.6 billion mixed-use
waterfront (ballpark and new arena), Columbus' 75-acre, $1 billion
Arena District, Cincinnati's "The Banks" $1 billion mixed-use Ohio
River shoreline development (ballpark and football stadium),
Detroit's 50-block, $1.2 billion mixed-use District Detroit (arena,
ballpark, and football stadium), and Kansas City's 12-block, $1 billion
Power and Light District (arena).[4] To these cities we should also add
San Diego's highly successful ballpark district,[5] Indianapolis' long-
standing downtown-wide sports facility focus, Toronto's half-dozen
sports venues concentrated in the heart of an already vibrant down-
town, and the significant real estate projects associated with
Atlanta's Truist Park and Inglewood's SoFi Stadium.

FirstEnergy Stadium, with its ten dates a year of occupancy for football games (together with several annual concerts or other special events) has not driven its own entertainment complex.

Letter Grade: B

4. Sports Facility Rankings

On February 2, 2019—three and a half years following the Browns' completion of their $120+ million stadium renovation project—Stadium Journey ranked FirstEnergy Stadium number 10 of a total of 31 facilities, behind more popular stadiums in Indianapolis, Baltimore, Atlanta, Philadelphia, Pittsburgh, New Orleans, New England, Seattle, and Houston. Apart from the facility itself, the article cited with approval the Browns' unmatched NFL experience.[6]

In May, 2023—four years after the unveiling of nearly $200 million worth of Cleveland's arena renovations—Stadium Journey ranked Rocket Mortgage FieldHouse the number-four NBA arena (four slots ahead of San Francisco's lavish new Chase Arena), citing the Cleveland facility's renovations and the vibrancy of its neighborhood.[7]

In December, 2022—six years following the completion of Progressive Field's $44 million renovation and the Indians' historic World Series matchup with the Chicago Cubs—Stadium Journey ranked Progressive Field as the nation's second-best ballpark (trailing only San Diego's Petco Park), citing affordability, access, and "a constantly improving stadium."[8] And, showing the 2022 ranking was no fluke, Stadium Journey's 2019 study rated Progressive Field number one.[9]

Letter Grade: A

5. Longevity

How likely is it that each Cleveland sports facility will remain intact a decade from now—or longer? That answer depends on the answers to several sub-questions: the level of upkeep, the extent of modernization, and the remaining lease term.

Cleveland may be the only American city to have enacted a 20-year dedicated maintenance stream covering all three of its major sports facilities. In May, 2014, Cuyahoga County voters passed a 20-year extension of the County sin tax which—though declining—is still expected to yield $12-13 million per year that Gateway will apply toward lease-required capital repairs to the ballpark and arena, and that the City can apply toward lease-required capital repairs to the football stadium.

Within the past decade, all three team owners have completed midterm upgrades to insure that their respective facilities remain economically competitive with more recently constructed facilities: the Haslam family (with the City's assistance) drove FirstEnergy Stadium's $120+ million 2014-2015 renovation, the Dolan family managed (and funded) Progressive Field's $44 million 2015-2016 renovation (supplemented with a Gateway-funded $20 million new scoreboard), and Dan Gilbert (with help from the City, the County, and Destination Cleveland) spurred Quicken Loans Arena's $185 million 2018-2019 renovation.

The leases to all three teams contain specific performance clauses requiring the teams to play all their home games in Cleveland throughout their respective lease terms. The Cavaliers lease expires in 2034, and the Browns lease expires in 2029. The Indians lease extension process—to December 31, 2036— was detailed in Chapter

10. This extension, coupled with the Cavaliers and Browns terms, supports an "A" grade on "Longevity."

Letter Grade: A

6. Downtown Locations/Walkability

As stated in a recent New York Times article entitled "Welcome to the Neighborhood: America's Sports Stadiums Are Moving Downtown":

> Like many cities, Sacramento's urban core needed some serious rethinking....
>
> No longer. Three years after (Vivek) Ranadivé, the owner of the (Sacramento) Kings, partnered with the city to scrape away a nearly empty downtown mall, and a year after he opened the (Golden 1 Center basketball) arena and the 1-million-square-foot (Downtown Commons development), Sacramento is a city reborn.
>
> The number of downtown jobs has increased 38 percent, according to the Downtown Sacramento Partnership, a city economic development group. In the last year, 27 new stores have opened and 23 others are scheduled to open this year. So much construction is happening that the city has decided to hire two dozen new employees to process applications and building permits.
>
> And Sacramento is not alone. Across the country, in more than a dozen cities, downtowns are being remade as developers abandon the suburbs to combine new sports arenas with mixed-used residential, retail and office space back in the city. The new projects are altering the financial formula for building stadiums and arenas by surrounding them not with mostly idle parking lots in suburban expanses, but with revenue-producing stores, offices and residences

capable of servicing the public debt used to help build these venues.[10]

In 2018, there were 13 North American cities with franchises in all four major sports leagues (baseball, basketball, football and hockey).[11] Of these cities, Detroit is the only one[12] with all four of their sports facilities located within a compact downtown district:

> With the NBA's Pistons announcing this week they will be relocating from Auburn Hills (34 miles north of downtown Detroit) to join the Red Wings in their new Little Caesars Arena, which itself is approximately a 5-6 block walk to both Comerica Park (home of the Tigers) and Ford Field (home of the Lions), Detroit's burgeoning sports and entertainment district is about to become the most compact and voluminous of its kind in America.[13]

Amongst the six cities with franchises in three of the major sports leagues, the cities with all three sports facilities located downtown are Toronto, Cleveland, Pittsburgh, and Houston. Combining the two lists, of the 19 North American cities having three or more major sports franchises, only five cities—Detroit, Toronto, Cleveland, Pittsburgh and Houston—have at least three sports facilities located in their downtown cores. These five cities are leaders in a downtown development trend that was accelerating rapidly until it was stalled—but not reversed—by the global pandemic of 2020-2021:

> The explosion in mixed-use developments like these is owed, in part, to the urban American economic renaissance. City populations grew faster from 2010 to 2016 than those in the suburbs, reversing a 60-year trend that started in 1950, according to census data. And cities — not suburbs — are the now primary generators

of the nation's economic growth, according to research compiled by the Federal Reserve.

"It's the one-square-mile effect," said Bruce Katz, an urban development specialist at the Brookings Institution. "Downtowns and midtowns possess an enormous amount of value in a relatively small geography."[14]

Cleveland's downtown sports facilities aren't just convenient because they are downtown; they are also located in walkable pedestrian environments. Unlike other facilities concentrated in urban settings, they are not surrounded by expansive parking lots. Chapin's 2004 article cited Baltimore for making this mistake:

> Somewhat perversely, instead of new development being catalyzed in the immediate district, areas surrounding Camden Yards have seen the opposite: clearing of land for surface parking lots (E. Cline, personal communication, May, 1998). These lots have spread into the Camden Industrial District to serve the massive influx of automobiles and buses on event days. The Maryland Stadium Authority has purchased or leased a number of parcels in the Camden Industrial District and paved them over for event parking (see Figure 2), much to the chagrin of local planners. Attendees also park on other undeveloped parcels, as well as along the streets of this district on event days. City planning staff expressed concern with the infiltration of parking because the city has promoted industrial and manufacturing development in this district, an area that remains best suited for industrial uses (J. French and J. Leviton, personal communication, August, 1998).[15]

Gateway planners anticipated the Baltimore parking lot experience and short-circuited it through the City's Public Land Protective

District that preserved historic buildings and prevented parking lot speculation. True, that decision did result in an onsite parking shortage; but that very shortage encouraged Gateway visitors to either walk to the sports facilities from their downtown offices (leaving their cars in their office parking spaces) or use public transportation.

Letter Grade: A

7. Amount of Public Support Dollars

Up until the 1950s, the majority of major sports facilities were privately financed. Since then, the trend has dramatically reversed; today, privately-built facilities are the exception rather than the role, and the few privately financed stadiums and arenas are clustered in large market regions.

Starting with baseball, when the San Francisco Giants' $357 million Pacific Bell Park (now known as AT&T Park) was opened in 2000, it was the first ballpark built without public funds since Dodger Stadium in 1962. But even the team's owners—who were spurred to action after seeing four separate referendums for public moneys fail between 1987 and 1992—conceded that the private financing was unique to the Bay Area's economic climate:

> The Giants say private financing only worked in their case because they built the park at a time when San Francisco and Silicon Valley were flush with cash from booming technology companies. "We had a very strong economy in the late 1990s, a strong company base and a storied franchise," says Giants chief operating officer Larry Baer, who assembled $75 million in sponsorships including $50 million in naming rights fees from Pacific Bell and $75 million from 15,000 charter seat licenses. Giants president Peter Magowan says most teams couldn't build a stadium without public funds, and

that even the Giants couldn't do it now. "You cannot expect a private ballpark to be built in Cincinnati or Milwaukee, there's not the economic base there. It's not the Silicon Valley," he says. "And we couldn't do it today. We were very lucky in our timing we had low interest rates and a very good economy."[16]

The following table[17] ranks the 30 MLB franchises in ascending order according to the amount of public dollars spent on the franchise's ballpark.

MLB FRANCHISE	TV HOMES IN NIELSEN MARKET	YEAR OPEN/ IMPROVE	PUBLIC COST ($ MILLIONS) OPEN/IMPROVE	TOTAL COST ($ MILLIONS) OPEN/IMPROVE
Boston Red Sox	2,425,440	1912/2022	0/0	0.45/400
Chicago Cubs	3,299,720	1914/2019	0/0	0.25/550
Los Angeles Dodgers	5,318,630	1962/2020	0/0	18/100
San Francisco Giants	2,451,640	2000	0	325
Oakland Athletics	2,451,640	1966	26	26
St. Louis Cardinals	1,189,890	2006	45	357
Arizona Diamondbacks	1,919,930	1998	75	354
Baltimore Orioles	1,108,010	1992	100	107
Detroit Tigers	1,739,380	2000	115	361
Los Angeles Angels	5,318,630	1966/1998	24/117	25/117
Tampa Bay Rays	1,879,760	1990	138	138
San Diego Padres	1,002,770	2004	139	285
Chicago White Sox	3,299,720	1991/2015	150/0	167/125
Colorado Rockies	1,589,560	1995/2014	162/0	215/11.5
New York Mets	7,074,750	2009	164	688
Philadelphia Phillies	2,869,580	2004	173	346
Houston Astros	2,467,140	2000	180	252
Pittsburgh Pirates	1,141,950	2001	197	237
Kansas City Royals	901,020	1973/2009	28/250	37/250
Cincinnati Reds	871,970	2003	261	291
Cleveland Guardians	1,447,310	1994/2016/2021	143.5/0/135	175/44/202
Milwaukee Brewers	868,500	2001	310	414
Toronto Blue Jays		1989/2023	344/0	570/300
Miami Marlins	1,677,850	2012	391	515
Minnesota Twins	1,730,430	2010	392	545
Atlanta Braves	2,449,460	2017	400	1,100
New York Yankees	7,074,750	2009	480	1,100
Texas Rangers	2,648,490	2020	500	1,200
Seattle Mariners	1,880,750	1999/2018	372/135	517/297
Washington Nationals	2,492,170	2008	611	611

Cleveland's total public investment of $278.5 million ($143.5 million toward the ballpark's original cost of $175 million plus zero public monies applied toward the 2016 renovation cost of $44 million plus

$135 million towards the 2021 lease extension) ranks it 10th highest in public costs. Note that most of the teams with the smallest ballpark public investments are located in large metro areas with large TV markets, while many of the teams with the large ballpark public investments are located in smaller Midwestern metro areas with smaller TV markets.

In football, the New York Giants' and New York Jets' $1.6 billion MetLife Stadium was privately financed, the San Francisco 49ers' $1.2 billion Levi Stadium in San Jose was significantly privately financed, and the $4+ billion joint Los Angeles Rams/Los Angeles Chargers SoFi Stadium in Inglewood, California was privately financed as part of a massive mixed-use real estate project.

The following table[18] ranks the 32 NFL franchises in ascending order according to the amount of public dollars spent on the franchise's stadium.

NFL FRANCHISE	TV HOMES IN NIELSEN MARKET	YEAR OPEN/ IMPROVE	PUBLIC COST ($ MILLIONS) OPEN/IMPROVE	TOTAL COST ($ MILLIONS) OPEN/IMPROVE
Miami Dolphins	1,677,850	1987/2016	0/0	115/500
New York Giants	7,074,750	2010	0	1,600
New York Jets	7,074,750	2010	0	1,600
Los Angeles Rams	5,318,630	2020	0	4,000+
Los Angeles Chargers	5,318,630	2020	0	4,000+
Washington Redskins	2,492,170	1997	70.5	250.5
New England Patriots	2,425,440	2002/2022	72/0	412/225
Buffalo Bills	592,750	1973/2013	22/54	22/110
San Francisco 49ers	2,451,640	2014	114	1,200
Carolina Panthers	1,145,270	1995/2015	55/75	247.7/205
Jacksonville Jaguars	700,890	1994	146	161
Detroit Lions	1,739,380	2002/2017	154.8/0	430/100
Tampa Bay Buccaneers	1,879,760	1998/2017	168.5/0	168.5/160
Green Bay Packers	415,890	1957/2003	1/169	1/295
Pittsburgh Steelers	1,141,950	2001	193.89	281
Philadelphia Eagles	2,869,580	2003/2014	199.68/0	512/125
Baltimore Ravens	1,108,010	1997/2009	200/0	229/120
Cleveland Browns	1,447,310	1999/2015	212/30	300/130
Houston Texans	2,467,140	2002	256.96	352
Kansas City Chiefs	901,020	1972/2010	28/263	33/388
Denver Broncos	1,589,560	2001	265.72	364
Tennessee Titans	1,030,650	1999	292	292
Seattle Seahawks	1,880,750	2002	299	360
New Orleans Saints	638,020	1966/2011	163/141	163/156
Arizona Cardinals	1,919,930	20062018	308/14	455/100
Indianapolis Colts	1,026,260	2008	375	750
Chicago Bears	3,299,720	2003	390	590
Cincinnati Bengals	871,970	2000	424.8	453
Dallas Cowboys	2,648,490	2009	444	1,150
Minnesota Vikings	1,730,430	2016	498	1,129
Atlanta Falcons	2,449,460	2017	600	1,600
Las Vegas Stadium	757,400	2020	750	2,000

Cleveland's total public investment of $242 million ($212 million toward the stadium's original cost of $300 million plus $30 million toward the 2015 renovation cost of $130 million) ranked in the mid-range of this chart (15th amongst 32 teams). And again, many of the teams with the smallest football stadium public investments are located in large metro areas with large TV markets, while most of the teams drawing the large football stadium public investments are located in smaller Midwestern metropolitan areas with smaller TV markets.

In basketball, the two significant privately-financed arenas are the Golden State Warriors' $1 billion new Chase Center under construction in downtown San Francisco and the New York Knicks' $1 billion Madison Square Garden renovation.

These and the other privately-financed facilities were built in cities with large regional populations and large regional TV markets. For medium-sized Midwestern cities with smaller TV markets, it's a much different story: there, the sports franchises have sufficient leverage (they can always threaten to relocate to another city) to demand and receive significant public support.

The following table[19] ranks the 30 NBA franchises in ascending order according to the amount of public dollars spent on the franchise's arena.

NBA FRANCHISE	TV HOMES IN NIELSEN MARKET	YEAR OPEN/ IMPROVE	PUBLIC COST ($ MILLIONS) OPEN/IMPROVE	TOTAL COST ($ MILLIONS) OPEN/IMPROVE
Boston Celtics	2,425,440	1995/2020	0/0	144/100
Chicago Bulls	3,299,720	1994	0	180
Denver Nuggets	1,589,560	1999	0	180
Toronto Raptors		1999	0	238
Los Angeles Lakers	5,318,630	1999	0	315
Los Angeles Clippers	5,318,630	1999	0	315
Golden State Warriors	2,451,640	2018	0	1,000
Washington Wizards	2,492,170	1997/2018	0/0	200/40
Miami Heat	1,677,850	1999	0	213
New York Knicks	7,074,750	1968/1991/2013	0/0/0	133/200/1,000
Utah Jazz	948,840	1991/2017	0/23	94/102
Philadelphia 76ers	2,869,580	1995/2022	35/0	186/250
Dallas Mavericks	2,648,490	2001	125	390
Minnesota Timberwolves	1,730,430	1990/2013	55/74	104/76
New Orleans Pelicans	638,020	1999/2016	84/50	114/50
San Antonio Spurs	924,480	2002	147	175
Houston Rockets	2,467,140	2003	175	175
Phoenix Suns	1,919,930	92/2003/2020	28/0/150	83/67/230
Oklahoma City Thunder	705,840	2002/2012	89/95	89/95
Cleveland Cavaliers	1,447,310	1994/2020	124/70	152/185
Charlotte Hornets	1,145,270	2005/2014	172/33.5	212/40
Memphis Grizzlies	649,360	2004	207	250
Portland Trailblazers	1,180,980	1995	218.94	262
Sacramento Kings	1,412,940	2016	223	558
Milwaukee Bucks	868,500	2018	250	500
Atlanta Hawks	2,449,460	1999/2016	150/142.5	150/192.5
Detroit Pistons	1,739,380	2017	324	862.9
Orlando Magic	1,531,130	2010	420	480
Indianapolis Pacers	1,026,260	1999/2019	178/ 295	178/360
Brooklyn Nets	7,074,750	2012	511	1,000

Cleveland's total public investment of $200 million ($130 million public monies applied toward the arena's original construction cost of $157 million plus $70 million public monies applied toward the 2020 renovation cost of $140 million) ranked 12th largest amongst the 30 NBA teams).

University of Michigan professor Judith Grant Long has performed what is arguably the most sophisticated cost comparison of major league sports facilities. In her 2013 book PUBLIC/PRIVATE PARTNERSHIPS FOR MAJOR LEAGUE SPORTS FACILITIES, she began by computing for each major league facility a "public capital cost" which is an indicator with three components: building, land and infrastructure. She adjusted the total of these components to year 2010 by "...using the Construction Cost Index (CCI) from *Engineering News Record* for building and infrastructure components, and the average inflation rate for the land component." To determine the public portion of this total capital cost, she subtracted "... private contributions from total building, land and infrastructure costs."[20]

Then she added an element she calls "Net Annual Public Cost" which was calculated as follows:

> The second part of the financial model, "net annual public cost," estimates the sum of all public expenditures over the expected life of the facility, minus or "net of" public revenues.... Where annual revenues exceed annual expenditures, the net annual public cost is negative, and represent a credit against the total public cost....Net annual costs are treated as occurring over a 30-year period, discounted to present value at 6 percent in 2010. The 30-year term was chosen because it closely approximates the average lease length for facilities currently in use..."[21]

Her revenue elements included rent, admission taxes, share of gate, premium seating, concessions, advertising, naming rights, and parking. Her expense elements included maintenance, capital improvements, municipal services, and foregone property tax revenues. Cleveland's three sports team leases did not fare well on Long's Net Annual Public Cost measure, probably due to most revenue items—with the exception of relatively high admissions taxes—being reserved to the teams, coupled with the public incurring high expenses on capital repairs and foregone property taxes.

When the dust settled, Cleveland's sports team leases ranked as follows based on several of Long's tables (with "1st" being the costliest):

SPORTS TEAM LEASE	PUBLIC CAPITAL COST RANK	PUBLIC % SHARE RANK	PUBLIC % SHARE OF CAPITAL COST
Indians[22]	13	14 (tie)	86
Browns[23]	11	10	103
Cavaliers[24]	6	9	88
Metropolitan Area[25]	8	20	93

Assessing all the above comparative costs data, I assign:

Letter Grade: C

8. Fairness of Public Support Dollars

Apart from the percentage of a sports facility's support provided from public dollars, there is a separate question: of the public support dollars that are provided, how fair are those support dollars when viewed from the perspective of a city or county resident? For example, funding via a county sales tax may be the most unfair measure because every county resident will pay sales taxes. Property taxes are also unfair: though not every county resident pays them—renters don't pay, at least not directly—, if you own any property in the county you will pay. City and county general fund payments and bond debt service payments are also relatively unfair because they impact every resident of these local governments.

At the other end of the fairness scale are those taxes paid only by attendees to a sporting event. The City admissions tax contributions approved by Cleveland City Council in 2017 as part of the Q Arena renovation are a good example: those contributions are a mixture of payments by Cavalier game attendees and payments by attendees at other Arena events. In short, if you don't attend Arena events, you will not be contributing to the City's Arena renovation share. Bed taxes are also fair to residents: they are paid by people (mostly nonresidents) who choose to stay at local hotels. Sin taxes—though they are clearly regressive in nature, disproportionately impacting low and moderate-income persons—are relatively fair in that a person can choose to avoid paying them by declining to consume alcohol or tobacco products.

How have these distinctions played out with Cleveland and Cuyahoga County citizens? From January 25 through February 3, 1985, The Plain Dealer/Gordon Black poll interviewed 684 people in Cleveland and Cuyahoga County measuring sentiments (with a 5% margin of error) toward building a domed stadium. A chart[22] depicting "The Most Acceptable Method to Finance a Dome" displayed the following percentage supports: Team & User Fees—65%; State Funds—34%; Restaurant & Hotel Tax— 30%; Tax Break For the Developers—28%; Sales Tax—15%; and Property Tax —7%. And recall that on May 8, 1984, County voters defeated a proposed domed stadium property tax by a 2-to-1 margin.

With these admittedly subjective fairness assumptions, let's take a look at how the public contributions to the region's major sports facilities actually played out over the years. The following table summarizes these contributions: the entries are approximate, and because they are not presented in present value terms they add up to a much greater total than the actual cost of the three facilities; that said, the entries can be used to demonstrate comparative magnitude of the respective sources.

SOURCE OF PUBLIC $	USE OF PUBLIC $	TERM	TOTAL # OF YEARS	AVERAGE ANNUAL $	TOTAL $ PAID
Sin tax	All facilities	1990-2034	45	13,000,000	585,000,000
County bonds	Arena	1991-2034	44	8,800,00	387,200,000
City parking tax	Football	1995-2029	35	10,000,000	350,000,000
City admissions tax	Arena	1992-2034	43	4,000,000	172,000,000
City admissions tax	Football	1995-2029	35	4,000,000	140,000,000
County bed tax	Arena	1991-2034	44	2,000,000	88,000,000
City motor vehicle lessor	Football	1995-2029	35	2,000,000	70,000,000
State capital money	All facilities	1992, 1996	n/a	n/a	62,500,000
County bed tax	Baseball	2022-2036	15	3,000,000	45,000,000
City admissions tax	Baseball	2022-2036	15	2,500,000	37,500,000
City parking rev bonds	Gateway	1992	n/a	n/a	37,000,000
City general fund	Football	2014-2028	15	2,000,000	30,000,000
State of Ohio	Baseball	2022	1	n/a	30,000,000
County general fund	Baseball	2022-2036	15	2,500,000	27,500,000
City garage sale	Baseball	2022-2036	15	2,000,000	25,000,000
Local government $	Gateway	1996-2016	20	500,000	10,000,000
City general fund	Gateway	1996-2005	10	300,000	3,000,000

There is some double-counting here, as the County relies in part on bed tax monies, and on admission tax payments from the City, to fund its annual Arena debt service payments.

Summarizing, over half the public dollars came from sources that were generally fair to the region's residents: sin taxes, admissions taxes, bed taxes, and motor vehicle lessor taxes. Another large portion—City parking taxes—were reasonably fair to County residents, particularly those who relied exclusively on public transportation.

Slightly more than one-quarter of the public moneys came from sources—County Arena bonds, City and County general funds, City parking revenue bonds, State capital moneys, local government funds—that would fall squarely upon a typical resident of the region.

And—given the double-counting on the County Arena bonds payments—the real percentage is less than one-fifth of the total public moneys.

Letter Grade: B

9. Adding Up the Scores

The following chart lists the scores for the eight performance indicators and calculates an overall score measuring Cleveland's performance measured against other cities with major sports franchises.

CATEGORY	LETTER GRADE
Reuse of Existing Buildings or Spaces	B+
New Construction Within the Surrounding District	C
Emergence of a New Entertainment or Sports Complex	B
Sports Facility Rankings	A
Longevity	A
Downtown Locations/Walkability	A
Amount of Public Support Dollars	C
Fairness of Public Support Dollars	B
TOTAL GRADE	B+

CHAPTER TWELVE

HOW CLEVELAND DID IT

In the preceding chapter, I discussed a number of indicators that demonstrated Cleveland's—and Cuyahoga County's—success in building and maintaining its major sports facilities. If civic leaders in other cities, as well as future local leaders *here*, are to learn from this success, it's appropriate to look at what led to the region's strong track record.

The Local Fan Bases

Successful political leaders know how to read their constituencies; they know that they cannot accomplish their own political goals without recognizing the priorities of the people who put them in office. Cleveland's priorities are not easily defined. Though at heart a blue-collar town, it also has a history of support for the arts: many of its most prosperous neighborhoods (Detroit-Shoreway, Collinwood, University Circle, Fairfax, Shaker Square) are anchored by impressive arts institutions. And its populist bent leads to an extraordinary concern for the underdogs of society: there is a reason why the Cleveland Foundation became the world's first community foundation.

That said, Clevelanders also define themselves by their passion for their sports teams. As Andy Billman explains in his director's take of ESPN's 30 for 30 documentary "Believeland:"

> "Believeland" is Cleveland to the core. It's the story of the fans whose love and loyalty have endured despite half a century of losing, and the spiritual and economic impact of sports in a city that has suffered more than its share of scorn. Above all, "Believeland" is a testament to the unique power of sports to create communal bonds of faith and love, regardless of the final score.

It's often said that Cleveland is first and foremost a "football town" and there's ample evidence to support this claim: historic Cleveland Browns attendance records and TV ratings, the team's unprecedented championship run from 1946-1955, Northeast Ohio's strong high school football teams, and the whole state's commitment to the Ohio State Buckeyes. There's a reason the NFL Pro Football Hall of Fame is sited in Canton, Ohio.

Despite the Browns' horrific two-decade stretch of losing football after the expansion team returned in 1999, the devoted fan base has not wavered. In the decade following the Browns' return to the NFL, their attendance ranked in the top-quarter of teams despite losing records in eight of those ten years and one sole playoff appearance. Over the next decade—a period of even worst on-field performance—they occupied the League's middle tier in attendance. In 2017, when they finished 0-16, CBS Sports still rated their fan base 14th in the League.

All things considered, there can be no doubt that the Browns' fan base ranks with the nation's elite football fan bases of the Green Bay Packers, the Dallas Cowboys, the New England Patriots, the New York Giants, and the Chicago Bears. Moreover, it's doubtful that any of these other fan bases would average 63,882 attendance per game (as the Browns did in 2017) in a challenging weather environment when the team's record over the past two years was 1-31. The Browns' hold on their community is not just sustainable: it is anchored deeper than the Stadium's pilings which extend to the bedrock underlying the sandy Lake Erie deposits.

The Cleveland Cavaliers' average attendance of 20,562 in the 2017-2018 season ranked second in the league, trailing only the Chicago Bulls. They maintained that status for the prior four seasons, coinciding with the return of LeBron James to the team for the 2014-2015 season. And in James' first tenure with the team (2004-2010), they consistently ranked in the League's top five in attendance. But what about the years when James wasn't packing them in? In the team's infancy in the Cleveland Arena days of the early 1970's, they averaged under 10,000 fans per game. There was a brief attendance spike coinciding with the team's "Miracle of Richfield" 1975-1976 playoff run and the several following years, but the period from 1978-1984 yielded some horrific teams that averaged as low as 3,916 fans per game in 1982-1983.

But the team and its fans revived in the late 1980's—with the core of Brad Daugherty, Mark Price, and Larry Nance—and, but for Michael Jordan and his Chicago Bulls, might have made a few NBA finals. The team's fortunes fell after Daugherty and Nance's last season in 1993-1994, but for several years after the fans showed up in force to see the brand-new Gund Arena. But the Arena's new glitter could mask a subpar basketball team for only so long, and by the

2002-2003 season the Cavaliers recorded the league's worst average attendance (11,496 per game).

On balance, over the years the Cavaliers fan base is better than average. It does not rate with the NBA's elite fan bases (in Boston, Chicago, San Antonio, Los Angeles, San Francisco, and Portland), but it certainly belongs in the next tier behind those leaders.

Historically, the Cleveland Indians' fan base has proven to be the most skeptical of the followers of the city's three major sports teams. When the team produces a truly compelling product, like the World Series champions of 1948 and the powerful and exciting 1990's teams that yielded the 455-game consecutive sellout streak, the fans have come out in league-record fashion. But, unlike Browns fans, Indians fans will not consistently show up at the ballpark to support a subpar product. Low attendance marks were quite understandable during the team's trudge through the baseball wilderness from 1960 through 1992, but they were much less defensible when the franchise fielded strong teams in the mid-1950's and in the early years of Terry Francona's management tenure (2013-2015). The latter stretch is largely explainable—though not justifiable—by the "Dolans are cheap" perception hangover deriving from the team's trading away of Cy Young winners C.C. Sabathia in 2008 and Cliff Lee in 2009.

On the team's performance in the Francona era, Peter Gammons has written:

> The Cleveland Indians have won 454 games the past five years, 22 more than the Boston Red Sox. In those years, the Indians spent $414M less in payroll than Boston, which at the start speaks volumes about how well the Indians have been run.[1]

Yet during that same tenure, the team averaged under 20,000 attendees per game in the first four of those years, finishing 28th, 29th, 29th, and 28th amongst MLB's 30 teams in attendance. Only in 2017 did attendance climb to a more respectable average of 25,285 attendees per game (ranking 22nd).

However, a baseball team's impact on its fan base cannot be measured by game day attendance numbers alone. Over the years, the Indians have maintained strong radio and TV numbers (in the 2016 season the Indians were fifth in Nielsen ratings, in 2017 they led Major League Baseball with a 9.22 Nielsen rating, and, even allowing for the larger size of some of the big city markets, Cleveland's household audience of 138,000 was fifth in the nation in 2017).[2]

Watching and listening statistics aside, walk down a city sidewalk on a spring or summer day and you are apt to hear Tom Hamilton's voice narrating an Indians game. Better yet, walk into the lounge of any senior living facility—and, with its aging population, Cleveland has a lot of them—and you will likely find a group of seniors engrossed in a Cleveland Indians telecast.

Political Leadership

Almost without exception throughout the past thirty years, Cleveland and Cuyahoga County's political leaders were savvy enough to recognize the clout of the sports team's fan bases and accommodate that clout into their decisions regarding sports facilities. During that time period, three leaders stood out through their multiple supportive actions on sports facilities: Cuyahoga County Commissioner Tim Hagan, and Cleveland Mayors Michael R.

White and Frank G. Jackson. Ironically, all three would disclaim a sports facility legacy: it was not a driving factor in any of their political ambitions.

Commissioner Hagan grew up in a politically-savvy family in Youngstown, Ohio, serving in the Army and working as a steel-worker prior to earning a degree from Cleveland State University in 1975. His next job—as a social worker in Youngstown—probably shaped his political views: he was an unabashed "Kennedy Democrat" who became friendly with Edward Kennedy and other members of that family. He was elected to the Cuyahoga County Board of Commissioners in 1981 and served for 16 years (1982-1998). During that tenure he played a key role in both launching the Gateway project and managing its 1995-1996 cost overrun challenge. He also rallied the County Commissioners to place the sin tax extension on the November, 1995 ballot, the approval of which became a key linchpin in funding a new football stadium.

Mayor White's priorities were education, economic development, community development, and equity. For him, the Gateway project was first and foremost an economic development engine. Then, when Art Modell made his infamous relocation announcement in Baltimore, he fired up the national Browns' fan base to unleash the unprecedented "Save the Browns" campaign that recaptured a football franchise for Cleveland inside of six months. No city in the nation has reclaimed its sports franchise in such a short time—before or since—and Mayor White's rare combination of traits (down-and-dirty street-fighting, brilliant political maneuvering, and boundless energy) were perfectly suited to this national stage,

But that campaign was as much about civic pride and self-respect as it was about a sports franchise, and his February, 1996, decision to settle with the Browns and the NFL was largely influenced by the hard work that lay ahead for him on the Cleveland schools in the balance of 1996.

Like Commissioner Hagan and Mayor White, Mayor Jackson approached the sports facility business somewhat reluctantly: as a City Councilman, he had voted against the Browns Stadium package in June, 1995. After serving 16 years as a City Councilman from 1990-2005 (including four years as City Council President), he ran for mayor in 2005 on a platform similar to Mayor White's (education, economic and community development) with a particular focus on improving quality of life for "the least of us." He won that election—and the next three mayoral elections in 2009, 2013, and 2017 —to become the longest serving mayor in Cleveland's history.

His particular strengths were municipal finance and an ability to stay calm and build and maintain effective coalitions in tackling the city's thorniest problems. He valued the City's relationships with the leaders of all three major sports franchises and understood the financial benefits of preserving the existing sports facilities for long tenures. He delicately managed City approvals of four controversial measures: the $120+ million FirstEnergy Stadium renovation, the 20-year sin tax extension approved by County voters in May, 2014, the $140 million Quicken Loans Arena renovation, and the Cleveland Indians lease extension.

The next tier of political leaders also played key roles in building and maintaining Cleveland's sports facilities; Mayor/Governor/U.S. Senator George V. Voinovich, City Council Presidents Jay Westbrook, Martin J. Sweeney, and Kevin Kelley, County Executive Armond Budish, and County Council Presidents Dan Brady and Pernell Jones.

Senator Voinovich applied his strong financial acumen in all three of his political roles (during his tenure in the Senate he became known as a "budget hawk") to ensure that the public always got a fair economic deal in its sports facility investments.

City Council President Westbrook, initially elected to City Council in 1980 on a populist plank infused with strong opposition to downtown tax abatements, risked angering many of his base supporters when—as Council President from 1990 to 1999—he rallied support amongst his Council colleagues for the Gateway project in 1990 and the Browns Stadium funding package in June, 1995.

County Councilman Sweeney served as a City Councilman from 1998 to 2014. During his tenure as City Council President from 2006-2014, he formed a strong alliance with Mayor Jackson— leading to a rare period of minimal mayoral/council strife in Cleveland City Government—and procured passage of the controversial $120+ million FirstEnergy Stadium renovation package in November, 2013. He served as a member of the Ohio House of Representatives from 2015 until 2018, and was appointed to Cuyahoga County Council in 2021.

Former City Council President Kevin Kelley was first elected to Council in 2005, and from 2015 through 2021 he served as Council President. Like Commissioner Hagan, he had a background in social work prior to seeking elective office. He obtained his law degree from Cleveland State University. He played a key role in promoting the sin tax extension campaign (including public debates against high-profile naysayers) that culminated in County voters' May, 2014, approval, and was a force both behind the scenes and out in front on the $140 million Quicken Loans Arena renovation and the Cleveland Indians lease extension.

County Executive Armond Budish negotiated and then shepherded the controversial Q deal legislation through numerous County Council sessions and brokered the August, 2017, compromise with the Greater Cleveland Congregation that set aside a referendum on the deal. His determination to preserve baseball in Cleveland and his patient approach were key factors in the Indians lease extension. And County Council President Dan Brady provided strong County leadership (partnering effectively with Kelley) on both the sin tax extension campaign and the Quicken Loans Arena renovation. He was a longstanding public servant, including Cleveland City Council, Ohio House of Representatives, and Ohio Senate terms.

Then-County Councilman Pernell Jones worked hard on the sin tax extension campaign in 2014 and more recently—as County Council President in 2021— spearheaded the Cleveland Indians lease extension through County Council.

Then there was sports facility critic Councilman Michael Polensek —who'd be appalled to find his name on this list—who gave the City's negotiating staff members strong ammo when they argued with their sports team counterparts for more City-friendly deals ("Even if we could get our mayor to do your deal, it'd never fly with Councilman Polensek and his ilk").

Team Owners and Staff

You can have great fans, strong political leaders, and a competitive stadium deal: but you can still lose your team if your owner develops wanderlust. Art Modell's civic history certainly didn't suggest he would abandon Cleveland. He'd volunteered to lead a business group that saved the city's Hotel Sheraton, and he'd leased Cleveland Stadium on terms—Roldo Bartimole's views notwithstanding—that were arguably more-city friendly than any other city's stadium deal.

But his front-office failings (years of poor drafts, leading to gross overspendings and bad decisions on the free agent market) plunged him into a deep financial hole. Then, seeing an unprecedented financial bonanza in Baltimore (offered by ruthless Maryland negotiators) coupled with some questionable assessments by his own management team, Modell opted to jettison his ties with the City of Cleveland.

Since then, the City of Cleveland and Cuyahoga County have been more fortunate in the owners that have taken control of the major sports franchises. The Lerner family owned the Browns from 1999 until 2012 (Al Lerner from 1999 until his 2002 death; son Randy Lerner thereafter). Though the Lerner's were not able to field competitive teams, they were strong civic and charitable partners.

Jimmy and Dee Haslam purchased the Browns for $1 billion in 2012, and their tenure has seen churning coach and general manager turnover and a very poor drafting record. The team's 54-107-1 record in the 2013-2022 decade was the second worst in the NFL (only Jacksonville was worse). But the Haslam's have made major civic contributions, including the funding of five new synthetic turf football fields for Cleveland high schools: James Ford Rhodes and John Marshall on the west side, and Glenville's Bump Taylor Field, JFK's Roye Kidd Field, and John Adams on the east side. They also helped fund a sixth field at Lonnie Burten Recreation Center.

Haslam's initial front office was confrontational, seeking major renegotiation of lease terms or even a possible new football stadium. Thankfully, the Haslam's curtailed this approach in early 2014, and since then the City and Browns staff worked more collaboratively on Stadium issues.

Dan Gilbert has owned the Cleveland Cavaliers since 2005 and he and predecessor owner Gordon Gund had already invested $69 million in Arena upgrades as of 2013. Then, Gilbert's willingness to invest in a *renovation* of the 24-year old Arena (at a time when owners in Sacramento and Milwaukee were negotiating for brand-new arenas at price-tags well over half a billion dollars) *and* his willingness to fund *half* of the $140 million renovation cost (the final tally will be approach 2/3, after Gilbert's decision to fund an additional $45 million of improvements privately), may not endear him to populist critics but ranks him among the most city-friendly owners in the NBA.

Gilbert was ably served by long-time (since 2003) Cavaliers and Quicken Loans Arena CEO Len Komoroski, who contributed 30 years of pro sports experience. The Cavaliers have also displayed a strong civic commitment. Several years ago, they refurbished the gymnasium and outer grounds at Fairfax Recreation Center, and as part of the Q deal they are refurbishing gym floors at each of the city's public high schools, as well as donating the net proceeds from all playoff watch parties to Habitat for Humanity.

The Dolan family purchased the Cleveland Indians from Dick Jacobs for $323 million in 1999. Larry Dolan and Paul Dolan have maintained a low public profile over the years, but they worked well with City government in their first twenty years of ownership. In recent years they have completed total ballfield renovations at Luke Easter Park (two fields), Gunning Recreation Center, Halloran Park, and Brookside Reservation. They are longstanding investors and participants in the Cleveland Baseball Federation and other youth baseball initiatives. They invested $44 million of their own dollars in the impressive 2015-2016 makeover of Progressive Field. And, as noted in the Peter Gammons article cited earlier in this Chapter, they've made a strong case for being Major League Baseball's best-run organization over the past five years.

However, the team's approach to the public sector changed in 2019 after the retirement of Dennis Lehman from his post as Executive Vice President, Business. As more fully detailed in Chapter 10, owner Paul Dolan and his front office adopted a more aggressive stance during negotiations on the team's lease extension, seeking public contributions exceeding those obtained in the three most recent MLB franchises lease extensions.

Private and Public-Sector Worker Bees

For a metropolitan area its size, Cleveland has been blessed with a disproportionate share of experienced professionals schooled in the nuances of pro sports facilities. In the private legal sector, there were Squire Sanders attorneys Fred Nance, David Goodman, Barbara Hawley, and Tim Cosgrove, ThompsonHine attorney Jeff Appelbaum, Gateway counsel Dennis Wilcox, and former Gateway board chair Craig Miller.

The public sector has a matching talent list. Knowledgeable City attorneys included Law Director Barbara Langhenry, Chief Corporate Counsel Rick Horvath, Chief Assistant Director of Law Rich Bertovich, Assistant Director of Law Debra Rosman, and County Law Director Greg Huth. Former Cuyahoga County Director of Law Robert Triozzi worked on sports facilities from both City and County perspectives.

Private sector financial experts included Tim Offtermatt (former Gateway chair and County financial advisor, and current Rock Hall CFO), Bob Franz (current County financial advisor), Downtown Cleveland Partnership's Deb Janik and P3 Development Advisors' Paul Komlosi. Gateway's Todd Greathouse understands that entity's long history, particularly in capital repairs. On the public finance side, former City Finance Director Sharon Dumas (who did double duty as Mayor Jackson's Chief of Staff from 2017-2021) and her bond expert Betsy Hruby had considerable sports facility experience and expertise.

In overall sports facility negotiations, key private participants were Nance, Carole Hoover, Tom Chema, Joe Roman, and communications/crisis management authority Nancy Lesic. On the public side of these negotiations, in addition to my roles, there were former County Chief of Staff Sharon Sobol Jordan, County Economic Growth and Opportunity Officer (and Gateway board member) Matt Carroll, former Stadium Project Manager Diane Downing, former City Chief Operating Officer Darnell Brown, and former City Chiefs of Development Chris Warren and Ed Rybka.

CHAPTER THIRTEEN

CITIES' REMEDIES TO LIMIT FRANCHISE RELOCATION

Suppose you are a city official in a location—like Cleveland—where your government has a good track record in dealing with a particular pro sports franchise: you have a number of years remaining on a lease that contains a specific performance clause requiring the sports team to play all its home games at your sports facility, your sports facility is either fairly new or—if not—you've made reasonable efforts to perform capital repairs and have presided over a mid-life modernization of the facility, your fans have turned out in reasonable numbers when compared to league averages, and your fans have shown reasonable interest in the team when measured by radio and TV ratings.

But, in derogation of the lease, your team's owner suddenly declares an intent to relocate the franchise to a potentially more profitable market area. What remedies are available to you to retain the team and thwart the intended relocation?

Specific Performance Lawsuit

Based on your lease, you can file a lawsuit seeking a temporary restraining order, followed, over time, with a preliminary injunction and, ultimately—following a trial on the merits—with a permanent injunction, each of which would compel the team to continue to play its home games at your sports facility for the duration of the lease.

The City of Cleveland took this route in November,1995, and was successful in earning a preliminary injunction from the trial judge. However, the City's February, 1996, settlement with the NFL included the dismissal of this case as well as other litigation amongst the parties. Had the City's injunction case proceeded to a trial on the merits, the Browns' Jones Day attorneys would have renewed their argument, first made during the preliminary injunction hearing, that the City's lease was not with the Browns but with Modell's Cleveland Stadium Corp.

A more recent example was the City of Seattle's 2008 lawsuit against team owner Professional Basketball Club, LLC ("PBC") to retain the Seattle Supersonics basketball franchise and prevent its relocation to Oklahoma City. The City's case is well-stated in its April, 2008 trial brief:

> In 1994, the City determined to pledge more than $80 million taxpayer dollars to rebuild what is now KeyArena to the specifications of the Seattle Sonics in exchange for the Sonics' promise to play all their home games there through the 2009-10 NBA Season. That policy decision and promise were memorialized in a Lease that included a provision acknowledging that "the obligations of the parties . . . are unique in nature; this Agreement may be specif-

ically enforced by either party." In 2006, PBC purchased the Sonics, contractually assumed the Sonics' obligations under the Lease, and promised in writing and orally to "honor" the Lease obligations. At the time of PBC's purchase, the City made clear its intent to hold the new Sonics' ownership to the Lease for its full term.

Less than a year later, PBC started trying to escape the Lease. First, in the spring of 2007, PBC asked the NBA about moving the team to Oklahoma City for the 2007-08 NBA season and contacted Oklahoma City to reserve arena dates. Immediately thereafter, PBC tried to buy its way out of the Lease, but Seattle Mayor Greg Nickels made the policy decision to reject that offer. In response to the City's decision, PBC initiated arbitration to breach the Lease and leave two years early. The City then filed this lawsuit consistent with its prior policy decisions to enforce the Lease rather than accept a buy-out. Here, the City seeks to enforce its contractual rights and to obtain the benefits, economic and intangible, that it bargained for when deciding to pledge taxpayer dollars in a completely renovated basketball arena. Those benefits are unique in nature and cannot reasonably be measured in monetary terms. Under these circumstances, the City is entitled to specifically enforce the Lease to prevent the Sonics' breach.

On the other hand, PBC asks this Court to ignore the City's contractual rights and let PBC breach the Lease. PBC wants out of the Lease because of claimed undue hardship. The facts say otherwise. PBC bought the Sonics knowing the team historically lost millions of dollars per year, and that such losses were expected to continue into the future. PBC exacerbated its financial losses by announcing before last season –three years prematurely according to the Lease –its intent to move the team to Oklahoma City. The announcement came on the heels of PBC's demand for a $500 million dollar publicly financed "world-class" arena that did not include a specific dollar contribution commitment from the PBC, nor a willingness to cover cost overruns —an effort, in other words, that PBC knew might (and indeed likely would) fail. PBC's billionaire owners understood the deal they were making. There is no justification for PBC to breach the Lease, ask the Court to rewrite the Lease to insert an escape clause that is not there, and take Seattle's 41-year history with the team to Oklahoma City.[1]

Though the case went to a six-day trial and the Court was on the verge of issuing a decision on whether the team would be required to play in Seattle for another two years, the litigants reached an August 19, 2008, settlement agreement which, among other terms, included a PBC initial payment to the City of $45 million and a subsequent contingent payment of $30 million. Yet for any municipal attorney planning a future injunction lawsuit, the Seattle trial docket is an excellent resource.

The most recent sports franchise injunction case was the City of Columbus, Ohio's lawsuit seeking to retain its Columbus Crew soccer franchise and prevent its relocation to Austin, Texas. The Crew had signed a 25-year lease with the City in 1998 after the City constructed the first soccer-specific stadium in the history of the Major Soccer League. But, like the Seattle case, the Columbus lawsuit settled before it went to trial: in this case, the settlement in occurred in December, 2018, after the League approved a new expansion franchise in Austin and then approved a bid by Jimmy and Dee Haslam, and local doctor Pete Edwards, to purchase the Crew franchise.

Ohio's Art Model Law

The City of Columbus had also alleged that the Crew violated Section 9.67 of the Ohio Revised Code (also known as the "Art Modell Law") which, among other requirements, provides that the owner of a pro sports team using a tax supported facility cannot relocate unless two conditions are met: 1) the host city consents, or 2) the team owner gives 6 months' notice and provides an opportunity for local entities to buy the team. Had the case not been settled, the Columbus lawsuit would have been the first legal test of the constitutionality of the Ohio law.

Antitrust, Tortious Interference with Contract and Related Claims

As previously noted in Chapter 4, in 1995, the City of Cleveland filed a second significant lawsuit in the Browns relocation dispute. This was the $300 million lawsuit against the Browns, Cleveland Stadium Corp., Modell, the Maryland Stadium Authority, and John Moag as defendants. The lawsuit claims included breach of contract, tortious interference, breach of fiduciary duty, and civil conspiracy. It would have been a fascinating trial, but Cleveland dismissed its suit when the City settled with the NFL in February, 1996. Over twenty years later, in April, 2017, the City of St. Louis sued the NFL alleging similar wrongs.

The St. Louis Convention Center, St. Louis City and St. Louis County is suing the Los Angeles Rams, owner Stan Kroenke and every NFL owner for an alleged $1 billion in damages caused by fraud, misrepresentation, breach of contract and tortious interference with a business expectancy. It's connected to the Rams leaving St. Louis for Los Angeles in January of 2016.[2]

The monetary stakes were huge:

"The plaintiffs are seeking a billion dollars in damages or more," NFL attorney Gerard Carmody said during the hearing.... Although the St. Louis plaintiffs seek reimbursement for wasted expenses arising from allegedly futile efforts to keep the Rams in St. Louis, the case apparently also will attempt to recover a slice of the enhanced value of the team resulting from a relocation that the plaintiffs believe happened in defiance of the NFL's applicable rules.

"Our damages relate to the violation of the relocation policy," lawyer Jim Bennett said during the hearing..... "The move, the relocation fee, the minimum increase in value to Mr. Kroenke, the minimum increase in value to all the other teams or defendants, the minimum increase in value to Mr. Kroenke's real estate empire, expenses that we incur based on their representations that they might actually think about the new stadium."

It seems like an aggressive position, to be sure. But the St. Louis plaintiffs have managed to fend off the efforts of the NFL to suck the case out of the civil justice system and into the business-friendly alternative method of arbitration. As Marc Ganis, a consultant with very close ties to the NFL, told Kaplan, "home cooking" has helped the St. Louis case survive. Of course it has; "home cooking" is a longstanding reality of the broader justice system....

Regardless, the St. Louis plaintiffs currently have a multi-billion-dollar tiger by the tail. Whether and to what extent they can hold on will be interesting to watch.[3]

Like Seattle's lawsuit against the Supersonics, the St. Louis case went a long way down the tracks. The Seattle case actually went to trial before settling, while St. Louis was less than two months away from the trial date when it reached its own massive $790 million settlement with the NFL defendants. In addition to reaping an unprecedented dollar award, the St. Louis plaintiffs served notice to the NFL and all other sports leagues that team relocation criteria cannot be ignored.

Congressional Legislation On Franchise Relocation

Of the major sports leagues, only the MLB is exempt from federal antitrust laws:

The exemption — which shields many of the activities of both Major League Baseball ("MLB") as well as the lower-ranked, so-called "minor leagues" from antitrust scrutiny — dates back to the United States Supreme Court's decision in the 1922 case of Federal Baseball Club of Baltimore, Inc. v. National League of Professional Baseball Clubs. In Federal Baseball, Justice Oliver Wendell Holmes wrote for a unanimous Court holding that under then-prevailing precedent, the business of "giving exhibitions of base ball" was neither interstate in nature nor commerce, and thus was not subject to the Sherman Antitrust Act. 259 US 200 1922.

See Haywood v. Nat'l Basketball Ass'n, 401 U.S. 1204 (1971) (holding that antitrust law applies to the activities of the National Basketball Association ("NBA")); Radovich v. Nat'l Football League, 346 U.S. 356 (1953) (same with respect to the National Football League ("NFL")).[4]

Professor Nathaniel Grow of the University of Indiana's Kelly School of Business argues that "baseball's antitrust exemption actually decreases the frequency with which MLB franchises place extortionate demands upon their host cities...for stadium subsidies;" and "allows MLB to place greater restrictions on franchise relocations than the other leagues, whose ability to regulate relocation has been curtailed by various antitrust rulings[5]...

Whereas only a single MLB franchise has relocated since 1972 — the 2005 move of the struggling Montreal Expos franchise to Washington D.C.— franchises in the other sports leagues have frequently relocated over the same time period. Specifically, in the last 40 years, both the NFL and NBA have had seven franchise relocations, while the NHL has seen ten franchises move.[6]"

Accordingly, Congress has more than once considered legislation that would grant the other major sports leagues a limited antitrust law exemption for the purpose of reducing franchise relocations. Perhaps the most notable attempt came in 1995:

On November 29, 1995, Congress' Subcommittee on Antitrust, Business Rights, and Competition of the Senate Committee on the Judiciary held hearings on sports franchise relocation. Four panels--federal policy makers, sports league commissioners, municipal authorities, and academics--presented testimony to the committee.

The Fans Rights Act, introduced by Senator John Glenn (D-Ohio), Senator Mike DeWine (R-OH), Congressman Louis Stokes (D-OH), and others, would give fans, communities, and sports leagues more control over sports franchise relocation. The Act would provide for a very narrow antitrust exemption shielding a professional sports league from a lawsuit if the league blocks a relocation; require that teams intending to relocate give a community 180 days' notice and hold public hearings during that time; and give the community an opportunity to present bona fide offers to purchase the team or induce it to stay.[7]

As noted above in Chapter 4, former NFL Commissioner Paul Tagliabue explained the NFL's concerns regarding franchise relocation—and sought potential antitrust immunity for the League—in a November 25, 1995, statement to the Committee. In arguing for limited antitrust immunity, he explained how the legal decisions tied the League's hands and left it powerless to prevent the Raiders' move from Oakland to Los Angeles in 1983, the Colts' move from Baltimore to Indianapolis in 1984, and the Rams' move from Los Angeles to St. Louis in 1995.

Cleveland Mayor Michael R. White also testified:

The 1990s have unveiled an alarming trend in stadium financing, For most of this century, cities only replaced stadiums when the facilities became structurally obsolete. Recently, however, owners are deserting perfectly sound structures on the alleged grounds that they are economically obsolete. ...The Browns decided to leave Cleveland despite the unquestionable fan loyalty to the Browns.... The betrayal of Cleveland touches a raw nerve not just in Northern Ohio, but all over America."[8]

The last congressional action on the 1995 Act was a referral to the The Senate Committee on Commerce, Science, and Transportation on November 30, 1995.

Congress next attempted to limit franchise free agency via the Professional Sports Relocation Act of 1998 (H.R. 3817, 105th Congress (1998), (a copy of which is included in Appendix 1). Like the 1995 Act, it would have granted limited antitrust liability to the major sports leagues. It was notable for the Congressional criteria that the leagues would have to consider during their relocation decision-making:

(1) The extent to which fan loyalty has been demonstrated during the tenure of the member team in the home territory (this is to be determined by fan attendance, ticket sales, and television ratings);

(2) The degree to which the owner of the member team has engaged in good faith negotiations enabling the team to retain its present location;

(3) The degree to which the ownership or management of the member team has contributed to any circumstance that might demonstrate the need for relocation;

(4) The extent to which the team has been a beneficiary of public support by means of any publicly financed playing facility, rent abatement or special tax treatment;

(5) The adequacy of the stadium or arena of the team and the willingness of authorities to remedy any deficiencies;

(6) Whether the team has incurred net operating losses, exclusive of depreciation or amortization, sufficient to threaten its financial viability;

(7) Whether any other member team in the league is located in the home territory of the team requesting relocation;

(8) Whether the member team wishes to relocate to a territory in which no other team in the league is located;

(9) Whether the stadium or arena authority, if public, is opposed to relocation;

(10) The effect that relocation will have on contracts, agreements and understandings between the member team and public and private parties.[9]

The 1998 Act was not enacted. Some believe this was a good thing. There are writers who disagree with the notion that franchise free agency can be curbed by granting limited antitrust immunity to the major sports leagues.[10] And the St. Louis and Oakland officials who recently brought suit against the NFL would probably be skeptical of any Congressional action that would loosen the reigns on the NFL.

But, twenty years removed, I believe that the 1998 Act deserves reconsideration. Its exemption from antitrust laws was expressly limited to relocation decision-making:

It shall not be unlawful under the antitrust laws for a professional sports league (or a member team of such league acting jointly with another member team of such league, under the authority of such league) to issue or enforce rules, or to enter into or carry out agreements, to permit or restrict the relocation of any such member team.[11]

The ten items listed in the Act's "Criteria to be Considered" are comprehensive. Though the NFL's existing criteria, to take one example, are not wholly different, the Act's grant of limited antitrust immunity would give league officials far more confidence to more aggressively enforce adherence to the criteria.

While embracing the 1998 Act as a helpful step forward, I retain some degree of distrust towards the sports leagues and their own roles in furthering franchise relocations. First, I will always remember Cleveland City Council's May 2, 1990, Finance Committee meeting when Dick Jacobs invited MLB Commissioner Fay Vincent to attend and testify before the Committee. I watched across the table while Commissioner Vincent summarized his league's team relocation criteria and —without naming Tampa by name—warned us all that Cleveland needed to act now or face the very real specter of team relocation.

Second, my attendance at three NFL owner meetings in early 1996 taught me that the protection of cities' treasuries is a non-factor when the owners vote on franchise relocations. To the contrary, in 1996, seeking to catch up to Major League Baseball, the NFL owners were determined to achieve new football stadiums for every franchise, with the cities bearing the brunt of the expense.

And while NFL Commissioner Paul Tagliabue, his then-deputy Roger Goodell, and the rest of their staff were professional and highly competent in their negotiations with Cleveland in 1996, their allegiance—then and now—was/is to the 32 owners and—as a group —those owners have not shown much empathy for the municipal finances of the cities that host their respective franchises. Consider this 2019 observation by political journalist Mark Leibovich after Las Vegas' decision to pledge $750 million of public monies toward the new Raiders stadium:

In the friendlier confines of the Membership, (Las Vegas Raiders owner Mark) Davis was being treated more like a conquering hero. Few maneuvers are more respected among NFL owners than finagling a sweet stadium deal from a sucker municipality.[12]

Third, the Clevelans Indians' injection of MLB CFO Bob Starkey into our lease extension discussions amounted to a not very subtle threat that if we didn't accede to *a* Indians demands, MLB would disapprove the lease extension (thereby clearing the path for a team relocation). While Starkey himself was not as blunt as the team, the implied threat hung over our discussions.

So Congressional action on legislation comparable to the 1998 Act is at best a partial solution to the problem of unfair franchise relocations. But it would at least do away with the primary excuse—fear of antitrust liability—cited by NFL and NBA league officials when they explain their alleged inability to control recalcitrant franchise owners.

Congressional Legislation Giving Tax Relief to Teams Investing in Sports Facilities

My second proposal for federal action is patterned on a highly successful 1976 law—Historic Tax Credits—that in the two decades following its passage had already leveraged "...more than $45 billion in private funds to create nearly 382,000 rehabilitated housing units, of which 24 percent are low and moderate-income (LMI) housing units.[13]" The program provides tax credits to property owners equal to 20 percent of the qualified rehabilitation expenditures.[14]

To be titled "The Tax Credit for Private Rehabilitation of Professional Sports Facilities Act of 2022" (a copy is included in Appendix 2), the legislation would provide to owners of pro sports facilities – and to qualifying long-term lessees of same—tax credits equal to 20 percent of their qualified rehabilitation expenditures. A rehabilitation project would qualify under the Act if the submitting taxpayer paid at least 65% of rehabilitation costs and the total expenditure on the project exceeded $50 million.

Pro sports team owners who own their sports facilities outright would have much to gain from passage of this legislation. Consider, as an example, the experience of the Ricketts family, owners of the Chicago Cubs baseball franchise and Wrigley Field. After a seven-year wait for the filing of paperwork, they qualified Wrigley for federal landmark status in the National Register of Historic Places. That, in turn, qualified those taxpayers to receive historic tax credits for a portion of their $1 billion expenditures refurbishing the ballpark. The family, which had originally sought public monies for the project, ultimately settled for the tax relief.[15]

Baseball franchise owners of the Los Angeles Angels, Los Angeles Dodgers, San Francisco Giants, St. Louis Cardinals, and Boston Red Sox would be vey interested in a new federal tax incentive to supplement their private investments in their sports facilities. But the vast majority of pro sports franchises *lease* their sports facilities from public owners, and these owners are the primary target of my proposed legislation. Lessees would qualify if their leases provide as follows:

- A public entity is the owner/lessor of the sports facility;
- The lease has a remaining term of at least 15 years;

- The lease contains a specific performance clause obligating the lessee to play not less than 90% of its home games in the sports facility; and
- The lease does not include a "state of the art clause" requiring lessor, or any other public entity, to spend monies to maintain the sports facility at a level equal to or better than a stated percentage of other facilities located within the applicable pro sports league

We Need a Sense of Urgency

The vast number of sports facilities newly-built in the 1990s and early 2000s are nearing their 20th or 25th anniversaries. Sports franchises and their respective leagues will continue to demand extraordinary public subsidies, either via demands for new facilities (as with Atlanta, Arlington, and Oakland) or via high public investments coincident with lease extensions (as with Cleveland's baseball franchise). The franchises' usual lever will be a threat—sometimes explicit, sometimes veiled, but always lurking—to relocate the team to another city.

Absent Congressional action, local governments will continue to play the role of abused spouses. Just as the NFL, NBA, and MLB have adopted rules to achieve balance and competitiveness *within* their leagues, it is past time for Congress to legislate to achieve a competitive balance between those sports leagues and the local governments that supply the leagues' fans and media support.

AFTERWORD

There is a clear consensus amongst sports facility experts on what is wrong with the business environments entrapping small market cities such as Cleveland. Consider three separate statements of the problem, the first coming from Neil deMause and Joanna Cagan in 1998:

> The effective blackmail that professional teams wield over cities is not good, it is not correct, and it is not eternal. It is the consequence of a particular state of affairs in which public agencies have become beholden to private power. It can be changed, and it's worth changing.[1]

Next were economists James Quirk and Rodney Fort in 1999:

> Sports leagues have learned to use their monopoly powers to coerce host cities into building expensive publicly financed stadiums and arenas with accompanying sweetheart rental agreements. Cities that refuse to do this are threatened with the loss of

their teams, and the threats have been enforced by league action authorizing the moves of franchises elsewhere. The expansion policies of leagues are geared to adding new teams at a rate designed to protect the value of existing franchises and to minimize competition among teams within the league, while carefully husbanding credible threats of relocation against the current host cities in the league. Expansion fees are set at levels that transfer most of the prospective monopoly profits of new teams back to the league.[2]

Third, from University of Michigan professor Judith Grant Long in 2013:

Leagues are...able to set the price of expansion teams by maintaining scarcity, and at the same time, giving their existing owners the option to be the first to move into a new market, or under certain circumstances, to move out of troubled ones. Teams in search of better markets often pursue lucrative public subsidy packages to support new facility construction as part of the relocation rationale. Teams have also generally moved in concert with population growth trends from north to south, east to west, from declining markets to growing markets, from shared markets to unshared markets, and in the case of the NFL Oakland Raiders, from one market to another and back again.[3]

Long's 2013 statement was written prior to the Raiders football team relocating, yet again, to Las Vegas, thereby reaffirming the points made earlier in her statement.

The first quote, from deMause and Cagan's book FIELD OF DREAMS, was the concluding paragraph of the authors' "Afterword: Winning Isn't Everything?" That Afterword also praised the work of local activist groups in the cities of Cleveland, Detroit, Minneapolis, Chicago and Seattle:

> For the activists fighting block by block and referendum by refer-
> endum to put an end to sports subsidies, seeking small victories in
> the larger defeats has become a familiar pursuit.[4]

But to the adjective "familiar" I would add two more adjectives: "naïve and misdirected." Corporate welfare is not going away any time soon. For nearly a century, cities have waged economic war against each other by piling on corporate subsidies to attract or retain businesses and industries. In the last half-century, wealthy sports franchise owners joined the parade of businesses seeking taxpayer dollars for their operations. They are making up for lost time with a vengeance: recent demands upon taxpayers in Atlanta, Arlington and Oakland have been almost punitive in nature.

A more realistic advocacy goal is to *reduce* corporate welfare rather than *end* it. This can be done through a two-pronged approach: reduce the local government's *percentage share* of project costs via Congressional action; and reduce the *overall cost* of the sports facility project by choosing rehabilitation over new construction.

Reduce Local Governments' Percentage Share of Project Costs

The history of local activists' challenges to sports subsidies followed one of two paths. When the activists lost their local battles, the team owner simply pocketed his or her desired sports subsidy and moved on with his or her project. In the rarer cases when the activists persuaded their elected leaders to "just say no," the usual outcome (Houston Oilers, San Diego Chargers, Seattle Supersonics) was the team owner carrying out his or her threat and relocating the franchise to a city that *was* willing to support the desired subsidy.

A more concentrated *national focus* on sports franchise free agency might have prevented the worst justified owner decisions, such as:

- The Oakland Raiders' 1982 relocation to Los Angeles;
- The Baltimore Colts' 1984 relocation to Indianapolis;
- The Cleveland Browns' 1996 relocation to Baltimore;
- The Houston Oilers' 1996 relocation to Nashville;
- The Seattle Supersonics' 2008 relocation to Oklahoma City;
- The St. Louis Rams' 2016 relocation to Los Angeles;
- The San Diego Chargers' 2017 relocation to Los Angeles; and
- The Oakland Raiders' 2020 relocation to Las Vegas.

The United States Congress—and not local government—is the best venue for the fight to reduce local governments' percentage share of sports facility costs. The federal laws and court decisions as they currently stand amount to a stacked deck that heavily favor sports leagues and their owners against municipal treasuries. That won't change until:

1. We demand that our Congressional representatives correct a national template that now allows sports franchise free agency—with its attendant subsidy competitions—to continue to pit city against city; and
2. Those Congressional representatives respond by enacting corrective legislation such as that I described in Chapter 13.

Reduce Sports Facility Costs By Choosing Preservation Over New Construction

Going forward, local activist groups should focus their efforts and activities on "preservation of existing sports facilities" and extending their useful lives. Let's return to the cathedral/stadium analogy. Why do we regard a well-built cathedral as something that should last through the ages, but think of a sports stadium as economically obsolete if it's not replaced with a new facility every twenty-five years? If local activists focus on this issue, and hold their local elected officials accountable for premature replacement of perfectly good sports facilities, they can play a far more useful role in our civic dialogue.

The FIELD OF SCHEMES authors identified several activist groups of this nature, including the Tiger Stadium Fan Club (with its Cochrane Plan to upgrade Tiger Stadium) and the Save Our Sox group/South Armor Square Neighborhood Association (united by their desire to renovate and preserve historic Comiskey Park in Chicago). Though each of these efforts proved unsuccessful, I would argue that they were at least fighting for the right issue.

History Enhances Clevelanders' Sports Experiences

A sports venue's history matters to more than activists and scholars. Fans care about it, and Cleveland is proof positive. Since staging a Billy Joel concert on its October, 1994 opening night, the Rocket Mortgage FieldHouse has served as Northeast Ohio's premier concert venue. Memorable performances by Paul McCartney, Bruce Springsteen, Lady Gaga, and many others have occurred there.

It hosted the U.S. Figure Skating Championships in 2000 and 2009, and games of the NCAA Men's and Women's Division I Basketball

Championship (including the Women's Final Four in 2007). It was the site for the 1997 and 2022 NBA All-Star Games, including celebrations marking the 50th and 75th anniversary of the establishment of the NBA.

As for the principal tenant— the Cleveland Cavaliers—they have played exciting NBA Finals games at the venue in 2007, 2015, 2016, 2017, and 2018. The team's first appearance at the Finals in 2007 was enabled by a memorable Game 6 of the Eastern Conference Finals. As reported by the Associated Press:

> For the first time in a long time, championship-starved Cleveland has something to feel good about. The Cavaliers, once the punch line to jokes and Michael Jordan's favorite foil, are Eastern Conference champions -- and on their way to the NBA Finals. Lugging an entire region's hopes with him on every trip to the basket, James had 20 points and 14 rebounds, and unflappable rookie Daniel Gibson added 31 points -- 19 in the fourth quarter -- to give the Cavaliers a 98-82 victory in Game 6 against the Detroit Pistons.[5]

Though the Cavaliers' 2016 NBA Championship was earned in Game 7 at Oracle Arena in Oakland, the Game 6 win at the Field-House—led by James with 41 points and Kyrie Irving with 23— was nearly as exciting. Suffice to say that the FieldHouse has become a community icon in its three decades of existence.

The same can be said for Progressive Field. Beginning with opening day in April, 1994, when Wayne Kirby's sharp single to left earned the ballpark an inaugural extra-inning win against the Randy Johnson-led Seattle Mariners, and continuing through the remarkable streak of 455 straight sellouts in the 1990's, the unique architecture of Cleveland's ballpark has witnessed some special moments:

- The left field bleachers where catcher Tony Pena homered in extra innings against the Boston Red Sox in October, 1995, to deliver the Indians' first post-season win in 47 years;
- The right-centerfield stands where catcher Sandy Alomar lined a home run against Yankees relief ace Mariano Rivera to propel the team towards the 1997 World Series;
- The pitcher's mound where a swarm of midges disrupted Yankee pitcher Joba Chamberlain, leading to an improbable extra inning win over the Yankees during the team's progression to the 2007 American League Championship Series;
- The upper deck near the right field foul pole where Jason Giambi deposited a walk-off home run against the Chicago White Sox in the midst of the team's season-ending ten-game winning streak that earned manager Terry Francona a playoff berth in his 2013 inaugural season in Cleveland; and
- The left field plaza where Rajai Davis lined his game-tying two-run home run off Cubs relief ace Aroldis Chapman in the eighth inning of Game 7 of the 2016 World Series. Per Wikipedia, "Game 7 of the series would go down as a classic, with some calling it the greatest Game 7 in World Series history, comparing it to 1924, 1960, 1991, 1997, and 2001 for its drama and tension."[6]

The latter three events remain immensely popular YouTube searches. Like Rocket Mortgage Fieldhouse, Progressive Field has earned its status as one of Cleveland's most popular landmarks.

Cleveland Browns Stadium cannot come close to the Gateway venues when it comes to memorable events. Its history has had the misfortune to coincide with the Browns' *three winning seasons*—with only one playoff win—since its September 12, 1999 opening day which, perhaps prophetically, featured a 43-0 loss to the Pittsburgh Steelers. By contrast, in the first fifty years (1946-1995) of the team's existence, Browns fans had only borne *12 losing seasons*.

But let's remember that the current football field footprint nearly matches the Cleveland Municipal Stadium's field footprint (just as the City's restored League Park field matches the footprint of the original field). As noted in Chapter 4, this bow to history was a factor in retaining a lakefront location for the City's football stadium. Accordingly, for fans like me who are old enough to remember the team's glory days, a look around the Stadium recalls:

- The west end zone where Lou Groza kicked his game-winning field goal to give the Browns a League Championship in their inaugural 1950 NFL season;
- The same end zone that witnessed Gary Collins' three touchdown catches in the Browns' 27-0 upset win over the Baltimore Colts in the December, 1964, NFL Championship game;
- The same end zone that, regrettably, bears the taint as the locale of John Elway's touchdown pass that tied the game and enabled the Denver Broncos to achieve an overtime win that sent them—and not the Browns—to the 1987 Super Bowl;
- The east end zone (by design) is—and was—the site of the legendary "Dawg Pound" bleacher area that was a hallmark of the Browns' superb late 1980s teams.

It Won't Get Any Easier

Nationally, the stakes are getting higher and higher. In the NFL, "keeping up with the Jones'" is proving challenging for some owners:

Certain owners, (Dallas Cowboys owner Jerry) Jones said, resent the wave of stunning new stadiums being built around the league. They get up in the meetings, these small-thinking owners do, and complain about the arms race mentality. They feel pressured to keep up with the biggest and grandest new venues their partners are building in other cities. Why is it necessary to spend so much on stadiums when the league derives 60 percent of its revenue from TV rights?[7]

The "arms-race mentality" shows no signs of slackening. Consider three recent projects:

- The expected $1 billion public obligation on the new Buffalo Bills football stadium;
- The expected $1.26 billion public obligation on the new Tennessee Titans football stadium (replacing an existing stadium not yet 25 years old[8])
- Kansas City Royals owner John Sherman's request for a new downtown ballpark to replace the highly rated and well-maintained Kaufmann Stadium.[9]

Of these and other examples, it is the City of Oakland—having lost its football and basketball franchises, and now battling to retain its baseball franchise—that stands out as Ground Zero in the national dilemma of sports franchise free agency. As a long-time local writer asked in 2015:

How much more disrespect can Oakland tolerate from its ungrateful three sports franchises?" Dave Newhouse, a retired longtime columnist for The Oakland Tribune, wrote recently in an essay published in Bay Area newspapers. "There isn't another sports town anywhere that has enjoyed more success or endured more grief from its sports tenants than Oakland, the carpetbagger capital of America."[10]

As previously noted, in April, 2021, MLB told the A's to "consider other markets" and declared the existing ballpark site unacceptable.[11] But why? Though the A's owners wanted to demolish Oakland Coliseum and build a new waterfront ballpark at Howard Terminal, that site carried with it the above-cited $855 million public infrastructure cost, and there are other reasons for skepticism.[12] Could a remodeled and renovated Coliseum have been a more economical solution? As originally built—that is, prior to the 1995 addition of 20,000 seats via the "Mount Davis" wall of football seating—the Coliseum was well-suited for baseball and had a splendid view of Oakland hills. The New York Times made this point in a 2015 article:

> Part of what makes O.co Coliseum a relatively inhospitable place to watch baseball is the wall of seats and suites that were built 20 years ago to entice the Raiders to return from Los Angeles, where the owner Al Davis took them in 1982. They block what had been a serene view of the Oakland hills beyond the outfield and eliminated the type of pavilion that so many new ballparks now relish.[13]

With the exit of the football team, "Mount Davis" could have been demolished and the original vista restored. That action, coupled with a major overhaul of the Coliseum's overall infrastructure, might have yielded a splendid baseball facility at a lower cost than a new facility. While MLB understandably called out local elected officials for the slow pace of Oakland's stadium deliberations, the league office overplayed its hand by eliminating the existing ballpark site as a potential solution.

The present and future leaders of Cleveland and Cuyahoga County should keep a close watch on what happens in Oakland and Las Vegas, and remember the legal strategies used by St. Louis in its successful lawsuit against the NFL. And they should learn from what worked—and what didn't work—in the facility-preservation efforts in other towns.

Northeast Ohio has three centrally-located sports facilities in good repair, and each facility has undergone a midlife renovation and repurposing to make it competitive with more recently constructed structures. Each of these sports facilities can and should enjoy lives comparable to Fenway Park in Boston, Wrigley Field in Chicago, and Lambeau Field in Green Bay. In turn, if the citizens of Cleveland and Cuyahoga County accept this worthy goal—and hold future elected officials accountable for its realization—their region will remain a national leader in sports facility decision-making.

ACKNOWLEDGMENTS

Between New Hanover County, North Carolina and Cleveland, Ohio, I spent 33 years of my career in government employment. From my start in Wilmington, North Carolina in 1980, I regarded the meetings I attended as equivalents of college lectures, and I applied my college-note-taking-practices to record the conversations in long-hand script. Consequently, when I retired from the City of Cleveland in June, 2017, my accumulated notes filled an entire 3 ½-foot-long bookshelf.

That same year, Cleveland Mayor Frank Jackson and Cuyahoga County Executive Armond Budish asked me to serve as their joint appointee on the board of the Gateway Economic Development Corporation of Greater Cleveland. I agreed and—now having time available—began preparing for my board role by reviewing my notes covering past public decisions on our community's sports facilities.

What was originally intended as a refresher course turned into something much bigger. As I reviewed my notes, I began to believe that my accounts of elected officials' sports facility decisions may be useful to college students who were considering governmental careers. Accordingly, my review expanded to cover every sports facility encounter since I joined the Cleveland Law Department in 1988.

That proved to be a lot of activity. As I stated in the Preface, I sought out every opportunity: my upbringing as a Cleveland sports fan had hard-wired me for these kinds of projects. But merely wanting to participate would not have made it so: without the support of my bosses—and the mayors I served under—I could not have experienced the inside stories that I have shared in this book.

My first Law Department supervisors—Section Chief June Wiener and the late Law Director Marilyn Zack—entrusted me with major responsibilities during my first six months in the Cleveland Law Department, including a standing assignment to City Council's Finance Committee (where I had a front row seat to Council President George Forbes' tactics and techniques) and an assignment to the Cleveland Municipal Stadium lease. Those excellent attorneys and my next Law Director, Craig Miller, taught me a whole range of negotiating practices.

Though I didn't serve directly under the late Mayor George V. Voinovich, I had enough meetings with him to learn his governing style. He was then and would be for the rest of his career—as Governor of Ohio and United States Senator—a devoted "budgetary hawk," and his fervor for his government's strong financial standing always insured that his chief financial advisors would be major power brokers. Through his relationship with Council President George Forbes, he taught me a great deal about power sharing. Congressional leaders today would do well to follow Senator Voinovich's example of moving across the aisle to forge partnerships regardless of political affiliations.

I did have the opportunity to serve directly under Mayors Michael R. White and Frank G. Jackson. In most American cities, senior mayoral staff members have dual responsibilities: managing the pressing city issues of the moment, while always keeping an eye on the impact those city issues might have on your mayor's longer term political ambitions: state senator, governor, U.S. Senator, what have you. For the nearly eighteen years I served directly under Mayors White and Jackson, I was never burdened with the second responsibility. Mayors White and Jackson were unique in caring *only* about what was best for Clevelanders. The political part of my jobs was thus simpler than what my colleagues in other cities faced.

I am grateful for the sports facility duties that all three mayors gave me, and for their confidence in my ability to fulfill those assignments. I had my share of missteps along the way, and each mayor was appropriately direct in calling me to account for my errors. But I was fortunate to have grown up with a strict (but humorous) father who taught me how to work for demanding leaders.

I first got to know County Executive Armond Budish during the deliberations on the Q deal, where his political courage and persistence kept the transaction from unravelling at the end. He showed faith in my judgment by making me a joint appointee to the Gateway Board, and took aggressive steps to keep the baseball team at the table in our lease extension negotiations.

I worked for and learned from other political leaders, including (alphabetically) Dan Brady, Tony Brancatelli, Joe Cimperman, Phyllis Cleveland, George Forbes, Blaine Griffin, Pernel Jones, Jr., Kevin Kelley, Kerry McCormack, Dale Miller, Terrell Pruitt, James Rokakis, Chris Ronayne, Sabra Pierce Scott, Cheryl Stephens, Martin Sweeney, Jay Westbrook, and Matt Zone. And I have been, and am now, pleased to serve with my past and current Gateway board colleagues Ahmed Abonamah, Terry Agosta, Matt Carroll, Dave Ebersole, Ron King, and Davida Russell,

My upbringing in Cleveland suburbs imbued me with lifelong fandom for the city's sports teams, and I'm sure my career would have eventually touched pro sports in some fashion. But there was in my case a special incentive to participate in these kinds of public decisions. My brother David—one year younger than me and the best athlete in our family—died way too early in 1978 at age 24 after a 2 ½ year battle with schizophrenia. From then on, I sought out connections between my work and Cleveland sports teams as a kind of tribute to his memory. David's full story deserved its own separate treatment, and I have attempted to do that via a screenplay that will hopefully spring to life someday in the form of a motion picture.

In the tasks described in this book, I was honored to work with and learn from some of Cleveland's brightest and skilled attorneys and public servants. In alphabetical order, these leaders included Jeff Appelbaum, Rich Bertovich, Darnell and Terri Hamilton Brown, Bob Brown, Matt Carroll, Tom Chema, Fred Collier, Tim Cosgrove, Tony Coyne, James DeRosa, Tim Donovan, Diane Downing, Therese Sweeney Drake, Sharon Dumas, Lee Friedman, Bob Franz, Jim Gentile, Dave Gilbert, Todd Greathouse, Carole Hoover, Rick Horvath, Betsy Hruby, Greg Huth, Deb Janik, Barbara Langhenry, Nancy Lesic, Mary Louise Madigan, Joe Marinucci, Bill Mason, Trevor McAleer, Valarie McCall, Marty McGann, Craig Miller, Hunter Morrison, Fred Nance, Joe Nanni, Tracey Nichols, Tim Offtermatt, Jeff Patterson, Albert Ratner, Joe Roman, Debra Rosman, Ed Rybka, Baiju Shah, Scott Simpkins, Bob Smith, Sharon Sobol Jordan, Steve Strnisha, Felton Thomas, Dr. Jerry Sue Thornton, Robert Triozzi, Chris and Linda Warren, Dennis Wilcox, Tom Yablonsky, Brian Zimmerman, and Ann Zoller.

I am indebted to Nancy Lesic for volunteering to review and edit the first draft of my manuscript. As a participant in many of the book's events, she was uniquely qualified to perform this task. Also, as those events transpired, I often visited my favorite local tavern, Great Lakes Brewing Company. To owners Pat and Dan Conway, and to bartenders Corin Moloughney, Kevin Graham, and Carrie Komandt, I give thanks for keeping my spirits high and my perspective grounded.

My friends also provided companionship and encouragement. Thanks to Solomon Balraj and Lisa Williams, Patrick and Debbie Berry, Bob Brown and Susan Berger, Cheryl Davis, Diane Downing, Sharon Dumas, Dan and Connie Cevasco, Don and Linda Colon, Lee Friedman, Marty Flask, Al Gulley, Glenn and Janet Harbeck, Marvin Hayes, Jerome Howard, Todd Hunt, Barbara Langhenry, Gerald Linderman, Dan McMullen, Kathy Linderman, Ken Lurie, Tarra Petras, Dr. Monyka Price, Estelle Price, Barb Price-Willoth, Harold Reeder, Sharon Sobol Jordan, Dan and Wendy Stummer, David and Linda Stummer, Richie and Rhonda Stummer, Bill Verhamme, Chris and Linda Warren, Barry Withers, Eric and Jenny Wobser, Jason and Courtney Wood, and Rick Werner, Eleanor Werner, and Caroline Werner,

My father, Victor David Silliman, passed away at age 56 in 1984 in Wilmington, North Carolina. I am grateful for the work ethic he instilled in his sons Ken, David and Jim. My mother, Virginia Gale Silliman, and my brother, James Allen Silliman, both live in Wilmington, North Carolina. We are a tight-knit family, and since my retirement in 2017 I've been able to spend much more time with them in Wilmington. They continue to provide me support in my written endeavors.

Lastly, it's been nearly 50 years since I graduated from Case Western Reserve University with a Bachelor of Arts in Urban and Environmental Studies. I remember how, as a student interested in urban affairs, I sought out books that depicted day to day experiences in local government. I am hopeful that this book can provide such real-life experiences to the college students of today and tomorrow.

Ken Silliman

June, 2023

NOTES

PREFACE

1. Ty Shalter, "Why NFL Stadiums Are the Modern-Day Cathedral, BLEACHER REPORT, April 26, 2012.
2. JAMES A. TOMAN, CLEVELAND STADIUM: SIXTY YEARS OF MEMORIES, Revised Edition 1994, p. 17.
3. See, e.g., R.A. Baade, "Is there an economic rationale for subsidizing sports stadiums?, 1987, THE HEARTLAND INSTITUTE; D. Coates and B. Humphreys, "Do Economists Reach a Conclusion on Subsidies for Sports Franchises, Stadiums, and Mega-Events," 2008, ECON. JOURNAL WATCH 5(3), pages 294-315; R.G. Noll and A. Zimbalist, "The organization of sports leagues," 2003, OXFORD REVIEW OF ECONOMIC POLICY 19(4) pages 531-551; JAMES QUIRK AND RODNEY FORT, HARD BALL: THE ABUSE OF POWER IN PRO TEAM SPORTS (1999); and ROSENTRAUB, MAJOR LEAGUE LOSERS: THE REAL COST OF SPORTS AND WHO'S PAYING FOR IT (1997).
4. See JOANNA CAGAN AND NEIL DEMAUSE, FIELD OF SCHEMES: HOW THE GREAT STADIUM SWINDLE TURNS PUBLIC MONEY INTO PRIVATE PROFIT (1998); Kevin Clark Forsythe, "The Stadium Game Pittsburgh Style: Observations on the Latest Round of Publicly Financed Sports Stadia in Steel Town, U.S.A.; and Comparisons with 28 Other Major League Teams," 10 MARQUETTE SPORTS LAW REVIEW 237 (2000); and JUDITH GRANT LONG, PUBLIC/PRIVATE PARTNERSHIPS FOR MAJOR LEAGUE SPORTS FACILITIES (2013).
5. Forsythe, supra note 4.
6. MICHAEL SCHATZKI WITH WAYNE R. COFFEY, NEGOTIATION: THE ART OF GETTING WHAT YOU WANT (1981), page 35.
7. Id. at page 41.
8. Id. at page 34.
9. Alan Peters and Peter Fisher, "The Failure of Economic Development Incentives," JOURNAL OF THE AMERICAN PLANNING ASSOCIATION, Volume 70, No. 1, Winter 2004, pages 27, 35-36.
10. "... it could be argued that since the mid-1980s, the concept of sport reimaging has been embraced by a large number of developed cities with a new intensity and purpose. These cities.... have indulged in what has become known as place marketing (Madsen 1992), which involves striving to sell the image of a place so as to make it more attractive to economic enterprises, tourists and inhabitants (Philo and Kearns 1993: 3). Due to the contemporary dominance of the media and the

popularity and exposure devoted to sport, it has become common for cities in the US, and increasingly in the UK, to use sport as a vehicle for city image enhancement." Andrew Smith, "Sporting a new image? Sports-based regeneration strategies as a means of enhancing the image of the city tourist destination," in CHRIS GRATTON AND IAN HENRY, SPORT IN THE CITY: THE ROLE OF SPORT IN ECONOMIC AND SOCIAL REGENERATION, 2001, pp. 127-148

11. Id.

12. JOANNA CAGAN AND NEIL DEMAUSE, supra note 4 at page ix.

13. JUDITH GRANT LONG, supra note 4 at page xiii.

CHAPTER 1

1. TOM L. JOHNSON, edited by ELIZABETH J. HAUSER, MY STORY (1993), page li.

2. Michael D. Roberts, "A Century of Building," CLEVELAND SCENE, November 24, 2004.

3. See generally Norman Krumholz, "Government, Equity, Redistribution and the Practice of Urban Planning," in W. DENNIS KEATING, NORMAN KRUMHOLZ, & DAVID C. PERRY, Editors, CLEVELAND: A METROPOLITAN READER (1995), page 311.

4. Roldo Bartimole, "Who Governs: The Corporate Hand," in W. DENNIS KEATING, NORMAN KRUMHOLZ, & DAVID C. PERRY, Editors, CLEVELAND: A METROPOLITAN READER (1995), page 168.

5. Roldo Bartimole, "30 Years of Shaming Deals, Point of View, Volume 30 No. 12 and Volume 31 No. 1, page 15.

CHAPTER 2

1. JAMES A. TOMAN, CLEVELAND STADIUM: SIXTY YEARS OF MEMORIES (1987), pages 6-8.

2. Id. at page 21.

3. Id. at page 22.

4. The sources of information for the respective years are as follows, with all referenced ordinances and board of control resolutions being from the City of Cleveland as reported in that city's The City Record: 1936 (Workers Progress Administration project), 1939 (author estimate of amount spent by Indians per term in lease), 1944 (bonds issued pursuant to Ordinance No. 1231-44, passed October 30, 1944; public improvement made pursuant to Ordinance No. 121-45, passed February 9, 1945), 1945 (Board of Control Resolution No. 224-45, adopted August 11, 1945), 1947 (Board of Control Resolution No. 918-47, adopted July 23, 1947), 1948 (TOMAN, supra Note 1 at page 26), 1949 (Board of Control Resolution No. 194-49, adopted March 16, 1949 pursuant to the authority of Ordinance

No. 22-49, passed February 7, 1949; Board of Control Resolution No. 464-49, adopted June 15, 1949), 1949-50 (TOMAN, supra Note 1 at pages 26,29; John J. Lodudco, Executive Secretary, Department of Public Properties, City of Cleveland, "American Institute of Park Executives Panel Discussion on 'Management of Public Stadiums and Arenas"), 1950 (TOMAN, supra Note 1 at page 29). 1953 (Board of Control Resolution No. 228-93, adopted April 8, 1952; Board of Control Resolution No. 87-53, adopted February 4, 1953 (Board of Control Resolution No. 692-53, adopted September 6, 1953), 1954 (Board of Control Resolution No. 405-55, adopted June 1, 1955 pursuant to the authority of Ordinance No. 1643-54, passed June 28, 1054; Board of Control Resolution No. 343-55, adopted May 11, 1955 pursuant to the authority of Ordinance No. 1643-54, passed June 28, 1954), 1958 (Board of Control Resolution No. 713-58, adopted October 1, 1958; Board of Control Resolution No. 799-58, adopted October 1, 1958), 1960 (Board of Control Resolution No. 261-60, adopted April 13, 1960 pursuant to the authority of Ordinance No. 1566-59, passed June 29, 1959), 1961 (Board of Control Resolution No. 891-61, adopted October 18, 1961 pursuant to the authority of Ordinance No. 2135-60, passed October 31, 1960), 1965 (Board of Control Resolution No. 143-65, adopted March 4, 1965 pursuant to the authority of Ordinance No. 2649-64, passed December 14, 1964; Board of Control Resolution No. 617-65, adopted August 16, 1965 pursuant to the authority of Ordinance No. 1855-65, passed July 12, 1965), 1966 (TOMAN, supra Note 1 at page30).

5. TOMAN, supra Note 1 at page 39.
6. "Can Nick Mileti Make the Cavaliers Go?" CLEVELAND MAGAZINE, October 1974.
7. "The Rise and Fall of Richfield Coliseum," THE TRUST FOR PUBLIC LAND MAGAZINE, Fall 1989.

CHAPTER 3

1. Interview of George Voinovich, quoted in JACK TORRY, ENDLESS SUMMERS: THE FALL AND RISE OF THE CLEVELAND INDIANS (1995), pages 216-218.
2. MICHAEL G. POPLAR with JAMES A. TOMAN, FUMBLE: THE BROWNS, MODELL AND THE MOVE- AN INSIDER'S STORY (1997), page 138.
3. TORRY, supra note 1 at page 220.
4. TERRY PLUTO AND TOM HAMILTON, GLORY DAYS IN TRIBE TOWN: THE CLEVELAND INDIANS AND JACOBS FIELD, 1994-1997 (2014), page 36.
5. TORRY, supra note 1 at page 204. For a more thorough oral history of this time period, see Tom Chema's March 11,2020 interview with 92.3 THE FAN at https://www.audacy.com/923thefan/articles/tom-chema-gateway-group-revitalizing-down town-cleveland
6. POPLAR AND TOMAN, supra note 2 at page 165.

7. TORRY, supra note 1 at page 221.

8. TORRY, id. at page 223.

9. TORRY, id. at pages 223-224.

10. See generally TORRY, id. at pages 224-225.

11. Roldo Bartimole, "Dick Jacobs—He Loved Money But Also Life," REALNEO.US, November 21, 2007.

12. TORRY, supra note 1 at page 224.

13. JOANNA CAGAN AND NEIL DEMAUSE, FIELD OF SCHEMES: HOW THE GREAT STADIUM SWINDLE TURNS PUBLIC MONEY INTO PRIVATE PROFIT (1998), page 16, citing newspaper ad, The Plain Dealer, May 3, 1990.

14. JOHN HELYAR, LORDS OF THE REALM (1994), page 439.

15. Id. at page 495.

16. Bob Becker and Lou Mio, "Baseball Chief opposes city losing Indians, but says move is possible, "The Plain Dealer, May 3, 1990, page 1-A.

17. TORRY, supra note 1 at page 229.

18. Timothy S. Chapin, "Sports Facilities as Urban Redevelopment Catalysts: Baltimore's Camden Yards and Cleveland's Gateway," JOURNAL OF THE AMERICAN PLANNING ASSOCIATION, Vol. 79, No. 1, Spring 2004, page 194.

19. Id. at page 202.

20. Id. at page 202.

21. The summary of Gateway's construction process from 1990-1994 is drawn from JeĿrey R. Appelbaum, "Building Gateway: The Role of Project Construction Counsel," CLEVELAND BAR JOURNAL June-July 1994, and Keith A. Asmus and JeĿrey R. Appelbaum, "Building Gateway: Resolving Project Labor and Employment Issues," CLEVELAND BAR JOURNAL September 1994.

22. Barbara Hawley, Squire Sanders & Dempsey fax to Ken Silliman, February 2, 1996.

23. Jack DeVries, "Cleveland's Crowning Jewel," in GAMEFACE INDIANS SCOREBOOK MAGAZINE:OPENING DAY 1994, page 38.

24. POPLAR AND TOMAN, supra note 2 at page 237.

25. Roldo Bartimole, "Boyle, Hagan morally deficient again," POINT OF VIEW, Volume 28, No. 7, December 9, 1995.

26. Roldo Bartimole, "Gunds Sandbag Politicians," POINT OF VIEW, Volume __, No. __, August __, 1995.

27. TERRY PLUTO AND TOM HAMILTON, supra Note 4 at pages 99-101.

28. JON MORGAN, GLORY FOR SALE (1997), page 269.

29. PLUTO AND HAMILTON, supra note 4 at pages 280-281.

30. See generally Id. at pages 320-321

31. Chris D. Davies, "Assessing the Indians talent development,"www.letsgotribe.com, June 4,2018.

32. JUDITH GRANT LONG, PUBLIC/PRIVATE PARTNERSHIPS FOR MAJOR LEAGUE SPORTS FACILITIES (2013), page 110.

33. City of Cleveland Department of Public Works, Division of Parking Facilities, Report on Audit of Financial Statements for the Fiscal Year Ending December 31,

2019, page 31.

CHAPTER 4

1. MICHAEL G. POPLAR with JAMES A. TOMAN, FUMBLE: THE BROWNS, MODELL AND THE MOVE (1997), p. 133.
2. Roldo Bartimole, Sweetheart Modell" POINT OF VIEW, Volume 20, Number 20, June 11, 1988, page 2.
3. POPLAR and TOMAN, supra note 1 at page 136.
4. Id. at pp. 136-137.
5. Roldo Bartimole, "Establishment frets: Modell cries," POINT OF VIEW, Volume 21, Number 12, February 11, 1989, page 2.
6. POPLAR with TOMAN, supra note 1 at page 300.
7. Id. at page 15.
8. Id. at page 145.
9. Id. at page 190.
10. Id. at page 320.
11. Id. at page 326. See also Id. at page 325, concluding that the Browns' finances would have been improved by "a better drafting record between 1986 and 1993."
12. Id. at pages 326-327.
13. Id. at page 207.
14. Id. at pages 305-306, 320.
15. Notice and Statement of Reasons of the Cleveland Browns supporting Relocation of Franchise to Baltimore, page 12, November 4, 1995.
16. POPLAR with TOMAN, supra note 1 at page 235.
17. ROSENTRAUB, MAJOR LEAGUE LOSERS: THE REAL COST OF SPORTS AND WHO'S PAYING FOR IT (1999), pages 66-67.
18. JON MORGAN, GLORY FOR SALE (1997), page 157.
19. Id. at page 255.
20. Mayor Michael R. White, Stadium Task Force Meeting, May 17, 2017.
21. Id.
22. DAVID HALBERSTAM, THE BEST AND THE BRIGHTEST (1969), page 5.
23. MORGAN, supra note 18 at page 256.
24. See generally Id. at pages 258-261.
25. Id. at page 262.
26. My description of this meeting is derived from the account given by MORGAN, supra note 18 at page 249
27. POPLAR with TOMAN, supra note 1 at pages 317-318.
28. Stephen Phillips, "City reworked the numbers as clock ticked down," THE PLAIN DEALER, November 8, 1995,.
29. Tim Green, "The American Dream," Forward to MORGAN, supra note 18 at page i.

30. John Helyar, "*Browns Blues*: In New NFL, Moves Get a Lot of Attention OL the Field as Well," THE WALL STRRET JOURNAL, Friday, December 15, 1995.
31. Id.
32. MORGAN, supra note 18 at pages 274-275.
33. Jim Konkoly, "Cuyahoga voters 'stick it to Modell,'" EUCLID SUN JOURNAL, November 9, 1995.
34. Stephen KoL and Mark Rollenhagen, "Browns told: Stay put!" THE PLAIN DEALER, November 25, 1995, page 1-A.
35. V. David Sartin, "White, fans launch drive to recover the Browns," THE PLAIN DEALER, November 10, 1995.
36. Tony Grossi, "Owners to take Browns vote Jan. 17," THE PLAIN DEALER, November 26, 1995.
37. MORGAN, supra note 18 at page 162.
38. Id. at 181-182.
39. Id. at 119.
40. Statement of Paul Tagliabue, Commissioner of the National Football League, Before the Subcommittee on Antitrust, Business Rights and Competition of the Committee on the Judiciary of the United States Senate (November 29, 1995), page 6.
41. Id.
42. Id. at pages 7-8.
43. See generally Id. at pages 9-14.
44. "26 Teams Burst the Cap," THE PLAIN DEALER, January 2, 1996.
45. POPLAR with TOMAN, supra note 1 at page 294.
46. Charles Babington, "For Stadiums Under Scrutiny, Lawmakers say Browns, P.G. May Have to Pay Up," WASHINGTON POST, November 15, 1995, page B1.
47. *See* Michael Abramowitz, "A Few Determined Men Made Stadium Dreams Come True," THE WASHINGTON POST, April 14, 1996. *See also* MORGAN, supra note 18 at page 300.
48. The accounts in this paragraph are drawn from Stephen KoL, "Browns fans deliver a hit: Contingent appeals for owner loyalty," THE PLAIN DEALER, January 17, 1996, page 8-A.
49. Timothy Heider and Stephen KoL, "NFL owners expected to delay vote on Browns: Some want to check options against Modell," THE PLAIN DEALER, January 17, 1996, page 1-A.
50. Stephen KoL, Timothy Heider, and Tony Grossi, "Owners plan vote on Browns in 3 weeks," THE PLAIN DEALER, January 19, 1996, page1-A.
51. Tony Grossi, "NFL owners in a quandary over Browns, Cleveland pleas," THE PLAIN DEALER, January 19, 1996, page 10-A.
52. Id.
53. MORGAN, supra note 18 at page 286.
54. Id.
55. Kristen E. Knauf, *If You Build It, Will They Stay? An Examination of State-of-the-Art Clauses in NFL Stadium Leases*, 20 MARQUETTE SPORTS LAW REVIEW 479,

486, citing LEASE AGREEMENT BY AND BETWEEN THE BOARD OF COMMISSIONERS OF HAMILTON COUNTY, OHIO AND CINCINNATI BENGALS, INC., May 29, 1997 art. 12.3-12.4; *Chiefs, Royals Plan to Stay Put*, SPORTS BUS. J., Nov.15, 2004, at 28; see also *City, Chargers Reach Middle Ground*, SPORTS BUS. J., July 12, 2004, at 32.

56. See, e.g., Patrick Rishe, *St. Louis Fans Should Direct Blame Towards 1994 Lease and Not Stan Kroenke*, FORBES MAGAZINE, January 6, 2016.

57. MORGAN, supra note 18 at page 287.

58. See generally Id. at pages 287-288.

59. Id. at pages 291, 292.

60. https://www.thebreakers.co/about-breakers/

61. MARK LEIBOVICH, BIG GAME: THE NFL IN DANGEROUS TIMES (2018), page 29.

62. See Courtney Astolfi, "Majority of Clevelanders want FirstEnergy Stadium to stay put, prefer renovation over new stadium," November 22, 2022, https://www.cleveland.com/news/2022/11/majority-of-greater-clevelanders-want-firstenergy-stadium-to-stay-put-prefer-renovation-over-new-stadium.html

63. KoL, Heider and Grossi, supra note 50.

64. Id.

65. Terry Pluto has asserted that the NFL stalled the Brown's ownership decision to "drive up the price" and allow other teams to use the threat of relocation to Cleveland as "leverage... to get new stadiums and better leases." TERRY PLUTO, FALSE START: HOW THE NEW BROWNS WERE SET UP TO FAIL (2004), page 36.

66. MORGAN, supra note 18 at page 311.

67. Richard Sandomir, "PRO FOOTBALL: The Price of Cleveland's Heart," NEW YORK TIMES, September 2, 1998.

68. Tony Grossi, "Lerner buys new Browns: $530 million record-setting deal," THE PLAIN DEALER, September 9, 1998, page A-1.

69. Don Pierson, "$700 million Buys Houston an NFL Expansion Team," THE CHICAGO TRIBUNE, October 7, 1999.

70. JOANNA CAGAN AND NEIL DEMAUSE, FIELD OF SCHEMES: HOW THE GREAT STADIUM SWINDLE TURNS PUBLIC MONEY INTO PRIVATE PROFIT (1998), page 106.

71. Christian D'Andrea, "The Browns' 4 1st-round NFL Draft busts in 3 years is a record that may stand forever," sbnation.com, June 27, 2018.

72. Steven Ruiz, "Grading every NFL team's draft performance over the last five years," ftw.usatoday.com, April 26, 2017.

73. Vinny Iyer, "NFL Draft Grades: Best, Worst of 2018 Picks," The Sporting News, April 29, 2018, https://www.sportingnews.com/us/nfl/list/nfl-draft-2018-picks-grades-best-worst-winners-losers/17xeclajzey1x1kb7ljx7t1eoe/16

74. Andy Benoit, "NFL Draft 2019 Grades: Analyzing All 32 Teams' Draft Picks," Sports Illustrated, April 27, 2019, https://www.si.com/nfl/2019/04/27/nfl-draft-2019-team-grades-picks-analysis

75. See, e.g., Pete Smith, "Don't Hire John Dorsey As Your Team's General Manager, si.com, December 2, 2020,

    https://www.si.com/nfl/browns/browns-maven-features/dont-hire-john-dorsey#:
-:text=Reports%20suggest%20teams%20are%20considering,don't%20want%
20to%20make.

CHAPTER 5

1. "Quicken Loans Arena in "WIKIPEDIA;" "About Quicken Loans Arena," at theqarena.com.
2. Greater Cleveland Partnership, "Protect the Public's Investment" Power Point presentation to Cuyahoga County Council, January 21, 2013, Slide # 40.
3. Thomas Ott, "Cleveland City Council Oks $5.8 million for stadium repairs," THE PLAIN DEALER, February 7, 2012.
4. Id.
5. Craig Calcaterra, "The Braves are leaving Turner Field after the 2016 season," mlb.nbcsports.com, November 11, 2013.
6. Mark Naymik, "Cleveland Browns and City of Cleveland announce deal on Firtst-Energy Stadium financing," THE PLAIN DEALER, November 19, 2013, page 1A.
7. Eric Sandy, "Dispatches from Cuyahoga County's Public Sin Tax Meeting," clevelandscene.com, January 21, 2014.
8. Cleveland Frowns, "Grassroots Coalition announces campaign to defeat Cuyahoga County sin tax renewal (Issue 7) this May," www.clevelandfrowns.com, March 12, 2014.
9. Sam Allard, "Spin Tax: With an Organized Opposition Raising Questions, the Sin Tax Debate Heats Up," clevelandscene.com, April 2, 2014.
10. Sam Allard, "Sin Tax Passes, but Opposition is Just Getting Started," clevelandscene.com, May 7, 2014.
11. Protecting the Public's Investment: Gateway Economic Development Corporation: Major Capital Repairs (October 27, 2015 Power Point Presentation to Cuyahoga County Council).
12. Kevin Kleps, "Gateway board meeting gives interesting look at upgrades to Progressive Field, the Q," crainscleveland.com, May 26, 2016.
13. Gateway Economic Development Corporation of Greater Cleveland, Quicken Loans (Arena) Major Capitol as of April 30, 2018 and Progressive Field Major Capitol as of April 30, 2018.
14. The annual debt service payments over the twelve-year term range from a high of $7,035,774.58 in 2016 to a low of $6,510,000 in 2027. The 2018 payment will be $6,919,000. See County of Cuyahoga Fiscal Office, Annual Informational Statement, September 26, 2016, pages 60-61.
15. Totals are derived from slides 16-19 of Gateway/Indians Meeting PowerPoint (prepared by Cleveland Indians), September 17, 2018

16. Cleveland Cavaliers Five Year Capital Repairs Estimate Submitted to Gateway Economic Development Corporation of Greater Cleveland.

17. Sam Allard, "Sin Tax Funds Rapidly Depleting, Yet Stadiums Continue to Seek Major Upgrades," CLEVELAND SCENE July 11-17, 2018, page 7.

18. Id.

19. Courtney Astolfi, "Cuyahoga County Council considers $40M bond issue to reimburse Cavs for arena repairs," THE PLAIN DEALER, May 29, 2019.

20. Resolution No. R2019-0125 and Resolution No. 2019-0126 were each heard and passed on June 11, 2019.

21. Nbodnar 1,"FirstEnergy Stadium, home of the Browns, will get $10 million in repairs, upgrades," August 17, 2016, https://www.neosportsinsiders.com/firstenergy-stadium-home-browns-will-get-10-million-repairs-upgrades/

22. Jordan Vandenburge, "City Council approves $12 million for First Energy Stadium repairs, upgrades," TV News 5, December 9, 2020, https://www.neosportsinsiders.com/firstenergy-stadium-home-browns-will-get-10-million-repairs-upgrades/

23. Id.

24. Courtney Astolfi, "New pedestrian ramps at FirstEnergy Stadium among $10 million in slated taxpayer funded repairs," THE PLAIN DEALER, June 10, 2022.

CHAPTER 6

1. David Budin, "I Can't Wait (White on White: Cleveland's New Mayor Speaks Out)," NORTERN OHIO LIVE, February 1990, page 32, 34.

2. Erick Trickey, "It's Time to Stop Underestimating Frank Jackson", CLEVELAND MAGAZINE, February 16, 2013.

3. Mark Naymik, "Cleveland Browns and City of Cleveland announce deal on Firtst-Energy Stadium financing," THE PLAIN DEALER, November 19, 2013, page 1A.

4. Id.

5. Id.

6. Leila Atassi, "Cleveland City Council members challenge city's obligation to pay for FirstEnergy Stadium improvements, THE PLAIN DEALER, November 20, 2017.

7. Leila Atassi, "Cleveland Browns Improvement Plan for FirstEnergy Stadium before City Council Today (LIVE Coverage). Cleveland.com, November 25, 2013.

8. Leila Atassi, "Cleveland City Council Approves Financing for upgrades to FirstEnergy Stadium," Cleveland.com, November 25, 2013.

9. Id.

10. Matt Goul, "Is it time to think about new stadium?: Browns' lease runs through 2029," THE PLAIN DEALER, May 4, 2018, page A1.

11. Mary Kay Cabot, "Haslam's say Browns will wear new uniforms in 2020 and they'll keep the stadium's location," THE PLAIN DEALER, May 27, 2019.

12. Compare Kaitlin Durbin, "Cleveland Browns reportedly want new $1 billion stadium, likely publicly funded,"

https://www.cleveland.com/news/2022/06/cleveland-browns-reportedly-want-new-1-billion-stadium-likely-publicly-funded.html, June 20, 2022; Ken Prendergast, "Sources: Browns want new stadium; Mayor wants community input," https://neo-trans.blog/2023/02/27/sources-browns-want-new-stadium-mayor-wants-community-input/, February 27, 2023; Brent Larkin, "Hold onto your wallets, taxpayers. The Browns are about to come knocking," March 12, 2023, https://www.cleveland.com/opinion/2023/03/hold-onto-your-wallets-taxpayers-the-browns-owners-are-about-to-come-knocking-brent-larkin.html, Chris Easterling, "Jimmy and Dee Haslam dispute desire for new stadium, stand by renovation," March 29, 2023, https://www.beaconjournal.com/story/sports/pro/browns/2023/03/29/jimmy-dee-haslam-renovation-not-new-stadium-firstenergy-justin-bibb-cleveland-browns-developmen/70048920007/, Mary Kay Cabot, "Jimmy and Dee Haslam 'are committed to redoing' FirstEnergy Stadium, believe a revitalized waterfront is critical to Cleveland's future, " March 29, 2023, https://www.cleveland.com/browns/2023/03/jimmy-and-dee-haslam-are-committed-to-redoing-firstenergy-stadium-believe-a-revitalized-waterfront-is-critical-to-clevelands-future.html.

13. Tim Newcomb, "Plans Progressing for Tennessee Titans to build $2.2 Billion Domed Stadium, https://www.forbes.com/sites/timnewcomb/2022/10/17/plans-progressing-for-tennessee-titans-to-build-22b-domed-stadium/?sh=6f0176745027, October 17, 2022.

14. See Bob Mendes, "Reject the Proposed Stadium Deal," February 14, 2023, https://static1.squarespace.com/static/5e39b7a79f189676b3a81ccd/t/63ec26b96b5d8100b484f24d/1676420793838/stadium+deal+memo+feb+2023.pdf. See also Neil deMause, " Nashville votes to spend $1.26 billion on new Titans stadium to avoid having to spend $??? On renovations," December 22, 2022, https://www.fieldofschemes.com/category/nfl/tennessee-titans/ .

15. Steve Litt, "Cleveland proposes North Coast Development Authority with power to realize big lakefront dreams," April 13, 2023, https://www.cleveland.com/news/2023/04/cleveland-proposes-north-coast-development-authority-with-power-to-realize-big-lakefront-dreams.html

16. "Cleveland Mayor Justin Bibb gives his thoughts on potential new stadium for the Cleveland Browns," WKYC, April 19, 2023, https://www.youtube.com/watch?v=Nez6EeKQcWg

CHAPTER 7

1. The Chicago Tribune, "NBA Arenas ranked," December 8, 2014.

2. Peter Lane Taylor, "Why Cleveland Is America's Hottest City Right Now," www.forbes.com, October 27, 2016.

3. Sam Allard, "Everything You Need to Know About the Quicken Loans Arena Transformation," clevelandscene.com, December 14, 2016.

4. Sam Allard, "#NOTAllin: Regional Faith-based Coalition Announces Opposition to Q Renovations," clevelandscene.com, January 12, 2017.

5. Sam Allard, "Heated Deliberations Begin for the Q Renovation Plan," cleveland-scene.com, February 22, 2017.

6. The sources of the data for the respective cities are: http:///www.espn.com/nba/story/_/id/14666181/golden-state-warriors-new-arena-called-chase-center; http://www.nytimes.com/2013/10/25/sports/garden-renovations-come-with-a-tug-of-war.html; http://www.good4utah.com/news/local-news/slc-will-pay-22-million-for-arena-renovations; http://www.cleveland.com/opinion/index.ssf/2017/02/tightly-crafted-county-deal-tohtml#incart-river-home; http://www.charlotteobserver.com/sports/nba/charlotte-hornets/article9246866.html; http://www.citadel-builders.com/Projects/New-Orleans-Arena.html; http://www.espn.com/nba/story_/id/9893324/minnesota-timberwolves-give-97m-facelift-target-center; http://questia.com/newspaper/1P2-27788534/oklahoma-city-arena-renovation-bids-below-expectations; http://www.usatoday.com/story/sports/nba/2016/11/01/atlanta-hawks-philips-arena-renovations/93129048/; http://www.tmj4.com/news/local-news/milwaukee-bucks-new-arena-construction-on-schedule; http://www.sacbee.com/news/local/city-arena/article36414231.html; and http://www.nydailynews.com/life-style/real-estate/barclays-center-owner-city-drop-debt-article-1.1206050.

7. Sam Allard, "City Council Begins Q Deal Deliberations, Cavs' Cheerleaders Are No-Shows," clevelandscene.com, March 28, 2017.

8. Robert Higgs, "Cleveland City Council approves deal for renovations to The Q," THE PLAIN DEALER, April 25, 2017, page ___.

9. Robert Higgs, "SEIU to back challengers to incumbents in Cleveland City Council election," cleveland.com, July 19, 2017.

10. Robert Higgs, "Ohio Supreme Court rules Cleveland must accept referendum petitions on upgrades at the Q," THE PLAIN DEALER, August 11, 2017, page A1.

11. Sam Allard, "The Q Deal is Alive and Well—How GCC Compromised to Resuscitate It," clevelandscene.com, August 31, 2017.

12. Id.

13. Plain Dealer Editorial Board, "Time to move on after compromises reached on The Q," THE PLAIN DEALER, August 31, 2017, page A15.

14. See generally Courtney Astolfi, "Cavaliers to spend $45 million more on upgrades at The Q," THE PLAIN DEALER, September 19, 2018, page A-7.

15. Jay Miller, "Cavs add $45 million to Quicken Loans Arena renovation," crainscleveland.com, September 18, 2018.

16. Kevin Kleps, "Two-year renovation of Quicken Loans Arena will result in a deduction of about 1,000 seats," crainscleveland.com, September 18, 2018.

17. Id.

18. Hannah Drown, "Renovated Rocket Mortgage FieldHouse is now open," THE PLAIN DEALER, September 29, 2019, page A7.

19. Courtney Astolfi, "Cavs CEO talks about arena renovation," THE PLAIN DEALER, September 28, 2019, page A!0.

20. Editorial Board Roundtable, "Is public financing of our sports venues worth the cost?" THE PLAIN DEALER, September 28, 2019, page A20.

21. Sam Allard, "Sin Tax Funds Rapidly Depleting, Yet Stadiums Continue to Seek Major Upgrades," CLEVELAND SCENE, Volume 49, Issue 2, July 11-17, 2018, page 8.

22. Sam Allard, "Ugggggggggggggggggggghhhhhhhhhhhhhhhh," CLEVELAND SCENE, February 28, 2020.

CHAPTER 8

1. Michelle Jarboe, "Cleveland Indians detail multimillion-dollar renovation plans, seat cuts at Progressive Field," THE PLAIN DEALER, August 8, 2014.

2. Jim Pete, "Progressive Field skyrockets to MLB's fifth-best ballpark in 2016," waitingfornextyear.com, October 22, 2016.

3. Scott Sargent, "Photos: First look at "The Corner" at Progressive Field," waitingfornextyear.com, April 7, 2015

4. Scott Sargent, "Progressive Field's renovations crank the social aspects up a few more notches," waitingfornextyear.com, March 6, 2016

5. Id.

6. Jacob Bogage, "Major League Baseball Wants to Expand. Montreal Wants Its Expos Back." CHICAGO TRIBUNE, July 25, 2018.

7. Sergei Klobnikov, "Minor League Baseball's Most Valuable Teams," FORBES, July 5, 2016.

8. Camryn Justice, "All-Star Week in Cleveland breaks records with Play Ball Park, viewership," News5Cleveland, July 12, 2019.

9. Id.

10. The City taxes on hotels, income, parking and admissions totaled $8.87 million annually; the County taxes on sales, hotels and property totaled $3.57 million annually.

11. "Bad Moon Rising," composed by John Fogerty, published by Jondora Music.

12. ccMy primary data source for this table is National Sports Law Institute of Marquette University Law School, "Sports Facility Reports: Major League Baseball, Appendix 1 to Sports Facility Reports, Volume 13," Copyright 2012. I also consulted Kevin Clark Forsythe, "The Stadium Game Pittsburgh Style: Observations on the Latest Round of Publicly Financed Sports Stadia in Steel Town, U.S.A.; and Comparisons with 28 Other Major League Teams," 10 MARQUETTE SPORTS LAW REVIEW 237 (2000), at Appendix VII, pages 267-282. Data on the three most recent MLB franchise lease extensions in Denver, Houston and Seattle came from, respectively, Neil deMause, "Rockies get land rights for lease extension, nobody actually seems to be scammed this time," FIELD OF SCHEMES BLOG, March 31, 2017, http://www.fieldofschemes.com/2017/03/31/12295/rockies-get-land-rights-for-lease-extension-nobody-actually-seems-to-be-scammed-this-time/, Matt Young, "Astros extend Minute Maid Park lease through 2050," HOUSTON CHRONICLE, July 9, 2018; and Zach Spedden, "Seattle Mariners Ink 25-Year Lease Extension," BASEBALL DIGEST, December 11, 2018.

13. Matt Loede, "Indians TV Ratings Sky-High Among All of MLB, Set to Wrap Up 4th Straight Season In the Top Three," SI CLEVELAND BASEEBALL INSIDER, September 9, 2020, https://www.si.com/mlb/indians/news/indians-tv-ratings-sky-high-among-all-of-mlb-set-to-wrap-up-4th-straight-season-in-the-top-three. See also Maury Brown, "Early Regional Sports Network TV Ratings And Ad Sales For MLB Are Up Compared With 2019," August 6, 2020, https://www.forbes.com/sites/maurybrown/2020/08/06/early-regional-sports-network-tv-ratings-and-ad-sales-for-mlb-are-up-compared-to-2019/#40b7a1cf3441.

14. Chris Cwik, "MLB ratings are up in 2020 thanks to women and younger fans," August 21, 2020, https://sports.yahoo.com/mlb-ratings-are-up-in-2020-thanks-to-women-and-younger-fans-202327251.html.

15. Barry M. Bloom, "Jeter's Marlins Endure Financial Losses and Covid-19 En Route to Third PlayoL Appearance," SPORTICO, September 29, 2020, https://www.sportico.com/leagues/baseball/2020/jeter-says-marlins-have-taken-a-financial-hit-because-of-the-coronavirus-1234613907/

16. Joe Henderson, "Covid-19 could throw curveball to Tampa Bay Rays stadium hopes," FLAPOL, May 14, 2020,
    https://floridapolitics.com/archives/332605-joe-henderson-covid-19-could-throw-curveball-to-tampa-bay-rays-stadium-hopes

17. Marc Bona, "What were the top 5 viewed Cleveland Indians games on Sports Time Ohio." October 3, 2020, https://www.cleveland.com/entertainment/2020/10/what-were-the-top-5-viewed-cleveland-indians-games-on- sportstime-ohio.html. See also Maury Brown. "MLB Sees Local TV And Streaming Viewership Up Over 4% For 2020,"FORBES, October 4, 2020, https://www.forbes.com/sites/maurybrown/2020/10/04/mlb-sees-local-tv-and-streaming-viewership-up-over-4-for-2020/#6a9234c33dac.

18. https://www.wkyc.com/video/news/local/the-future-of-progressive-field-with-changes-on-the-horizon/95-c 0998a-e41c-46cc-bf01-2be182cb1589

19. Associated Press, "MLB announces change to minor league structure featuring 120-team regional alignment," ESPN.COM, February 12, 2021, https://www.espn.com/mlb/story/_/id/30887636/mlb-announces-changes-minor-league-structure-featuring-120-team-regional-alignment

20. Courtney Astolfi, "Progressive Field Pay Ball!" THE PLAIN DEALER, August 6, 2021, Page 1A.

21. Seth A. Richardson, " Cleveland mayoral candidates oLer varying levels of support to Progressive Field deal," https://www.cleveland.com/cityhall/2021/08/cleveland-mayoral-candidates-o er-varying-levels-of-support-to-progressive-field-deal.html

22. Id.

23. Id.

24. Sam Allard, "Local leaders announce deal hatched in private to continue pumping monet into progressive field," CLEVELAND SCENE, August 5, 2012, https://www.clevescene.com/scene-and-heard/archives/2021/08/05/local-leaders-announce-deal-hatched-in-private-to-continue-pumping-public-money-into-progressive-field

25. DeMause's assertion first appeared in his August 6, 2021 blog at https://www.fieldof
schemes.com/2021/08/06/17721/cleveland-o ers-dolan-285m-to-keep-the-guardians-
in-town-not-that-they-were-leaving-or-anything/ He based his math on an earlier
report that compared Phoenix expenditures with those of other lease extension
deals:

"Spending $168 million to get 15 extra guaranteed years of NBA basketball (or
whatever it is that the Suns play) comes to $11.2 million a year; how does that
compare with other sports lease extension deals?

• **Carolina Panthers:** $87.5 million for six years, $14.6 million a year
• **San Jose Sharks:** $100 million for eight years, $12.5 million a year
• **Atlanta Hawks:** $142.5 million for 18 years, $7.9 million a year
• **Tampa Bay Lightning**: $61 million for a 16-year extension, $3.8 million
a year
• **Colorado Rockies:** a bunch of land rights for close to market price for 30
years, $0 a year

So, not the worst lease extension deal ever, but close to it! And that's only if
you consider "fair" to be "what everyone else is paying," as opposed to, you
know, *fair*." https://www.fieldofschemes.com/2019/01/24/14555/phoenix-council-
successfully-lobbies-self-to-give-suns-owner-168m-for-new-furniture-air-condition
ing/ But DeMause failed to consider the 2007 Kansas City Royals deal, which by
my math (see Table at page __ infra) totals slightly more than the Indians agreement at $19,188,780 per year.

26. Kaitlin Durbin, "Progressive Field Renovation moves closer, public reaction
mixed," October 20, 2021, https://www.cleveland.com/news/2021/10/progressive-
field-renovation-moves-closer-to-vote-public-reaction-mixed.html

27. Sam Allard, "Cuyahoga County Council Passes Progressive Field Deal 9-1, Public
Spigot Continues to Spew Money for Pro Teams," November 10, 2021, https://m.
clevescene.com/scene-and-heard/archives/2021/11/10/county-council-passes-progres
sive-field-deal-9-1-public-spigot-continues-to-spew-money-for-pro-teams?fbclid=
IwAR19bAA7VzHOaXMiY8SLdHiySOoBUU26jg641yr4fmoo4RXTMjC5uT
BROwE

28. Sam Allard, "10 Things We Learned from Cleveland City Council's Mammoth
Progressive Field Deal Hearing, November 19, 2021, https://www.clevescene.com/
scene-and-heard/archives/2021/11/19/10-things-we-learned-from-cleveland-city-
councils-mammoth-progressive-field-deal-hearing

CHAPTER 9

1. Mike Rosenberg, "King County Council approves $135 million in taxpayer funds
for Mariners ballpark," THE SEATTLE TIMES, September 5, 2018.

2. Chris Daniels, "$135 million in public funding approved for Safeco Field improve-
ments, www.king5.com, September 17, 2018.

3. Associated Press, "Seattle City Council Approves KeyArena renovation," www. espn.com, September 24, 2018.

4. Emily Kaplan, "Seattle gets NHL expansion team, to debut in 2012-22 season," www.espn.com, December 4, 2018.

5. Seattle Weekly, "Safeco Field Funding Referendum Withdrawn," www.seattleweek ly.com. October 31, 2018.

6. Jessica Boehm, "Phoenix City Council delays $230M Suns arena renovation vote," THE ARIZONA REPUBLIC, December 12, 2018.

7. Id.

8. Rebecca L. Sanders, "Is the Phoenix Suns' arena deal worse than other cities' deals? You decide." THE ARIZONA REPUBLIC, December 14, 2018.

9. Id.

10. "Poll shows strong public support for Talking Stick Arena renovation plan, ARIZONA BUSINESS MAGAZINE (January 10, 2019).

11. Abe Kwok, "Phoenix approved a Suns renovation deal. But could it still head to voters?" ARIZONA REPUBLIC, January 24, 2019.

12. Jessica Boehm, "Anti-arena group drops referendum on Phoenix Suns arena funding," THE ARIZONA REPUBLIC, February 6, 2019.

13. Sam Donnellon, "As Philadelphia changes, Wells Fargo Center tries to change with it," THE INQUIRER, June 7, 2018.

14. Id.

15. Nate Taylor, "Pacers owner seeking major renovations to Bankers Life Fieldhouse," IndyStar.com, April 13, 2017.

16. Zach Spedden, "Indiana Governor Signs Bill with Bankers Life Fieldhouse Renovation Funds," ARENA DIGEST, May 1, 2019

17. Neil deMause," Pay-to-Play Is The Stadium Grift That Keeps On Giving," dead-spin.com/pay-to-play-is-the stadium-grift-that-keeps-on-giving—1834331811, April 29, 2019.

18. Martin J. Greenberg and Dennis Hughes, Jr., "Sports.comm: It takes a village to build a sports facility," 22 MARQUETTE SPORTS LAW REVIEW 92, 93 (2011).

19. Id. at page 101.

20. Id. at pages 102-103.

21. Id. at page 109, referencing an interview by Doug Foglsang with Jim Hopkins, Cleveland Assessor's Office on June 10, 2010.

22. Id.

23. Id.

24. Id.

25. Id. at page 110,

26. Id. at page 116.

27. Id. at page 112.

28. Id. at page 114.

29. Id. at page 121, citing JeL Little, *The Arena Chronicles Part IV- Arena Requires Public Participation*, HOCKEY WRITERS (February 8,2010).

30. Id. at page 123, citing David Wirick, Assessment of the Gross Economic Impact of the Arena District on Historic Columbus, JOHN GLENN SCHOOL OF PUBLIC AFFAIRS, July, 2008, at pages 1-2.

31. Id. at page 124, citing Caitlin Rother, *Promises of Padres are a Mixed Bag: Some Kept, Some Broken in Long Building Process*, SAN DIEGO UNION TRBUNE, April 5, 2004, at page A-1.

32. Bianca Barrigan, "Inglewood in talks to build new Clippers Arena across from NFL stadium," https://la.curbed.com/2017/6/15/15811564/clippers-arena-inglewood-nfl-stadium.

33. Greenberg and Hughes, supra note 18 at pages 118-120.

34. Id.

35. Id. at page 141.

36. Id. at pages 141-142.

37. Rob Reischel, "Green Bay Packers' Titletown District OL To Sensational Start," FORBES, July 22, 2018.

38. Greenberg and Hughes, supra Note 18 at pages 137-152.

39. Id. at pages 153-174.

40. Adam Sanford, Mister Lizzie, and Daniel Russell, "Financial support for new Rays stadium in better shape than previously announced," https://draysbay.com/2018/11/23.

41. John Romano, "For Rays, stadium deal isn't personal, it's just ruthless baseball business," TAMPA BAY TIMES, December 14, 2018.

42. Gabe Laques, "Rays' new stadium proposal dead—and clock ticking on alternatives to Tropicana Field," USA TODAY, December 12, 2018.

43. Scott Soshnick, "Can't Fill the Seats? MLB's Rays Decide to Shrink the Stadium," BLOOMBERG, January 4, 2019.

44. Daniel Russell, Ian Malinowski, and Mister Lizzie, "The consequences of going 'cashless' at Tropicana Field," https://www.draysbay.com/2019/1/28/18197257/tropicana-field-cahless-analysis-tampa-bay-rays.

45. Marc Topkin, "Rob Manfred: Rays' Montreal plan legitimate, gaining momentum," https://www.tampabay.com/sports/rays/2020/02/16/manfred-rays-montreal-plan-legitimate-gaining-momentum/

46. Marc Topkin, "MLB kills Rays' split-city plan with Montreal," TAMPA BAY TIMES, January 20, 2022.

47. Megan Cassidy, "Warriors must pay $40M in arena debt to Oakland, Alameda County, judge rules," SAN FRANCISCO CHRONICLE, October 29, 2018.

48. City of Oakland vs. Oakland Raiders, a California Limited Partnership, et.al., Complaint in United States District Court, Northern District of California, Oakland Division, Case No. 4:18-cv-07444, paragraphs 80 and 81.

49. "10 questions about the new Oakland A's ballpark and Coliseum plan—San Francisco Business Times," https://www.bizjournals.com/sanfrancisconews/2018/11/28/oakland-athletics-new-ballpark-coliseum-mlb.html.

50. Shayna Rubin, "Kaval says new stadium would allow A's to spend like never before," THE MERCURY NEWS, June 9, 2021, https://www.mercurynews.com/

2021/06/09/kaval-says-new-stadium-would-allow-as-to-spend-like-never-before/

51. Neil deMausse, "Alameda County board gripes about many unknowns of A's stadium tax plan, votes for it anyway," fieldofschemes.com, October 27, 2021.

52. Neil deMause, "A's make getting $500M+ in Vegas stadium funding team's priority, Oakland cuts oL talks," April 20, 2023, https://www.fieldofschemes.com/.

53. Id.

54. Mick Ackers, "Major-league deal: A's to purchase land near Strip for new ballpark," April 19, 2023, LAS VEGAS REVIEW-JOURNAL, https://www.reviewjournal.com/sports/athletics/major-league-deal-as-to-purchase-land-near-strip-for-new-ball park-2764701/.

55. Id.

56. Sandra Tan and Jonathan D. Epstein, "Everything on the Table as Pegulas Weigh Bills, Sabres stadium options," www.buLalonews.com, November 27, 2018.

57. Id.

58. A list of stadium improvements since opening day in August 1973 (note that the Pegula's bought the team in 2014) is provided in Didonato, "Highmark Stadium Condition Study: Rough Draft Submission," 2020/2021, page 8:

West End Suites (1993 & 1994) $ 8,000,000
Red Zone & Goal Line Clubs First Level (1994) $ 13,300,000
JumboTron (1994) $ 5,700,000
Field House (1995) $ 10,500,000
Dug Out Suites (1999) $ 10,500,000
Second Level Clubs (1999) $ 5,600,000
Training Facility & Admin. Offices (1999) $ 10,500,000
Sideline Clubs & Restroom Towers (1999) $ 19,000,000
Seating (Heated, Suite & Lower Bowl) (1999) $ 5,000,000
Repair of existing tunnel walls & Concrete repairs (2004) $ 1,500,000
Parking lot renovations (2004, 2005, 2008 - 2012) $ 6,000,000
New HD scoreboard (2007) $ 3,000,000
2013 Lease Improvement Project* $ 130,000,000
Grass Practice Field (2017) $ 5,000,000
Renovate Sideline Clubs (2018) $ 15,000,000
Replace Upper Deck Ribbon Board (2018) $ 1,300,000
TOTAL $ 249,900,000.

*The 2013 Lease Improvement Project included many upgrades throughout the Stadium including new video displays, additional concessions stands and restrooms and various elements to improve circulation and provide ADA access in and around the facility. This project also included the addition of 3 new buildings on site; the Commissary, Operations Building and the Bills Store.

59. Mike Rodak, "Bills' Kim Pegula: Financial outlook for new stadium not promising," www.espn.com, May 23, 2018.

60. John Wawrow," AP Exclusive: Bills propose 60,000-seat stadium by 2027", August 31, 2021, https://apnews.com/article/kathy-hochul-sports-nfl-business-buLalo-bills-77b347e94170316c76a9c9bd380b80ae

61. Id.
62. Marcel-Louis Jacques, "NFL Commissioner Goodell on what's needed in BuLalo: 'I think a new stadium is what's needed'", https://www.espn.com/nfl/story/_/id/32072905/think-new-stadium-needed
63. Neil deMause, "Friday roundup: Bills owners get their $ 1B in public stadium cash, triggering other NFL owners' salivary glands, " April 8, 2022, https://www.fieldof schemes.com/2022/04/08/18687/friday-roundup-bills-owners-get-their-1b-in-public-stadium-cash-triggering-other-nfl-owners-salivary-glands/
64. Joel Currier and Ben Fredrickson, "St. Louis, NFL agree to $790 million settlement in Rams lawsuit, Goodell approves," November 24, 2021, https://www.stlto day.com/sports/football/professional/st-louis-nfl-agree-to-790-million-settlement-in-rams-lawsuit-goodell-approves/article_020b5bde-3a33-557b-aa8c-870b4c562d03.html

CHAPTER 10

1. "Stadiums, while not prohibited to be funded by public money, were originally privately funded. With the notable exception of the Los Angeles Coliseum (built in 1923), Chicago's Soldier Field (1929) and Municipal Stadium in Cleveland (1931), all of which were built to attract the Olympics, all major league (MLB, NBA, NFL, NHL) stadiums were exclusively privately financed until 1953. That year, Milwaukee's taxpayers forked over $5 million to lure the Boston Braves to their city and County Stadium." A.J. Manuzzi, "Flagrant Foul: How Cities Subsidize Stadiums and Why They Shouldn't, " THE AMERICAN AGORA, May 27, 2019. https://www.americanagora.org/single-post/2019/05/27/flagrant-foul-how-cities-subsidize-stadiums-and-why-they-shouldn't.
2. JOANNA CAGAN AND NEIL DEMAUSE, FIELD OF SCHEMES: HOW THE GREAT STADIUM SWINDLE TURNS PUBLIC MONEY INTO PRIVATE PROFIT (1998), page 64.
3. See generally Id. at pages 62-83.
4. JON MORGAN, GLORY FOR SALE (1997), page 312.
5. Id. at pages 313-314, citing Robert Baade, "Professional Sports as Catalysts for Metropolitan Economic Development, 18 JOURNAL OF URBAN AFFAIRS pages 1-17 (1996).
6. Timothy S. Chapin, "Sports Facilities as Urban Redevelopment Catalysts," 70 JOURNAL OF THE AMERICAN PLANNING ASSOCIATION, Number 2, Spring 2004," pages193-194.
7. Id. at page 194.
8. Eric Boehm, "Atlanta Braves' New Stadium Is a Disaster for Taxpayers and Fans," reason.com, April 15, 2017.
9. CAGAN AND DEMAUSE, supra note 1 at page 187.
10. MORGAN, supra note 4 at page 321.

CHAPTER 11

1. Timothy S. Chapin, "Sports Facilities as Urban Redevelopment Catalysts: Baltimore's Camden Yards and Cleveland's Gateway," JOURNAL OF THE AMERICAN PLANNING ASSOCIATION, Vol. 79, No. 1, Spring 2004, pages 203-204.
2. Robert Higgs, "First Look: Cleveland, Browns owners propose grand park to link downtown to lakefront, develop land around FirstEnergy Stadium," cleveland.com, May 16, 2021, https://www.cleveland.com/metro/2021/05/first-look-cleveland-browns-owners-propose-grand-park-to-link-downtown-to-lakefront-develop-land-around-firstenergy-stadium.html?outputType=amp
3. Chapin, supra Note 1 at pages 204-205.
4. Keith Schneider, "Welcome to the Neighborhood: America's Sports Stadiums Are Moving Downtown, THE NEW YORK TIMES, January 10, 2018.
5. Morris Newman, "The Neighborhood That the Ballpark Built," THE NEW YORK TIMES, April 26, 2006.
6. Marc Viquez, "Stadium Journey's 2018 NFL Stadium Rankings," stadiumjourney.com, February 2, 2019.
7. "Stadium Journey's 2023 Ranking of the NBA Arenas," May 8, 2023, https://www.stadiumjourney.com/stadiums/stadium-journey-s-2023-ranking-of-the-nba-arenas.
8. "Stadium Journey 2022 Major League Baseball Stadium Ranking, December 25, 2022, https://www.stadiumjourney.com/stadiums/stadium-journey-2022-major-league-baseball-stadium-ranking
9. Stadium Journey, "Stadium Journey's 2019 Major League Baseball Ballpark Ranking," October 13, 2019, https://stadiumjourney.com/news/stadium -journeys-2019-major-league-baseball-ballpark-ranking/
10. Schneider, supra note 4.
11. See chart in the category 'List of teams by urban area' in "List of American and Canadian cities by number of major professional sports franchises," Wikipedia.org.
12. Patrick Rishe, "District Detroit: The Most Compact Sports District In America Is Revitalizing Downtown Detroit," forbes.com, November 24, 2016.
13. Id.
14. Schneider, supra note 4.
15. Chapin, supra note 1 at page 199.
16. The Associated Press, "Privately built Pacific Bell Park a curse to other teams," ljworld.com, October 22, 2002.
17. Data on Nielsen Markets is from "Local Television Market Universe Estimates," Estimate as of January 1, 2018, neilsen.com. Data on facility opening costs and public share of opening costs is primarily from National Sports Law Institute of Marquette University Law School, "Sports Facility Reports: Major League Baseball, Appendix 1 to Sports Facility Reports, Volume 13," Copyright 2012. The Chicago Cubs' Wrigley Field renovation data is drawn from Barry M. Bloom, "Wrigley Field Renovations Are Nothing Short of Spectacular," May 24, 2019, https://www.forbes.com/sites/barrymbloom/2019/05/24/wrigley-field-renovations-

are-nothing-short-of-spectacular/?sh=3b3da45b2eb5. The Boston Red Sox' renovation data for Fenway Park is drawn from Mark Fortier, "Fenway Preview: Red Sox Reveal New Food Options, Improvements Ahead of Home Opener," April 22,2022, https://www.nbcboston.com/news/local/red-sox-to-preview-fenway-park-improvements-ahead-of-home-opener/2692488/. The renovation data for Dodger Stadium is drawn from Mark Hickman, "$100 Million Renovation of Dodger Stadium is Complete," THE ARCHITECT'S NEWSPAPER, July 27, 2020, https://www.archpaper.com/2020/07/renovation-of-dodger-stadium-complete/. For renovations to the Chicago White Sox's Guaranteed Rate Field, data is drawn from "Guaranteed Rate Field," www.baseballinstadiums.com. The renovation data for the Colorado Rockies' Coors Field is drawn from "The Rooftop at Coors Field/ Denver CO: Can the renovation of an iconic stadium show immediate revenue gains?" https://www.mortenson.com/projects/the-rooftop-at-coors-field. Renovation data for the Toronto Blue Jays' Rogers Center is drawn from Bryan Murphy, "Rogers Centre Renovations: Blue Jays' Stadium gets major update ahead of 2023 home opener," April 11, 2023, https://www.msn.com/en-ca/sports/mlb/rogers-centre-renovations-blue-jays-stadium-gets-major-update-ahead-of-2023-home-opener/ar-AA19HYhM. Seattle's 2018 lease extension/renovation, data is taken from Zach Spedden, "Seattle Mariners Ink 25-Year Lease Extension," BALLPARK DIGEST, December 11, 2018 and Chris Daniel, "$135 million in public funding approved for Safeco Field improvements," www.king5.com, September 17, 2018.. For Atlanta's new ballpark, data is taken from Dan Klepal, "Cobb to borrow $376 million for SunTrust Park", https://www.ajc.com/news/local-govt--politics/cobb-borrow-376-million-for-suntrust-park/yEv6osd51CzK7YtuHWDVaO/. For Arlington's new Globe Life Field, data is taken from Bill Hanna, "What will you have to pay in Globe Life Field? Team studies aLordable seats," FORT WORTH STAR TELEGRAM, March 26, 2019.

18. Data on Nielsen Markets is from "Local Television Market Universe Estimates," Estimate as of January 1, 2018, neilsen.com. Data on facility opening costs and public share of opening costs is primarily from National Sports Law Institute of Marquette University Law School, "Sports Facility Reports: National Football League, Appendix 1 to Sports Facility Reports, Volume 12," Copyright 2011. Renovation data from Miami's Hard Rock Stadium is drawn from Zach Speddan, "The Evolution of Hard Rock Stadium," January 31, 2020, https://footballstadiumdigest.com/2020/01/the-evolution-of-hard-rock-stadium/. Renovation data for the BuLalo Bills' stadium is drawn from Daniel C. Vok, "NFL Plays OLense to Get Public Money for Stadiums," PEW CHARITABLE TRUST, April 22, 2013. Renovation data from Charlotte's Bank of America Stadium is drawn from Charlotte Observer StaL, " Emails shed light on Panthers' renovation project at Bank of America Stadium," CHARLOTTE OBSERVER, January 16, 2016, updated February 15, 2016. Renovation data for the Tampa Bay Buccaneers' renovation of Raymond James Stadium is drawn from Gil Arcia, "More renovations coming to Raymond James Stadium," March 13, 2018, www.bucsnation.com. Renovation data for the Baltimore Ravens' stadium is drawn from Kevin Lynch, "Ravens Eye Additional

Upgrades at M&T Bank Stadium, Better Connection to Casino District, January 11, 2002, www.southmore.com. Renovation data for the Detrit Lions' Ford Field is drawn from James Kozinn, " Go Inside Ford Field After Its $100 Million Renovation," ALSD. Renovation data for the Philadelphia Eagles' Lincoln Financial Field is drawn from Timothy Rapp, "Philadelphia Eagles Reveal $125 Million Plan for Lincoln Financial Field," BLEACHER REPORT, June 9, 2013. Renovation data for the Arizona Cardinals' stadium is drawn from Jim Fifield, "As training camp begins at Cardinals' stadium, work continues on $100 Million in upgrades," THE REPUBLIC, July 27, 2018.

19. Data on Nielsen Markets is from "Local Television Market Universe Estimates," Estimate as of January 1, 2018, neilsen.com. Data on facility opening costs and public share of opening costs is primarily from JUDITH GRANT LONG, PUBLIC/PRIVATE PARTNERSHIPS FOR MAJOR LEAGUE SPORTS FACILITES, 2013, Table 2.1 at pages 19-31, and secondarily from National Sports Law Institute of Marquette University Law School, "Sports Facility Reports: National Basketball Association, Appendix 1 to Sports Facility Reports, Volume 14," Copyright 2013. Data on $295 million public expenditures for Bankers Life Fieldhouse in Indianapolis is from Chris Sikich, "Deal to keep Pacers in town rises to $800 million to extend, operate Bankers Life Fieldhouse," THE INDIANAPOLIS STAR, April 12, 2019. Data on the $142.5 million public share for the Philips Arena renovation in Atlanta is from "Atlanta Hawks reach agreement on terms for renovation of Philips Arena," November 4, 2016. https://ocgnews.com/atlanta-hawks-reach-agreement-on-terms-for-renovation-of-philips-arena. Data for other arena renovations is from a table contained in Rebecca L. Sanders, "Is the Phoenix Suns' arena deal worse than other cities' deals? You decide," THE ARIZONA REPUBLIC, December 14, 2018.

20. JUDITH GRANT LONG, PUBLIC/PRIVATE PARTNERSHIPS FOR MAJOR LEAGUE SPORTS FACILITIES (2013), page 59.

21. Id, at pages 62-63.

22. V. David Sartin, "Taxpayers: Can we call it Freedome?" THE PLAIN DEALER, March 3, 1985, page 1-A.

CHAPTER 12

1. Peter Gammons, "The Cleveland Indians, best run team in professional sports," March 5, 2018 by Peter Gammons.

2. Maury Brown, "Here Are the 2017 MLB Prime Time Television Ratings for Each Team," forbes.com, October 10, 2017.

CHAPTER 13

1. City of Seattle v. Professional Basketball Club, LLC, Case No. 2:2007cv01620T, Trial Brief of the City of Seattle, Trial Docket Item #103, filed June 11,2008.

2. Sam Masterson, "New decision in $1 billion St. Louis vs NFL lawsuit will benefit St. Louis, legal analyst says," NEWS RADIO 1120, KMOX, March 11, 2021, https://www.audacy.com/kmox/local-sports/local/new-decision-st-louis-vs-nfl-lawsuit-will-benefit-st-louis

3. Mike Florio, "St. Louis wants more than $1 billion over Rams relocation," PRO FOOTBALL TALK, February 14, 2021, https://profootballtalk.nbcsports.com/2021/02/14/st-louis-wants-more-than-1-billion-over-rams-relocation/

4. Nathaniel Grow, "In Defense of Baseball's Antitrust Law Exemption," 49 AM. BUS. L. J. 211 (2012).

5. The other leagues are constrained by two antitrust decisions, Los Angeles Memorial Coliseum Commission v. National Football League, 726 F. 2d 1381 (9th Cir. 1984), and National Basketball Association v. San Diego Clippers Basketball Club, 108 815 F.2d 562 (9th Cir. 1987).

6. Grow, supra note 4.

7. "Should Congress Stop the Bidding War for Sports Franchises?" *Heartland Policy Studies* #74-77 (Chicago, IL: The Heartland Institute, August 1996).

8. Id.

9. H.R. 3817, 105th Congress, Section 4 (1998), discussed in Michele Cotrupe, "Curbing Franchise Free Agency: The Professional Sports Franchise Relocation Act of 1998," 9 DEPAUL JOURNAL OF TECHNOLOGY & INTELLECTUAL PROPERTY LAW 165, 180-181 (1998).

10. See, e.g., Sanjay Jose Mullick, "Browns to Baltimore: Franchise Free Agency and the New Economics of the NFL," 7 MARQUETTE SPORTS LAW JOURNAL 1 (1996).

11. H.R. 3817, 105th Congress, Section 3 (1998).

12. MARK LEIBOVICH, BIG GAME: THE NFL IN DANGEROUS TIMES 204 (2019). Cleveland writer Terry Pluto formed an identical impression of the NFL owners when he attended a 1998 meeting:

    "I went to the NFL meetings in Dallas, where the league began the hustle of the Browns.... The meeting was held at the Dallas Hyatt Airport. I walked through the lobby, talking to the owners about the Browns. I have never been around a group that seemed so self-important and had so little regard for the customers.... Their pomposity and arrogance was appalling, even by the blatant standards of pro sports."

    TERRY PLUTO, FALSE START: HOW THE NEW BROWNS WERE SET UP TO FAIL (2004), pages 25-26.

13. Comptroller of the Currency, Administrator of National Banks, U.S, Department of the Treasury, "Historic Tax Credits: Bringing New Life to Older Communities,"

COMMUNITY DEVELOPMENT INSIGHTS, November 2008, https://www.novoco.com/sites/default/files/atoms/files/occ_insights_htc_1108.pdf

14. 26 UNITED STATES CODE Section 46.

15. Jesse Rogers, "Wrigley Field given federal landmark status," espn.com, November 19, 2020. https://www.espn.com/mlb/story/_/id/30347853/sources-wrigley-gield-given-federal-landmark-status.

AFTERWORD

1. JOANNA CAGAN AND NEIL DEMAUSE, FIELD OF SCHEMES: HOW THE GREAT STADIUM SWINDLE TURNS PUBLIC MONEY INTO PRIVATE PROFIT (1998), P. 200.

2. JAMES QUIRK AND RODNEY FORT, HARD BALL; THE ABUSE OF POWER IN PRO TEAM SPORTS (1999), page 173.

3. JUDITH GRANT LONG, PUBLIC/PRIVATE PARTNERSHIPS FOR MAJOR LEAGUE SPORTS FACILITIES (2013), page 44.

4. Id. at p. 199.

5. Associated Press, "Gibson's 31 points, James' balanced play, puts Cavs in the NBA Finals," June 3, 2007.

6. https://en.wikipedia.org/wiki/2016_World_Series#Game_7, citing Foster, Jason. "The 10 most memorable Game 7s in World Series history, ranked". Chicago: Sporting News. Retrieved December 23, 2016.

7. MARK LEIBOVICH, BIG GAME: THE NFL IN DANGEROUS TIMES (2018), page 161.

8. Neil DeMause," Consultant finds Titans' $1.8 billion stadium renovation wishlist would cost $1.8 billion," https://www.fieldofschemes.com/2022/11/07/19315/consultant-finds-titans-1-8b-stadium-renovation-wishlist-would-cost-1-8b/

9. Neil DeMause, "Royals owner Sherman wants $1 billion for a new downtown stadium? In this economy?," https://www.fieldofschemes.com/2022/11/07/19315/consultant-finds-titans-1-8b-stadium-renovation-wishlist-would-cost-1-8b/

10. John Branch, "Oakland is Home to Championship Teams, All of Them Looking to Leave," NEW YORK TIMES, June 6, 2015.

11. JeL Passan, "Oakland A's to start look at relocating elsewhere," ESPN, May 11, 2021, https://www.espn.com/mlb/story/_/id/31427293/oakland-athletics-start-looking-relocating-elsewhere-sources-say

12. Andy Dollich, "Dollich: Oakland A's Howard Terminal ballpark plan is fantasy: sports business consultant and former Oakland A's executive explains why team's plans won't pan out," THE MERCURY NEWS, December 19, 2018.

13. Branch, supra note 10.

APPENDIX I

105th CONGRESS

2nd Session

H. R. 3817

To exempt professional sports leagues from liability under the antitrust laws for certain conduct relating to the relocation of their respective member teams; to establish procedures and remedies applicable to such leagues with respect to the relocation of such teams, and for other purposes.

IN THE HOUSE OF REPRESENTATIVES

May 7, 1998

Mr. Meehan (for himself and Mr. Bryant) introduced the following bill; which was referred to the Committee on the Judiciary, and in addition to the Committee on Commerce, for a period to be subsequently determined by the Speaker, in each case for consideration of such provisions as fall within the jurisdiction of the committee concerned

A BILL

To exempt professional sports leagues from liability under the antitrust laws for certain conduct relating to the relocation of their respective member teams; to establish procedures and remedies applicable to such leagues with respect to the relocation of such teams, and for other purposes.

Be it enacted by the Senate and House of Representatives of the United States of America in Congress assembled,

SECTION 1. SHORT TITLE.

This Act may be cited as the ``Professional Sports Franchise Relocation Act of 1998''.

SEC. 2. DEFINITIONS.

For purposes of this section:

(1) Antitrust laws.--The term ``antitrust laws''--

(A) has the meaning given it in subsection (a) of the first section of the Clayton Act (15 U.S.C. 12(a)), except that such term includes section 5 of the Federal Trade Commission Act (15 U.S.C. 45) to the extent such section 5 applies to unfair methods of competition; and

(B) includes any State law similar to the laws referred to in subparagraph (A).

(2) Home territory.--The term ``home territory'' means the geographic metropolitan area within which a member team

operates and plays the majority of its home games.

(3) Interested party.--The term ``interested party'' includes, with respect to a member team--

(A) any political subdivision of a State that provides, or has provided, financial assistance, including tax abatement, for facilities (including a stadium or arena) in which the member team plays;

(B) a representative of the political subdivision with jurisdiction over the geographic area in which the stadium or arena of the member team is located;

(C) the member team;

(D) the owner or operator of a stadium or arena of the member team; and

(E) any other person who is determined by the sports league of the member team to be an affected party.

(4) Member team.--The term ``member team'' means a team of professional athletes--

(A) organized to play professional football, basketball, soccer, or hockey; and

(B) that is a member of a professional sports league.

(5) Person.--The term ``person'' means any individual, partnership, corporation, or unincorporated association, any combination or association thereof, or any State or political subdivision of a State.

(6) Professional sports league.--The term ``professional sports league'' means an association that--

(A) is composed of 2 or more member teams;

(B) regulates the contests and exhibitions of its member teams; and

(C) has been engaged in competition in a particular sport for a period of more than 7 years.

(7) Stadium; arena.--The terms ``stadium'' and ``arena''

mean the principal physical facility within which a member team

plays the majority of its home games.

SEC. 3. INAPPLICABILITY OF THE ANTITRUST LAWS.

It shall not be unlawful under the antitrust laws for a

professional sports league (or a member team of such league acting

jointly with another member team of such league, under the authority of

such league) to issue or enforce rules, or to enter into or carry out

agreements, to permit or to restrict the relocation of any such member

team.

SEC. 4. PROCEDURAL REQUIREMENTS.

(a) Request for Approval.--

(1) In general.--Not later than 210 days before the

commencement of the season in which a member team proposes to

play in a new location, any person seeking to change the home

territory of the member team shall submit a request for

approval of the proposed change to the appropriate professional

sports league.

(2) Requirements.--Each request for approval submitted

under paragraph (1) shall--

(A) be in writing;

(B) be delivered in person or by certified mail to

each interested party not later than 30 days after
submission to the appropriate professional sports
league under paragraph (1);

(C) be made available by the date specified in
subparagraph (B) to the news media;

(D) be published by the date specified in
subparagraph (B) in 1 or more newspapers of general
circulation in the home territory of the member team;
and

(E) contain--

(i) an identification of the proposed
location of the member team;

(ii) a summary of the reasons for the
change in home territory, taking into
consideration the criteria described in
subsection (b)(2);

(iii) the date on which the proposed change
is intended to become effective; and

(iv) a detailed description of--

(I) the requirements specified in
this subsection applicable to the

submission of such request;

(II) the procedures specified in subsection (b) applicable to requests submitted under this subsection;

(III) the requirements specified in subsection (c) applicable to decisions on such requests;

(IV) the requirements specified in subsection (d) applicable to notice of decisions on such requests; and

(V) the relief available under section 5 to a prevailing interested party.

(b) Procedures.--

(1) Establishment.--Each professional sports league shall establish rules and procedures for approving or disapproving requests submitted under subsection (a), that shall--

(A) include criteria to be considered by the professional sports league in approving or disapproving such requests; and

(B) be made available upon request to any

interested party.

(2) Criteria to be considered.--The criteria described in paragraph (1)(A) shall include--

(A) the extent to which fan loyalty to and support for the member team has been demonstrated, through attendance, ticket sales, and television ratings, during the tenure of the member team in the home territory;

(B) the degree to which the member team has engaged in good faith negotiations with appropriate persons concerning the terms and conditions under which the member team might continue to play its games in its current home territory;

(C) the degree to which the ownership or management of the member team has contributed to any circumstance that might demonstrate the need for the relocation of the member team;

(D) the extent to which the member team has, directly or indirectly, received public financial support by means of any publicly financed playing facility, rent abatement, special tax treatment, any other form of public financial support, any other public benefits not generally available to businesses as a whole within the jurisdiction, and the extent to which such support continues;

(E) the adequacy of the stadium or arena of the member team, and the willingness of the stadium or arena authority and the local government to remedy any deficiencies in the stadium or arena;

(F) whether the member team has incurred net operating losses, exclusive of depreciation or amortization, sufficient to threaten the continued financial viability of the member team;

(G) whether any other member team in the professional sports league is located in the home territory of the member team;

(H) whether the member team proposes to relocate to a territory in which no other member team in the professional sports league is located;

(I) whether the stadium or arena authority, if public, is opposed to the relocation;

(J) the effect that relocation will have on

contracts, agreements, or understandings between the member team and public and private parties; and

(K) any other criteria considered to be appropriate by the professional sports league.

(c) Decision.--In determining whether to approve or disapprove a proposed request submitted under subsection (a), the professional sports league shall--

(1) ensure that the requirements of subsection (a) have been satisfied;

(2) conduct a hearing at which interested parties shall be afforded an opportunity to submit written testimony and exhibits; and

(3) keep a written record of such hearing and any testimony and exhibits submitted under paragraph (2).

(d) Notice of Decision.--Not later than 5 days after making a decision to approve or disapprove a request submitted under subsection

(a), the professional sports league shall provide to each interested party, make available to the news media, and publish in a newspaper described in subsection (a)(2)(D), a notice that includes--

(1) a statement of such decision; and

(2) a detailed description of--

(A) the requirements specified in subsection (a) applicable to the submission of such request;

(B) the procedures specified in subsection (b) applicable to the request submitted under subsection (a);

(C) the requirements specified in subsection (c) applicable to the decision on such request;

(D) the requirements specified in this subsection applicable to notice of the decision on such request; and

(E) the relief available under section 5 to a prevailing interested party.

SEC. 5. JUDICIAL REVIEW.

(a) In General.--Compliance by a professional sports league with section 4 may be reviewed in a civil action commenced by an interested

party, but only in accordance with this section.

(b) Venue; Time Limitation.--Not later than 21 days after a professional sports league complies with section 4(d), a civil action under subsection (a) may be commenced in any judicial district of the

United States, excluding a judicial district--

(1) established in the State that contains--

(A) the home territory of the member team with

respect to which such action is commenced; or

(B) the proposed location of the member team; or

(2) that includes any geographical area that is less than

75 miles from any part of such home territory.

(c) Relief.--If the plaintiff prevails in a civil action commenced

under subsection (a) against a professional sports league, the court

shall enjoin such league--

(1) to vacate the decision of such league to approve or

disapprove the request by the member team involved to change

its home territory; and

(2) not to approve or disapprove such request until such

league complies with section 4.

SEC. 6. EFFECTIVE DATE; APPLICATION OF AMENDMENTS.

(a) Effective Date.--Except as provided in subsection (b), this Act shall take effect on the date of the enactment of this Act.

(b) Application of Amendments.--This Act shall not apply with

respect to conduct occurring before the date of the enactment of this

Act.

APPENDIX II

An Act

To amend 26 United States Code Section 46 and to add a new Section 26 United States Code Section 48E to encourage private rehabilitation of professional sports facilities

SECTION 1, SHORT TITLE

This Act may be cited as the "Tax Credit for Private Rehabilitation of Professional Sports Facilities Act of 2022."

SECTION 2. ADDING A NEW SUBSECTION (7) TO 26 UNITED STATES CODE SECTION 46 ENTITLED "THE

PROFESSIONAL SPORTS FACILITY REHABILITATION CREDIT."

(a) IN GENERAL—26 United States Code Section 46 is amended to add a new subsection (7) entitled "The Professional Sports Facility Rehabilitation Credit."

SECTION 3. ADDING A NEW SECTION 48E TO 26 UNITED STATES CODE ENTITLED "PRIVATE REHABILITATION OF PROFESSIONAL SPORTS FACILITY CREDIT"

(a) IN GENERAL—26 United States Code is amended to add a new Subsection 48E.

SEC. 48E. PRIVATE REHABILITATION OF PROFESSIONAL SPORTS FACILITY CREDIT

(a) GENERAL RULE

(1) In General

For purposes of Section 46, for any taxable year during the 5-year period beginning in the taxable year in which a qualified rehabilitated sports facility is placed in service, the rehabilitation credit for such year is an amount equal to the ratable share for such year.

(2) Ratable Share

For purposes of paragraph (1), the ratable share for any taxable year during the period described in such paragraph is the amount equal to 20 percent of the qualified rehabilitation expenditures with respect to the qualified rehabilitated sports facility, as allocated ratably to each year during such period.

(b) When expenditures taken into account

Qualified rehabilitation expenditures with respect to any qualified rehabilitated sports facility shall be taken into account for the taxable year in which such qualified rehabilitated sports facility is placed in service.

(c) Definitions

(1) Qualified rehabilitated sports facility

(A) In general

The term "qualified rehabilitated sports facility" means any professional sports facility (and its structural components) if

(i)   Such sports facility has been substantially rehabilitated;

(ii)   Such sports facility was placed in service before the beginning of the rehabilitation; and

(iii)   Such sports facility is at least 20 years old.

(B) Substantially rehabilitated defined

(i)   In general

For purposes of subparagraph A (1) a sports facility shall be treated as being substantially rehabilitated only if the qualified rehabilitation expenditures during the 24-month period selected by the taxpayer (at the time and in the manner prescribed by the regulations) and ending with or within the taxable year exceed the greater of:

(I)   The adjusted basis of such sports facility (and its structural components); or

(II) $50,000,000.

The adjusted basis of the sports facility (and its structural components) shall be determined as of the beginning of the 1st day of such 24-month period, or of the holding period of the sports facility whichever is later. For purposes of the preceding sentence, the determination of the beginning of the holding period shall be made without regard to any reconstruction by the taxpayer in connection with the rehabilitation.

(ii)   Special rule for phased rehabilitation

In the case of any rehabilitation which may reasonably be expected to be completed in phases set forth in architectural plans and specifications completed before the rehabilitation begins, clause (i) shall be applied by substituting "60-month period" for "24-month period."

(iii)   Qualifying lessees

Lessees of a sports facility qualify if

(I)   The owner/lessor is a public entity;

(II)   The remaining lease term exceeds 15 years;

(III)   The lease contains a specific performance clause requiring lessee to play at least 90% of its home games at the sports facility;

(IV)   The lease does not include a "state of the art clause" requiring lessor, or any other public entity, to spend money to maintain the sports facility at a level equal to or better than a stated percentage of sports facilities used by other franchises located within the lessee's professional sports league.

(iv)   Reconstruction

Rehabilitation includes reconstruction.

(2) Qualified rehabilitation expenditures defined

(A) In general

The term qualified rehabilitation expenditure means any amount properly chargeable to capital account for property for which depreciation is allowable under section 168 and which is a qualified sports facility rehabilitation project.

(3) Qualified sports facility rehabilitation project defined

(A) In general

The term "qualified sports facility rehabilitation project" means a project in which a professional sports franchise pays more than 65% of the qualified rehabilitation expenditures for a qualified rehabilitated sports facility.

INDEX

C

Printed in the USA
CPSIA information can be obtained
at www.ICGtesting.com
LVHW050215020823
754143LV00033B/168/J